Madonna © Redferns/Michel Linssen

Mary J. Blige © Redferns/Mick Hutson

Debbie Harry © Pennie Smith

Billie Holiday © Redferns/Beryl Bryden

Alanis Morissette © Redferns/James Dittiger

Lauryn Hill © Redferns/Paul Bergen

Janis Joplin © Redferns/Elliott Landy

Britney Spears © Redferns/Paul Bergen

Diana Ross © Redferns/Tom Hanley

# She Bop II

# She Bop II

The Definitive History of Women in
Rock, Pop and Soul

## LUCY O'BRIEN

continuum
LONDON • NEW YORK

**CONTINUUM**
The Tower Building, 11 York Road, London, SE1 7NX
370 Lexington Avenue, New York, NY 10017-6503

First edition published as *She Bop* in Great Britain by Penguin Books 1995
This edition published by Continuum 2002

**British Library Cataloguing-in-Publication Data**
A catalogue record for this book is available from the British Library.

ISBN 0-8264-5776-2 (paperback)

Typeset by Kenneth Burnley, Wirral, Cheshire
Printed and bound in Great Britain by CPD Wales, Ebbw Vale.

# Contents

# Acknowledgements

Many thanks to all the women who were interviewed for this book, and particularly to Tori Amos, Cyndi Lauper (Ms She Bop herself!), Suzanne Vega, Kristin Hersh, Miriam Makeba, Vicki Wickham, Peggy Seeger, Gracie Cole, Adele Bertei, Rosetta Reitz and Regine Moylett for being so helpful.

I also thank Fred Dellar for his invaluable support and patience, Ann Munday, Charles Shaar Murray, Jools Holland, Neville Farmer, Delilah Jackson and her Black Patti Archive, Paula Shutkever, Gaylene Martin, Pat Baird, David Terrill, Tony Gregory, Victoria Rutherford, Marilyn Botheras, Pennie Smith, Emily Andersen, Val Wilmer, Mick Patrick for access to his awe-inspiring knowledge of 1960s girl groups, and Lucy Duran, Debbie Golt, Alexa Dalby and Lois Darlington for their help with the Oye Mi Canto chapter. Thanks also to my family.

Special thanks to Ann, Naomi and Paul, and Fenton and Randy at World of Wonder for their hospitality when I was in New York, to Soul Coughing for making me laugh, and to Cathy Capozzi in Boston for showing me just how hard girls can rock.

And lastly, a big Yo! to all my girlfriends, the best a girl could wish for.

# Prologue

IT ALL BEGAN IN 1979, when a girl gang got together, spurred by the political activism that exploded that year after the Conservative General Election victory. They were from Southampton, a city perched at the top of the Solent, a day's crossing away from Le Havre, France, and home of the QE2. It was a town of former glories, with sprawling docks, where cargo ships once unloaded exotic cargo and luxury liners would slide in from abroad. Bombed remorselessly during the Second World War, Southampton had a detached, prefabricated air long after the bleak restructuring of the post-war years. Ken Russell, the maverick film director, was born there, as was comedian Benny Hill – but like all good So'tonites, they escaped early. 'I'm from Southampton' doesn't quite have the same ring as 'I'm a Geordie' or 'I'm from Glasgow'. It was never cool or hip to come from Southampton – but maybe that was a blessing, as it became important to invent your own identity.

In the late 1970s Southampton had a culture bypass. Excitement, allure, difference, were all things to be resourcefully manufactured in a recession-hit area where venues had closed down and nightclubs, apart from a second-rate one for divorcees, didn't exist. Into that vacuum leaped The Catholic Girls (before the Frank Zappa song, incidentally). Tina was our Siouxsie Sioux – hair dyed jet black, a member of the Anti-Nazi League, always wearing black when the school uniform was navy blue. Maddy, whimsical yet astute, and her older sister Judith, then a nihilist and the one most openly unimpressed with authority, were both hunt saboteurs and members of the environmental group Friends of the Earth. And me, casually leaving copies of *Spare Rib* on the school common-room table and putting up feminist posters ('You start off sinking into his arms, only to end up with your arms in the sink') in the hope that I could convert 200 convent-educated sixth formers to The Cause.

We produced a school magazine named *Within These Walls* (after a TV drama about a women's prison), set up a young feminist group called College Women's Action Group that lasted four meetings, attended one boring meeting of the Labour Party Young Socialists and went on the Corrie Bill anti-abortion march in London. Corrie was a Scottish MP seeking to limit abortion rights, who in 1978 looked perilously close to getting his way. Our school dutifully closed its anti-abortion ranks, leaving the few dissenters sticking out like bumps on a log. The most vocal of that number, Maddy, Judith, me and Tina, took the train to London and joined the march to Hyde Park.

This particular day was a flashpoint for us, as we fell in behind an open lorry crammed with two Leeds bands – The Gang Of Four and Delta 5. Their music was melodic, raw, cheeky, dissonant and marked by the distinctive use of a harmonium, an unlikely punk instrument. Seeing them squashed in a mêlée of singing and dancing on the back of the lorry was an inspiration. The next day Maddy said loudly at lunchtime, 'I'm bored. Let's form a band.' Tina went out and bought a harmonium. Maddy purchased a pair of drumsticks. For several months that was all she had, tapping on table tops and the backs of chairs. Being seventeen-year-old schoolgirls, we didn't have much money to buy instruments, so we made cakes and earrings, sold them at school and bought a drum kit between us on hire purchase. Drums, being the biggest instrument, had to be secured first. Then with savings from Saturday jobs, Judith got a bass guitar from Woolworths, I bought a synthesizer and Tina a microphone. We were The Catholic Girls, and we were set.

True to the tradition of punk spontaneity, there we were one Friday evening on stage at the Joiners Arms in Southampton, having had two weeks to write four songs and assemble some chords. I walked on with my knees knocking through my tight jeans, my bare feet crammed into black 1950s suede stilettos, a dark blazer adorned with a few pet badges (the anarchist feminist fist, the Anti-Nazi League arrow, the Gang of Four logo). The stage was two feet high, but it might as well have been a stadium. In front of us was a sea of expectant faces, some amused, some interested, some nakedly hostile, all there to 'check out the chick band'. Judith led with a few chords and we launched into 'Bored Housewife', our first song that opened with the immortal phrase:

> 'She's become resigned to life,
> She's become a lonely wife . . .'

Simple words, but they expressed all that we didn't want to be. We didn't want to be sealed within the living tomb of marriage and domestic slavery; we didn't want to be told what we could and couldn't do with our bodies by the Catholic religion; we didn't relish the idea of being relegated to the small-talk sidelines in groups of men, just because we were girls and therefore 'less interesting'. All this and more went into our songs, experiments in sound that were laughed at, derided, but also loved and admired.

In those gawky, nascent stages, it wasn't so much what we sounded like but what we stood for that mattered. No one told us that we would eventually get to know our instruments, improve and play them like they were part of us. No one told us that the ideas would eventually gel, the songs come easier and easier, the presentation more slick, confident and loud. No one told us that promoters would rip us off blind, that boy bands would try and fuck us under the guise of chivalrous respect, that skinheads would come to our gigs, shout abuse at us, overturn the tables, throw bricks through the windows and beat us up; no one told us that we would pay for our own studio time and be included on a compilation album, yet wouldn't see a penny of the profit (what profit?); no one told us that if we'd hung on to the nugget we had – ourselves, our youth, our sex, our music, our untutored, naïve difference – we'd have been one of the hottest properties in the business; no one told us that other girls would both love us and hate us, caught between admiring what we were doing and ostracizing what they saw as a threat; no one told us that we would have one of the most exciting years of our lives, that none of us would need boyfriends – as The Voodoo Queens sang later, why go out with boys when you had guitars? – that we would realize a dream (we could do it!) . . . but most of all, no one told us that there were other girls out there too, apart from one sharp woman journalist who came to a gig we played in Bournemouth and said to us after the show: 'You're very raw, you remind me of The Slits when they first started. You've definitely got something.'

After a year I left the band to go to university in Leeds. The Catholic Girls transmuted into Almost Cruelty, continued for a while longer before juddering to a halt. I played with a few Leeds bands, including an all-girl outfit making a massacre out of Dusty Springfield songs that was the McLarenesque brainchild of The Mekons' Kevin Lycett, then gave up performing to write instead, combining twin interests of music and feminism; Judith pushed through a Women's Studies strand on her Philosophy degree course and raised twin sons; Maddy went to study horticulture at Kew and became an expert on carnivorous plants, while Tina became a social worker. The youthful enthusiasm that gave us the courage to 'have a go' faltered through lack of support, without the resources of a major urban network like London or Manchester; but most importantly, it was our lack of confidence as girls isolated on an all-male scene that led to a sense of being besieged and beleaguered. If Riot Grrrl, the inventive, energetic, flawed yet ultimately knowing fanzine/girl-band network of the early 1990s had existed fifteen years earlier, the future of The Catholic Girls might have been very different.

Being in a band gives you instant power. No wonder boys love it. The day after our first gig at the Joiners Arms, we walked into the Lord Louis, the pub on the seafront frequented by all the local punks, and we were magically accepted. We could hold conversations with boy bands about guitar riffs, synthesizers, high hats and rehearsal space. We could swap dates – 'We're playing Pokesdown on the 15th . . . we're doing a gig in

Bournemouth next week.' We could trade demo tapes, and support them at gigs (always as the novelty all-girl act, of course); we could walk together into a major league Joy Division or Siouxsie and The Banshees concert, and people would whisper, 'There's the Catholic Girls.' We were Somebody. We were part of The Brotherhood. We were empowered.

*For Malcolm and Bubba*

# Introduction

'I'm glad there's a lot of babes doing this shit because it's kind of lonely out there. Just bring on the bands, you know?'
CHRISSIE HYNDE, quoted in *Rolling Stone* by Mim Udovitch, 1994

IN THE SIX YEARS since *She Bop* was first published, some key changes have occurred for women in rock. From being under-researched, there is now a wide range of writing on the subject – so much so that US girl band Le Tigre chanted on stage in 2000: 'Not another book about women in rock!' Yet despite fresh perspectives and new information, there is still a need to document women's musical history, because it is periodically buried. When interviewing a young organizer of Glasgow's 2001 Ladyfest event, for instance, I was shocked to discover that she came across Riot Grrrl through reading *She Bop* as part of a college course, even though the movement had been a major flashpoint five years earlier. As far as the mainstream media was concerned, once it was 'over', Riot Grrrl hardly existed.

In the same way that artists like Janis Joplin and Bonnie Raitt diligently uncovered stories of the 1920s blueswomen, many of today's rocker girls are discovering that there were women punk bands by reading about it in fanzines or alternative underground media. Whether Riot Grrls, rappers, or 1970s and 1980s soul singers, female performers are still being written out of 'official' pop history. As long as women are sidelined by the Rock 'n' Roll Hall of Fame, or TV retrospectives, or magazine anthologies, in favour of the male canon, there will be a need for more material on their achievements.

*She Bop II* is a major update on the original, with many new interviews and an extra chapter on millennial trends such as

Girlpower, Alanis Morissette and Lilith Fair rock, 'organic' soulstresses like Erykah Badu and Lauryn Hill, and the rise of pop divas such as Mariah Carey and Britney Spears. In working on the second edition, I was cheered to realize how many older women were reinventing themselves, with artists like Patti Smith, Deborah Harry, Joni Mitchell, Stevie Nicks and Yoko Ono proving that nothing, from childrearing to personal tragedy, had suppressed their creative expression. There was a place for them to come back.

When girl guitar bands and singer/songwriters were in the ascendant in the late 1980s/early 1990s, there was a noticeable lack of analytical material about women in rock and pop. (I use the word 'pop' in its widest sense: it signals the point when an artist becomes mainstream, a 'star' in whatever genre, be it rap, reggae, rock or swing.) For decades women have been the addendum in the history of pop, with information on them sporadic and inconsistent. In 1992, having spent eight years as a music writer, I decided to draw all the strands together. From 1984, when I co-wrote a cover story for the feminist magazine *Spare Rib* on women in the music industry and was shocked to discover just how few of them had record deals or were in the charts compared to men, I made a point of interviewing female artists whenever I could. As a journalist on *New Musical Express* (*NME*) in the 1980s, I tried to get more in-depth coverage of female acts with a feminist perspective, which did not really become fashionable until the early 1990s.

This book, fuelled by over 250 interviews in the US and Britain conducted between 1984 and 2001, and countless secondary sources, is not a straightforward chronological history; rather, I have examined themes, trends and genres. First of all I have tried to establish how women, whether as performers or working behind the scenes, have negotiated their place within the music industry. To each of them I put the question, 'How do you express yourself?' The response was startling. From the sassiest soul singer to the most hardcore rocker, all would blink, take a pause and think. Some cried. And I realized how much women have been written about in terms of what film-maker Penelope Spheeris has dubbed the 'Marilyn Monroe Damage' – that is, primarily as men-pleasing angels, victims or problem personalities – rather than in terms of their body of work.

But do women necessarily become victims of a system that militates against them? All those I spoke to had a singular sense of purpose and were able to give a clear appraisal of their role. It was as if obstacles such as racism and sexism had demanded such self-definition.

Certain themes came up again and again. Cissy Houston's support of her daughter Whitney, for instance, showed how the mother/daughter relationship can often empower women within pop – on many occasions mothers, whether through general influence or direct management, have acted as buffers between their daughters and a business that notoriously misunderstands how women want to express themselves. Also emerging from the interviews was a sense of the crucial importance of women as role models, whether it was Joan of Arc, lauded by Sinéad O'Connor for being a 'good soldier', or Billie Holiday, whose voice was, for Cyndi Lauper, that of the Universal Mother, or Aretha Franklin, admired by Ethiopian artist Aster Aweke for her verve and technique.

*She Bop II* is not a cheerleading account, however. Underlying women's success are their ambivalence and competitiveness with each other, the spur and assertion of difference in every genre, from Riot Grrrl 'gender traitor' accusations to the nail-scratching strictures of romantic pop. The impulse to define themselves as musicians first, women later has meant that solidarity is by no means automatic. In 1994, for instance, Madonna claimed, 'There's a whole generation of women . . . who cannot bring themselves to say anything positive about me . . . they want to kill you off because they want their independence from you.'[1]

Despite the catch-all labelling that arose precisely because high-profile women were so rare in rock and pop, female artists continue to resist being packaged into that generic mushy lump known as 'women in rock'. Retaining individuality and personal expression while still reaching out to other women has been a challenge, creating a spiky, contradictory, yet extremely creative, fusion.

As I was writing this book I envisaged a shimmering stave, a grid, a network, with women's voices weaving in and out – some angry, some sad, some self-pitying, some defiant – till *She Bop II* became as much an expression of them all, their own manifesto. In the recounting, an inevitable imbalance occurs. Because female artists have historically been steered into the role of decorative front-women, a disproportionate number of them are vocalists. But as more and more form their own guitar groups and enter traditional fields of excellence such as jazz, their presence as instrumentalists should eventually be recognized.

Women have played a part in the construction of modern-day pop, from blues to rock and soul. They have been at the forefront of the promotion of new formats – whether it was Billie Holiday, churning out 45s just after the juke-box was invented, or Donna Summer, making disco hits with the new 12-inch single in the 1970s. They have always been at the nexus of cult and mass market – for instance, it was vaudeville blueswomen who in a sense sold the blues to a wider audience, because of their stage-craft and show-womanship; and it has always been female consumers who turn bands into big sellers once they have reached past their fan base. Initially rooted in the alternative college rock circuit, REM, for instance, did not really 'break' until the early 1990s, when women began to buy their albums.

In *She Bop II* I have taken a close look at how women have created and consumed pop in their own image and focused on musical genres – because it is in Bessie Smith's singing that there are clues to what it was like to be in the rough world of 1920s vaudeville; it is through Holiday's narcotic jazz slur that there is a sense of alienation and distance from a world that favoured a slick, white, anodyne image; it is in Dusty Springfield's taut notes, Chrissie Hynde's jangling rock guitar or Courtney Love's emotive rasp that there is the impression of both embattled strength and fragility; and in the girl-group sound, that of The

Ronettes, The Supremes, The Crystals, that there exists the sheer joy and pain of being a Girl.

From the blues to 1940s swing to MTV, I have examined issues that have confronted women at various stage in the development of pop. How do women deal with stardom? How do they negotiate everything from contracts to, as Suzanne Vega put it, 'the Cleavage Question'? I have looked at the impact of racial segregation on music in the 1940s and 1950s, where rigid definitions for women were set (i.e., black women sing of gritty emotional reality, channelled into the 'race' record or R&B chart, while white women sing sweet and surface and gain access to mainstream chart exposure). I have taken apart the crystallized myths of the 1960s girl-group era, interviewing key personalities such as Mary Wilson, Martha Reeves and Ellie Greenwich. I have asked, 'Was punk really women's liberation? And whatever happened to the rock chick, post-Joplin, post-Patti Smith – did she just become a parody?'

I have also explored the areas of power for women in pop: Why have women colonized the singer/songwriter genre, formed their own sorority within gospel music or immortalized the role of the disco diva? And at the apex of the pop mainstream, just why was Madonna so successful? Going behind the scenes to find out exactly how an image is constructed, I have examined how much women are tyrannized by the Image Question and the impact this has on their work. Female artists have learned to be ingenious, devising a multitude of strategies to confront or bypass this issue – whether it's Madonna's outright twist on the blonde sex bimbo, or Annie Lennox's androgynous man in a suit. There is also the question of lesbian sexuality, how coming out of the closet is considered tantamount to commercial suicide. k.d. lang publicly saying she was gay in the early 1990s may have allayed this fear, but many lesbians still felt obliged to enter into an elaborate charade of disguise, bluff and counterbluff.

As crucial to the experience of women in pop is their influence 'from the margins' (i.e., away from the mainstream chart scene). Music grows through the incorporation of different beats and sounds from 'the street', and female rappers have formed their own vanguard. Theirs is a fascinating story: not just because the overt display of male rapper bravado has enabled them to be similarly overt and therefore step into their own power, but also because, placed in a wider context, in their generation they're echoing the themes, imagery and energy of black American women writers such as Alice Walker and Toni Morrison.

Reaching international stature, female world-music artists, too, have become important voices – whether it is that of Oumou Sangaré, with her sharp feminist message to young women in Mali, a country where arranged marriages render them male possessions; or of Angélique Kidjo, transplanted from Benin, making a career in the West; or of Zimbabwe's Stella Chiweshe, with her vision of a cross-cultural music 'happening' that will do nothing less than save the world. Women are marginalized when their geographical location is outside the epicentre of North American and British pop. They are also sidelined and penalized for being political. Why is it harder for women in protest pop to be seen as heroes? Why can't they be universal? To answer this question I have looked not only at women such as Joan Baez, Peggy Seeger, Miriam Makeba and Michelle Shocked, who have directed their political protest outward, but also at female artists who have investigated their inner pain and madness, from Sinéad O'Connor to PJ Harvey, Kristin Hersh and Chaka Khan.

There is an examination of women in the industry – the managers, executives, publicists, journalists, producers and A&R women who work in the power-broking areas. Like female performers, they have their own stories of day-to-day sexism, and, in the engine room of the business, their fight to be valued, recognized and promoted is just as gritty. Explored is the scandal of the industry 'brain drain', women fed up with hitting their heads against the vinyl ceiling leaving the corporate sphere to set up as independents. Assessed also is their progress within companies: how effective is their gradual 'infiltration' of key corporate positions? Despite, as one insider says, 'management training courses and a large amount of goodwill' in the progressive 1990s, with the threat of recession looming in the 'noughties', many working in the industry had reverted back to the 'old boy's network'. With so few women at executive level, particularly in the UK, there is still room for radical change.

I have also looked at the role of women as consumers, an area so far surprisingly under-researched despite the fact that female buyers are an increasingly influential group. They may not be seen as 'active consumers', whether of hardware (i.e., stereos) or software (i.e., albums), but there exists among women a huge underground tape network, a language and appreciation of music that is more private, less openly competitive but intrinsically their own. It is a question of confidence. Young men list music as their primary focus and means of identity – before sport, before TV, before cinema – while women cite fashion as most important, with music an ambivalent second.

The concluding chapter focuses on millennial Girlpower: not just the commercial Spice Girl variety, but the grassroots impact of female singer/songwriters in every genre telling their truth – whether it's Alanis Morissette screaming at a treacherous ex-love, or Tori Amos challenging rapper Eminem, or Erykah Badu singing about her pot belly and her reality rhymes.

Music is a political issue. It allows the listener to plug into powerful baseline emotions – be they anger, sadness, confusion, lust or joy. Music invites full-scale participation in life, and with knowledge comes empowerment. All the women interviewed for this book have found music, at some stage, to be a personally liberating force. Whether as performers, business people or as fans, they have learned to use music to describe, define and give meaning to their life. Music can motivate mass crowds or touch one person in a darkened room. Without such experience surely women are, as in many areas of life, cut off from the source of their power. As women move further to the centre of the industry, to shape it for themselves, the way music is consumed, performed and read will be totally transformed.

LUCY O'BRIEN
London, 2002

# Riffin' the Scotch

FROM BLUES TO THE JAZZ AGE

**1**

BLUES IS THE BASELINE OF MODERN POP, the twelve-bar language that underlies all current genres – from rock 'n' roll to soul and reggae. Its origins lie in Africa, through fragments of tribal chants or the voice of the village storyteller. Transported with the slave trade to plantations in the Caribbean or tobacco and cotton fields in the American South, its rhythms mingled with dominant white church or folk music. Gospel can be heard in the 'call and response' (the call of the featured singer, the response of the audience), in the 'field hollers' and chain-gang songs of those building railroads, digging ditches or picking crops. Repetitive team labour required the declarative song structure of spirituals, whereas the blues, more contemplative and solitary, arose from a meditative approach to work – that of the dirt farmer, for instance, following a mule-drawn plough, singing to lighten his spirits in the face of monotonous grind. Blues also had a place in the quiet hours of evening, or Saturday-night dances after a week of toil.

Although many histories of the blues hardly mention the contribution of women, the music was central to their experience. If not in the fields, they often worked alone – cleaning, tending the garden, cooking, bringing up children – and blues were the lullabies they sang, standards rooted in tribal memory, or songs as slow articulations of their own lives. Evidence of this is reflected in the recorded subject-matter of female blues artists – not only do they sing about relationships, but they also use the domestic imagery of cooking (as Memphis Minnie's 'I'm Gonna Bake My Biscuits', for instance) growing plants, making honey or keeping hens. Blues told their story just as accurately as it did that of the male sharecropper.

After the abolition of slavery in 1807 and the 1860s civil war that finally killed it off, there was mass migration of blacks from South to North. In 1850 there were 300 blacks in Chicago; this number swelled to 300,000 by 1900, increasing tenfold over the next five decades. With this trend the raw guitar blues of the rural South was brought to the cities, where it transmuted into a more sophisticated combo style with singers accompanied by piano, drums, bass and horns or harmonicas. It was the fusion of vaudeville with rural and urban blues that created the blueprint for the modern pop star, and women like Ma Rainey, Mamie Smith and Bessie Smith set the standard.

## Gimme a Pigfoot

Though female entertainers were among the first business-women, their success was hard-earned. As late as 1870 in the US and 1880 in Britain women who sold anything for a living were not deemed 'respectable'. In the early 1900s entertainment was one of the few professions open to women, but it was a risky avenue. A woman on stage was considered to be little more than a prostitute, so most aspiring singers or musicians performed in the privacy of their own parlour with a piano and sheet music, and those who played for pay had to take the consequences. Women led a rough, rollicking existence in turn-of-the-century minstrelsy and vaudeville, with only a few artists such as Ada Overton Walker or Sissieretta Jones (alias Black Patti and Her Troubadours) temporarily breaking through. It wasn't until the rise of recording and the blues that women were catapulted into a wider market.

Until Ma Rainey dominated the scene most of the vaudeville stars, such as George Walker and Bert Williams, were male. Ma Rainey was the first woman really to popularize blues in America. Born Gertrude Pridgett in 1886, the second of five children in a Columbus, Georgia, family, Rainey made her musical debut at fourteen in a local talent show. Four years later she married minstrel show manager Will 'Pa' Rainey, to become star of his roadshow, The Rabbit Foot Minstrels. She and Pa were billed as 'Rainey and Rainey, Assassinators of the Blues', before she travelled with her own group, The Georgia Jazz Band. Dubbed 'the ugliest woman in showbusiness', with her bulging eyes and gold teeth, Rainey was still a tough, self-possessed ironist, captivating audiences with the direct folksy purity of her music. She was blueswoman as mother and preacher, communicating directly to the crowd, moving from burning righteousness to outright sauce within the same song. Posing, strutting, laughing and moaning, she glorified herself with rhinestones, gold bracelets and horsehair wigs, while one of her favourite pieces of jewellery was a long chain of twenty-dollar gold pieces. Despite constant touring state to state in her rickety house-trailer (a wooden caravan perched on top of an automobile) from Chicago in the North to oil camps in Texas and Mobile in the Gulf, she remained close to the direct simplicity of her country blues, never allowing them to become 'citified'. Rainey cautioned naïve girls to 'Trust No Man' and sympathized with hard-working men on the 'Levee Camp Moan'. Casting herself as documentor, adviser and prophet, she transformed the nature of the minstrel/vaudeville circuit.

Women following Rainey's path were aided by the rise of the 'race' record. In 1920 black composer Perry Bradford convinced the white executives of an ambitious young record company called Okeh that there was a black market as yet uncatered for. They recorded black singer Mamie Smith as an experiment, expecting her version of 'Crazy Blues' to make a modest sum of money, but within six months it sold over half a million copies to the black community. Realizing there was a whole new market, major companies began to release 'race' records on separate catalogues – music by black artists for black consumers – tripping over themselves to sign new blues talent. In the rush, women initially came out on top.

New York's Black Swan label signed newcomer Ethel Waters, while Paramount in Chicago released records by Ma Rainey, Ida Cox and Alberta Hunter, a feisty young woman who also wrote her own blues songs, one of which, 'Downhearted Blues', became a hit for Bessie Smith. Many had a background in

vaudeville, which immediately gave them glamorous, popular appeal. Smith, for instance, was not purely a blues artist, having a wide repertoire in revues, theatre and film, but along with other female recording stars in their 1920s heyday, she brought blues into the mainstream. Because so many female artists flooded the market, the top headliners were given nicknames to distinguish them – Ma Rainey was billed 'Mother of the Blues', for instance, while Clara Smith was 'Queen of the Moaners', Lucille Hegamin was the 'Chicago Cyclone' and Sippie Wallace the 'Texas Nightingale'. They became pop heroines, admired for their verve and independence. Ida Cox, for instance, wrote her own material, hired all her musicians and toured the country with a revue of sixteen chorus girls, comics and back-up singers.

Stories of luxurious lives and dazzling retinues filtered through to an awestruck audience, and in tune with the 1920s taste for high glamour, the blues goddesses were for a decade far more successful than their male counterparts. Few of them achieved longevity, however, while none were given the degree of acclaim accorded to white artists, or indeed the male country blues artists that followed them. The prime blues years are considered to be 1927–33, *after* the period of the classic vaudeville blueswomen, a devaluation consistent with the notion that men were better at most jobs, particularly as musicians. Part of the reason for the women's sudden invisibility was also economic: a top blueswoman was more expensive than a country bluesman. At her peak Bessie Smith was earning $200 per usable side at Columbia, whereas a male country blues star such as Barbecue Bob, recording on the same label, received $15 per side.

Smith may have been a high earner, but many of her peers were not paid their due, some didn't know what royalties were, while others took the dollar pittance they earned per recording with gratitude. When blues went out of vogue with the arrival of swing, female singers were left with little investment. Mamie Smith, for instance, who appeared in movies and made nearly a hundred records in seven years, died penniless in 1946. Because few careers survived, the achievements of these women were buried and forgotten. Ma Rainey was an exception, investing money in two Georgia theatres, and retiring to live with her family six years before her death. To retrieve gems from this lost era, much painstaking work was done from the late 1970s onwards by individuals like singer Bonnie Raitt, with the Blues Foundation, and New York archivist and label owner Rosetta Reitz. In fact, if it hadn't been for the immense power of Bessie Smith, a singer whose music, nearly lost to oblivion, was resurrected during the 1960s, it would have been easy to assume that early women blues artists, like women composers, painters and playwrights, had never existed.

A competitive perfectionist, Bessie Smith frequently 'carved' the recordings of her contemporaries by remodelling and improving blues songs that other singers had only recently issued. Once this was established a proportion of 'race' consumers would hold back until her version of a song was released. Determined to keep an edge of originality, Smith introduced to blues-singing a new level of professionalism and expertise. Her version of 'Moonshine Blues', for instance, reinterprets and develops Ma Rainey's original. Rainey sings about drunken despair in a rough, forceful, autobiographical style, while Smith takes the sentiment and rounds out the feeling through well-placed phrasing and emphasis on musical structure, a technique that later endeared her to jazz enthusiasts.

There is dispute about how much she was influenced by Rainey – Smith gave her little acknowledgement once she became successful – but it was Rainey who spotted Smith as a poor Tennessee street singer with singular talent, employing her in The Rabbit Foot Minstrels as a chorus girl in 1912. Smith stayed with the company for a year before branching out on her own, performing on the hardy black vaudeville circuit, the Theater Owners' Booking Association. Though she worked everywhere from field tents to honkytonks, it wasn't until she began recording at twenty-five years old that her fame was established.

By the time she reached the studio, travelling-show experience had given her a wide repertoire, but, according to Frank Walker, the A&R 'Judge' who signed her to Columbia in 1923, she arrived for the first session 'tall and fat and scared to death'. She had already been rejected by three companies, nervous of her uncompromising style. Smith's skill, though, lay in her ability to marry raw expression with sophisticated phrasing. Her first cut, 'T'Ain't Nobody's Business If I Do', rang with a world-weary yet vulnerable knowingness, becoming an early anthem of women's independence.

Like Rainey, Smith had lavish tastes, dressing herself in outrageous sequinned gowns and ostrich plumes. Famed for her parties, she would flock into a bar after a show with her retinue and lay hundred-dollar bills on the counter. Tough if crossed and fiercely loyal, she sang and fought hard for her money – but just as soon as she got it she spent it, supporting a large extended family. Smith had several husbands, but they could never control her or her bisexual affairs. She drew female followers to her because of her assertiveness, in much the same way that Madonna would many decades later. Madonna may claim to be the first pop star to talk openly about sex, but sixty years earlier Smith was just as explicit, echoing other women blues artists in songs of sexual pleasure – whether it was jaunty and playful, searching for her 'jelly roll' in 'Kitchen Man', succumbing to the musty, elemental, guilt-ridden world of the devil in 'Blue Spirit Blues', or frustrated and yearning for her man in 'He's Got Me Goin''. Smith's enduring impact was shown, too, in the dusty grit and intensity of 1990s rap/singer Me'Shell NdegéOcello, who posed for concert posters in the style of a 1920s cross-dressing blueswoman.

Unlike her tenacious rival Ethel Waters, an ambitious blues stylist who levered herself out of the 'race' ghetto to Broadway and Hollywood, Smith had no intention of modifying her act for white people. Her first white audience appalled her because of its restraint, and she disdained the metropolitan dinner party set who tried to court her. As Elaine Feinstein says in her brief, appreciative biography: 'the very qualities which make [Smith] a splendid symbol of resistance to white definitions damaged her choices.'[1]

When in the mid-1930s blues declined in popularity and the Depression took hold, Smith was nearly wiped out. She began drinking heavily and was deeply affected when her husband Jack Gee left her for the entertainer Gertrude Saunders. Columbia producer John Hammond rediscovered her in a Philadelphia dive, singing pornographic songs for tips, and persuaded her to make a comeback. 'She was a big-boned woman, and a fairly heavy woman,' he recalled. 'Moved beautifully.'[2] Just as her career was picking up again, in 1937, she died in a car accident during a whistle-stop tour of the South, on Route 61, south of Memphis. The story – which later proved unfounded – raged for years that she was turned away from a white hospital, fuelling the Bessie Smith blues myth of racism and injustice. A (needlessly) fatal accident silenced her, when she should have been in her prime.

## I'm Gonna Bake My Biscuits

'The traditional view of women singing blues was that they were moaning and groaning for lost love. I discovered a lot of independent songs from the 1920s with titles like "Ain't Much Good

In The Best Of Men Nowadays", "Movin' On Out Of Here" or "You Can't Sleep In My Bed",' says Rosetta Reitz.[3] Her downtown New York apartment is jammed from floor to ceiling with records, books, pictures, posters and papers of female blues and jazz artists – an archivist's dream.

'As I started to retrieve women in jazz, the question arose, why was I finding blues songs saying "I bake the best jelly roll in town" or "I got the sweetest cabbage"? That is not a victim speaking. Why do I as a white woman in America have the notion that those women are victims? Because it was the victim stuff that was reissued. My biggest coup was a test-pressing of Ida Cox's called "One Hour Mama" that was never even issued. She's saying, I may need one hour or maybe four before I'm through; using the most beautiful metaphors she gives specific instructions about her requirements. Is it by conspiracy or accident that these songs were suppressed?'

Much female blues output celebrated women's sexuality and strength, a dynamism that in later decades was seen as crude and embarrassing, if not downright challenging. Far more palatable was the familiar image of the downtrodden black woman bemoaning her lot. When Ida Cox proudly sang 'I'm A Big Fat Mama', it meant that she was not suffering from tuberculosis and was therefore healthy. Feinstein argues, 'All blues singers were . . . outside the society in which they lived. Blues comes from that sense of not being at the centre, "from nothingness, from want, from desire", as WC Handy put it. Bessie became the incarnation of that "absence, darkness, death".'[4] 'Absence and death' is one, possibly romanticized, reading of the blues, but equally strong within the music lies a sturdy strand of optimism.

It wasn't only female vocalists who influenced the blues and later jazz, however, but long-unacknowledged instrumentalists. Female pianists abound – maybe because the piano was a traditionally 'acceptable' instrument for women. An early mama, Mamie Desdoumes, for instance, packed out whore-houses in Storyville, New Orleans, with her piano song blues, playing spirited tunes although two of the fingers in her right hand had

Blues guitarist
and singer
**Memphis Minnie**:
'about the best
thing goin' in the
woman line'.
(Michael Ochs
Archives/Redferns)

been cut off. Lovie Austin, writer of Bessie Smith's 'Graveyard Blues', was also a major Chicago session pianist throughout the 1920s, backing many Paramount artists including Ma Rainey, Ida Cox and Ethel Waters. She was famous for performing with a cigarette in her mouth, playing with her left hand and writing music for the next act with her right.

Women guitarists were far more unusual. Memphis Minnie is a key example of a blues guitarist and songwriter whose career spanned the two main phases of early blues – from the 'classic' vaudeville and country era of the 1920s to the development of the urban combo-style Chicago and electric blues of the 1930s and 1940s. Minnie more than adapted to changing guitar styles; she innovated, immediately grasping changes while other blues artists took time to learn new techniques.

Born in 1897 into a large Louisiana sharecropper's family, Minnie was given her first guitar at the age of five. When the family moved to Walls, Mississippi, in 1904 she regularly ran away to Memphis's Beale Street to listen to blues players, and started to perform herself. At the junction of three states, Memphis integrated old and new styles, urban and rural – symbolic of her interpretation of the blues.

Unlike the female vaudeville stars Minnie performed in the streets and parks as well as on the stage – an unusual and risky route for a woman to take. From the start of her career she travelled a great deal from her home base of Chicago, and her music echoes this basic, hard-working, down-home ethos. It's Minnie who sings about street-hustling, crime and ill health, as well as baking biscuits or feeding her roosters. Her classic song 'Hustlin' Woman Blues', for instance, expresses the danger and tension of prostitutes earning a dollar on the streets, while 'Memphis Minnie-Jitis Blues' raises the spectre of meningitis, along with TB then a major killer in the black community.

While Smith and Rainey emphasized the vaudeville in blues, Minnie was a dedicated documenter of domestic life. A highly competitive guitarist, she once beat the legendary Big Bill Broonzy in a 1933 contest, and was carried aloft by the crowd. She liked to play with other male instrumentalists, often keeping herself apart from women, and countered her little-girl persona by drinking hard, 'cussin'' like a sailor and driving flash automobiles. Her recorded output is prodigious – between 1930 and 1960 she recorded over 200 sides for various labels including Columbia, Vocalion, Decca and Bluebird. Even after a stroke had confined her to a wheelchair for thirteen years before her death in 1973, Minnie still tried to play. By then she had already made an impact; blues artists as diverse as Muddy Waters, Big Mama Thornton and Chuck Berry have acknowledged her as a major influence. Bluesman Bukka White recalled, 'You know, she got fat as a butterball . . . and all she do is sit in her wheelchair and cry and cry. But in her time, she was really something. She was about the best thing goin' in the woman line . . .'[5]

Blues may have gone underground when modern dance bands became popular from 1935, but its essence could be heard in swing, a manipulation of rhythm partly invented by Louis Armstrong, who in the early 1920s placed a note slightly before the beat, behind it, or ignored bar lines altogether. This style was developed by the composer/bandleader Duke Ellington, whose skill lay in voicing and tonal colour in the big-band mode. Central to swing is a sense of improvising with the beat. Its greatest vocal exponent was a woman – Billie Holiday.

## Strange Fruit

'You never heard singing so slow, so lazy, with such a drawl. It ain't the blues. I don't know what it is, but you go to hear her . . .'
MC RALPH COOPER recommending Billie Holiday to Apollo Theater manager Frank Schiffman, quoted in *Lady Sings the Blues*, by Billie Holiday and William Dufty

'Billie Holiday used to sing in her day of "My Man Who Treats Me Mean" and all that kind of material. But I don't see Negro men that way. I prefer to sing "Strong Man". I am a black woman . . . and I no longer see trite songs as an expression of our social existence.'
ABBEY LINCOLN, jazz singer and movie actress, quoted in *Billie Holiday, Her Life and Times*, by John White

'I know she is my sister in tears, if not in blood . . . There is an existential correctness about everything she ever said or sung about being a woman. She documented for all time the experience of loss that is so characteristic in a black woman's life.'
Writer MICHELLE WALLACE talking on *Arena: The Long Night of Lady Day*, 1984

Billie Holiday was the Mother of lullaby. Her soothing, sedated voice welded echoes of the old classic blues with the new sophisticated structure of swing. She created a sweet, haunting, lush, lotus-eating world, with the narcotics that lulled her exerting their own deadly ripe force on the listener. 'Her greatest unconscious art . . . was the way in which she poisoned popular song,' wrote critic Ian Penman.[6] Holiday's critical impact lay in the manner in which she turned the banal into the acidic, reworking the standards until they were either unrecognizable or gleamed like new, recasting a song each time she sang it. This was her revenge on the songpluggers who gave black artists the leftovers that other performers didn't want.

She was a sharp dresser, describing herself in her young days as a 'hip kitty'. Like all great female artists, her gift was in

**Billie Holiday**
in London, 1958:
pretty and a
'hip kitty'.
(Beryl Bryden/
Redferns)

presentation as well as performance. Holiday used the power of every kind of language – music, clothes and words – to convey a wholeness, an originality of self-expression. There is a picture of her taken shortly before her death, preparing for her last appearance in England. She is in a dressing room, half-eaten supper on a plate, hair scraped back and shining, bent over, unaware of the camera, applying foundation to her face. Her fingers are stained with hair grease – but as ever her make-up is impeccable; she has a look of concentration and her hands are messy, but there is a labour of love that has gone into putting her face together, out of habit, a long respectful habit for the audience. Although her drug problem meant that she didn't always get there, her intentions were whole. There is the feeling that this pre-show preparation has been long, deliberate and, like her singing, very, very slow – a weary application of self, of identity, taking longer and longer to put together.

'I was a woman when I was sixteen. I was big for my age, with big breasts, big bones, a big fat healthy broad, that's all,' Holiday said in her autobiography *Lady Sings the Blues*.[7] Even though in her last years she was thin and gaunt, inside Holiday was always 'the big fat broad, that's all'. Conscious of every gesture she made and each word she spoke, she exercised self-awareness right up to her eyebrows. In the same way that analysis has been made of Madonna's belly button, Holiday's eyebrows are a work of art and self-definition: arch, beautifully painted black half-moons that frame her coolly intelligent, distant eyes – a shape that announces both sophistication and artifice.

Holiday was the bridge between the vaudeville mamas and the era of jazz swing, when a burgeoning record industry demanded mass-media star quality. When there were pretty girl singers aplenty, musical knowledge and respect for the past gave one the edge. As a young teenager Holiday would clean at her local brothel so she could play classic 78s on their Victrola, listening to Louis Armstrong and Bessie Smith over and over again.

She had a language, too: a colourful, idiosyncratic and private code that she spoke with Lester Young, the seminal jazz saxophonist with whom she had a platonic yet intimate, even symbiotic, relationship. A 'grey boy' was a white man, an attractive girl a 'poundcake', and 'just play vanilla, man' meant delivering the music unembellished and unembroidered. Holiday's vocabulary was forceful, mocking and vulgar; she would, according to writer and friend Maya Angelou, use common words casually in new arrangements. More than just jive talk, it was Holiday's articulation of her world: in the same way she rendered the popular caustic, so she saw savage euphemism in 'white' language – a socialite, for instance, was a 'whore', an executive a 'thief', while a playboy was a 'faggot' and a deb a 'dyke'. 'Sometimes when I messed up, the fur and feathers would fly so you'd think nobody around there ever called a spade a spade before,' Holiday said of the confusion over her 'street' world and the world of café 'high society', where she sometimes performed.[8] She talked in *film noir* language, her autobiography reading like the character of a private detective – the sharp, streetwise loner as cool star in his own drama.

Holiday's medium was also heroin. It gave her words their narcotic slur, that self-possessed, surreal worldliness. 'Grass was sold on street corners,' recalled singer Thelma Carpenter. 'No one had to knock anyone over the head to get loaded . . . Musicians were smoking pot, but nobody was sticking their-selves in the arm.'[9] The reality, though, for many was cheap heroin and a heroic status. Holiday began her career without drugs, but was eventually seduced by heroin's oversweet, velvety power. She has often been described as a victim, vulnerable to low-life pushers and gold-diggers, but she was also actively captivated by the drug's mystique. It didn't just serve as an anaesthetic, it brought her immense pleasure – filled out her vision of the jazz world as something separate, cool and eerily heavy, superior to the white mainstream – as it did for jazz peers such as Charlie Parker. They were the vanguard of new black jazzers for whom, according to pianist Hampton Hawes, 'rebellion was a lonely thing'.

Coupled with alcohol, however, addiction slowly killed her art as surely as it did her physical self. Like overripe fruit, her talent began to decay. In the last years of her career, during a three-hour recording session she would actually record for forty-five minutes, while the rest of the time she had to drink a bottle of Napoleon brandy to open up her voice and assemble herself to sing. Inevitably the abuse intensified her feelings of paranoia and helplessness, but, as she sang in 'Ain't Nobody's Business', rather than being that of a simple victim her life was her drama, a supreme invention of self that has subsequently cast itself like a huge, enigmatic shadow over women's images of themselves in pop.

Although no birth certificates have been found, Holiday claimed she was born Eleanora Fagan in Baltimore, Maryland, in 1915 to a thirteen-year-old mother and fifteen-year-old father, and recalls her mother as 'a child bringing up a child'. Even if the story isn't true, it gives substance to the myth. Disruption and hardship certainly figured early: she was regularly beaten by her cousin Ida, raped by a neighbour at the age of ten, and severely traumatized by being sent to a Catholic

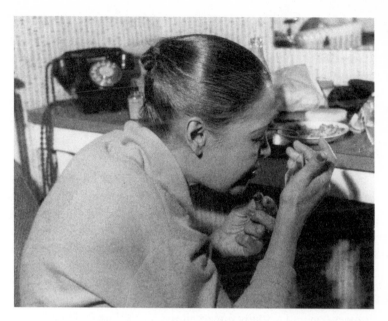

reformatory where the Mother Superior forced her to spend the night locked in a room with the body of a dead girl in a coffin. By thirteen she had moved to Harlem, working as a 'twenty-dollar call girl . . . more than I could make in a damn month as a maid'.[10]

Once she left hustling to earn money singing at local clubs, however, she was soon discovered by John Hammond, who produced her first record for Columbia, the 1933 session with a nine-piece Benny Goodman band that included a light, feisty rendition of 'Riffin' The Scotch'. Considered to be her prime years, the period 1933–40 saw her career boosted by the invention of the juke-box. Juke-boxes were first brought out in 1934, and by the following year 200,000 were in existence. The passing of Prohibition in 1933 meant that thousands of bars serving black customers installed Homer Capehart's invention, and Hammond was able to convince his boss Harry Grey (head of the American Record Company, later CBS) that there was a vast new market to be tapped. Discs aimed at the 'race' juke-box trade could be produced cheaply, with six or seven musicians accompanying a singer who made the pop tunes of the day accessible to black audiences. Holiday fulfilled this role, recording about a hundred records up to 1942 with sidemen who also happened to be the best jazz players of the era. Records sold an average of 3,000 each, and for early sessions Holiday received $25 flat per side. Few realized at the time that these cheap, cheerful arrangements would constitute the main body of her work, selling as classics over sixty years later.

By 1944 she had begun working for Decca, singing to lush strings and full orchestral arrangements. This material is less stark and powerful, widely seen as belonging to her 'slushy era'. It was also when her addiction took hold and she was regularly tailed by narcotics police. A spell in Federal reformatory through 1947 left her with a criminal record and a stigma that triggered a spiral of decline. Her last decade was marked by intermittent, erratic TV and concert appearances. Hounded until she died in 1959 from liver trouble and cardiac arrest, she was arrested for possession and actually fingerprinted on her hospital bed.

Jazz singer Annie Ross, one of the friends who were with her to the end, told me in 1994 that to know Holiday was

'frightening, emotional, wonderful, nerve-wracking. She was my idol and it was an honour to help her, look after her. She was a victim of the culture at the time. I'm sure there were many people in America then of a different class and colour able to take drugs and lead relatively normal lives but her livelihood was taken away when they denied her a cabaret card.'[11]

The feisty Scots-born Ross came from a family of vaudevillians and was a Hollywood child star at eleven, playing Judy Garland's younger sister in *Presenting Lily Mars*. By her early twenties Ross was subbing for Billie Holiday at the New York Apollo, and performing in Europe, playing to beatniks on the Left Bank. 'It was a time of great creation, when you just wanted to sing all night. To me a song was like painting – you'd do a minimalist sketch, then embellish it with tasteful colours.' Ross described the allure of heroin in the milieu of 1950s bohemianism. 'Yeh, sure, I tried everything I could get my hands on. When you're young you think you'll live for ever. Also, you were in another world, a buffer against the world, you were being hip and cool. Less was known about it then.'

It's been said that Anita O'Day, a jazz singer with a widely publicized drug habit, was less badly treated than Holiday because she was white. In fact O'Day regularly ran the gauntlet of the police, and because she was a lesser-known star, often had to take the risk of buying on the streets rather than wait for pushers to show up in her dressing room. The connection between O'Day and Holiday was small and sad; the only time they really met was when they scored together and Holiday shot 10CC into her feet, enough heroin to fill a small tuna can. 'I wasn't only in awe of her singing. I was in awe of her habit,' O'Day recalled in her autobiography.[12] Despite racial differences, O'Day and Holiday were both singled out and scorched by social disapproval because they were women – as Harry Shapiro says in *Waiting for the Man*, his study on drugs in pop music: 'Once hooked on heroin, the woman is stigmatized as more "deviant" than her male counterpart, because she is seen to be challenging the status quo by not fulfilling her role as dutiful wife and mother.'[13]

Like Holiday, O'Day did not have a positive experience of being mothered. Born in 1919 in a working-class district of Chicago, O'Day was treated as 'excess baggage' by her mother, an undemonstrative, defeated woman abandoned early by O'Day's father. Growing up into a 'hip, swinging chick' who hid her pain with a hard-boiled attitude, O'Day took part in gruelling professional Walkathon contests from the age of fifteen, earning what she could in the 'endurance business'. A unique stylist with an ear for original jazz phrasing, O'Day began performing in various Chicago combos before finding fame with Gene Krupa's band in 1941. Though widely respected in the business, her long career was marked in the 1950s and 1960s by drinking and heroin abuse. Far from expansion, heroin for Holiday and O'Day meant a constriction of their creative worlds – drugs narrowed their experience down to living on an emotional subsistence level, with everything geared towards the next hit, or who would supply that next hit.

'I'd sing songs when I was high and then have to relearn them when I was straight,' said O'Day.

Ironically both found being in prison a kind of retreat, the only time they were able to eat regularly and get enough sleep – away from chasing their habit and the rigours of the road. Even when they had periods off drugs (and O'Day kicked the habit altogether in 1966 after a frightening overdose), the stigma remained. O'Day writes with distaste about the 'rubberneckers' who turned up at her gigs to see a female junkie. Holiday, too, campaigned in her autobiography for more humane treatment of addicts. In an era when there was no energetic, politicized women's movement to support them, these female artists were out on their own.

While Holiday's tragic life was a reflection of her confused yet headstrong choices, she was also very sensitive to racism, feeling that she was a pawn in a hostile political game. Her experience as a lone black woman singing for a white band when she joined Artie Shaw in 1938 proved to be alienating and traumatic. While touring below the Mason–Dixon Line, Holiday would have to urinate in bushes while the white musicians could avail themselves of hotel rest-rooms. Audiences complained about a black singer with a white band, and ballroom managers wouldn't allow Holiday to sit on stage between numbers. Shaw unhappily compromised by hiring a white singer, Helen Forrest, and keeping Holiday, but it was a financial strain. It's a testament to the musicians' high regard for Lady Day that they each contributed $10 a week towards her salary.

It was when Holiday left the band in 1939 to open at the pioneering mixed-race club Café Society that she first sang the Lewis Allen lynching poem 'Strange Fruit', which would make her famous to a whole new audience, the left and celebrity intelligentsia. Every time she sang it Holiday elicited an ecstatic reaction – but her bitterness remained. Racism isolated and demeaned her. In *New Orleans*, for instance, her first Hollywood picture, she was reduced to playing the role of a maid caught red-handed by the angry mistress of the house singing at the piano. 'It was a real drag going to Hollywood and becoming a make-believe maid,' she recalled. 'Maid was the pits.'[14]

Holiday was dependent not only on the pushers who brought her the 'white gardenias and white junk', but on her white patrons. Even Hammond, a tireless promoter of black music, was always the one in the authoritative position. Born to a wealthy New York family, as a young man he would bribe the family chauffeur to drive him round Harlem. He did not have to suffer the fear and limitations of racism first-hand. Jazz artist Mary Lou Williams said shortly before her death in 1981, 'How many women do you know who can go out on the road and not eat properly for thirty days? And how many women do you know will go back for sandwiches in a town where they're lynching blacks? I've been through hell at times.'[15]

Holiday's own hell later became the touchstone for black women's experience. It is difficult now to extract genuine resonance from her myth, told and retold countless times with that predominantly white media definition of 'authenticity'. But emerging from a mass of detail and the sensationalist legend is the sense of a thoughtful woman thoroughly in control of her art, building from catharsis a complex musical expression. Her style has since profoundly influenced generations of female performers. As 1980s star Cyndi Lauper once said, 'Billie Holiday is the sound of my mother, the Universal Mother.' Her impact lay in a combination of impeccable phrasing and instinct. Pianist Johnny Guarnieri once recalled an instance of her perfect timing, when she said to him during a rehearsal, 'Gimme four bars.' He played four bars. Nothing. Thinking she had missed her cue, he started again. 'Suddenly I felt a tap on the back of my head and I heard her say, "Don't worry 'bout me – I'll be there."'[16]

### How High the Moon?

If Holiday was the victim, plagued by contradiction, Ella Fitzgerald was the 'straight cat' who reaped the benefits. A different example of black female experience, Fitzgerald was as open and melodiously joyful as Holiday was languid and introspective. While the latter was Lady Day, the Queen of Jazz, Fitzgerald, is the survivor, the genre's elder stateswoman.

Like Holiday she had a deprived upbringing, as an orphan in the guardianship of her aunt. Born in 1918, she grew up in New York City, entering amateur Apollo contests from her teenage years. In 1934 she was discovered by Chick Webb, legendary hunchback jazz drummer and bandleader, and writer of 'Stompin' At The Savoy'. An immediate hit with jazz fans, she reached the wider public in 1938 with her enormous hit record 'A-Tisket A-Tasket', an adaptation with Al Feldman of an 1879 nursery rhyme. After Webb's death in 1939, she fronted the band for three years before going solo, hitting the *Billboard* charts on Decca with The Ink Spots, Louis Jordan and pop-flavoured hits like 1946's 'Stone Cold Dead In The Market'.

Without a guiding force or mentor during these years she lost her way, and it was said that, like her taste in men, her predilection for trite novelty songs was 'terrible'. Inside the large-boned, slightly gawky woman was still an insecure orphan starving for love and recognition. She received this attention in a much more structured way when jazz buff and label owner Norman Granz signed her to Verve. Seeing the potential in her warm, solid phrasing and superbly rounded voice, he encouraged her to record and reinterpret American classic standards and showtunes.

Thriving under his guidance, she was catapulted to world fame: the *Songbook* series, issued in double-disc sets between 1956 and 1959, showed Fitzgerald winging her way through the best of Cole Porter, Rodgers and Hart, and George and Ira Gershwin, investing each song with breathtaking vitality and humour. The shy worrier who stayed in her room between sets rather than socializing with the musicians was transformed through song. Not only did she display great abilities as a mimic, but she also made the cool bebop of the 1950s accessible by vocalizing it, using her voice like an instrument. Marlene Verplanck, a top US nightclub singer who started in the 1950s with the Tommy Dorsey band, enjoys interpreting the American Song Book (a general term used to describe standards by great American composers such as Porter and Berlin), and sees Fitzgerald as a major influence: 'She swings so hard,' Verplanck told me. 'She's a spontaneous singer who never in her life sang a wrong note. When improvising, some people are not always within the chord structure of the song. I don't think Ella has ever sung a wrong note. She's happy about it, she has a good time!'[17]

Taking swing to the heart of the mainstream, in 1957 she became the first black artist to headline at New York's Copacabana. Her pioneering scat predates the vocal gymnastics of later eras, in which stars like Whitney Houston and Mariah Carey race around the octaves yet somehow render their material meaningless. By comparison Fitzgerald makes every deft note pulsate. While Holiday focused in on rhythm and a kind of minimalist interpretation, Fitzgerald opened jazz swing right out, finding joy in the melody.

Fitzgerald toured consistently, on the road sometimes for fifty weeks of the year. This arduous schedule took its toll: she nearly lost her eyesight and had to wear glasses. Yet this didn't deter her. While Holiday died prematurely in 1959, Fitzgerald's career flowered as she became older, reaching her prime time in her 1970s tour of the jazz festivals. Despite the fact that by 1962 she had topped more polls than any other female singer in history, and in 1966 *Harper's Bazaar* listed her among the '100 Most Accomplished Women of the Twentieth Century', the private Fitzgerald was perceived as 'ordinary'. Although she was briefly in the headlines in the early 1990s when, disastrously, she had to have both legs amputated, she was rarely connected with the lurid drugs-and-tragedy stories that are so readily used to define women performers. Reluctant to buy into self-aggrandizement, she also disliked being referred to as legendary: 'It makes me feel like a relic.'

In 1988 Quincy Jones approached her to work on his *Back On The Block* album, a celebration of Afro-American music featuring a cross-section of stars from Miles Davis and Sarah Vaughan to rap artists Kool Moe Dee and Big Daddy Kane. Though initially reticent, Fitzgerald was persuaded to take part, enjoying her opportunity to 'be current'. There is a glorious, vibrant picture taken by photographer Annie Leibovitz at the time, which shows Fitzgerald wearing wicked white horn-rimmed sunglasses and a tailored but saucy scarlet suit, her hair almost bouncing off her head. For Fitzgerald musical excellence meant she not only survived but thrived. 'She wasn't at all shy and retiring,' Leibovitz told me later. 'I was playing Michael Jackson's *Bad* while taking the picture, and Ella kept saying, "I'm Bad!"'[18] When she died in 1996, she was celebrated as one of the most joyful female jazz icons.

## Sweethearts of Rhythm

Fitzgerald and Holiday were central figures in the swing era – but what of the women instrumentalists? Behind many great jazz players there was often a woman. Lester Young, for instance, was taught the fundamentals of the saxophone by his sister Irma, while he gained valuable experience playing in a band with his mother. Lil Hardin Armstrong, a famous pianist in the 1920s known as 'Jazz Wonder Child', was married to Louis for over ten years. Though they worked together and she encouraged him to become a solo star, she herself led numerous all-male and all-female bands in the early 1930s. A house pianist at Decca, with a postgraduate degree from New York College of Music, Armstrong composed over 150 pieces of music during her lifetime. She continued to play her loud, strong rhythmic style right up to 1971 when, at the age of sixty-nine, she died on stage while taking part in a live TV tribute to her late former husband.

Despite being an established star in her own right before her younger brother Cab, Blanche Calloway was passed over by Irving Mills's influential booking organization, suffering terrible financial insecurity. She bounced back in the 1930s with top players known as her 'Joy Boys', but never quite had Cab's success. Perhaps the most famous of female bandleaders to emerge in the pre-swing era was trumpet player Valaida Snow. She has been compared to Louis Armstrong, but emotional problems reputedly arising from being interned in Europe in a Second World War prison camp traumatized her to such an extent that she never fulfilled her potential. Hazel Scott, too, was a highly influential musician and social symbol of the black bourgeoisie. A Trinidad-born child prodigy whose mother once played with Lil Hardin Armstrong, she started performing solo at the integrated Café Society in 1940, adding a controversial jazz interpretation to classical music. Confident and elegant, her career spanned forty-five years, including Broadway, Hollywood, her own TV shows, and a collection of best-selling albums.

Aside from individual artists, all-women bands had a rich and varied history, despite their lack of chart success. From before the turn of the twentieth century, there were female vaudeville troupes, ladies' jazz bands, and all-woman dance orchestras. In 1927, for instance, trumpeter Leona Henderson led her female ensemble with the billing 'The Twelve Vampires – Twelve Girls Who Can Play Real Dance Music'. The year 1935 saw members of black women's jazz band The Harlem Playgirls go on to play with the renowned International Sweethearts of Rhythm, who dominated the women's dance-band scene throughout the 1930s and 1940s.

Women's bands were often formed as a response to the difficulty of getting access to the male jazz world – yet they were dismissed as gimmicks or novelty acts. Sometimes women acquiesced to pressure, emphasizing their physical allure over musicianship, as in one group billed 'The Band With A Bosom'. Many female musicians therefore resisted women's bands *per se* as a professional tactic. Oft-compared to Artie Shaw, clarinettist Ann Dupont, for instance, led all-male bands from 1939, after announcing that she was through with all-women outfits.

Taking a more positive view was Sarah McLawler, a Kentucky-born child prodigy who began playing piano at six, later winning scholarships to Jordan Conservatory and Chicago's Fisk University. 'I decided to help women all I can – whatever way I can help younger women – to inspire them,' she says.[19] She began entertaining as a teenager in the early 1940s, travelling the South with her father's permission in Lucky Millinder's band. 'I was a skinny brat. Had me an organdy dress with yellow socks and a ribbon, a sweet little girl featured with big old guys. They protected me, told me to eat my vitamins. In the 1940s then showbiz was very glamorous. All the clubs had chorus lines, dancers, comedians and complete productions.'

This experience proved useful when she moved to Chicago to join her sister, who worked as a songwriter. McLawler would play at a cocktail lounge in State Street, doing 'double duty' because she was broke. 'I liked to play late at night with gamblers and big-money people, I'd make a lot of tips. I'd be riding the subway at four in the morning with pockets full of money praying, Please God, let me get home safely.' After some years as a 'single', McLawler decided to form an all-woman small combo. 'There were lots of girls in big bands like the Sweethearts of Rhythm, but none out there expounding on their instruments like Dizzy or Miles in small groups. I heard about a new club opening uptown on the Southside, called Blue Heaven, and talked the manager into bringing in girl musicians to kick the place up.'

Leading some of the finest all-woman small combos of the day, McLawler drew talent from all-black big bands such as Darlings of Rhythm and The Harlem Playgirls. ' "Fix yourself up," I told them. "Look nice, be glamorous and play." ' One of her most famous groups was The Syncoettes, playing as a top draw in Chicago and New York between 1948 and 1953. The momentum faltered when one of her best members, tenor saxophonist Lula Roberts, died of spinal meningitis, and McLawler found her hard to replace. Discouraged by the number of women she heard who could not really play, McLawler worked again as a single before teaming up with her husband, violinist Richard Otto, until his death in 1979.

In the early 1990s she was still performing regularly in New York City. The night I met her, she was appearing at the Novotel in mid-town Manhattan, playing an array of jazz and popular standards, and, true to her word about encouraging other women, she invited a young female horn player, Deborah Sandoval-Thurlow, to join her for a few numbers. Although McLawler and her 1940s combos were treated with respect by other musicians, she feels that they never got the critical recognition they deserved. 'It made no difference how good we were, we were always seen as a novelty. I've not been recognized for the work and pioneering I've done.' She is clear about the cost of being a pioneer: 'My throat was closed, my hands was swollen. I'd play matinées and evening till two every morning on the chitlin circuit. If you wanna break a group send 'em to Atlantic City chitlin circuit. *That's* work'.

Despite a few individuals who managed to break through, bands of the swing era were generally no-go for women. For many their only route into the business was through all-female ensembles, particularly in Britain.

## There'll Be Bluebirds over the White Cliffs of Dover

'I still can't believe she's not here. I haven't taken her number out of my phone book. I can't,' drummer Chrissie Lee told me shortly after the death of her former boss and mentor Ivy Benson, the legendary female bandleader who died in May 1993 after a long, battling career.[20] Ivy's story is unique in British showbusiness. Although there have always been women's bands, from the early 1940s the Ivy Benson band was one of the major routes for women instrumentalists into jazz and studio work in Britain. While women in the States were making inroads into jazz and swing through such major performers as Holiday and Fitzgerald, and female dance bands like the International Sweethearts of Rhythm, their British sisters were some way behind.

As Charlie Gillett says in *The Sound of the City*, 'Britain has had little sense, in the twentieth century, of its own popular culture.'[21] Apart from surviving strains of nineteenth-century folk styles, until the Second World War British popular music was centred first on the light opera and variety of music hall, the brass-band network, and then the only radio station, BBC's Light Entertainment, which featured crooning and derivative dance-band sounds. The main roles for women in this area were either cloying or comic.

Gracie Fields, whose releases gave her record companies a steady income during the Depression, was Britain's first singer of modern popular music. As a music-hall and film star, the

Rochdale lass presented an image that was rousing, clean-living and slightly gawky. With her direct, humorous delivery, she set a trend for female singers as heroines of the working class, a role taken up by Vera Lynn in the 1940s during the Blitz. Standards like 'White Cliffs Of Dover' and 'We'll Meet Again' rallied listeners round the radio in a peculiarly British way. The blonde bouffanted Lynn was the reassuring gal who would make you a cup of tea and soothe with song. Through her lively request programme *Sincerely Yours*, a radio link between men serving overseas and anxious families at home, Lynn was dubbed 'The Forces' Sweetheart'.

In the same way that the Second World War opened up job opportunities for women through munition work, so it created a space for women in the music business. A charismatic, forceful figure, Ivy Benson took advantage of the vacuum created briefly during the war when many male musicians were conscripted, slotting her girls into club and variety tours and leading them into the job as the BBC's resident dance band. She also went on extensive ENSA (Entertainments National Services Association) dates in Europe and the Middle East, earning the distinction of performing more concerts to troops overseas than any other artist.

A great enabler, Benson once said proudly: 'I took a girl from a pie factory once, and made her a bass guitarist.'[22] Born in Leeds, the daughter of 'Digger' Benson, a trombonist with the Leeds Symphony Orchestra, Ivy was playing piano in working men's clubs at the age of eight and sax with the local British Legion band at fourteen. After stints with Edna Croudfoot's Rhythm Girls and Teddy Joyce's 'Girl Friends', Ivy decided to branch out on her own. Determined to make a mark in popular music, she spotted a gap in the market – i.e., women – and, creating a big band that was on a par with the major male bands of the day, took it much further than novelty status. Hers was the Ivy League, a kind of music school for girls in an era when 'the weaker sex' were not expected to play anything stronger than the parlour violin. 'There were girls before, but it's to do with the impact one makes. Suddenly one will come out of the blue – Ivy was that one. People will always remember what Ivy stood for, and the fact that she blazed a trail for them all,' says Gracie Cole, a quiet, taciturn woman and dedicated musician who played lead trumpet with Benson in the 1940s before going on to form her own All Girl Orchestra.[23]

'The first thing Ivy did when I joined the band was take me to London to Boosey & Hawkes, the most famous music shop in the world, and buy me a trumpet,' says Cole, who until then had been a star cornet player in northern brass bands. 'She wrote asking me to join her in 1940 – I didn't until 1945, but she'd had her eye on me all along.'

Like a mother hen, Benson took full responsibility for her 'girls'. When playing to troops during the war, sometimes the band would socialize in the officers' club after a concert. 'Ivy would go on the piano, play for atmosphere and a few requests. Boys would dance with girls, but at a certain time she'd put her hat on and say, "OK girls, we're ready!" She'd stand there and have us filing past like a roll call. There was no question of hanky panky – she was very strict, especially with girls under sixteen.' Part of this gentle yet firm surveillance was to protect her own interests: it was always a source of disappointment to Benson that she kept losing good female players to marriage and pregnancy.

Although she nurtured talent, she knew when she had to let it go gracefully. 'One of the first things to remember . . . is certain instruments consider themselves very hard to replace and one is tempted to do anything to keep them, even spend sleepless nights. Do not let it happen to you,' Benson replied to Cole, when in the 1950s the latter decided to form a women's band and wrote to Benson for the name of a good drummer. 'Remember the only important person in the outfit is yourself, and you pay the salaries, and you call the tune.'[24]

Cole was cheered to receive a letter full of advice – '"Don't make the mistakes I did, love." You could hear her Yorkshire accent!' – but after some successful tours with her female outfit, she soon noticed the lack of support and understanding when she went back to playing in male bands. Her time as the only woman in The Squadronaires was truncated because one trumpet player in particular, Ron Simmonds, found it hard to play with a woman on lead:

'He criticized my playing, would chat to others and ignore me, as if I didn't exist. I had to really control myself and my playing because I knew he'd have had a ball if I cracked a note. It got to a point where I gave up rather than play in those conditions. He said later he was envious because I was a famous player while he was up-and-coming at the time, and that made him mad. He was prejudiced, pure and simple.'

Benson was a useful conduit for women keen to be serious instrumentalists. Sheila Tracy, a trombonist with Benson between 1956 and 1958 who went on to form the brass girl duo The Tracy Sisters, remembers her period with the band as invaluable:

**Ivy Benson** conducting her All Girl Orchestra with Gracie Cole as soloist on Christmas Day 1945. Broadcast live from Hamburg, the show was relayed to England immediately following the King's Speech. (Gracie Cole's private collection)

'Ivy was a good leader because she was strict. I was put on lead trombone one night. It came to the last number at one in the morning, and she brought out an arrangement of "Rose Marie" – it had a top C in it and I cracked it. It was a bit of a solo, and I cracked it! She came down on me like a ton of bricks. Next morning I got up and said, "I'm handing in my notice."'[25]

Nevertheless, the confrontation gave Tracy the added incentive to put her duo on the road, the experience with Benson giving her the poise and musicianship needed to cope with a rumbustious variety circuit.

Benson recognized women's need to be not only 'as good as' men, but exceptional. Tracy, for instance, never wanted to play the 'acceptable' instruments for women. 'I was sitting in the orchestra as a Royal Academy student in the late 1940s, fourth desk of the second fiddle, scraping away, surrounded by women. I looked up at the brass where there wasn't a woman in sight; all men were sitting up there. I thought it'd be rather nice to sit up there.' A bright, enthusiastic woman in clothes of impeccable cut, Tracy knew then that there was no reason to hold herself back. She took up the trombone because 'it was more manly. I didn't fancy all these namby-pamby female things like violins.'

Don Lusher, a trombone player with many of the big bands, including Ted Heath's, admits that it was difficult for women instrumentalists to get work. 'We had nothing against having girls in a band . . . but you've got to remember it was a pretty high standard in those days. And maybe it wasn't as fashionable for girls then.'[26] Tracy recalls that the amount of prejudice against women was stifling. 'Women were rubbished,' she says, '"She looks pretty, but don't expect her to play the same way as a man" – that was the attitude. It's not true today because there are so many good girl musicians now in colleges. In my day jazz was absolutely taboo.'

Benson got her break during the war, but it was hard won. 'When the BBC made Ivy their resident house band all hell broke loose, because it was the plum job in the country. The male bandleaders didn't want to know her, they loathed her guts. And the reviews for the first broadcast were vitriolic.'

Adored by the troops and the general public though, Benson became a British star, more popular even than Vera Lynn. Although she could have capitalized on her popularity with US troops by going to America after the war, she stayed in Britain to consolidate her position. 'Then every door slammed in her face. Even the BBC turned its back on her, and with the band circuit booked up, there was nowhere to go. A committee of band-leaders was set up and they all closed ranks, saying, "We're not having Ivy Benson in." She said, "Don't you want me in? Forget it, I don't want to be in!"'

Benson survived by playing American bases and holiday camps before returning to the main circuit by the 1950s. Until recently much of her achievement has been overlooked, but her 1960s drummer Chrissie Lee was keeping the spirit alive well into the 1990s with her own sixteen-piece big band. 'I formed it after seeing a TV documentary on Ivy in the late '80s,' she said. 'I thought, we can't let this go. I want to push this further afield. We have to let the world know what British girls are doing, and we will!'

In the 1940s swing enshrined women's position as vocal stars, and as 1950s pop developed, they were invested with greater power, yet, paradoxically, even greater limitations. The next decade was about how women fought, negotiated and expressed that glittering role.

# Stupid Cupid

## DREAM BABES IN 1950S POP

**2**

'In 1943 I saw a film called *Orchestra Wives*. I wore my hair like one of the stars, Ann Rutherford, parted in the middle and cascading down. She won the good-looking trumpet player George Montgomery in the Glenn Miller band. I put myself right into that picture. Everything happened to me just like that. I got into the best band in the country, married a good-looking trumpet player and that was that. Pity it didn't end happily.'

    LITA ROZA, singing star and British post-war pin-up, author interview, London, 1993

## Peaches and Cream

By enabling them to do men's jobs, the Second World War may have temporarily given women a sense of freedom, but once 'the boys' came back they were manoeuvred out of the labour force back into the home. Because so many women became house-wives again with a sense of reluctance, their role had to be sugared and heavily sold. One of the most effective ways to market the image of domesticated femininity was through post-war pop – an ideal personified in Doris Day, the wholesome peroxide-blonde Hollywood star who began her career in 1940s big-band singing, with million-sellers such as 'My Dreams Are Getting Better' and 'Sentimental Journey'. Her métier in the 1950s was big hit musicals like *Calamity Jane* and *The Pajama Game*, or dramatic biopics such as *Love Me or Leave Me*, where she starred alongside James Cagney as glamorous gangster moll singer Ruth Etting.

Day presented a screen version of ideal womanhood, while women working more in popular music also played out a role of glamour and glitz, severely criticized if they stepped out of that rigid category. Not wanting to be cast as a 'peaches and cream' big-band trinket when she was working with Gene Krupa, singer Anita O'Day set a new trend for female singers on the road by wearing a shirt and band jacket on stage instead of a gown. 'I want them to listen to me, not look at me. I want to be treated like another musician,' she argued.[1] Krupa allowed her to 'dress down' for concerts that weren't in theatres or ballrooms, but for many years she was considered to be 'mannish' because she refused to be mere bandstand decoration.

The 'gown' question meant that women working in big bands were set apart from the male musicians, which inevitably bred an atmosphere of suspicion. Although they had more work opportunities than women musicians, big-band vocalists often felt they were there on male sufferance. It took guts to stay in a career that could be very isolating. Women had to work doubly hard to 'earn' their place. 'Musicians are strange,' says Lita Roza, one of the biggest British stars of the 1950s. 'They either like you or they don't. They've always considered female singers a boil on the face of God knows what, a necessary evil. I had a genuine rapport with them, probably because I wasn't a time-waster – they knew I was a professional, there to do a job. We got in and out. I never hung them up.'[2]

Women in the music business have always had to be singular and self-aware to avoid stereotyping, but in the 1940s and 1950s, when roles were much more restricted, self-belief had to be even more unshakeable – a rare commodity. The first woman in the UK to get a chart No. 1 with 'How Much Is That Doggie In The Window' in 1953 ('I sang that song once and I shall never sing it again: I was what you'd call "a sophisticated singer"'), Roza was cool and resourceful from the moment she walked unaccompanied into a pantomime audition in Liverpool at the age of eleven. It was her chutzpah that led her to the job as singer in the early 1950s for *the* top British big band, after she impressed the bandleader Ted Heath:

'I'd sent a demo to Ted and he invited me to audition one day when he was rehearsing his band at the London Palladium. After I sang he said, "How would you like to go on tonight?" I think he expected me to fall back in a faint. I said, "I'd like it." I went home, got a cocktail dress and came back. I went on that night and according to all the trade papers, I stopped the show.'

While most top female singers up to the end of the 1940s were usually attached to big bands, by the next decade they were emerging as soloists and stars. After leaving Ted Heath, Roza became a star in her own right, her smouldering half-Spanish eyes and robust yet silky vocals making her a favourite with pop audiences throughout the 1950s. Billed as 'THE GIRL WITH THE PIN UP VOICE', Roza was voted by *Melody Maker* the Most Popular Girl Singer every year between 1951 and 1956.

The fluffy 1950s Baby Doll image of flouncy gowns and cosmetic smiles belied a hard-working reality. Roza's experience of constant, exhausting touring was typical. In 1956 she ended up doing thirteen shows in one night, for instance, when performing for British troops stranded in Suez. 'I sang in garages, hotels, bars. I performed with my hair in pincurls! They didn't care, as long as they were being entertained. It was a wonderful experience, but, God, was I drained – I was dead when we got back to Britain.' Another day on the same tour, the captain of the Firth of Forth supply ship invited Roza on board for coffee. She asked her manager if she would have to sing. 'No, it's 10 a.m., we have to fly out at 2 p.m.,' was the reply.

'When we got to the ship I was piped aboard. I've never seen so many men – they were on the funnels, they were on the rails, everywhere! I had my hair in pincurls and felt dreadful. The first thing I was asked when I set foot on the deck, "Where would you like the piano Miss Roza?" I thought I was going for coffee! I did the show, but, God, was I glad to get home.'

Ivy Benson's band was a rare example of women working in solidarity, but more often the experience was as a lone female. Elaine Delmar, daughter of the famous black bandleader Leslie 'Jiver' Hutchinson, recalls touring on the Northern club circuit at seventeen in the late 1950s, organizing her own itineraries.

'I'd do a gig and go home on the milk train. Sometimes I'd play two or three clubs a night. It makes today's audiences seem easy. I've had whole audiences crossing over the club to get their meat pies. There'd be lots of booze, lots of smoke and rowdiness – the chairman of the club would come on stage saying, "Come on, give her a bit of support, give the poor cow a chance!" Dreadful.'[3]

By the early 1990s she had thoroughly 'paid her dues', performing when it suited her on a more relaxed, sophisticated jazz nightclub scene. After the years of grind, she admitted her career had never felt better.

International stars, too, were not exempt from punishing schedules. One eight-week period playing with the Count Basie band at the Strand Theater on Broadway, for instance, Billie Holiday performed five shows a day, seven days a week. 'You can go dressing-room crazy,' she once said.

Because the early pop business was a tough prospect in terms of prejudice and sheer working hours, women who stayed the course have an air of relaxed confidence. They have already proved themselves a hundred times over. One performer who exuded this like a wry secret was Marion Montgomery, a Mississippi belle who settled in Britain in the mid-1960s when she married a musician in the Johnny Dankworth Orchestra. Until then she had worked the clubs of the American South, sometimes as a white woman fronting an all-black band. Her father was very much opposed to a singing career, she explained in a genteel Southern accent, because, when she started in the 1950s, the jazz scene in particular was considered close to criminal.

'The first gig I did I thought, God, if you were trying to get me out of the business you sure pulled out all the stops. It was six strippers and me. All the waitresses tried to teach me to B-drink: that's where you walk up to some guy who's sittin' there, say, "Hello, d'you want to buy me a drink?" You sit down and they bring you some kind of crap in a glass, charging him a fortune for it. One night I eventually did it, and it turned out to be an undercover policeman. Luckily he screamed with laughter. The girls had set me up, 'cos they knew I wouldn't get into trouble. In a sense, when you're young your innocence protects.'[4]

## Dreamboats

One of the era's biggest stars, Peggy Lee combined that sense of innocence with classy ambivalence and assiduous career moves. Though rooted in jazz swing her striking image – ice-blond hair and refreshing delivery – marked her out as a potential pop siren from the beginning. In the first eighteen years of her career she had over forty hits, from 'Mañana' to 'Waitin' For The Train To Come In'. Many women singers tried, but none have touched the seductive sparse tension of her 1958 hit 'Fever'.

Born 'poor white trash' in Jamestown, North Dakota, and abused by her stepmother, Norma Delores Egstrom achieved a superb reinvention of self when she took the stage name Peggy Lee and went West to carve out a singing career in California. Oddly detached and quietly charming, she was not easily fazed – even when she got her first big break as vocalist with Benny Goodman. When he came to hear her sing in a vocal trio at a Chicago hotel, the sharp, dry bandleader gave nothing away. 'I was sure he didn't like me,' recalls Lee in her autobiography. 'He just stared at me and chewed his tongue. After the show, though, he said simply: "Come to work, and wear something pretty."'[5]

After two years and several hits with Goodman, she left to get married and become a housewife. Bored with retirement, she soon started recording again, with stints on Capitol and Decca. As well as featuring regularly in the Top Ten with songs like 'Lover' (1952) and 'Fever', she was a prolific songwriter, contributing to the soundtrack of the 1955 Disney film *Lady and the Tramp*, and co-writing with 'greats' including Ellington, Quincy Jones and composer Cy Coleman. Lee acted according to the part mapped out for her, genteelly seizing photo opportunities with high-profile friends like Nat King Cole, Frank Sinatra, Bing Crosby and, in later years, President Ronald Reagan. Unafraid of kitsch, she embraced the wackier elements of stardom; as when she flew over Los Angeles in a helicopter with Julie Andrews and tossed a six-foot bag of rose petals over her daughter's house. Or the time she set pale blue birds in delicate cages on each table for a ballroom gala evening in Texas. As soon as Lee started singing, so did they.

Lee had access to the mainstream in a way that was denied her contemporary Billie Holiday. This was not only due to the fact that Lee was white and Holiday black, but that Lee conformed to a 'Good Girl' standard. She had no publicly unattractive addictions or weaknesses. Frequently plagued by ill health and, in later years, often hospitalized, she took 'the show must go on' motto to extremes, once even performing with a broken pelvis. Holiday self-destructed while Lee spent much of her life in a battle to stay alive – one that she finally lost in January 2002. This fight was made easier by her acceptance into a white mainstream that championed a woman who observed protocol and played ambassador – joshing with and subtly orchestrating the male network around her so that she would never be rejected.

**Peggy Lee** in Lake Tahoe, 1953 – the bridge between 1940s swing and 1950s Dream Babe pop star. (Bob Willoughby/ Redferns)

As economic restraints on touring big bands signalled the decline of the swing era, popular taste shifted to smaller combos and individual artists, and there was greater pressure on women visibly to be stars. Lee was the bridge between the 'hip' era of white 1940s swing and its transmutation into 1950s pop. 'The 1950s were a big time for clothes,' she said with characteristic understatement.[6] There is a picture on the bill poster for a New York Basin Street East engagement that illustrates this appeal: the words 'Peggy's back' are set beside a dramatic shot of Lee turned away from the camera, with shining coiffured hair and drop diamond earrings, sheathed in a glistening white dress that reveals most of her bare back. With breathtaking directness it spells Glamour.

In the early pop industry, beauty was constructed in order to dazzle. Elaine Delmar remembers:

'In those days it was the sequinned gowns with a very tight waist. I'd go to a dealer and buy them for £200, £300. They were made by a wonderful dressmaker. And these gowns were *built*. You had to have someone pull you into it. Beautiful workmanship. If you bought one it could last you ten years.'

There was an element of bravado in how expensive a girl could get her dress, and the bigger the star the dearer the sequins. When British star Alma Cogan first approached bandleader Ted Heath, his advice was: 'Remember two things. First, when you sing a song you must mean every word of it. Next, you must always dress beautifully.'[7]

Cogan took this literally. 'Dress designer Lily Anthony took three months stitching and embroidering 12,750 rhinestone and *diamanté* beads into an intricate lace bodice' read a press release at the height of her fame in the mid-1950s, just before an appearance on the premier TV show *Sunday Night at the Palladium*. 'The beading forms part of the most fabulous "powder puff" skirted gown ever designed for a television appearance.'[8]

Only in pop can a dress be a marathon Event. Cogan travelled in Rolls-Royce cars that had to have space for her dresses. She left the stage door one evening wearing a dress covered in green feathers, but by the time she had passed through 2,000 fans to get to the car, she didn't have a feather left, having been plucked like a chicken. For the Royal Variety Performance in 1955, she was worried about upstaging the Queen with a vast mauve crinoline dress sporting 14,000 beads. Luckily Her Majesty remarked, 'What a wonderful dress you are wearing, Miss Cogan.'[9]

In contrast to that of her mother, a slightly raddled merry widow who smoked cheroots and wore her lipstick in a vivid bow, Cogan's camp, ornate image required meticulous upkeep. In daily life Cogan wore muted cashmere, but on stage she created a complete 1950s fantasy, a combination of Dior's New Look and Girl Next Door.

With her regal glitz, Cogan was the first British female TV singing star to become more than derivative of American pop. Her main rival, the Belfast charmer Ruby Murray, who assaulted the charts with reassuring ballads like 'Danny Boy' and 'When Irish Eyes Are Smiling', lacked Cogan's charisma. Even though in 1955 Murray had five hits holding simultaneous Top Twenty positions, Cogan was more popular, the first female singer to have her own major TV series, broadcast on ITV between 1959 and 1961. She took her vocation seriously, as vocalist, entertainer and hostess.

Mistress of bouncy trivia, Cogan made comic novelty hits and light ballads, releasing her first record 'To Be Worthy Of You' in 1952, and reaching No. 1 three years later with 'Dreamboat'. Famed for her Kensington-flat parties, she entertained all the celebrities of the day, from Noel Coward and Cary Grant to John Lennon, who called her 'Sarah Sequin'. Her star status lasted until TV began to kill off the variety-theatre circuit that sustained her. When the hits died (among her final records, 'He Just Couldn't Resist Her With Her Pocket Transistor' was a 1960 Japanese No. 1), Cogan toured fanatically, collapsing while in Sweden in 1966 and dying a few months later. The girl with 'the giggle in her voice' died of stomach cancer at the age of thirty-four. Cogan epitomized the 1950s Baby Doll, unable to escape the image that crystallized and drove her.

Connie Francis played out a similar role as America's biggest 1950s female star. She courted male approval, but in the end it tragically didn't offer the protection she needed. Born Concetta Rosa Maria Franconero in 1938 in Newark, New Jersey, she was singing in variety shows and on local TV by the age of ten. Taking cues from her strict Italian father (Francis recorded her first hit 'Who's Sorry Now' in 1958 at his suggestion), then from the industry as a whole, Francis sustained a run of twenty-two Top Twenty MGM hits in six years from 1958 to 1963. Featured in Hollywood movies aimed directly at the new teen market, such as *Where the Boys Are* and *Follow the Boys*, she set the trend for the cute white female star. Light songs such as 'Lipstick On Your Collar' and oldies rearranged with glimpses of rock 'n' roll guitar licks meant that she spanned the adult market and the burgeoning younger generation.

Throughout her career Francis released over sixty albums, including compilations. She branched out into cabaret in the late 1960s, and worked hard doing charity work for CARE, USO and UNICEF. In 1974, having had a model showbusiness career, she was raped and robbed at knife-point following a performance at Westbury Music Fair in New York State. After a long hiatus, she performed a warmly received comeback at Westbury in 1981, but never regained ground, her life after the crime dogged by problems. Such an act of male violence must have made her career as pop's Good Girl seem meaningless.

## I Want to Be Evil

The 1950s Baby Doll was very much a phenomenon of the white mainstream. Though few black women achieved such broad popularity, they were paradoxically able to project a more realistic image, perhaps because of racist notions about black people being closer to a gritty, emotional truth. The segregated nature of music marketing also meant that black women had considerably less access to the mainstream. Fifties rock 'n' roll star Big Mama Thornton, for instance, had a No. 1 R&B hit in 1953 with 'Hound Dog', but its success was eclipsed three years later by Elvis Presley's version, which went into the pop Top Forty.

Black female artists hardly skimmed these charts unless, like Lena Horne or Eartha Kitt, they were lighter-skinned. Horne's success in the 1940s was crucial for black women in America. Vaudeville star Josephine Baker twenty years earlier had to go to Europe to succeed, while Horne, fêted as the 'New Negro' of the Harlem Renaissance, was both street smart and a symbol of the rising black bourgeoisie – the first black woman fully to 'cross over' into the international club cabaret scene. Her grandmother Cora Calhoun Horne was a militant suffragette and Urban League NAACP (National Association for the Advancement of Colored People) activist who left behind a political legacy for the younger woman to emulate. Elegant and intelligent, Horne began her career as a singer/dancer at the Cotton Club in 1934, touring with Noble Sissle and then recording in small groups with leading swingers of the day like Teddy Wilson and Artie Shaw.

Horne achieved worldwide fame during the 1940s after she went to Hollywood and became the first black actor to negotiate her own contract, refusing to play undignified roles like the maid or the jungle native. Although starring in box-office successes such as *Cabin in the Sky*, *Stormy Weather* and *Ziegfeld Follies*, Horne was never a studio pussycat. A complex heroine, she did not supply easy answers for either side of the racial divide. In the 1950s, an era intolerant of interracial marriage, her career suffered because she spoke out against prejudice, and married her white accompanist Lennie Hayton. During the 1960s, however, a more militant younger generation criticized the former wife of black boxer Joe Louis as selling out to the supper rooms. Horne's reply was to the point: 'I can't get up in a nightclub in a $1,000 dress and start singing "Let My People Go".'[10]

Horne's appeal, too, was complicated. A Second World War pin-up, she matured throughout the 1950s in a manner that spoke to both sexes. 'She does not flatly sing suggestive stuff, and makes no obvious pass at male audiences,' remarked

*Esquire*'s Robert Ruark. 'She does rather direct her mood at women, who seem more allied with her . . . that true love is harder on girls than boys.'[11] In later years it hurt Horne to realize how arid her early performances had been, the result of trying to keep dignity and cool reserve while at the same time being accepted by white audiences. It was a difficult card to play, and one that resulted in sparse work throughout the 1970s. She was rewarded, though, with respect from younger singers. One night in 1972 she was visited backstage at the San Francisco Circle Star Theater by Dionne Warwick, Lola Falona and Mary Wilson – three stars who'd formed Bravo, an unofficial association of female singers. Presenting her with a ring, they thanked her for being the trail-blazer who made it easier for them to pursue their careers.

Almost ten years later, Horne proved that she had longevity when at the age of sixty-four, the initial six-week run of her Broadway show *Lena Horne: The Lady and Her Music* was extended for fourteen months. It closed in June 1982 with a record 333 sold-out performances, the longest-running one-person show in the history of Broadway. Possessing a delicate glamour that worked easily in the white mainstream, Horne's blackness, her sense of being the Other, meant still that she was never stuck in the Baby Doll caricature that so limited Cogan and Francis.

Eartha Kitt was an altogether racier proposition. Haunted by the memory of a cotton plantation owner who overshadowed her childhood with his grim catchphrase: 'Nigger's a fool, nigger's a fool', a man who took on Brothers Grimm-monster proportions in her rags-to-riches fairy tale, she was determined from an early age to reinvent herself as the epitome of class and cool. This became translated at the peak of her career as an insecure arrogance, but her antagonistic behaviour was the result of trying to control a world that, when she was a girl, so devastatingly controlled her.

At sixty-six, slim, scary and bright as a button, Kitt's ferocious cool was the response to that bitch of a showbusiness in which a 'yella girl' never properly belonged. 'When my career took off in the 1950s it was difficult for women in general, but particularly brown-skinned women. The William Morris Agency said to me, "Yes, you're a beautiful, talented, intelligent woman who's got everything going for you, but we don't know what to do with you",' she told me in 1994.[12]

Not white enough to be a mainstream commercial act, yet not black enough to slot into the emerging soul movement of the black community, Kitt fell between pedestals, fashioning a bizarre act that was half Catwoman, half sultry striptease and brilliantly humorous styling. Despite almost grudging agreement on the part of a series of major labels (Capitol, MCA, RCA) to put out her material – 'Record companies thought I was strange. They said my voice was too weird and nobody would accept it' – Kitt had huge hits with songs like 'Uska Dara' (sung partly in Turkish), 'C'est Si Bon', 'I Want To Be Evil' and 'Santa Baby'.

Born Eartha Mae in 1928, a sharecropper's daughter in the backwoods of South Carolina, she was abandoned by her mother to an adoptive family who victimized her because of her light skin. Always the ugly 'yella girl', Kitt set out to prove herself attractive for the rest of her life. 'Yes, I was abused, used and accused, but you used it as manure to be constructive about yourself. I didn't fall by the wayside,' she says. It was as if she turned early experiences of sexual abuse by her adoptive mother on to the world. Behind the feline sexuality of the Catwoman pose that made her famous lay an element of hostility and aggression – a camp, 'vamp' image that crackled against the conservatism of 1950s pop culture, and led Orson Welles to call her 'the most exciting woman in the world'.

Sent to live with an aunt in New York, the teenage Kitt left high school to become a seamstress in a Brooklyn factory. She inveigled her way into the Katherine Dunham dance troupe, and ended up becoming a featured dancer, travelling through Europe and Mexico. Like Josephine Baker before her, Kitt was captivated by Europe's seeming cultural sophistication, far removed from the racist South where she had grown up. This manifested itself in the affectation of her voice, a haughty,

**Eartha Kitt**
on US date, 1989:
Catwoman, 'yella
girl' and seasoned
'rich man's
entertainer'.
(Ebet Roberts/
Redferns)

playful purr that suited the exotica of her Eurasian temptress.

When Kitt sang 'I Wanna Be Evil', you believed her. Only black girls could be bad and make it sexy: Doris Day had to have a shadow side, and Kitt was it – fulfilling the potent myth of black woman as morally dubious and sexually adventurous. Her career in the States didn't take off until her Broadway appearance in *New Faces of 1952*, in which she mixed sex with sharp humour. Her main means of promotion were through expensive nightclubs, movies, and TV talk shows. 'They called me the *crème de la crème* of café society,' she says, 'which meant that I was a rich man's entertainer.' Though her act was risqué, Kitt insisted that she never took her clothes off:

'Not for my job. I wore skimpy clothes as a dancer, and I'd strip off a gown to flex my muscles. I'd have a bikini brassiere underneath to go into a dance number. I consider myself to be sensual rather than sexy. Sexy is something you act up. You wear *décolleté* dresses with bosoms hanging out, your belly button or *derrière* showing. That to me is not sexy, it's just vulgar.

The 'Bad Girl' stance served her, while simultaneously limiting her. Although Kitt's celebrity status gave her access to philosophers and Heads of State, from Albert Einstein to India's Prime Minister Nehru, when she denounced the Johnson administration involvement in Vietnam she was reputedly blacklisted by the FBI. Once her career peaked with the arrival of rock 'n' roll, she was pushed further into the cold in the 1960s when, like Lena Horne, she crossed the racial divide, marrying white businessman William McDonald.

By the early 1990s, Kitt was back in favour with the White House, using the opportunity of a gala dinner there to berate President Clinton about high taxation. Kitt also lobbied for campaigns such as Project Ongrowing, an urban allotment initiative for 'street people'. 'I'm related to this. I worked on farms all summer as a kid – this project is part of me.' Cultivating the soil was important for Kitt. In the spirit of her name Eartha, it connected her with the sharecropper's urchin inside. 'People call you tough when you're really just shy and timid,' she said to me. 'You're afraid of being rejected. I can walk into a room and I'm so scared I give the impression of not enjoying it. After you get acquainted with a couple of people though, and they treat you all right, then it's fine.'

Kitt deliberately put a distance between 'Bad' stage Eartha and quiet homely Eartha to guard herself against the intrusive aspects of fame. By contrast Judy Garland was an artist who lived the diva role in the same Broadway/cabaret society, but without respite or reserve. When it became too overwhelming she drowned herself in alcohol and painkillers. Kitt meanwhile saved herself with a protective humour that gave her fairy-tale life its realistic grounding.

## La Vie en Rose

The cabaret tradition looked to Europe for its sophistication, and to Paris in particular, the city that spawned one of its greatest exponents, Edith Piaf. Taking the tortured torch song to extremes, Piaf lived out the tragic romanticism of her life, her interpretation of popular song infusing the pop ballad for decades to come. A street singer from the age of fifteen, Piaf honed her trade in the vaudeville theatres of 1930s Paris. Christened *'la môme Piaf'* ('the waif sparrow') by her first employer, Louis Leplée, who was later killed in a gang-related murder, the diminutive Piaf sang songs of love, loss and degradation amid the slums and sea ports in raw, unembellished tones, the full melancholy nature of her delivery winning audiences worldwide. Most successful in the late 1940s and early 1950s, she made standards of such love paeans as 'La Vie En Rose' and 'Hymne À L'Amour'. Popular music creates most impact in the telling of stories, and the tale of her life became inextricably linked with the pathos of her material. 'Piaf was a street singer, like rap artists now,' says the 1990s French *chanteuse* Liane Foley. 'She started out with no comfort, no money, she sang in the street. She was revolutionary – she sang mostly love stories and she sang the misery of the world.'[13]

Piaf had an excellent ear for good songwriters, and though, like many women in pop who died young, she has been presented as a victim, hopelessly addicted to painkillers and unsuitable men, Piaf was also a woman uncharacteristically in control of her career, at one time purportedly one of the highest-paid entertainers in the world, third only to Sinatra and Bing Crosby. On stage she milked and manipulated the rapport she had with an audience – in one performance shortly before her death she collapsed but the show still had to go on. In a moment of bathos someone tried to drag her off stage, but she fully surrendered herself to the melodrama, clutching hold of a piano leg, wailing that she had to finish and could not disappoint the crowd. Off stage she could also be a brisk operator, acting as mentor to many young male singers of the day; under her patronage for instance, the careers of Yves Montand and Charles Aznavour took off. Her emotional masochism was also tempered by a strong rebellious streak. During the war she worked for the Resistance, smuggling POWs from camps under the noses of the Gestapo.

Piaf is a pop heroine on a par with Joan of Arc. Her contribution has been to widen the scope of pop ballad, introducing *chanson* to the international language. Her tours of America in the 1940s and 1950s were key to this development. At first the US was slow to react to her minimalist theatrical style, but through diligent touring of the small intimate club network, Piaf in the little black dress became a symbol of a mordant, delicate sensuality in an era when the mainstream was gorging itself on the blonde-bombshell dynamic of pin-up stars like Betty Grable.

An Americanized version of Piaf's style grew on Broadway – the baroque flourishes of Judy Garland and in later decades the unabashed romance of Barbra Streisand (see Chapter 14). Torch in its pure form has been kept alive more in European pop, with artists like Foley in France, Germany's Ute Lemper and Carmel in England displaying very different styles. Lemper, for instance, harks back to the brooding bohemianism of Lotte Lenya and 1930s Berlin street cabaret with her interpretation of satirical playwright and songwriter Kurt Weill, while Carmel wraps her soaring voice around a combination of French pop and the blues. A major star in France by the late 1980s, Carmel told me, 'I want to shift away from the swing emphasis of pop and things American by opening up new ground in what I term "the song". It's music with more European influences. Musically I'd like to stand on my own territory.'[14]

In 1989 Carmel (Scunthorpe-born Carmen McCourt) could smile knowingly at me and say with confidence that she was mixing up genres, thereby not obeying the rules of the market. Three decades earlier three women in particular found them-

selves either stranded or bouncing between categories. All origi-
nators, Dinah Washington, Dusty Springfield and Nina Simone
felt a deep unease at their prescribed roles. Each had a musical
sensibility that went beyond the Baby Doll stylists. Performers
like Connie Francis, Lena Horne and Alma Cogan may have
sparkled and inspired, but none of them were making unheard-
of connections. Washington, Springfield and Simone, each in
their own way, were plugging deep into the undercurrents of
R&B and pop opera that would surface in the 1960s. They were
women anticipating change and transgressing boundaries, yet at
the same time frustrated by the obstacles of race and sex. In
order to transcend those categories, they had to work some
magic.

## Do Nothing Till You Hear from Me

She was called a witch because of her charm, her ability to
enchant and seduce through song. Dinah Washington was the
missing link between the blues and swing of the 1940s and the
glorious technicolor of 1960s R&B. Able to swerve from sexually
frank blues authenticity to smooth chart pop, Washington had a
warmth that imbued every song that she chose to transform.
Unlike that of other performers of her era, her style does not
date. It is typical of Washington's genius that she took the
mannered wit and gentility of a 1930s English musical hit and
turned it into a full-throated paean to an older woman's lust and
longing. It was her rendering of the Noel Coward original 'Mad
About The Boy' that tore through an early 1990s Levi's commercial soundtrack, the class, rawness and gloss of her voice
resonating decades after her death.

'Dinah had the ego of an ox but Ruth Jones was a sweet little
girl,' once said sax player Eddie Chamblee, one of her many
husbands. Ruth Jones was the little girl from the South Side of
Chicago who travelled with her mother Gertrude performing
gospel recitals on the early-1930s church circuit. By the age of
fourteen she was choir director and church piano player, and for
a year sang with Gertrude in the Sallie Martin Gospel Singers,

the first all-female gospel group. By 1942, at the age of seventeen, she had changed her name to Dinah, married for the first time, and started singing outside gospel. Much to her mother's chagrin (Gertrude considered all blues to be the devil's music), Washington's early recordings are rooted in the blues, drawing on the straightforward delivery of Chicago blueswomen she had grown up with, like Georgia White. She began performing in the secular world with the Lionel Hampton band, but by 1943 was singing on her own.

Between 1949 and 1961 Washington had nearly thirty R&B hits on Mercury Records, beginning with Leonard Feather's 'Baby Get Lost', a magnificent song of sauce and disdain where she tells her suitor to play it her way or vanish. Whether it was singing to the thrill of her dentist's 'drill' in the explicit innuendo of 'Long John Blues', cutting through with assurance the schmaltzy strings of 'What A Difference A Day Makes', or asking frankly whether she was just his latest flame on 'It's Too Soon To Know', Washington conveyed the essence of female desires.

A powerful mentor and businesswoman, shortly before her death Washington had launched her own booking agency, Queen Attractions, handling Sammy Davis Jr, Aretha Franklin and Muhammad Ali, and was thinking of establishing a scholarship fund to help young singers. She did much to resurrect the blues artist Bessie Smith by recording *The Bessie Smith Songbook*. She owned her own restaurant in Detroit and a charitable concern, the Ballantine Belles. Like many stars, however, Washington had a flip side: extravagant, brash and gunslinging. Along with peroxide-blond wigs, she had a penchant for crystal chandeliers, mink toilet-seat covers and men – there may be some dispute about whether she had seven or nine husbands, but it's clear she had a large appetite for life.

Though ebullient and robust, she operated from a baseline of insecurity. In an era before anorexia nervosa was 'officially' recognized, Washington was addicted to slimming pills and tranquillizers, going through wild fluctuations in weight. When she died at the age of thirty-nine in 1963 of an overdose of pills and alcohol, she weighed only five stone (seventy pounds). She died in Detroit, just as Motown was breaking. More than any black artist before her, Washington had taken great strides sweeping black music without compromise into the mainstream. Had she lived, she would have continued to resist category and enrich music's vocabulary – but the strain of pleasing the crowd as well as straddling the divide between jazz/blues improvisation and the art of pop proved to be too much.

## A Single Woman

Nina Simone is another black woman who moved between genres with absolute assurance. While Washington worked magic with the seductive chimera of her playful delivery, Simone cast a direct spell over her audience. Simone's version of the Screamin' Jay Hawkins original 'I Put A Spell On You' still chills with its intense overtones of desperation, charm and voodoo. A commanding musician, she has been to the edge many times, fighting through marginalization, prejudice and her personal torment to create something fierce with integrity.

In 1992 she was a slightly ravaged sixty-year-old diva, sitting in a West End hotel room wearing a curious négligé-cum-evening gown, her hair swept back, her lower lip trembling, her eyes proud. When I arrived to interview her she was scolding her publicist for not ensuring that copies of her autobiography *I Put A Spell On You* were in the shops. 'But it's not out yet,' said the PR with enforced politeness.

'I don't care,' was Miss Simone's reply. 'They should be in the shops, and I want to see the money for them.'

Low-down promoter or high-class publicist – to Princesse Noire they were the same thing – people out to cheat her. Thinking Simone had forgotten about me I ostentatiously fiddled with my Walkman. In mid-harangue Simone briefly turned to me. 'I'll be with you,' she said kindly, before concluding her rap.

'I hate showbusiness,' she claimed, after the PR had gone. 'It's hard. You never know if you're gonna get your money. There's

**Nina Simone**
at Ronnie Scott's,
London, 1984:
'I Put A Spell On
You'.
(Val Wilmer)

different hotels, different airplanes, bad food. When it's all finished you have people pirating your records and stealing from you. The poor always ask you for money; they think you lead a special Cinderella life. It's all nonsense.'[15]

Simone's life has been one long, erratic saga of being misunderstood. A one-time classical musician, she should have been a world-famous concert pianist, but instead poverty and prejudice led her to the pop world and a showbusiness format that has never been taxing enough for her. The disdain shows. She wouldn't be seen dead in a video blow-drying her hair like Diana Ross, or dancing on the ceiling, Lionel Richie style. A self-contained legend, she has carved out a powerful personal sound of blues, classics and soulful hymns – from 'I Loves You Porgy' to the phenomenally successful 'My Baby Just Cares For Me'.

Her life-story is packed with 'should have beens'. She should have become America's first black classical pianist, but the only realistic route open for a poor unknown black girl in the 1950s was supper-club swing or a strong dose of the blues. She should have been happily married with 2.2 kids and a white picket fence. Instead the rigours of the road left her with two failed marriages and a string of abandoned lovers. She swears that, could she live her life over again, she would have married her first boyfriend and had babies. 'I maybe would have continued with my music, if he'd allowed me to.'

It is difficult to imagine the star who danced naked in a Liberian disco and attempted to seduce Louis Farrakhan buckling down to the role of obedient wife. Like a seasoned connoisseur she was candid about what she admired in a man. 'I don't want a fat man. I can't stand that, can't stand his snoring. I want him tall and thin and tender. Aware of how to make love. He must be rich, or have some money, so he doesn't envy mine. He must love sports. Love to dance. Love music. Preferably black. If I can get him.'

A haughty but oddly vulnerable woman, Simone asserted herself so early on that acquiescence never came easy. Born Eunice Waymon in 1932, the sixth child of a Methodist preacher's family in Tryon, North Carolina, Simone hopped on to the piano stool at two and a half and, like a little-girl Mozart, played her mother's favourite hymn note-perfect. Her mother, a stern, distant minister, then channelled Simone into a life of musical excellence.

At six she was playing church revivals, in her teens she was sent to an exclusive, mainly white, private school for girls with a top academic record, and her hometown launched a fund to finance her musical training. After a year's scholarship at New York's Juilliard School of Music, it was expected Simone would win a place at the elite Curtis Institute in Philadelphia. 'There was a lot of black pride and money invested in me.'

Despite her brilliance, the young Eunice was rejected. Even though many claimed it was a racist decision, she felt humiliated. Reluctantly turning her back on the classical world ('How was I going to be the first black concert pianist in my spare time?') she changed her name – a Hispanic boyfriend kept calling her Nina, Spanish for 'little girl', so that stuck, and Simone she adopted after the French actress Simone Signoret. She then began performing popular songs in bars to earn money for further tuition. Early bitter disappointment was to infuse her music, creating a sense of tragedy as stagey as it was magnificent. For her first gig, a downtown dive in Atlantic City full of 'drunken Irish bums', she played sitting erect in a chiffon gown, her hair and face meticulously made up. A big-boned woman with wide shoulders and a strangely regal face, Simone always took her diva role seriously.

Beginning to attract a young, hip, beatnik audience, Simone moved to New York and in 1957 signed her first record contract with the Bethlehem label without looking at the small print – a mistake that would cost her over a million dollars in royalty wars. Simone never had a smooth relationship with money. At times dogged by debt, and hounded by the American tax authorities for ten years for not filing tax returns, Simone became extra vigilant about getting paid.

Despite her feigned indifference to the entertainment world, through years of relentless international touring Simone perfected the art of hypnotizing an audience, using both intense musical emotion and absolute silence. Although her voice in later years grew cracked and worn, she still had that calculated ability to mesmerize. A concert could be an assault of nerves – she has been known to harangue an inattentive crowd.

'Sometimes she's all right. Sometimes it's just torture,' says Stuart Lyon, a London promoter who worked on her 1989–90 concerts. His wariness was understandable: in 1984 Simone had been booked an extra few sell-out weeks at Ronnie Scott's club, and failed to turn up.

'You're always on edge, never quite sure which way it'll go. I remember having dinner with her once and she asked me about the singer Najma Akhtar: "How is that Asian girl? I really enjoyed her tape." I said, "She's doing well in France," and Nina suddenly spat out, "There you go, some other bitch riding on my coat tails!" She wouldn't speak to me for ten minutes. Talk about unpredictable. The audience tended to be adoring even if she abused them. Half the people expect that. She's unique, the last of the working divas."[16]

Though burned by her initial Bethlehem deal, it was a song re-released from her first album and used on a Chanel No. 5 commercial that was to be her biggest hit and led to a comeback in 1987. Simone believes 'My Baby Just Cares For Me' to be one of her slighter recordings, but it opened a whole new market to her music. Before that she was considered a left-field soul singer who'd had her day. She had spent the 1970s drifting, from Africa to Switzerland, to an attempted suicide in London, to ending up broke in Paris. Success in the 1980s gave her back her self-respect.

Simone's highest point was in the 1960s, supporting the civil rights movement, penning such classics as 'Mississippi Goddam' and 'Young, Gifted And Black'. Friends with James Baldwin, Stokely Carmichael and Miriam Makeba, she was one of the first black American entertainers to 'rediscover' her African roots, spending four years in Liberia. The year 1993 saw further success with the release of a new album on Warners, *A Single Woman*. She sang of living alone, and how that hadn't always been easy. A kind of dignified reprise, it featured sleevenotes by the American writer and poet Ntozake Shange:

'Not unlike the mythic *Charlie Parker With Strings*, this album found Nina Simone, her deep and sensate voice, nestled among arrangements featuring strings and guitars, allowing the power of her vocals to float and penetrate our realities at will . . . evidence that a politically conscious life may not be correct, but may be rich in moments and memories, as when Nina sings, as only she can, "Love's been good to me".'

Although devotees were delighted, Simone pointed out to me at the time that her music doesn't come easy. 'These days I have no inspiration to write. Two months ago I wrote two tunes. I was pushed by the fact there's money in it – that gives me inspiration to write.' She was flattered that film star Bridget Fonda, as the tough heroine in the 1993 US remake of *Nikita*, found such solace in her music. Six Simone songs were used on the sound-track.

True inspiration, though, came back when she returned to her classical roots. One evening in 1992, for instance, she played

The Beatles' 'The Long And Winding Road' with the Boston Symphony Orchestra. 'It brought back a lot of memories and I cried, because that was the happiest I'd been with my music in about ten years.'

## I Only Want to Be with You

Dusty Springfield was another witch on the cusp of two worlds, a shape shifter who began her career as a 1950s Baby Doll, yet bursting from within was a sultry soul singer deeply attached to the blues. When Springfield was eleven, her convent-school teacher asked the class what they wanted to do when they were older. 'I want to be a blues singer,' Springfield piped up. Despite gaping differences in terms of race, history and musical environment, a middle-class Home Counties Catholic girl in the 1940s called Mary O'Brien found Bessie Smith. An old schoolfriend, Angela Dean, recalled a school talent contest in which she, Springfield and another girl performed a song. 'Mary [Dusty] did all the arrangements, the guitar and the harmonies. She chose "St Louis Blues", which we in all our innocence sang. The nuns walked out in disgust. They thought it too raunchy!'[17]

Even after she left school and became a star, Springfield had continually to rein herself in for the 'delicacies' of a white audience, in accordance with the strictures of mainstream pop. 'Everything was so well-pronounced, the diction had to be correct. It was also fast and panic-stricken. You had to sing like that in those days of Light Entertainment,' recalls Riss Chantelle, prime mover of The Lana Sisters, the female vocal trio she formed after playing guitar with Ivy Benson. 'I'd put an advert in the paper, and Dusty answered. She was a well-educated girl. When someone writes a good letter you know they'll fit in.'[18]

Briefly successful in the late 1950s, The Lana Sisters – Springfield, Chantelle and Lynne Abrams – were a key attraction on the variety TV/theatre circuit. After signing to Fontana they issued an array of songs like 'Chimes Of Arcady' and '(Seven Little Girls) Sitting On The Back Seat', busy pop tunes

**Dusty Springfield** rehearsing for *Ready Steady Go!*, London, 1964: blonde 1960s mod icon. (Val Wilmer/ Redferns)

dripping with breathy harmonies. 'It was my group – I booked it, sang in it, drove it,' says Chantelle. 'We'd go to Denmark Street [London's Tin Pan Alley] and before we could get out of the car, publishers would be rushing to us saying, Here's a song for your next broadcast. We came back from town laden with acetates.'

For The Sisters, though, it was a struggle to avoid trivial material. 'We were trying to make it good-class pop with jazz-minded phrasing. We'd have got a lot further, but in 1959 we had the onslaught of the rock 'n' roll boys. We were raring to go, but having to compete against all these boys – Tommy Steele, Cliff Richard – the 2 I's coffee bar was brimming over with them. We had to fight our way through.'

After gaining a few years' experience in The Lana Sisters, Springfield moved on to perform innocuous bushy-tailed folk pop with her brother Tom in The Springfields. By the time she launched herself solo in 1963, she already had a Grand Plan. 'She saw showbusiness as a job. Like a solicitor or an accountant,' says Chantelle. More than that, Springfield had a musical mission. 'I was struggling to establish something in England that hadn't been done before,' she told me in 1988, when she was still living a life of exile in Los Angeles. 'No one could use those musical influences I heard in my head. Now the British music industry is 2,000 times better, with singers like Annie Lennox and Alison Moyet. In the 1960s there was no one like Sinéad O'Connor. She's fabulous, young and Irish. Where was she in the 1960s?'[19]

Back then Springfield was on her own, a white British girl frustrated with studio musicians who couldn't approximate the sound she needed in order to flourish. Paradoxically, it is this tension between a desire to create searing soul and the pull towards acceptable pop – the fact that she felt this dichotomy so sharply – that makes her sound so distinctive. In the late 1980s when post-modern pop duo The Pet Shop Boys drew her out of California obscurity to record 'What Have I Done To Deserve This?' Springfield didn't understand what they wanted until it struck her: 'They didn't want me to DO anything, they just wanted the sound of my voice. It was that simple!'

That sound of transient pain and husky promise on her international solo debut 'I Only Want To Be With You' was the start of seven hectic, exhausting years marked by twenty UK and European hits. As the major female contender in the celebrated 'British Invasion', she also had six hits Stateside. Despite her bouffant hairdo and drag artiste mascara, Springfield was as much part of the early mod scene, appearing regularly on the pioneering pop show *Ready Steady Go!* dramatically throwing herself into the studio crowd. When Mick Jagger was considered a joke by the style cognoscenti, Springfield had 'cred', defying barriers, working to ensure that her fans acknowledged black American soul and R&B. Resisting the British fixation with dollybird pop *à la* Cilla Black and Sandie Shaw was an uphill struggle, but her vocals were rooted in soul, and many from

Martha Reeves to Mary Wells assumed she was black. Staying 'true to the faith', in 1968 Springfield recorded the classic soul album *Dusty In Memphis* for the US Atlantic label, and 1970's *A Brand New Me*, produced by the Philadelphia Gamble & Huff team, earned her the dubious title of blue-eyed soul singer: 'a pigeon-hole term coined in 1969 which stuck'.

Tired of the British music business, with a private life under siege from the tabloids, Springfield decamped in 1974 to Los Angeles, thinking it was there that she could pursue her musical dream. America's vastness, along with the segregated nature of its music industry, bewildered her, and she was steered by ill-advised management into glitzy supper-club cabaret. Her career faltered, and apart from intermittent, unsatisfying albums, Springfield spent the 1970s lost and alone. While many agree that the problems were of her own making, Springfield suffered from being a trail-blazer, trying to articulate R&B torch song in an era when white girls were not supposed to express raw 'black' emotion.

The 1980s and 1990s were kinder to her: resurrected through The Pet Shop Boys, she began recording again, with the highly acclaimed albums *Reputation* (1990) and *Dusty In Nashville* (1995). In 1988 she appeared in a TV commercial for the orange-juice drink Britvic 55, espousing 'The Real Thing'. Like Simone and Washington, whose sound has enough 'authenticity' to sell classic products, Springfield's drive for musical excellence meant the barriers of pop acceptability were broken. It wasn't until she died tragically of breast cancer in 1999, at the age of 59, that her genius was finally acknowledged. Stars worldwide, including Cher, Elton John and The Pet Shop Boys, paid tribute to Springfield as one of the finest female vocalists of her generation.

Dinah Washington, Nina Simone and Dusty Springfield presaged the 1960s, an era when pop was to explode, splintering those Baby Doll myths right along with it.

# 3 The Real Thing

'We were our own Disney World. The Supremes, The Four Tops, The Temptations – we were the rides, we touched the world.'
MARY WILSON of The Supremes, author interview, Los Angeles, 1993

COCA-COLA, LEVI JEANS and the 1960s girl-group sound are 'The Real Thing' – that high-pitched, humming, nasal, husky, teen-girl sound derived from gospel and soul, yet so unique. Like the white-label underground of techno-house records in the 1990s, girl groups were on the cutting edge of 1960s pop, issued by small independent labels and sent on to the market from one week to the next. One song, like The Chiffons' 'He's So Fine', might become a classic, lasting decades after its release. Another would die within two weeks, to crumble in a vault until resurrected for specialist CD compilations in the 1980s and 1990s.

The girl-group sound was clearly identifiable: like punk, it blasted the market for a short period before mutating, maturing and becoming assimilated into mainstream pop. Like punk or house music, its impact was considerable. It articulated the *Zeitgeist*, the fresh ebullient hope of the early 1960s; it feminized rock and provided the basis for the 1960s beat groups of the famed 'British Invasion', particularly The Beatles. The demise of the girl-group era is often blamed on The Fab Four; it's ironic that in appropriating the girl-group sound a male band inadvertently destroyed it through their own success. In the same way that a white person (Elvis) made millions out of the previously segregated blues, so it took a male band to capitalize on the female-group sound, and when they moved on to rock, their teen muses were left behind. Male beat groups from The Beatles to Manfred Mann drew on the girl-group sound to achieve a kind of permanency, while the women, apart from Diana Ross and Ronnie Spector (who were stars), were considered throwaway. \\

But as with anyone who dies young and leaves a shimmering corpse, there is a fascination about the genre that has lasted decades after its death. Girl groups, from The Shirelles to The Supremes, have mythic status. Woven into the mythology surrounding the manufacture of that grand sound are a dozen or so fairy-tale characters: the Beauty and the Beast, Phil Spector and Ronnie the Ronette kissed a frog and he turned into her deadly Prince Charming, her Bluebeard; the Ugly Sisters, Diana Ross and Flo, a kind of demented Snow White and Rose Red in bitter rivalry; Darlene Love, the Cinderella, always at the hearth – she shall go to the ball! – still waiting for her glass slipper.

A myth is a 'narrative involving supernatural or fancied persons, embodying popular ideas or social phenomena'.[1] Women love telling stories – they read them to children at night, they relate them to girlfriends in the ladies' room – the girl-group era is a gigantic narrative full of morality tales locked up like charms in a crystallized sound. The real women of the cast – Martha Reeves who takes her Vandellas touring on a hard-working nostalgia circuit of gay clubs and family venues; The Crystals' LaLa Brooks who became a Muslim, changed her name to Sakinah Muhammed, settled in Britain and in 1987 was threatened with deportation; Arlene Smith, lead singer of The Chantels, who now teaches elementary school in the Bronx and does community work with children of drug users – are separate from the polished myths that surround them. In order to penetrate those myths, it's necessary to go back and look at the fiercely competitive conditions within which they worked.

## Tycoons of Teen

Small record labels often form a cluster, a buzz and an identity around which things happen. No matter how tiny the original group of enthusiasts, entrepreneurs and artists – from that stars and then a myth can be built. The luminous girl sound was centred round the independents Red Bird, Dimension, Philles, Scepter, Laurie and, of course, Motown. Not all their product was exclusively girl group, but it was an area in which each specialized. Major labels such as Columbia, Mercury, Brunswick, RCA and Liberty tried to launch their own girl groups – RCA in particular, with Reparata and The Delrons – but few of them had major hits. As with any street craze, the majors were too large to react quickly enough to the taste and demand of a fickle, volatile market.

Girl groups had most success with the songwriters, labels and producers who focused completely on their sound. Feeding the small labels were three main husband-and-wife songwriting teams: Gerry Goffin and Carole King, Ellie Greenwich and Jeff Barry, along with Barry Mann and Cynthia Weil, all based in New York's centre of song publishing, the Brill Building. Although other writers figured on the scene, until Motown these three partnerships were the nucleus of the girl-group industry.

'You're out there as a kid, barrelling along doing your thing. Then twenty years later your songs get used in commercials, basketball games, all over TV . . . that's neat,' says Ellie Greenwich. Thirty years after her success writing hits for groups like The Crystals and The Ronettes, the writer of 'Be My Baby', 'Then He Kissed Me' and 'Leader Of The Pack' recalls,

'It was wonderful, really simple. At that time anyone could walk into the door of a publishing office and be heard. Jeff and I worked with Leiber & Stoller [publishers] and built their little stable with Phil Spector. Little families were created, people helped each other out. If we had an idea for a song a record company liked they'd say, "Here's $5,000, let's take a shot." There was a spontaneity about the process. For instance, I did background singing for Lesley Gore. One day I wrote "The Look Of Love" in the back of a cab; I called her producer Quincy Jones the next day, then had lunch with her without a demo – just sat at the piano playing the song. The next week she was in the studio recording it. It was the era of singles – talk about excitement! It was the music business, now it's the music *business*.'[2]

Back in 1957, five years before Greenwich became the jewel in
Leiber & Stoller's glossy crown, the girl-group business was in
its early, raw stages. Post-war pop consisted mainly of white solo
artists like Connie Francis singing more adult novelty and light
satire, or rigorously jolly groups such as The Chordettes and The
McGuire Sisters, who had No. 1 hits with 'Sincerely' and
'Sugartime'. This trend shifted when The Chantels, four
teenagers from New York, issued 'Maybe' on George Goldner's
End label. The song reached No. 15 in the national pop charts, a
considerable feat for an unknown black girl group. Their
winning sound was a combination of doowop street-corner
harmonics, rattling drums, Gregorian chant and Arlene Smith's
lead vocals, teased way up high at a time when commercial
voices were still mid or low range. Though taking its cues from
male doowop, the song broke through to huge untapped
territory in its articulation of teen-girl concerns and romance.

This budding genre, however, didn't reach fruition until
1960, when The Shirelles came out with a follow-up to their Top
Forty tickler 'Tonight's The Night'. Released on Florence
Greenberg's Scepter label, 'Will You Still Love Me Tomorrow?'
was the first girl-group single to reach No. 1, launching an
overnight onslaught of girl-group frenzy. The Shirelles laid the
blueprint for the 1960s sound – girlish vocals fraught with adolescent idealism and pain, plus quirky arrangements embellished
by strings and a dramatic drumbeat. 'The most important thing
about this music, the reason it spoke to us so powerfully, was
that it gave voice to all of the warring selves inside us struggling,
blindly and with a crushing sense of insecurity, to forge
something resembling a coherent identity . . . ,' says writer Susan
Douglas. 'In the early 1960s, pop music became the one area of
popular culture in which adolescent female voices could be
clearly heard.'[3]

Certain songs were flashpoints: Little Eva's 'Loco-Motion',
with Eva Boyd's robust, sweet vocals bubbling over rhythm; the
urgent certainty and compulsion of The Exciters' 'Tell Him';
and The Crystals' heartfelt 'He's A Rebel', marking the first
major success for a young, obsessive producer, Phil Spector. All

these songs struck in 1962, the year the girl-group scene hit financial paydirt.

Spector is rightly credited as being the architect of the Wall of Sound, in songs such as The Crystals' 'Then He Kissed Me' and The Ronettes' 'Be My Baby', though many claim that all he did was take existing musical structures and simply build harmonic overload – layer upon layer. His genius was in switching around pop's vocabulary to create clearly identifiable songs rather than piled noise. For instance, he introduced the minor keys of jazz into pop for dramatic effect, and brought in Wagnerian elements of *Sturm und Drang*. Between 1961 and 1965 Spector had seventeen records in the Top Forty, and with ten million sales at the age of twenty-three, he was dubbed the 'first tycoon of teen' by writer Tom Wolfe. The studio was his factory of experimentation, churning out mass commercial appeal. Greenwich recalls:

'Oh gee. I think he was out of his skull, totally. He was always making weird noises and he was always late. My first meeting with him, I sat waiting from 2 p.m. until he showed up four hours later at 6 p.m. I start playing him a song and he's looking in the mirror, making noises, walking up and down. Eventually I slammed down the piano saying, "When you're ready to listen, come in." I told people afterwards, I don't care if it's Spector, the guy's crazy and very rude. Next time I met him by accident. I'd written "The Boy I Want To Marry" and he wanted to produce it for Darlene Love. It was really funny, because he walked in, saw me and said, "It's you!" I looked at my watch. "Four hours late, Phil."

'But it worked, it was funny. He was very erratic, but on a creative level, terrific. I found him fascinating – he was like a little Svengali, very dominating. He's slight of stature, and he had a terrible background, but made up for whatever inadequacies he felt with a powerful presence, a controlling need. I was very young then and found him vulnerable. He felt Jeff and I to be the most sensitive writers to work with. We knew when to leave him alone, he felt comfortable with us.'

A canny Spector also knew that his main songwriting team had talent that would be hard to replace. The female artists on his Philles label were treated with less respect. The Crystals, five young girls from Brooklyn, started out singing the songs they recorded, but were soon cheated out of royalties when Spector hired a session singer, Darlene Love, to record songs like 'He's A

Rebel' and 'He's Sure The Boy I Love' for a flat studio fee. The girls had to tour and front No. 1 hits that they had not even recorded, yet couldn't leave Spector because he owned their name. Fostering an air of insecurity and dependency, he played one artist off against another – promising Love, for instance, a singer with probably the most powerful pop voice of her generation, a solo career, yet issuing a track she recorded solo under The Crystals' name. 'After "He's A Rebel" I wanted a contract,' Love said later. 'I wanted royalties they were three cents a record in those days, or something ridiculous like that. Well, I never got what I felt was due to me.'[4]

I saw Love thirty years later, performing her 'biographical' concert Portrait Of A Singer, at New York's Bottom Line. Gracious, vivacious and singing with a permanently startled look, she only referred to those early frustrating years once, when she introduced herself as 'the most successful "unknown" singer in the history of music'.

The daughter of a Pentecostal preacher, Love's voice combines gospel fire with a sense of street-teen innocence. It was a style honed from the age of sixteen, when, as Darlene Wright, she joined a girl group called The Blossoms and became one of the hardest-working session singers in Los Angeles. The Blossoms' versatility meant that they could accompany black and white artists in a range of styles, from Duane Eddy to Doris Day. After meeting Spector in 1962 she soon became his number-one vocalist, singing lead on fifteen hits (for other acts) and supervising the backing vocals for at least three dozen other songs. The more she fought for a solo contract and due recognition, the more he relegated her to the background. 'The singers were nothing to Phil,' she recalled. 'He used to say it was all about "his music". So I'd say, "If it's all about your music, why aren't you making instrumentals?"'[5]

By the late 1960s Love had stopped singing for Spector but was left with no concrete solo identity. After ten years backing Dionne Warwick, and a prospective solo deal with hip 1970s soul label Philadelphia International that came to nothing, Love ended up earning a living as a cleaner. It got to the point where if she was driving and heard one of her songs on the radio, she would stop the car, break down and cry.

After a slow, gritty climb back into the business, during which Love had to pawn her jewellery and sing on cruise ships, by the late 1980s she was on tour with Cher and recording sessions with Whitney Houston. Her *Bottom Line* show finally gave her the recognition that had eluded her for so long.

In the 1960s Love was a major talent in a minor role, but the girls who fronted the groups weren't necessarily the best. It has been observed by many industry insiders that groups like The Shirelles and The Ronettes were not great singers. Their working conditions, however, were hardly ideal. Young, inexperienced women were often not consulted on marketing or recording decisions, while job insecurity made it difficult for them to flourish.

Those women who could get work as instrumentalists fared better, achieving a self-sufficiency that was rare in the business. Carol Kaye, for instance, a key studio guitarist whose trademark Fender bass sound is on countless hits by acts ranging from The Supremes to The Beach Boys, had steady work for decades. Originally a bebop jazz guitarist who opted for studio sessions to support three children and an ageing mother, during the 1960s Kaye was 'the hottest thing in town'. Among the two hundred or so session players, she was considered part of the elite, nicknamed 'The Wrecking Crew'. Although she was a white woman playing R&B, she has always maintained that she had the respect of male musicians and was never the victim of prejudice.

Whether or not it was because she was white, Kaye's position as an exceptional instrumentalist was relatively secure, whereas most black female vocalists had to work knowing they could easily be replaced. Even Spector's flagship group The Ronettes suffered this insecurity. Three light-skinned, street-tough New York black girls, sisters Veronica (Ronnie) and Estelle Bennett and cousin Nedra Talley, they were the first female superstars of rock 'n' roll, touring with The Beatles and The Rolling Stones, causing fandemonium wherever they performed. 'There were a lot of girl groups back then, but they had the toughest sound of

Estelle, Veronica
and Nedra,
**The Ronettes**,
in 1964: three
streetwise New
York girls meet DJ
Alan Freeman on
the British ITV
programme *They
Sold a Million*.
(Mick Patrick's
private collection)

all,' recalled star Billy Joel. '"Be My Baby" oozed sex . . .
Ronnie's voice – it sounds almost lubricated. It's got that smell
to it, like sweat and garlic.'[6]

Their mini street-pop symphonies – 'Be My Baby', 'Baby I
Love You' and 'Walking In The Rain' – plugged into deep levels
of teenage passion. 'I wanted to be the Marilyn Monroe of
Spanish Harlem,' said Ronnie Spector, who prepared herself for
stardom even as a little girl. At the peak of their fame in the early
1960s, The Ronettes were the girls every teenager looked up to.

'We were like three goddesses up there, it was incredible,' Spector later recalled, 'We'd pile the hair higher and higher, and extend our eyeliner . . .'[7] She was also grooming herself for Prince Charming, and when one of the most powerful men in showbusiness turned his attention on her, she fully reciprocated. With Ronnie, though, Spector's paranoid insecurity reared its head. By the time he married her in 1966, he was burned out, he had made many enemies in the business and his empire was crumbling. In an effort to control those closest to him while everything around was disintegrating, Spector kept Ronnie away from the studio, locked in their twenty-three-room mansion in Los Angeles. When he allowed her out on her own, he forced her to drive with a blow-up plastic man on the seat next to her – supposedly to deter any would-be suitors. He would play the film *Citizen Kane* to her over and over again, identifying with Charles Foster, the anti-hero tycoon who takes a talentless nightclub singer and tries to turn her into an opera star.

Despite his high-art ambitions, Spector could sink pretty low. By now a victim who would drink herself into a stupor, Ronnie colluded in the masochistic fantasy to such an extent that it took her husband to beat her to the ground and call her 'a nigger cunt' to make her flee. Singer Gloria Jones and Darlene Love met Ronnie soon after her divorce. 'We looked at her like, "What happened",' said Jones. 'Ronnie was like the cheerleader in the old days, happy-go-lucky. Phil took that away from her.'[8]

After a period of obscurity in the 1970s, Ronnie made several attempts at a solo comeback, with a glam-punk vamp image in 1979 and a more retro nostalgic outing with CBS in 1988. Both faltered, through not only poor material, but also Ronnie's own failure of nerve. Her story echoes the familiar girl-group tale of brief meteoric success, followed by lack of career development and crushing ignominy.

She came back again fighting in 2001, working on an album with Joey Ramone (who called Spector 'the original bad girl of rock 'n' roll'.[9] She lashed out at those who said she had been Spector's puppet. 'It's such a myth that's been going around for years that Phil was our Svengali. He was producing and writing (but) you also had to have that lead singer, and that was me.' She came to the conclusion that Spector was jealous of her audience. 'I can't sing *any* of my hits on any TV show. He's taken all that away. I've been in litigation for fourteen years and in a way he's doing me a favour 'cos it keeps me going,' she remonstrated. 'I refuse to let anyone *erase* me like I never existed.'[10]

## Leader of the Pack

The Shangri-Las' story was almost as dramatic and seedy as their songs. Their svengali was a cult, eccentric producer from Long Island called George 'Shadow' Morton (so-called because he would disappear for spells of time), who masterminded the pathos of their first hit 'Remember (Walkin' In The Sand)', complete with crying seagulls. Leased to Red Bird Records via Ellie Greenwich, who was a schoolfriend of Morton's, the song went to No. 5 in 1964. This brought a whole new dimension to the girl-group sound, the concept of girl-talk as pop opera. Inspired by its success, Red Bird teamed Morton with Greenwich and Barry for the follow-up 'Leader Of The Pack', a motorbike tragedy where the heroine's rebel boyfriend is killed in a high-speed crash. A song featuring the technique of call and response, it is one of the most heart-wrenching classics in girl-pop history. For me and my friends, who encountered it second time around when it shot into the UK charts in the early 1970s, this was our pre-teen drama, the one we learned the words to – right down to every tear and every rev of that deadly motorbike.

'That was a little soap opera,' says Greenwich. 'I hear people singing it now, and it makes me feel proud.' The Shangri-Las were lead singer Betty Weiss, her sister Mary, and twins Marge and Mary Ann Ganser, streetwise kids from Queens who epitomized the white girl-group sound – slightly nasal, crystal-clear, talking tough. Although obedient during the flush of their early career, once it peaked after their last Top Ten hit 'I Can Never Go Home Anymore' in 1965, The Shangri-Las lost their direction. Betty had left the group, while the remaining three aimlessly toured the country without management or adequate

record company support. Strange reports of gun-running, kidnapping and drug overdoses underlined the sadness of their 1970s obscurity. Despite eleven hits, they never realized their potential – maybe because their use of pop banter and serious girl-talk was too ahead of its time. A fitting epitaph, their last single 'Past, Present And Future', a spoken-word song that 'bubbled under' in 1966, was described by critic Richard Williams as 'one of the most mysterious and moving tracks in all of pop'.[11]

Altogether more wholesome, Lesley Gore presented an image of white suburban Jewish Americanism that slotted more comfortably in the pages of teen magazines. Ironically, she delivered a message that was far more feminist than the helpless-girlfriend status of The Shangri-Las. 'You Don't Own Me', one girl's determined caution to a possessive boyfriend delivered by Gore with an air of self-contained independence, hit the Top Five in 1963. This followed three huge hits, the first of which, the gloriously spoilt teen queen anthem 'It's My Party', went straight to No. 1 earlier that year. Discovered by producer Quincy Jones while still at high school in New Jersey, Gore marked the transition of white female solo artists from the over-sugared, careful tones of the 1950s to fully fledged 1960s soul/pop. She was one of the few women in the girl-group era to be marketed as a magazine personality and role model.

Such success was much easier for white women in an industry where black performers were considered to be 'minority' interest vocal vehicles for girl-group songs rather than their main exponents. It took an all-black, independent company to tip the balance – Berry Gordy's Motown. Even when his label was a baby Detroit office, Gordy nursed the ambition of launching a black female diva on a par with such white mainstream stars of his era as Debbie Reynolds or Doris Day.

The experiment began with Mary Wells, Motown's first female star, and the first artist to give them an international profile when 'My Guy' went to No. 1 in the UK in 1964. Wells had the intelligence and sense of class that Gordy was looking for, but she was lured away from the label and signed to Twentieth Century Fox on the (unfulfilled) promise of a film contract. A stylized 1960s 'sharp girl' with her huge eyes, tight mohair skirts and a walk, Wells left Motown in 1964 when she refused to renew the contract she had signed at the age of seventeen. Without Smokey Robinson's focused attention as producer and writer her career foundered, with unremarkable stints on various labels throughout the 1960s and 1970s. She died of throat cancer in 1992 after decades of litigation with Motown. Although bitter for a long time, she recognized the importance of the label, once saying: 'Until Motown, in Detroit, there were three big careers for a black girl. Babies, factories or daywork. Period.'[12]

Even though Gordy was an enabler, he did not encourage solidarity or independence among his female artists. 'I guess people at Motown figured, if we can disunite The Marvelettes, we can fight them,' said Gladys Horton, founder member of the group.[13] She was the one to take the girls' reconstructed blues song 'Please Mr Postman' to Berry Gordy, which after some treatment by Motown producers became a No. 1 hit in 1961. The Marvelettes went on to have several Top Ten hits, including 'Beechwood 4-5789', but within eighteen months of their initial success, Gordy lost interest and the group dropped from the charts. Although they were able vocalists and arrangers, Horton felt that Motown looked down on them as naïve 'hicks from the sticks'. Coming from the dirt-track town Inkster, Michigan, they lacked the sophistication of the other female acts. 'We weren't pretty city girls from the projects like The Supremes, with nice clothes and make-up on and long nails,' she said. 'We had no experience of life at all.'

Motown became a conduit for upward mobility with the establishment of its famed charm school under the tutelage of Maxine Powell, a dignified lady whose task it was to smooth out the 'street' from her girls. For artists like Martha Reeves, this was a challenge. 'I had been captain of my cheering team and a tomboy. I had very little grace, and no idea how to be charming – I just knew I could sing,' Reeves said in 1994. Sitting in a London hotel suite smoking roll-ups and dressed in a brightly coloured jacket and gold chains, she may not have been the epitome of taste, yet she still exuded grace and poise, giving everyone full attention and courteously greeting the waitress.

'I remember Miss Powell gave a speech to all the girls in the class – The Marvelettes, Mary Wells, Claudette Robinson, us and The Supremes, we were all gathered together. "You're not the prettiest girls in the world," she said. "You're not the best singers. But what I'm going to teach you will give you all the charm, finesse and glamour you need to take you through the rest of your life." We rolled around on the floor with laughter. She stayed firm. "It'll take you all over the world, if you apply yourself." She gave us handsome tips that I use even today. I'll always be grateful to her. She made us walk down the stairs with books on our heads, sit on stools without falling off, keep our knees together. I loved the Motown experience, I feel I graduated from university – between the choreography from Cholly Atkins, the music director Maurice King and the charm school of Miss Powell – I feel I got the best education any performer could get. All young, upcoming talent needs people expert in their field to show them the ropes.'[14]

Reeves hasn't always been so sanguine. For many years she was locked in disputes with Motown over royalties, and once said, according to writer Gerri Hirshey, 'I think I was the first person at Motown to ask where the money was going. And that made me a enemy. Did I find out? Honey, I found my way to the door.' Reeves now denies she said that. Feeling her views have been misrepresented, she is usually reluctant to give interviews, but decided to speak out on this occasion partly as a way of laying the battles to rest and partly to get due acknowledgement as one of the key female players in the driving force of Motown. Starting there as a secretary, Reeves had a practical, working knowledge of the company that made her less content to just sing and look decorative.

'My relationship was with the producers and musicians. I wasn't an artist or a groupie. I became the A&R secretary: there were sixteen guys in the department and no women. I started keeping records because they weren't. Not only did I love the music, I had compassion for the musicians, I knew how to handle the producers. I think it helped my tracks – I had some of the hottest tracks that came out of Motown, "Nowhere To Run" and "Dancing In The Street" speak for themselves. That was only because I got to know the guys writing them, they looked out for me real good.'

Martha and The Vandellas certainly had some of Motown's 'blackest' tracks. Reeves's earthy soul voice took girl-group music into a darker, more funky vein – released amid the mid-1960s turmoil of US race riots and civic unrest, Vandellas songs encapsulated the frenzied upheaval of the time. Although she says that the No. 1 worldwide hit 'Dancing In The Street' was only about 'dancing, getting people united as one again', against the backdrop of the Detroit riots, many took its message to be radical. That radical essence was still there when she performed live in the early 1990s. She and two sisters, Lois and Delphine, were in a Brixton club doing what amounted to a nostalgia show, and when they launched into 'Nowhere To Run' the crowd roared. Thirty years dropped before our eyes, as we felt the heat of that intense 1960s soul maelstrom. A song she must have sung a thousand times before lived anew.

Though she had a talent Gordy respected – the run of Vandellas hits continued until 1967 – Reeves was not the glitzy superstar material he had in mind. Too pushy and outspoken, she defended her Vandellas at every turn and fought for session musicians to be properly paid. It grieved her that even while her group were at the peak of their success, Gordy focused his attention on the 'no hit' Supremes.

'Nobody was competing at first. We were all hopefuls, all wannabes. We were sisters, and the early Motown Revues were like camping tours or girl scouts. We ate together, we grew together, we learned together . . . you can't take that away. The rivalry started when the groups were separated off, and Berry selected Diana Ross and The Supremes as his favourite pet group. I guess we were all trying to contend for his affection.'

Gordy has been condemned for his treatment of The Vandellas, The Marvelettes, and indeed The Velvelettes, another Motown girl group who scored a classic hit in 1964 with 'Needle In A Haystack', but he had a clear idea of the girl group he wanted to take 'uptown', and these acts did not have the finesse needed to get there. He didn't waste time, and went straight for it when he saw it. Was that cold ruthlessness, or professional instinct? Snobbery within Motown meant the country gals, those with the rougher edges, didn't fit – but if that was the criterion, maybe they were on the wrong label. It wasn't just the rawness that mattered. Although she was one of the finest soul singers of her generation, scoring hits with The Pips like the original 'I Heard It Through The Grapevine' and 'Help Me Make It Through The Night', Motown act Gladys Knight was too experienced, her delivery almost too mature. It wasn't until she left Motown in 1973 (amid legal difficulties over royalties) for Buddah Records that her career fully flourished. Songs such as 'Midnight Train To Georgia' and 'The Best Thing That Ever Happened To Me' showed an adult range and depth. In contrast, Gordy's glittering female icon had to have a girlish innocence that would slot perfectly into the young, aspiring pop market. Impossible hopes and expectations were projected on to Motown, and in its search for prestige those who couldn't be groomed into compliance inevitably would remain in the background.

The hunch he had about Miss Ross proved to be correct – even though it took three years to get there. In 1964 The Supremes' second single 'Where Did Our Love Go' went straight to No. 1, starting a record run of thirty hit singles up to 1972, twelve of which reached No. 1. One of the first black acts to play New York's Copacabana, they were soul divas who sold massively to the white mainstream and did more to sustain the girl-group myth than all their forerunners and rivals combined.

'We were our own Disney World,' Mary Wilson said, thirty years after that first No. 1. 'The Supremes, The Four Tops, The Temptations – we were the rides, we touched the world.'[15] The Supremes were the fairy-tale ideal, role models for the aspiring female fans who made up a large proportion of their record buyers. Ross in particular was adept at ladies' talk, exuding the appeal of the girl in the class who dressed the best, knew the best make-up tips, how to get your man, how to get the best man. She appeared open and vulnerable without laying herself on the line, a role that she still performs today.

Although chat-show host Oprah Winfrey tried to pin Ross down during an interview in 1993 on the eve of publication of her unrevealing autobiography *Secrets of a Sparrow*, Ross would not be drawn, protesting, 'The girls ignored me in the dressing room and that hurt . . . but, hey, let's not get negative!' Over the years Ross has made several attempts to rehabilitate her reputation, mainly since 1986 when Mary Wilson published her memoirs *Dreamgirl: My Life as a Supreme*, in which she claimed Ross was manipulative, selfish and duplicitous. She also said that Ross was unmoved when Florence Ballard, the third original member of The Supremes, who had the strongest soul voice, was sacked from the group. Ballard resented the fact that she was pushed into the background, while Ross, by then Gordy's mistress, was brought into the limelight. Although nasal and peculiar, Ross's voice was distinctive, and it became The Supremes' trademark, at the expense of Ballard. As blunt and upfront as Ross was tactical, Ballard didn't endear herself to the

The young **Supremes** on *Ready Steady Go!*, London, 1964 (note a young Gary Glitter in the background!): the first soul divas to sell massively to the mainstream. (Val Wilmer/ Redferns)

Motown godfathers early on when she loudly remarked about Gordy: 'Ain't that the man who rips his artists off?'

Overweight and drinking to numb her depression, Ballard was forced to leave in 1967. The name of the group was then changed to Diana Ross and The Supremes, emphasizing Motown's decision to single out Ross as the star artist. Her solo career came to fruition when she quit the group in 1970 and went solo, while The Supremes went on to have a few more hits like 'Floy Joy' and 'Automatically Sunshine' with Jean Terrell at the helm. Meanwhile Ballard's career and health deteriorated. She lived alone on welfare, memories and drink until 1976 when she died of a heart attack at the age of thirty-two. Her death punctured the myth of the three Detroit princesses from the projects, highlighting a grittier story of female friendship and rivalry. Wilson told me:

'I have a huge portrait of Flo near my bed. I wake up every morning and her eyes stare at me. Our friendship never changes, it's very spiritual. She's as alive as ever. I felt the loss when Flo left – that was the end. The connection between the three of us had been broken. It was a very hard time because I was still in the group trying to keep my head above water. I was just sorting out where I wanted to go.'

She remained through line-up changes to the bitter end of The Supremes, touring under the name long after the group had been officially disbanded by Motown, having to get accustomed to a lower profile after a decade at the top of the charts. Ross by comparison kept up the superstar momentum, working diligently to fulfil the promise that Gordy saw in her. She employed an expensive, supportive team around her, averaged a major hit a year throughout the 1970s and 1980s, appeared on Broadway and starred in movies, notably the 1972 biopic *Lady Sings the Blues*, where her portrayal of Billie Holiday was highly acclaimed. One of the main lessons Wilson learned was how divisive and unfair the industry could be:

'If you work with friends you have to try and communicate even when it's not the easiest thing to do, especially in business matters. Business gets in the way and you lose a friendship that shouldn't have been lost. That was true with Diana, but money has nothing to do with what we feel inside for each other. The business happened so fast it got out of our hands. But I know in my heart she loves me and I love her.'

On the subject Ross is curt and clear. 'Mary's book seemed to say that if her life didn't work, it was because I left The Supremes. If Florence Ballard left the group because she was unhappy, I didn't know about it,' she said in 1993. 'If a person's life isn't working, they want to blame someone else. I'd rather take responsibility for my own life. I no longer see Mary.'[16]

Like many women who were stars in the girl-group era, Wilson is still searching for that elusive record deal. She plays corporate dates and gala events for nostalgia fans, and wrote a second book, *Supreme Faith: Someday We'll Be Together*, about her experience as a woman coping with the 1960s legacy. 'It's a comeback book, about the woman's plight – what happens after women have been major stars. I also do a lecture called "Dare to Dream", which is inspirational and motivational, a lesson in what you should and shouldn't do.'

She finds it frustrating when 'people see you one way and want to keep you that way', and it hurts when record companies say she is a has-been. Maybe Wilson lacked Ross's audacity; she didn't make enough noise. But then, she smiles to herself, 'Berry always said I was a quiet rebel. A classy lady rebel.'

## Natural Woman

Another strand of R&B that went deeper than the girl-group sound was the gospel-derived dynamics of deep Southern soul – a grainy, gutsy genre spearheaded by Aretha Franklin and Stax label artists such as Carla Thomas and Mavis Staples (of the famous family Staples Singers). These artists, together with blues belter Etta James ('Soulful Miss Peaches') on Chess, paved the way for full-throated stars like Patti LaBelle and Tina Turner.

Gospel was one of the main influences on rock 'n' roll and modern soul. Turn-of-the-century black American pentecostal churches added instrumentation and tempo changes to 'Hillbilly hymns', creating a raw, exciting, devotional music that by the 1920s was being performed outside the church in touring gospel groups. The son of a minister, Thomas A. Dorsey was one of the first to commercialize gospel, selling revivalist songs or ballads for pennies. He toured with Ma Rainey and discovered Clara Ward and Mahalia Jackson, dedicating his life to gospel within the church.

When gospel was incorporated into the wild rhythms of rock 'n' roll and the screams of male artists like Little Richard and Screamin' Jay Hawkins, the religious community was scandalized. Nervous of the secular world destroying their 'sanctified' style, gospel churches have always had an uneasy, if not hostile, attitude towards the pop business.

With church congregations consisting largely of women and children, the contribution of women to gospel, and in turn blues

**Sister Rosetta Tharpe**
at Fairfield Hall, Croydon, in 1964: star of gospel music's rich sorority. (Val Wilmer)

and jazz, is huge. It's not surprising therefore that it was a woman, Chicago-based Sister Rosetta Tharpe, who first tried to dissolve the line between sacred and secular. The daughter of a missionary, Tharpe began her controversial career singing gospel songs in a Cab Calloway show at the Cotton Club in 1938, stylizing and rephrasing the music for a jazz audience.

The elders of the church were outraged, but Tharpe maintained that the Lord was ready to listen wherever He was addressed. The music easily crossed boundaries: when historian Rosetta Reitz asked the great blues shouter and churchwoman Sippie Wallace what the difference was between gospel and blues, she replied, 'Honey, there ain't no difference. In the church we say Jesus, and in the blues we say baby.'[17]

Tharpe consistently collapsed the two, thus expanding the whole concept of 'the church', by appearing in the 'race' (later R&B) charts throughout the 1940s with such hits as 'Rock Me', 'Shout, Sister, Shout' and 'Trouble In Mind'. Her vocals were rich and uplifting, her guitar-playing innovative, and her taste in glitz unashamed. In 1951 she held her third wedding in Washington DC's Griffith Stadium with 20,000 paying guests, most of whom were women. The wedding included a concert and a

$5,000 firework display featuring a 20-foot reproduction of Tharpe strumming her guitar. When she was past fifty, she performed in an orange wig, jeans, high heels and an ostrich feather boa, bringing an unrepentant gospel style to the heart of the mainstream right up to her death in 1973.

Unlike Tharpe the other great gospel singer of the 1940s and 1950s, Mahalia Jackson, never played Harlem's 'devil' venue the Apollo. Treading the sacred path all her life, she campaigned against the 'cheapening' of pop gospel in nightclubs and resisted the attempts of bandleaders like Louis Armstrong to turn her into a jazz singer. Although she was often compared to the powerful blues artist Bessie Smith, and secretly listened to her records, Jackson saw nothing to recommend the genre. 'Blues are the songs of despair. Gospel songs are the songs of hope. When you sing gospel you have a feeling there is a cure for what's wrong,' she once said.[18]

Born the daughter of a clergyman in New Orleans in 1911, Jackson came from a large, impoverished but self-respecting family, leaving school early to work as a laundress. At sixteen she came to Chicago, her majestic, soaring contralto making her a key soloist in the Baptist church. By 1946 she was recording, with her song 'Move On Up A Little Higher' selling over two million copies. She played New York's Carnegie Hall, sang at the inauguration of President Kennedy, and added her voice to the civil rights movement, performing before 200,000 demonstrators at the Lincoln Memorial in 1963.

Tharpe translated gospel idiom for a pop sphere with fun and flamboyance, while Jackson conveyed the simple dignity of its message. When she sang 'I'm Going To Live The Life I Sing About In My Song' or 'When I Wake Up In Glory', Jackson conveyed blues, pathos, a rich spirituality and a magnificence of vision. After her death in 1972 the funeral was that befitting a Head of State, with thousands paying tribute and mourners including Sammy Davis Jr, who read a tribute from President Nixon, Ella Fitzgerald and Coretta King, wife of Dr Martin Luther. And over the body a young Aretha Franklin sang 'Gracious Lord, Take My Hand'.

## 'Retha, Rap and Revolt

Franklin combined Tharpe's commercial sensibility with Jackson's gospel purity to create the greatest voice of the 1960s soul generation. When her first Atlantic single 'I Ain't Never Loved A Man (The Way I Love You)' hit No. 1 in the R&B charts, No. 5 on *Billboard* in 1967, the girl-group sound grew up overnight. Heralding the arrival of the new, mature street-hip woman, Franklin drew the strength and conviction of her sound from the church that spawned her.

Gospel is the great Mother, the church a repository of women's memory, nurture, liberation and catharsis. Its moral codes may be strict, but it is a place where women feel safe in a full expression of self. When Franklin's father, the Reverend C.L., who in the mid-1950s could command up to $4,000 fees for an appearance on the gospel circuit, let loose his million-dollar roar, working women would surrender themselves to ecstatic prayer, some having to be carried away by strong-armed nurses.

Franklin learned early on to respect and express this powerful female intuition. At six years old she lost her real mother when Barbara Siggers walked out on her five children, dying four years later. For years Franklin felt the loss, keeping her mother's hairbrush with a few hairs in it as a small bleak memento. The women of the church became her substitute mothers and musical inspiration: Mahalia Jackson and Clara Ward would drop by the Reverend's house to dispense spare ribs, vocal tuition and guidance. 'Clara knew. She knew I had to sing,' said Franklin. By contrast with the women of Motown, preened in chiffon for a white male-defined acceptance, women gospel singers' first communion was with the Lord, who, thank goodness, wasn't visibly censorious about a generous girth, the length of a leg or the modulation of a voice. 'You know you understand gospel when you get a feel for the wholeness of the sound,' says Cissy Houston, mother of Whitney, and long-time friend and backing singer with Franklin.

Born in 1942 in Memphis, Franklin grew up in Detroit where

**Aretha Franklin**
in  New York
recording studio,
1966 – ushering in
a new era of raw
inspirational 1960s
soul.
(Chuck Stewart/
Redferns)

her father had assumed pastorship of the New Bethel Baptist
church. Although she sang solos in church from the age of nine,
she was a shy child, with wide, watchful eyes. She would practise
singing through the night with sisters Carolyn and Erma, but it
wasn't until she saw Sam Cooke singing in the church one night,
then headlining the Detroit Flame Show bar the next, that she
knew she wanted to 'go pop'. 'I guess I figured if Sam could do
it, I could, too.'

It wasn't just her religion that was at odds with the commercial pop world Franklin took on, but also her gutsy woman-ness
which she had to tone down for its etiolated, camera-conscious
gaze. Early in her career she was bumped off the *Ed Sullivan
Show* because her gown was apparently too low cut. 'It was a
beautiful gown . . . but I don't think at that time they had seen a

black woman on network TV showing as much cleavage,' she said.'[19] This theme reared its head again in 1993 when columnist Liz Smith wrote that Franklin was 'too bosomy' for the revealing dress she wore on a TV special. Franklin, always sensitive about her profile, was hurt by the comment. Although she sang best with her stomach muscles relaxed, pressure to present the *de rigueur* sylph-like figure meant that she sometimes compromised her sound by singing from the throat. Producer Tom Dowd noted this, saying, 'I would much rather record Aretha whenever she sat down and accompanied herself than have her . . . stand up and sing, because there was a difference in the vitality of the character singing. It was like night and day, a different human being entirely – her whole timing, her whole temperament.'[20]

It was Atlantic producer Jerry Wexler who understood the need for Franklin to be as 'bosomy' as possible, in attitude as well as dress style. She had been a powerful 'underground scam' in their New York studios for three or four years. 'I'd been watching her on Columbia, and when she came to Muscle Shoals I said, "Let this sound emerge and be heard and not make it palatable".'[21] Although she was gospel princess and daddy's girl, Franklin was rough and a rebel. At fifteen she was a single mother, with a second son arriving two years later. Teenage pregnancy, though, did not stop her from pursuing her career, as by the age of eighteen she was in New York where John Hammond, the A&R producer who had recorded Bessie Smith and discovered Billie Holiday, signed her to Columbia on the strength of a raw demo. Franklin spent the first half of the 1960s singing directionless showtunes, R&B jazz and pop, the label trying to mould her into a black Barbra Streisand. When her contract wasn't renewed in 1966, Wexler seized the opportunity to sign her to Atlantic.

It was as if she had spent her Columbia years in waiting: Atlantic, the label that had made a name for itself with a crossover of prolific blues and soul artists like Ray Charles, LaVern Baker, Ruth Brown, Otis Redding and Solomon Burke, created the ideal conditions for Franklin to emerge unfettered and direct, as a star. 'I Ain't Never Loved A Man' was followed by the No. 1 hit 'Respect', a classic of joyful self-determination that has since been interpreted as everything from anti-racist anthem to feminist call-to-arms. Going from 'zero, zip to national treasure' within three months, Franklin let fly, scoring fourteen hits in two years. By 1994 she had recorded fifty-eight albums and won fifteen Grammys (including a Grammy Lifetime Achievement Award), more than any other female performer in history.

Despite the high profile her career has included periods of retreat and reclusiveness. In 1969, for instance, at the height of her fame she cancelled a tour and withdrew from the secular business to electrify audiences back at her father's church. In 1972 she released *Amazing Grace*, the gospel album that won her a Grammy for Best Soul Gospel Performance. The rest of the 1970s saw her faltering in the face of disco, the hits tapering off as her great soul voice had nowhere to go. It wasn't until the early 1980s, when she signed to Arista and a fresh team, that she reached high points again – such as the raw rocking of *Jump To It* and *Who's Zoomin' Who*, and the duet 'Sisters Are Doin' It For Themselves' with Annie Lennox. As elements of the church were liberalized throughout the 1980s, the question of separation between gospel and secular for Franklin became less literal, more an existential one. Instead of pop being impure and unholy, it was less 'real'. Franklin may have played the MTV market, but she was uncomfortable with its artifice. When Diana Ross approached her as a famous sister saying, 'We really need to know each other . . . it's ridiculous we've never taken time to know each other,' Franklin rebuffed her, uninterested in celebrity protocol.

Franklin released a number of albums in the 1990s, but though offerings like 1998's *A Rose Is Still A Rose* showed she was still in fine voice, the material was bland and unmemorable. When she took to the stage during VH1's *Divas Live!* series of concerts in 2000, what people remembered and celebrated was her gritty contribution to soul music, not the over-produced confection of some of her later songs.

It is the notion of what's 'real' that tears through Franklin's music, with the church acting as a powerful source of truth'. Paradoxically, the separate world of gospel allows a woman to be more of who she is, while global pop entails a subtle diminution of self.

## Here Come the Girls

While the girl-group sound beat a swathe through definitions of chart pop, there were very few solo female stars in America. Apart from Franklin, who dominated the gritty, declarative end of the soul spectrum, the only other top female singles artist was Dionne Warwick, whose warm, subtle voice set her more in the international cabaret league. A former session singer in the trio The Gospelaires with sister Dee Dee and cousin Cissy Houston (mother of Whitney), Warwick was discovered in the early 1960s by songwriter Burt Bacharach and became the perfect showcase for the material he and his partner, Hal David, penned. From 1962's 'Don't Make Me Over' thirty-three of her first thirty-seven hits, including 'Walk On By' and 'You'll Never Get To Heaven', were written by them. 'Anyone I've worked with has taken into consideration who I am. They have written songs they feel I can do, and still maintain who I am,' Warwick said in 1988, explaining how she managed to keep an individual style. 'When I first started working with Bacharach & David, they were the songwriters and I was the interpreter. Any of the producers I've worked with since has had to take a similar method.'[22]

Bacharach & David also had a great deal of success in Britain, where female solo singers rather than girl groups dominated the charts. By 1964 it was fashionable in the British record industry to copy the American girl-group sound with a slightly cleaner home version. Each of the four major companies had their token girl star, groomed for acceptable family pop entertainment: Dusty Springfield on Philips; Cilla Black, the wise-cracking cloakroom girl from the Liverpool Cavern Club who was a friend of The Beatles, on EMI; Sandie Shaw on Pye; and Lulu on Decca. The tradition of the British female singer with the reassuring 'girl next door' image had been set during the Second

World War when a bouffant-haired Vera Lynn became the Forces' Sweetheart. Her optimistic delivery and lush orchestrations were followed by the crooning ballads and novelty pop of the 1950s, with singers such as Ruby Murray, Alma Cogan and the young Petula Clark continuing the trend for British girls to sing light and sweet, or saucy, like The Beverly Sisters. It was really The Vernons Girls, by sheer force of numbers, who began to open up alternative avenues for women. Originally clerical staff at Vernons Football Pools Company in Liverpool who sang in the organization's choir, sixteen girls emerged in the late 1950s as a group in their own right, becoming resident performers on the ITV rock 'n' roll show *Oh Boy!*, and backing such artists as Cliff Richard, Marty Wilde and Dickie Pride.

After the lavish ballgowns and restrained delivery of earlier female artists, The Vernons Girls, with their rib-tight sweaters, short skirts and energized presentation, created a stunning visual impact. Though they continued as a trio in the early 1960s, recording strong and at times eccentric pop, they were considered ahead of their time. It wasn't until acts like The Crystals and The Ronettes had succeeded in America that British companies decided to take a risk on more upbeat female pop artists. 'In the '60s it was very difficult to launch the career of a female singer,' says Dave Shrimpton, a former Philips employee. 'Girl singers were tried and promoted but we had a higher success rate with male acts like Cliff Richard and Adam Faith. It seemed women were less likely to be played on the radio, less likely to be accepted.'[23]

It would have helped, had their material been better. Despite the revolution of The Beatles, the tradition of an artist having to rely on outside songwriters or US cover versions was still very strong. Many women were not given access to the hits or hitmakers of the day, and no matter how well the artist was promoted, weak material worked against a high chart profile. Sandie Shaw later remarked to me that 'women weren't considered the big meat'.

As we saw in the previous chapter, Dusty Springfield was anxious to break out of British pop's squeaky-clean restrictions.

Aspiring towards longevity and international status, she kept ahead by releasing only original material as singles. It meant she created more work for herself, but as her manager Vic Billings said: 'It was hard in the early stages. We had floods of material and a load of crap, but it was easier later on, especially when we had a good relationship with songwriters like Burt Bacharach and Carole King.'[24] She also used the strong backing vocals of US expatriates like Madeline Bell, Doris Troy and former Ikette, P. P. Arnold. From the sidelines these gospel soul sisters taught Springfield a great deal, and she repaid the compliment by recording backing vocals for them, under the name Gladys Thong.

Springfield also marked out her individuality through image. Billie Davis, a beat girl singer who had a huge hit in 1963 with a cover version of The Exciters' 'Tell Him', recalls:

'Dusty was very serious about what she was doing. She was very trendy. It was important for girls not to dress in a cabaret style – flamboyant gowns, that kind of thing. Dusty and myself were able to communicate with what the kids were wearing, and the make-up. I had black leather miniskirts . . . not terribly short, but simple. I used to like black sweaters and trousers, sort of street-style. Dusty moved on later to Darnell, though, and was expected to dress in designer gowns for places like Talk Of The Town.'

Davis remembers the *Ready Steady Go!* audience as being obsessively discerning.

'They were a mod audience. There was a strict dress code. For instance, everybody had this thing about "Stan's", a shoemaker in Chelsea who could make the most pointy shoes in Britain. And all the girls were adopting Dusty's panda-eyed look. At the time we used shoe polish, and had great difficulty getting it off!'[25]

While the British girls were sharp dressers, they had to scrabble among themselves for hit material that went deeper than the sugary 'girl next door' sound. There was also competition to 'break' America. Apart from Vera Lynn, who topped the US charts for nine weeks in 1952 with 'Auf Wiederseh'n, Sweetheart', and Petula Clark, who had fifteen major hits in the States in the mid-1960s, including two No. 1s, British artists found that their quirkiness (and sometimes inferior productions) didn't translate overseas. Low-profile Stateside, however, enabled them to pilfer hot American tracks for the British market.

Warwick was reputedly miffed that Cilla Black would record cover versions of her US hits before she had time to release them in the UK. Skilfully promoted by The Beatles' manager Brian Epstein to the top of the charts with such hits as 'Anyone Who Had A Heart' and 'You're My World', Black had a bawling Mersey magic and a mod bob. Dubbed 'The Only Bird in a Beat Boy's World', she had a feisty charm that saw her through the comparatively lean days of 1970s cabaret and panto before she re-emerged as an 1980s TV celebrity. While Black may have had hits and Northern credibility, she acknowledged later that it was Springfield who had the most international potential. 'You've gorra remember, she was our icon. You ask any girl singer from the 1950s and they'll say Dusty was the guv'nor.'[26]

Lulu, the diminutive yet raw singer who emerged from Dennistoun Palace in Glasgow's East End, enjoyed a higher profile in the States when her song from the 1967 film *To Sir with Love* went to No. 1. She had been a major star in Britain since 1964 with her version of The Isley Brothers' 'Shout'. 'I loved black American music, especially Motown. It was hot,' Lulu said in 1988 when she was starring in a South London pantomime as Peter Pan. Then, it seemed as if her career had been relegated to the 'second division' oldies circuit of summer seasons and panto, but in the 1990s she was back in the British Top Ten with some credible dance singles and hit albums. Like Springfield she had an instinctive feel for R&B that propelled her out of insipid girl-singer category.

Sandie Shaw was also a consistent hit-maker, with a strong selection of songs penned mainly by writer Chris Andrews. Shaw's 'There's Always Something There To Remind Me' was the first of fifteen Top Forty placings, but after her ill-advised Eurovision hit 'Puppet On A String' her career faltered and she didn't emerge again until the 1980s with a completely different punk-inspired sound. Collaborating with such artists as The Smiths and The Jesus and Mary Chain, she announced, 'I'm the only '60s performer making contemporary music. Also I'm an artist. I don't think it's right to do the circuit, going to people just for the money . . . I want to communicate with people.'[27]

By the mid-1960s British girls did have a distinctive, sparky sound, but getting noticed was an uphill struggle. Most of the working British acts were male beat groups, riding on the crest of the wave created by The Beatles and The Rolling Stones. Amid this 'serious' talent, women were viewed as ineffectual. The Fab girl Four – Dusty, Cilla, Sandie and Lulu – received major record company support, but beyond a female figurehead little commitment was shown to other women on the roster, with the result that there was a vigorous underground female pop scene.

Many women occupied a kind of 'second division' pop status, releasing inspired one-offs or occasional cult classics, while even larger numbers threw in their lot with session singing. A cluster of beat-girl belters including Billie Davis, Barry St John and Beryl Marsden opted for straight R&B. 'There weren't a lot of female singers around because they couldn't associate themselves with the songs. The majority of female singers that had made the charts were Susan Maughan-types – pretty songs and party clothes. But in Liverpool you had to be one of the boys,' says Beryl Marsden.[28] Briefly signed to Decca, Marsden sang warm bouncy numbers like The Shirelles' 'Everybody Loves A Lover', but never made much impact with a British market fixated on America – the 'Real Thing'. Several girl groups like Goldie and The Gingerbreads appeared brandishing instruments, but they were always treated as novelties – and sometimes a girl would pop up in an all-male band looking distinctly odd, like Honey Lantree playing drums with The Honeycombs on their one-off hit 'Have I The Right' – 'Leadfoot Lantree', as she was unkindly dubbed by the 1960s pop fraternity.

What the beat girls were grasping for was something to define them as separate from their parents' generation. In the same way that the US girl groups articulated the intensity of being

**Marianne
Faithfull**
in London, 1976 –
vamp or victim?
(David Redfern/
Redferns)

**Marianne Faithfull** in London, 1976 – vamp or victim? (David Redfern/ Redferns)

teenagers, so British acts were trying to establish a sound independent of both America and their own popular music past.
'What got me at seventeen was that I could see The Stones were
making it up as they went along. There was a chance that WE
were going to make this, that it wasn't our parents. When
Andrew [Loog Oldham, the Rolling Stones' manager] turned
up, I got a really strong feeling that this had not been done
before,' says Marianne Faithfull, the ex-convent schoolgirl who
had a hit in 1964 with 'As Tears Go By' and became famous for
being Mick Jagger's girlfriend.[29]

Though she had flowing golden hair, a fresh face and spoke in
dulcet folky tones, Faithfull symbolized a loss of innocence,
teetering on the edge of 1960s teen pop and psychedelic rock.

Her image of youth and startled naïvety was undercut by sexually frank pictures such as Terry O'Neill's shot of her in black lace and suspenders, and the role she played in Jack Cardiff's bizarre film *Girl on a Motorcycle*, where her leather biker suit was literally whipped off by a ringmaster as she rode bareback in a circus. This taint of excess was compounded after the 1967 police drug bust at Keith Richards's house when the spotlight focused on Faithfull as 'THE GIRL IN A FUR SKIN RUG' and 'NAKED GIRL AT STONES PARTY', an incident mythologized by rumours of cunnilingus and a Mars bar. 'It's a stereotype, I'm nothing like that. I'm much too repressed sexually,' she says.

With lurid sex-and-drugs stories Faithfull may have distanced herself from her parents' generation, but it was at the expense of her music.

'When I finally did run off with Mick, I felt I should stop working, because he was such a great star. I was incredibly jealous of Mick's talent, but there was nothing I could do about that. I bit the bullet, put my ambition on hold and did what was required, which was to be there, and to give him everything I had . . . I was proud and honoured to do it. What I didn't like was that I was then perceived as the "rock chick". There must have been something magical about us as a couple, neither of us realized (well, maybe he did, he's awfully clever). Something caught the public imagination. It still does. I find that very hard now.'

It wasn't until Faithfull re-emerged in 1979 with bite and bile in her husky voice on the punk-influenced *Broken English* album that the true toll of those years could be calculated. She had travelled from pop confection to raw artist via street-heroin addiction, and there was an element of drama in her 'victim' status – 'Life has used me as its personal punch-bag,' she said. But A&R consultant Kate Hyman, who was then Faithfull's personal assistant, remembers her as far stronger than that. 'It was a crazy time because she was constantly being harassed by the police. She had a very bad reputation in England but was trying to get her records done, trying to work. She was a very smart woman who basically didn't conform. I learned early on that's what you got for not conforming – a bad reputation.'[30]

Like a weatherbeaten diva, Faithfull had an instinctive capacity for survival. Her musical output was sporadic, but always intriguing – such as 1987's *Strange Weather*, an album of standards spanning several decades and every composer from Kurt Weill to Paul McCartney. She was a rock artist, hamstrung by that 1960s image of meek pop-star girlfriend, eternally trying to break free from her past.

As the 1960s wore on, from the girl groups to the beat girls to the gospel swingers, women in pop were beginning to carve out a definition for themselves that was closer to the street than ever before, more in tune with their voice, their experience. The period has been stamped with the authority of 'The Real Thing' because it emerged as a genuine, glorious flashpoint within the record industry. As Atlantic producer Tom Dowd remarked, pop evolution is like a series of explosions – each one creating a whole new set of tangents. It was no longer, 'This is white, this is black; this is jazz, this is pop.' But, like punk over ten years later, because the industry couldn't fully control this Pandora's Box, in the wake of girl-group success many careers foundered. Their death was partly due to the rise of 1970s rock, an era when male supergroups took over and the Rock Chick, as troubled victim and visionary, was born.

# Can the Can

## WHATEVER HAPPENED TO THE ROCK CHICK?

**4**

### Homecoming Queen

'How can I say this without sounding sexist? Janis was one of the guys. When I was with her, there was no sense of she's female, I'm male . . . Her male balance was as strong as my female balance. We both acknowledged that place, the other side of our sexual whole.'

Producer PAUL ROTHCHILD, quoted in *Love, Janis*, by Laura Joplin

'Sexism killed her. People kept saying that she was just "one of the guys" . . . that's a real sexist bullshit trip, 'cause that was fuckin' her head around . . . she was one of the women. She was a strong, groovy woman. Smart, you know? But she got fucked around.'

Former lover and musician, COUNTRY JOE MCDONALD, quoted in *A Star is Torn*, by Robyn Archer and Diana Simmonds

One afternoon in September 1970, Janis Joplin walked out of LA's Sunset Sound studio with her Full Tilt Boogie crew. Walking up to the band's car, she turned and looked at the group of men, wondering who should drive. 'Who's got the biggest balls?' she asked. Then after a pause she answered, 'I do.'

Victim, visionary and Valkyrie, Joplin was dubbed 'the first pin-up hippy girl' and 'first major girl sex symbol in rock'. She expressed the confusion of a woman raised with the repressive sexual codes of the 1950s, yet embracing the bewildering lack of boundaries that came with 1960s hippy counter-culture. Before the supposed sexual liberation of the 1960s, 'good girls' didn't, and 'bad girls' did. Joplin tested this dichotomy, not just in her sexuality, but through her music and the way she lived her life on the cusp of a regressive era and a youth revolution.

The first white woman to negotiate the explosive, murky depths of psychedelic rock 'n' roll, Joplin made up the rules and suffered for it. The 'serious', grown-up rock that emerged in the late 1960s from a composite of beat groups, the blues and an elevation of the Unwashed musician as 'artist' created an elite male scene based on guitar virtuosity, rambling lyrics and an ability to get stoned. On entering this world, Joplin saw no other option than to imitate. But in drawing on that sound to accompany the full force of her unfettered blues voice, she created something startlingly original – driven, expansive, out of control. When Joplin stood on stage and screamed out 'Piece Of My Heart', there was a sense of megalithic rock being resung and reinterpreted through a woman's perspective .

Her brief, fiery four-year career symbolized the most extreme dilemma for women in rock 'n' roll – how to compete with men, yet not lose a valuable sense of self. Despite her rockin', cussin' and swearin' stance Joplin once made a concerted application to the girls' club when, in 1965, she temporarily returned home from wild living in San Francisco, scraped her hair back into a demure bun, dressed down, applied make-up and warned friends to watch their language. Though that period seemed out of character, it showed how Joplin's rebel activity was not simply about being 'one of the lads'. It was as much a reaction to the 1950s prom-queen brand of femininity that excluded her during those crucial teenage years. She had been a bright, co-operative child before adolescent hormones raged in her body, sending her complexion into a ravage red of acne. A heavy girl with a gutsy voice who wanted to take her space in the world, she found it impossible to squeeze into the rigours of decorative small-town femininity. Although part of her longed to join this aloof sorority of womanhood, she cast herself in a role so anti-social, so anti-traditional femininity, that she would never have to compete. Ironically, taking on a straightforward male rock 'n' roll persona made it easier for her to strive for superiority among men.

Born in 1943 in Port Arthur, Texas, Joplin was brought up by a liberal middle-class family baffled by her headstrong, destructive lifestyle. But as in the song 'Get It While You Can' on her final album *Pearl*, Joplin felt driven to seize every opportunity and experience that came her way. Despite attempts to under-

stand her, Dorothy and Seth Joplin found their eldest daughter's unique creativity overwhelming. Aware of their disappointment in her, even when she was high on heroin Joplin would write home to mother for Betty Crocker cook-books and advice on how to be a Good Daughter. Her younger sister Laura recalls in her memoir *Love, Janis* how one evening the family came to see Joplin in concert. They stood in the doorway of the Avalon ballroom in San Francisco as if poised between two worlds, bewildered by the light show and the stoned atmosphere that seemed to shut them out.

In pursuing a rock career Joplin had to become separate from her family and jettison the small-town 1950s values that she found limiting. A teenage loner who expressed herself through poetry and painting, Joplin decided to develop her singing career early on, leaving home in 1960 to sing in Houston bars and clubs. One of her first big breaks was a regular gig in Austin performing at a gas station turned beer bar run by Kenneth Threadgill, a hang-out for country music 'outlaws'. By 1966 she had moved permanently to the West Coast, falling in love with the Haight Ashbury hippy scene of San Francisco, and teaming up with the band Big Brother and The Holding Company. With Joplin on vocals, bassist Peter Albin, drummer David Getz, and James Gurley and Sam Andrew on guitar, they became a Bay area sensation, but it wasn't until their appearance at Monterey Pop festival in 1967 that they were snapped up by Columbia Records and launched to overnight fame.

The first annual Monterey International Pop Festival was an event unimaginable today, a non-profit gathering where money made would be distributed 'for the betterment of pop music'. The festival was marked by pop pyrotechnics: Pete Townshend smashed his guitar, while Jimi Hendrix set fire to his. In a sense rock died before it had begun, a revolutionary force that, like punk and hardcore techno later, burned itself out within a brief period. In 1967 50,000 young people passed through San Francisco, taking advantage of the free food and free housing provided by the 'Council for the Summer of Love'. 'Free' became a buzz word, while love, sex and peace seemed limitless. Haight, however, attracted not only 'free lovers' but hustlers, losers and unhappy rejects seeking solace in drugs. With new psychedelic highs like STP giving people a three-day trip to hell, San Francisco General Hospital was treating 750 bad trips a month. The rate of venereal disease went up sixfold in one year. Then heroin invaded a sub-culture that was psychologically defenceless against it, because being cool meant being high.

Joplin took drinking and drug-taking to extremes, once telling her stylist Linda Gravenites to make her a handbag 'big enough for a book and a bottle'. Despite her intake, though, she was a musical professional, dedicated in live performance and eager to learn in the studio. The problem lay in her inability to set boundaries: on stage she made the mistake of turning herself inside-out for her fans, trying to be everything they expected her to be. 'Her insecurity made her a great performer because she needed the return that she got,' Gravenites recalled.[1] A good friend of hers, legendary 'scene queen' Suzy Creamcheese, told me how she and Joplin would go to bars and drink tequila: 'She'd lick her thumb with salt and squeeze lime down her throat and shoot a tequila. She had this ritual *down*.'[2] A fan once asked her, 'D'you like what you're doing?' 'I wrote the part!' she quipped back. Joplin could also be headstrong and undiscriminating in her choice of men: her fiancé Seth Morgan, for instance, was an unstable conman from a privileged background. He died twenty years after her in a motorcycle crash, high on alcohol, cocaine and Percodan, with his girlfriend beating him on the back crying desperately for him to 'slow down'.

Though Joplin's chaotic emotional drive was similar to Morgan's, playing havoc with her personal life, Joplin found it easier to focus it in her music. By 1969, with a No. 1 hit album and a Top Ten R&B hit (a cover of Erma Franklin's 'Piece Of My Heart') under her belt, Joplin had outgrown her Big Brothers. Taking Andrew with her, she formed The Kozmic Blues Band for the album *I Got Dem Ol' Kozmic Blues Again*. When she became a star in her own right with the ability to hire and fire musicians, Joplin initially found it hard to tell the men what to do, a typical expression of her lack of confidence as a woman. This was gradually dispelled as she developed business acumen and an even stronger musical direction, disbanding Kozmic Blues to form Full Tilt Boogie Band for the recording of *Pearl* in 1970. By then she was taking less drugs and had started to settle down with her dogs in a redwood house in Marin County. Less dominated by her screaming stage persona, Joplin began to produce the finest material of her career.

On 3 October 1970, after a long day recording at the garage-like Sunset Studios in LA, she retired to her motel room and accidentally injected a lethal dose of pure heroin. The album she had been working on was nearly complete. Released posthumously in 1971, in its combination of tenderness, anguish, slippery funk and sophisticated blues *Pearl* became a monument to her unique talent.

Hearing her old recordings in scrappy mono you can trace a development – from the unstructured abandon and amateur production of 'Piece Of My Heart' to the warm, assured tones of 'Me And Bobby McGee' and 'Move Over'. Bessie Smith was her

idol, and in many ways Joplin lived in her far-off footsteps, making a connection with an underprivileged black woman from the 1930s through voice. Songs such as the psychedelic blues of 'Summertime' and the authentically honed 'Turtle Blues' sound like outright tributes. It's not surprising that Joplin stumped up the money for a Bessie Smith memorial stone. Joplin often said she wished she was black, not so much in a clumsy, naïve appropriation of black culture, but as a way to understand and reach something within herself, a depth of tensile feeling that was denied by her white prom-queen small-town upbringing. The bridge to that emotion was in the power of her voice. Once warned that such a hurtling style meant her voice wouldn't last long, Joplin quipped that she didn't want to be an inferior performer so that she could be inferior longer.

Joplin's struggle was one of identity and integration. Her masculine and feminine sides vied for attention: sometimes it was out-and-out war, sometimes her sense of being a woman came to the fore, with her long, electrifying hair, her love of flamboyant, sensual clothes and the aesthetic sense with which she decorated her home. At other times she 'ran with the gang', outswearing and outdrinking the next man, proud that she could hold her liquor Texan-style. This duality expressed itself too in her bisexuality, two sides that were often out of synch.

'My impression of Janis was that there were a lot of people living off her. She was a great spirit, a dynamite performer and a really needy human being,' recalls Suzy Creamcheese.

'She had people around her egging her on. She wanted to be the toughest "drink-you-under-the-table" girl. She always had a female companion who tried to run her gate, to make sure she didn't die. That went on for a long time, until Linda (Gravenites) had had enough. You couldn't help but love Janis, she was so generous and fun. But she was in serious need of protection, if not rehab. There wasn't a lot of rehab in those days, no one thought anybody was going to *die* from it.'[3]

She died too young to gain support from the second wave of feminism that hit in the early 1970s, rescuing many a 'bad girl' from oblivion. Despite the myth that surrounds her and the death that ironically glorified her, had Joplin lived, she could have been an astute, mature voice in the women's movement. She was intelligent, witty and well-read, yet isolated, pushing back gender boundaries ahead of her time. When she died at twenty-seven, she was still growing up, coming to terms with her identity, trying to kick her heroin addiction. If she had been part of a network of like-minded women, she might well have been alive today. Instead, she became rock's first female star casualty.

## Surrealistic Pillow

In the history of supergroup stadium rock, only a handful of women have emerged with any lasting impact. As opposed to the more deliberately left-field confrontational style of punk and its antecedents, in this area, more than any other genre, there exists a glass ceiling for women. The codes of stadium rock are strict, based on a shared male-musician language of virtuosity and hierarchy. Had she survived, Joplin might well have got there. The only other women to reach supergroup status in the 1960s and 1970s were Grace Slick and Stevie Nicks.

From the same 1960s San Francisco hippy scene as Joplin,

Slick also went through problems with drugs and alcohol, but she survived. Unlike Joplin her viewpoint wasn't centred on an oppositional 'me against the world'. Benign, sarcastic, confident, she cut a graceful figure with her curiously long face, striking eyes and keen, commanding voice. Though she joined the band Jefferson Airplane after their first album, it was her songwriting and classically based composing that took the band to its dizzying height at the head of late 1960s counter-culture. Her controlled performance of surrealistic mayhem on 'White Rabbit' – a song about a psychedelic acid trip through the eyes of Lewis Carroll's Alice – made it an LSD classic. Whereas Joplin has often been seen as a pained victim, Slick was just plain groovy. In 1980, she recalled,

'The '60s was a sensual revolution. We figured the whole thing was going to go on and on and more people were going to take acid, more of us were going to get enlightened. It wasn't like peace and love kinda stuff, it was, Let's make music and screw around instead of making war. To a certain extent it was pretty arrogant and it was also the hedonism thing that said, If you get in the way of my fun, fuck you.'[4]

Despite drink problems, Slick came through the 1960s with hit-making potential intact. A former model from an upper-middle-class background in Chicago, Slick had moved to the West Coast with her first husband Jerry. Inspired by an early Airplane performance, the two formed the band Great Society, and it was two Society songs – 'White Rabbit' and 'Somebody To Love' – that Slick brought with her when she joined Jefferson Airplane. Her first album with them, *Surrealistic Pillow*, was released in 1967 and became an immediate Top Ten hit.

By the early 1970s the band had peaked creatively, and in 1974 Slick and guitarist Paul Kantner formed their own offshoot, Jefferson Starship, which had solid (if chequered) success till the mid-1980s, when it transmuted into Starship. In 1985 Slick was back in the charts again with the No. 1 hits 'We Built This City (On Rock 'N' Roll)' and 'Sara', appealing to a new, younger generation of fans. Despite Starship's generic soft rock, Slick has become a legendary personality in the business, a kind of graceful figurehead who survived by playing down gender differences, in contrast to Joplin who allowed them to tear her apart.

Another survivor from the era of 1960s and 1970s rock was Stevie Nicks, a silvery sweet vocalist and songwriter who joined Fleetwood Mac in 1974 with her partner Lindsey Buckingham. The following year their commercial songwriting skills took Fleetwood Mac from being a middle-range blues/rock band to the level of supergroup, with the Reprise label debut album *Fleetwood Mac*. In 1977 the band came into even stronger focus with the follow-up *Rumours*, which within two years sold twenty million copies worldwide. Nicks's voice, a confident mutation of folk/rock and aching melody, stood her in good stead when she launched a solo career in the early 1980s. She wasn't as success-ful without the band, however, and she had a long hiatus during which she was treated for chemical dependency. Within ten years she had become a parody of her former self, the archetypal blond-locked spacey Rock Chick in flowing dresses. New York gay club Jackie 60, a regular hang-out for drag queens in the early 1990s, used to have Stevie Nicks theme nights as a testament to how camp her image had become.

While male acts from The Rolling Stones to Bruce Spring-steen and U2 have remained in the limelight, hallowed every time they bring out a new album (sometimes ridiculed but never ignored), many rock chicks seem to have a brief, glorious spurt lasting a few years before fading either into parody or complete obscurity. In 1997, however, her career enjoyed a renaissance when she joined a reunited Fleetwood Mac for a tour and the album *The Dance*. She went on to release solo albums, including 2001's aptly named *Trouble in Shangrila*, a set of songs reflecting on her life. This album was special in that Nicks had teamed up with an array of younger female artists, such as Sheryl Crow, Sarah McLachlan and funky soulstress Macy Gray. Nicks obviously had an affinity with other women, defending Courtney Love when the grunge heroine was in dispute with her record label, and adopting a protective attitude towards Sheryl Crow. 'I can give her advice because I've already gone through everything she could possibly think of going through,' she once said frankly. 'She's like the little sister I never had.'[5] Little wonder that Nicks watched out for younger women artists – it had taken a long time for her own status to be restored.

In 1993 another former female legend re-emerged after two decades of silence. While Joplin and co. were expressing hippy abandon on the West Coast in the late 1960s, The Velvet Underground touted a more no-art, New York nihilist aesthetic. Despite the casual anti-hippy hero stance, they were firmly grounded in a rock sensibility. A vital component of the trademark of this 'seminal' band sound was Maureen (Moe) Tucker, one of the first serious female drummers on the rock scene and an understated heroine whose career is an example of how a woman can so easily 'disappear'.

## The Vanishing

'I've often wondered why so many women didn't join bands: especially when record sales back then were 80 per cent female. My inspiration was to do it rather than just sit and listen to it. Maybe it was considered too masculine to swing a guitar around,' Moe Tucker told me, shortly after the re-release of her solo album *Life In Exile After Abdication* in 1993.[6]

It's ironic that Tucker, careful, considerate and a self-confessed homebody, belonged to one of the biggest rock 'n' roll groups of all time, whose avant-garde atonality and songs about sexual surgery, smack and speed acted as the muse to countless college bands. Although a major member of The Velvet Underground, Tucker still felt she was there on sufferance – especially when guitarist John Cale raised objections to a 'chick' being in the band. 'I was glad he was outvoted,' she recalls. 'All the time I was in the band I was always conscious of doing my thing, moving gear, for instance, so I wouldn't be the chick sitting on the pavement saying everything was too heavy. I think John's scepticism got to me in that way.'

Born in 1944, Tucker grew up in Long Island, starting out as a computer operator who practised the drums in her bedroom at night just because she liked the sound. 'I really liked African

drumming, and from there I found myself listening to drums on records. At nineteen I bought a snare drum – that was all I could afford. Then a friend bought me a cymbal, four inches in diameter, so that gave me something else to smack. One day I came home and mum had bought me a $50 second-hand bass and snare.'

This is what Tucker played when Sterling Morrison, a friend of her brother's, called her up asking if she could replace their drummer in The Velvet Underground for one show. 'Lou Reed came to my house to see if I could keep a beat. That was suffi-cient for them, and after that job I just stayed.' Modest about her achievements, Tucker evolved a very distinctive drumming style, up-ending the bass drum and hitting it with mallets, a key element in the Velvets' package. 'I wasn't musically knowledge-able, so my drum parts were mine.' Artist and mentor Andy Warhol picked up on them early as the perfect soundtrack to his deadpan visual comments on fame and celebrity, and they were hired for his 1966 *Exploding Plastic Inevitable* shows, multi-media extravaganzas held in St Mark's Place, New York, as an East Coast answer to Ken Kesey's California Acid Test festivals. 'I liked Warhol very much; he was full of ideas, easy-going and ahead of his time. I enjoyed his friendship.'

Although she grew to like her, initially she wasn't so pleased when the enigmatic German songstress Nico joined them for their first album *The Velvet Underground & Nico.* 'She was a stunningly beautiful Nordic model – I was a goofball in shades,' remembers Tucker. 'We didn't have anything in common. Glamour was not my way. Men loved her but she was a schmuck from the start. With Lou and John there was this tension about control and that was understood by all of us as what made it work. She would watch out for who had the upper hand and side with them.' Nico fitted in as the dark female seducer, adding a whiff of European arthouse elegance to their brutal, fuzzy post-garage-rock sound. Singing songs of drugs and sado-masochism such as 'Heroin' and 'Venus In Furs', her pale, decoratively tragic air was a kind of inverted mirror to Tucker's equally pale, cool-tomboy image.

Tucker was no dilettante, however; her drumming was the band's steady backbone, and she outlasted Nico and John Cale, playing on two more albums (*White Light/ White Heat* and *The Velvet Underground*) before leaving in 1969 to give birth to her first child. That was when she vanished.

In the early 1970s Tucker married, moved with her husband to Phoenix, Arizona, and raised five children. When she was away from the band and the business, her musical involvement receded. 'At one point I played with a band for two weeks, but it was too much with all the kids, trying to rehearse, so I gave up.' After her marriage broke up, she moved with the children to live with her mother in Georgia. She couldn't get a job and ended up working in Wal-Mart for three years. It wasn't until the early 1980s, when she plucked up the courage to record again, that Tucker realized she even had a reputation she could trade on. 'I made a single, a version of The Shirelles' "Will You Still Love Me Tomorrow?" and I got up the courage to call record stores and try to sell it. I had a little speech prepared: "Hi, I'm Moe Tucker from The Velvet Underground . . . " I wanted to get the group's name in real fast before they hung up on me – but when I said my name, they knew who I was.'[7]

From there she eased herself back into the business, bit by bit, working around the children at vacation times or weekends – a 'slow melting-in'. She released her first solo album *Playin' Possum* on her own Trash label in 1982, and her next one, *Life In Exile After Abdication*, featured guest appearances from Lou Reed, Sonic Youth and Daniel Johnson, among others, garnering critical acclaim and securing her place in rock's 'pantheon'. Raw, experimental and witty, Tucker makes music that is still as inventive as her slightly offside world-view. By the early 1990s she was touring and recording more regularly, joining The Velvet Underground for an easy-going European nostalgia tour in 1993.

What is painful about her story is the fact that while members Lou Reed and John Cale went from strength to strength with solo careers following the Velvets, Tucker disappeared into suburban obscurity and near-poverty. Admittedly she chose to have children, but she did not welcome the enforced hiatus from music. This is an issue that comes up time and time again for women in the business, holding them back in much the same way it does in any career. While childcare is considered the preserve of the mother, along with the guilt attached to leaving children for any length of time, women artists are effectively prevented from working up to that stadium-star level – unless they are completely single-minded or have an excellent nanny.

'The first tour I did with my own band was six weeks long,' recalls Tucker. 'And I realized it was too long for everybody: my mother, my kids and me. I had to wait till the youngest kids were a lot older before I could go on the road longer than a month. Nappies, bath time, picking up kids from school – it'll never sell . . . it just ain't rock 'n' roll.'

## Bigger Than Jesus

'Rock 'n' roll is hard work, it's harder than being in the army. And your guitar is your machine gun; tour instruments are your implements of battle . . . you've gotta know your instruments.'
PATTI SMITH, quoted in *NME* by Tony Parsons, 1977

'She stands there, machine-gunning out her lines, singing a bit and talking a bit, in total control, riding it and steering it with a twist of a shoulder here, a flick of the wrist there – scaled down bird-like movements that carry an almost unbelievable degree of power.'
CHARLES SHAAR MURRAY, *NME*, 1975

'There's not anyone in this band that doesn't accept . . . the bend of the knee, the humility that comes with working with her, because she is the best. We feel very honoured to work with her.'
LENNY KAYE, guitarist of The Patti Smith Group, quoted in *NME* by Paul Morley, 1978

In 1964 Patti Smith graduated from high school to do piece-work in the basement of a non-union New Jersey factory. Miserable and alienated, Smith didn't get along with her co-workers, and took refuge in a book of poetry, *Illuminations* by Arthur Rimbaud. She was inspired not only by the words of the nineteenth-century romantic poet ('Woman will discover the unknown, will her word be different from ours? She will discover things that will be strange and unfathomable, repulsive, and delicate'), but also by his face, 'defiant and restless', which she taped to a pipe – 'Me and Rimbaud together in the bowels of the piss factory.'[8]

To Smith, Rimbaud expressed 'all the noble egoism of adolescence'. He was the keystone in her mental pyramid of heroes, a roster of men that included Dylan, Camus, Genet, John Lennon, Hank Williams and John Coltrane. Her only real female hero, Joan of Arc, was de-sexed as if Smith felt that true revolution rested on being male, or at least asexual. She understood the power of adolescence, its pure, fearless pursuit of an ideal, its yearning, its straining to *be*. It was this potent sense of isolation and ambition that she harnessed to rock 'n' roll, using the medium to plug directly into the heart of her audience.

'All through childhood I resisted the role of a confused skirt tagging the hero,' she once wrote. 'Instead I was searching for someone crossing the gender boundaries, someone both to be and to be with. I never wanted to be Wendy – I was more like Peter Pan. This was confusing stuff.'[9] Born in Chicago and

**Patti Smith**
in Amsterdam,
1979: 'Rock 'n' roll
is hard work; it's
harder than being
in the army.'
(Pennie Smith)

brought up in a blue-collar family in Pitman, in southern New Jersey, Smith always had a strong sense of self. 'When I was a kid, I had an absolute swagger about the future. I wasn't born to be a spectator.'

A child of the 1960s, Smith immersed herself in its growing pains: racial integration, the death of Kennedy, the acid revolution and Vietnam, to emerge in the New York-garage band scene of the early 1970s with a keen sense of 'new eyes on everything – gender, race, God. Borders were crossed, blurred, obliterated.'[10] With the fervour of a female Billy Graham, Smith became rock 'n' roll's preacher, its salvation. In identifying rock as a religious experience complete with a notion of ecstasy, working a crowd until they submit totally to the sensuality of just being, Smith articulated rock's power with greater eloquence and authority than any man before her. Maybe her vision had that sense of an unusual 'Greatness' because of her very position as The Other, the continual disaffected female adolescent. With her drawn, emaciated look and casual rejection of the trappings of femininity (rock photographer Pennie Smith says that Smith was one of the few women she enjoyed photographing 'because she never worried about looking pretty'), Smith still emanated a febrile, sexual tension through long hair, hacked raw like Keith Richards's, dark eyes and a sullen mouth.

Smith originally nursed thoughts of a literary career, giving poetry readings on the alternative Manhattan arts scene of the late 1960s. It wasn't until she roped in guitarist/writer Lenny Kaye in 1971 to provide musical accompaniment to her musings that her idea for a combination of rock and poetry took shape. By 1974 Smith had released her first single, 'Hey Joe'/'Piss Factory', with Television's Tom Verlaine on guitar, and assembled a fully fledged band – Lenny Kaye, Richard Sohl on piano, bassist Ivan Kral and drummer Jay Dee Daugherty. Every record label she approached turned her down, apart from Clive Davis's fledgling Arista, who decided to take a chance on her cutting, flexible vocals and the multi-rhythmic band. Produced by John Cale, her 1975 debut LP *Horses* included such classics as 'Break It Up' and a thundering, caustic version of Van

Morrison's 'Gloria'. The cover featured a Robert Mapplethorpe photograph of Smith wearing a white shirt, loose tie and jeans, her unadorned stare focused right at the camera. Though now its sprawling rhythms and self-referential lyrics sound dated, then it was a stunning, confrontational debut.

'My first question as a producer was, how do I capture this energy on record?' recalls John Cale. 'I had to take her physical presence into account, it's like putting Iggy Pop on record. There was a lot of power in Patti's use of language, in the way images collided. It wasn't easy. It was like an immutable force meeting an immovable object. Still, something creative came out of it.'[11]

Smith told me in 1996 that the experience was very challenging. 'I knew nothing about recording or being in the studio. I was very suspicious, very guarded and hard to work with, because I was so conscious of how I perceived rock 'n' roll. It was becoming over-produced, over-merchandised and too glamorous. I was trying to fight against all of that.

'I had all these ideas. I'd have seven different poems I'd want to put on seven different tracks, sometimes I only wanted three words from one. I was creating a sort of William Burroughs cut-up. Instead of throwing his hands up or being pissed at me, John got even crazier and more obsessive. It was like having two crazy poets dealing with showers of words. It was a great experience.'[12]

For the follow-up, the lukewarm *Radio Ethiopia*, she momentarily lost her nerve, shaken, too, by a serious accident on tour in Florida when she fell from a stadium stage and broke her neck. The year 1978, though, saw her 'resurrection' with the confident, glorious *Easter* album. The stand-out track 'Because The Night', co-written with her blue-collar New Jersey peer Bruce Springsteen, became her first and only major international hit, covered since by other artists including top alternative rock band 10,000 Maniacs fifteen years later.

By the time her fourth album *Wave* appeared in 1979 Smith said, 'I don't feel like a gawky kid looking up at legends any more. I feel equal to anyone in rock 'n' roll.' Confident that she had done all she set out to do, Smith married MC5 guitarist Fred 'Sonic' Smith, and moved with him to the suburbs of

Detroit to raise a family. She poked her head above the parapet again in 1988 with *Dream Of Life* on Arista, an album which didn't have her former bite.

Since her monumental success in the 1970s, opinion on Patti Smith has been revised several times. Was she a rock 'n' roll saint, an asexual hero, or a feminist sell-out? When in 1980 the 'great and the good' females of British punk, including members of The Slits, The Raincoats and The Au Pairs, assembled for an *NME* 'Women in Rock' round-table discussion, they agreed that artists like Patti Smith and Joan Armatrading were more of a threat than women who openly sold their sexuality in rock. According to The Passions' Barbara Black,

'They've actually denied they're feminists. They've said, "Oh yes, it's over there somewhere, but it's nothing to do with us. We're here because of our merits." Fair enough, but you know it's not true. I know when Patti Smith came over here there were loads of women who went to see her because of the way she is, her way of performing, and to deny her association, to me, is cowardly. I think they're lying to themselves when they say the women's movement has nothing to do with them.'[13]

Like self-styled asexual anti-heroine Polly Harvey (a rock artist often compared to Patti) fifteen years later, Smith was fighting labels, petrified of being cut down to size and exiled to what she felt was a gender ghetto. To her the route to rock freedom was male, but in twisting it to suit her vision she created something peculiarly intense and female. Reassuringly feminist it was not, yet the risks she took with slogans, words, myth and music were exhilarating – she was unafraid, and in her self-confessed heroic terms that in itself should have been a powerful role model.

It was her singularity and lack of public support for women that ultimately made her message less effective. An individual surrounded by a group of talented and influential men – Robert Mapplethorpe, John Cale, Tom Verlaine, Lenny Kaye, Bruce Springsteen – her position seemed unassailable and at the same time daunting. Many women at the time saw in Smith nothing they could usefully relate to. Others picked up on something untutored and elemental, something they didn't have words for, a desire. 'She shocked me the first time I saw her. Real old-fashioned shock . . . This 27-year-old skinny punk who hammered out dirty poetry and sang surreal folk songs. Who never smiled. Who was tough, sullen, bad, didn't give a damn . . . I felt both ravaged and exhilarated,' wrote Mademoiselle's Amy Gross.[14]

To ex-punk singer/songwriter Adele Bertei, who in the 1970s was singing blues in bars in Cleveland, Ohio, Smith was a brand-new role model.

'At the time music was about divas or rock goddesses. It was nothing to do with boyish little tykes like myself who could sing blues. I didn't think there'd ever be a place for me. Then Patti Smith came out with an album that rocked my universe. She was androgynous, outspoken, obviously well-educated and well-read. She became like a mentor to me. If she dropped references to Brancusi [the Romanian sculptor], I'd go out and find art books. If it was Rimbaud, I'd read him and learn about the French decadents. Because I didn't have much of an education, Smith in a sense was my first teacher.'[15]

By the early 1990s Smith's rock performance had become legendary, and a younger generation of female bands cited Smith as an influence without equivocation. Accompanying this, though, was a sense of disappointment about where she disappeared to. One of the greatest rock 'n' roll icons of the twentieth century retiring? to the suburbs? to raise a family? There was a sense that, like countless women before her, she opted out to have children. Maybe Smith's accident scarred her more deeply than she thought – literally lost in her own music, she had careened out into mid-air and nearly killed herself. Maybe a quiet family life seemed preferable to the gaudy, transcendental craziness of rock. After the fall, it seemed all her adolescent angst had been expressed and spent, that the warrior had retreated. 'I no longer have the need for angels,' she wrote in 1993. 'They have all been internalized.'

But come 1996, she rose again, phoenix-like, with the album *Gone Again*. Resonant with coruscating songs of love and loss, it was a quiet testament to her strength and fierce independence.

Both her husband and brother died tragically in 1994, and grief seemed to spur her on to a period of intense creativity. She published a book of poetry, *The Coral Sea*, dedicated to her late friend Robert Mapplethorpe, went on tour, and released a series of critically acclaimed albums, including 1998's *Dream of Life* and *Gung Ho* in 2000. For her, personal tragedy had acted as a galvanizing force. 'I cherish even the tragic things,' she says. 'I only have time for comedy and tragedy in my life, I don't have time for the middle ground.'[16]

### Can the Can

Patti Smith's brand of art rock crossed over to the mainstream and made her a stadium name, but the core of her appeal has always been with a college-based audience. What of the rock that's more consciously downmarket: mass market good-time riffs and chorus lines? When 1960s beat and pop rock transmuted into 1970s glam, the groups that held sway were predominantly male – from the pop extremes of Mud, Sweet, Slade and Gary Glitter to the more self-conscious artifice of David Bowie and Roxy Music. There was room in boho rock for Patti Smith to carve a place for herself as female prophet/poetess, while Joplin crashed on to a liberal hippy scene that at least paid lip service to women expressing themselves. The more riff-driven, head-banging basic end of rock, though, was male territory, like coal-mining and engine-driving.

When Suzi Quatro dived head first on to the scene in 1973, her first single 'Can The Can' went straight to No. 1 in the British charts the week of its release. 'It was a classic example of a record creating an artist, and "Can The Can" certainly created Suzi Quatro, after which she became a superstar,' says Mike Chapman, one half of Chinn & Chapman, the most successful British writer/producer team of the early 1970s.[17]

A diminutive fireball with a black-leather jumpsuit, towering platforms and a mean bass guitar slung low on her hips, Quatro screamed and stomped her way through the pile-driving pop excitement of 'Can The Can' – a song that Chapman freely

**Suzi Quatro**
at Hammersmith
Odeon, 1976: her
brand of brassneck
glitter rock
heralded a new
phase for 1970s
'chicks'.
(David Redfern/
Redferns)

admits 'has no meaning at all'. Although her heyday was just one golden year of such thumping follow-up hits as '48 Crash' and 'Devil Gate Drive', Quatro encapsulated a historic pop moment. No one had seen a girl like this before! Heard one like this! No one was quite certain who she was, what she was doing screaming madly on *Top of the Pops* and trying to jump through the stage, but whatever it was, it was exciting, it moved, it was in yer face.

'I was totally unique. A one-off,' Quatro told me twenty years later. 'I was a female playing a serious bass and leading a band of boys in a male-dominated industry. In other words, I held my own.'[18] *NME* heralded her arrival in 1973 with the declamatory headline: THIS IS SUZI QUATRO. SHE'S HEAVY. Though it seemed as if she had shot from nowhere, Quatro had in fact been playing bass and singing since 1964. She grew up in Detroit, learning a great deal from her father, a successful musician who led a number of Michigan-based units. One of five children who all learned to play a musical instrument, Quatro trained as a classical pianist and drummer before teaching herself bass guitar.

At fifteen she formed an all-girl group Suzi and The Pleasure Seekers with her sisters Patti, Nancy and Arlene, playing dance revues all over the US and touring bases in Vietnam. 'Motown was my first love. My original band The Pleasure Seekers did a complete Motown revue. I danced for a while on a TV show in which at least four Motown acts appeared, giving me the chance to learn the new routines first and show off at school.'

Top record producer Mickie Most discovered her singing in Detroit and brought her over to Britain, intent on drawing out her potential. It took a long time. Eighteen months after Quatro's arrival in London her debut single 'Rolling Stone' flopped, and Most had to call on capable friends Chinn & Chapman. 'I was terrified to take over where Mickie couldn't succeed, but I told him that if he was prepared to take the risk, I was game,' Chapman recalled. 'I think Mickie's problem with Suzi was that neither of them knew what her direction should be, and [that] finally came from "Can The Can" – when we had that song, Mickie had the image.'[19]

Despite criticism that she was a phenomenon moulded by men Quatro maintains,

'The style in "Can The Can" was me. I didn't have a role model, there were never any serious female musicians to model myself on – I only had my own instincts to go by. I've always screamed since I began in '64, it always wowed audiences. I insisted on wearing leather for my first release and Mickie came up with the idea of a jumpsuit. Mike's contribution was to provide the song and take me to the very top of my range, which created a very exciting sound. I can remember the hairs on the back of my neck standing up when I felt that we had indeed cut a No. 1.'

Claiming in early interviews that she had 'fought and scratched and clawed the whole way', Quatro is not shy when assessing her impact. 'Initially it opened up a lot of doors after I burst on the scene. It broke the taboo of women being taken seriously. Since then there don't seem to have been many good female musicians coming up.' Quatro's refusal to recognize the plethora of female guitar groups since punk may be due in part to her distance from the business. Her impact was immediate: there was rioting at her gigs and the tabloids sought sensational Quatro stories. When Chapman tried to take Quatro in a more generic American power-rock direction, he diluted the 'ball-breakin'' style that gave her Top Ten fame, and her chart career fizzled out soon after it exploded. She returned to the charts in the late 1970s with 'If You Can't Give Me Love' and 'She's In Love With You', but then became better remembered for her long-running TV part as the Fonz's sidekick Leatherface in *Happy Days*.

The measure of her success is in how often women mention her as an influence. Clearly infatuated with the leather and bass, a fledgling *NME* journalist Chrissie Hynde interviewed Quatro in 1974 in the ladies' toilets at a Reading gig ('Goodbye tits 'n' ass,' wrote a jubilant Hynde. 'Hello rock 'n' roll'), to emerge five years later and hit the UK charts with her own band, The Pretenders, her own leather and her own bass guitar.

Early-1980s renegade Joan Jett also took inspiration from Quatro's uncompromising stance, combining it with an appreciation of Gary Glitter and the Sex Pistols to come up with the massive 1982 No. 1 hit 'I Love Rock 'N' Roll'. Joan Jett, too, served a long apprenticeship, heading the much-ridiculed all-girl rock band The Runaways in the mid-1970s. Under the stewardship of legendary West Coast impresario Kim Fowley, the four girls (including guitarist Lita Ford who went on to build a successful solo career) were a bunch of LA teenagers 'partying and travelling round the world', not asking too intently where the money went. There was a dedicated live following for their raucous guitar rock, but that never translated into record sales, a fact worsened by constant press trivialization. 'I can take constructive criticism, but, boy, some of it was away over the top,' Jett said in 1982. 'I think The Runaways were just too honest. Girls act like that – girls drink, girls smoke and girls swear. If it would have been an all-guy band no one would have given a shit.'[20]

With the odds against them the group disbanded in 1979, and Jett regained her strength taking elements of punk into her 1980s version of baseline glam rock. No label would sign her after The Runaways, but through dogged determination and indie backing Jett made it back into the limelight with the old Arrows B side 'I Love Rock 'N' Roll'. It was with a pleasant sense of revenge that she and manager Kenny Laguna printed posters saying: 'EVERY MAJOR RECORD COMPANY SAID NO BUT TWO MILLION ROCK 'N' ROLL FANS SAID YES.' 'When they write the official book . . . I want to be in there,' she said. Don't worry, Joan, you have your place.

While Joan Jett was the pimply jet-lagged face of serious hard rockin', her early-1980s chart-bound counterpart Pat Benatar came across as more commercially acceptable and video-friendly. A Spandex-clad redhead with a determined chin, daughter of a Long Island opera singer and veteran of bar and lounge singing from her teens, Benatar continued the noble tradition of the rock chick, but in a manner palatable to the video age. Unlike the wayward, unpredictable talent of Joplin, Patti Smith, Joan Jett even, Benatar's talent was reliable, and she was hard-working, with a sort of fluffy-edged feisty sexiness – guaranteed to produce an album a year, like clockwork, right on the button. She understood the music-business game of longevity: put your records in the market place basically, and keep them coming.

She was rewarded with hit after hit, from 1981's 'Hit Me With Your Best Shot' to 'Invincible' in 1985, along with nine best-selling albums. Her heavy rock, peppered with clear pop melodies, was an astounding success in the States, but didn't translate overseas, particularly in a UK market allergic to power-chord riffs. Benatar's achievement was to take the earth-tremors of heavy metal and sell it back to America in a pop format. Although accommodating, she was never a floozy. When her record company Chrysalis airbrushed part of her top off for a *Billboard* advertisement, Benatar toned down the sexy stage image and cut her hair short. By 1991, acknowledging the limitations of her genre, she moved into grittier, less commercial 'jump blues' with her album *True Love*.

Apart from Benatar, the mainstream rock chick of the 1980s was notable by her absence. The arrival of MTV in 1981 meant that for five years at least women rockers were marginalized: you can't be sexy, visually delectable and seeking approval, *and* seriously shit-kickin', if you're female. Video demanded a certain pliable sexual representation of women and most fell into line, subverting it if they could with a touch of irony. One way of dealing with rock fantasy was to play the sex role to the hilt, invest it with a touch of aggression and heavy-metal swagger and, hey ho, you have the cartoon rock chick. Into this vacuum poured Tina Turner.

## Hatshepsut Takes the Throne

Turner has several weapons at her disposal: the constitution of a horse, good legs and a solid background in raunchy R&B. Allied to this is a penchant for a lion's mane of hair and outrageously red lipstick. Turner knows she's a ham and that this is show-business.

'People like me not just because I have big hair, lips and legs: I've got credibility,' Turner once said. Feeding into her pop-cartoon character is a complex personality. She may look like, and know how to sell, a one-dimensional image, but underneath the woman draws on harrowing experiences throughout the 1960s playing R&B with Ike Turner on the US chitlin circuit. Much has been made of the years he beat and bruised her before she finally fled one night in 1976, blood spattered over her white suit as she ran into a motel with 38 cents in her pocket. If Turner hadn't reached the stratospheric success she did in the 1980s, she could have remained a forgotten obscurity on the oldies circuit, her story just a catalogue of backstage beatings from a man too mind-numbed and brutalized to care. And she would have been another statistic, a woman caught in a sordid, closed world of domestic violence.

Despite living in poverty in the late 1970s when she was half a million dollars in debt and supporting her four children on food stamps, Turner was never tempted to go back to Ike and some kind of steady living. Instead she held out, scraping her own show together and touring it round the late-1970s cabaret circuit. Whether she saw possibilities beyond that is debatable, but when an opportunity came, Turner leaped on it. It wasn't until British designer-pop producers Heaven 17 persuaded her into the studio to record a cover version of The Temptations' 'Ball Of Confusion' for their 1981 nostalgia compilation album that she realized she could make the move away from oldies soul to a more commercial sound, wrapping her raunchy and emotional vocal style around such anthems as 'What's Love Got To Do With It?' and 'We Don't Need Another Hero'. Her 1984 debut solo album *Private Dancer* sold over ten million copies in two years, going on to become the fifth bestseller of all time.

She 'went public' with Ike's abuse in her 1986 autobiography *I, Tina,* written with *Rolling Stone*/MTV journalist Kurt Loder, and since then the story of her escape and survival has become part of her mythical pop character. Like a female Judge Dredd she has become the avenger, the comic-strip warrior – a role transferred to celluloid when she played the alien in rags and chain mail racing through the badlands of 1984's *Mad Max III – Beyond the Thunderdrome*. In 1992 she appeared in tabloid cartoon when the UK *Daily Mirror* ran a thirteen-week strip featuring Tina in battle with their space-travelling tough guy Garth. 'I'm thrilled,' she said. 'But I want it to be on the rough 'n' ready side. I'm a big fan of films like *Star Wars*, but I never imagine myself in the pretty ship that's well organized. I want to be in with Harrison Ford in the rough ship with all the raggedy bits.'[21]

Driving and defining that powerful image is an unglamorous

memory of the black eyes, the swollen nose, the broken jaw, reminding Turner of a time when she felt powerless. Although she partly co-operated with Brian Gibson's 1993 biopic *What's Love Got to Do with It?*, she was not happy dredging up the buried pain that still fuels her. If she could soar high enough and far enough, make big bucks and spend big bucks, surely she could escape the past. Hence the determination that filled those thirteen articulated lorries, those 125 shows at sixty-five stadiums and sixty arenas, those three and a half million people in nineteen countries. Those number-crunching world tours financed the $15,000 shopping sprees, living large as proof of escape from the early grind.

The first black woman to become a stadium rock star, Turner enjoyed fraternizing with Great White Blokes of rock like Mick Jagger, Bryan Adams, Rod Stewart and Dire Straits' Mark Knopfler. 'I felt I was the only girl in the playground with the guys. I was out there with the guys, playing ball!' This was infinitely preferable to the R&B slog that haunted her. Born in 1939 in Nut Bush, Tennessee, the daughter of field workers in a rural hamlet with fifty families, Turner once said, 'I came from the grit of the earth. Black people are close to the earth, close to the beginnings, and this is why we still know how to enjoy ourselves.'[22] Mixed with that pride are the childhood memories of seeing a woman stabbed to death on the sidewalk in a lovers' row, and a woman knifing her father in the groin. She learned that emotions were suppressed till they exploded, that life was a continual tense negotiation with danger. People have criticized Turner for turning her back on her roots, but she said simply: 'To me, a lot of rhythm and blues is depressing. The culture from which it descends is depressing.'[23]

A more positive influence on Turner's upbringing was her maternal grandmother, a Navaho Indian who dipped snuff, chewed tobacco and worked as a healer. Years later, in the midst of the most gruelling years with Ike's revue, Turner remembered Mama Georgie's calm spirituality, finding her own kind of mental salvation in Nichiren Shoshu Buddhism. Meditation coupled with a belief in reincarnation gave her energy and

strength. The story of the Egyptian pharaoh Queen Hatshepsut, who took the throne from her brother, is particularly significant for her as she believes that she was the queen, now paying a debt in this life. 'I was a slave to Ike because before I had enslaved him.'

Though she is happy with the raunchy image she projects, it is also a stereotype that defines her. Women admire Turner's energetic independence, the fact that she was still rockin' after the age of fifty, still showing off her legs with assorted micro-dresses, and that she never resorted to plastic surgery – but there is a contradiction in this role. Male artists talk about her respect-fully, yet Turner is still never seen as a serious rock star. She symbolizes fun, parody, a whacking great voice and a potent sexuality. She feels that people have got the wrong impression of her from her stage show: 'Strutting about in some tiny skirt, some men presume you are up for grabs. Well, I'm not and never was . . . I was never vulgar.' She would have loved to play a female Indiana Jones, but in her movie career she couldn't get beyond the Mad Acid Queen in Ken Russell's 1976 film *Tommy*. Even in the early 1990s, after her part in *Mad Max III* and a decade of phenomenal success, she said, 'All the roles Hollywood offers me are hookers.'

Deep within her was the chaste Baptist girl desperate to sing as a way out. Brash white rock was her upward mobility, because to her as a child it was always white folks who had a desirable life. 'Sex [for black people] was a sneaky thing in cars and sheds; white people's love, like I saw in the movies, seemed prettier and more romantic.'[24] Although Turner's rock chick parody appears easy, it is the result of decades of hard graft and multi-faceted experience. The shame is that she could never be a real stadium hero like Bruce Springsteen, articulating the messy truth and injustice of her former life. For a woman at her age and stage, parody became her strongest and safest card.

## Tramps and Thieves

The Queen of 1980s Rock Chicks had to be Cher. Born
Cherilyn Sarkasian LaPierre in California in 1946, she was a
disciple of Phil Spector, singing sessions with The Ronettes in
his studio before teaming up with the young writer/producer
Sonny Bono. While Janis Joplin thundered her way to fame as a
genuine Haight Ashbury blues rocker, the groovy married
couple Sonny and Cher presented an image of hippydom that
was far more palatable for a TV audience, singing reassuring pop
hits such as 'I Got You Babe'. Cher began to toughen up once
she launched a solo career, with early 1970s hits like 'Gypsies,
Tramps And Thieves' and 'Half-Breed' showing a darker, more
biting edge. By the late 1970s she had split up with Bono and
was beginning to experiment with heavy rock.

She developed a dual role as singer and movie actress,
starring in films such as *Silkwood*, *The Witches of Eastwick* and
*Moonstruck*, and it seemed natural to collapse the two jobs. With
her cascading hair, rear-end tattoo, fish-net stockings, black
leather jackets and well-publicized romances with young heavy
metal heroes such as Bon Jovi's Richie Sambora, it was as if she
was playing the role of rock star. By the time of her huge 1989
hit 'If I Could Turn Back Time', she had become the ultimate
cartoon rock chick, unafraid of self-parody and outrageous
artifice, her music a secondary force. In 1998 her hit album
*Believe*, characterized by vocoder vocal and disco beats,
cemented her image as a camp stylist rather than serious rock
singer.

Within the stadium rock hierarchy women find it hard to be
'promoted' on musical merit. 'A female singer has a place, but if
you're a female musician you're breaking into a special enclave,
and it changes their attitude,' says Joy Askew, a top keyboard
player and solo artist in her own right who has toured with
everyone from Peter Gabriel to Rodney Crowell, Joe Jackson
and Laurie Anderson.[25] It was while on Gabriel's 'Secret World'
tour in 1993 that Askew most felt the keen edge of male muso
elitism:

'It wasn't just a question of playing the piano and grooving along – underneath the stage they had two enormous twin towers of equipment with 60-foot midi lines. I was covering all the brass, all the background vocals, as well as playing keyboards. I didn't have time to josh with the drummer. After six months the band refused to play with me, saying I wasn't any good. I felt the rift was to do with a woman penetrating an all-male enclave. Big gigs are like that – they're about money, prestige and keeping a reputation in the world arena.'

Only a handful of female musicians have managed to penetrate this core on their own terms. When they signed to Decca in the 1960s Goldie and The Gingerbreads were the first all-girl band on a major label, while Fanny were lone riders in the early 1970s. Raised on a diet of Led Zeppelin covers, sisters Ann and Nancy Wilson were soon to follow, achieving success in the late 1970s and 1980s in Heart, a mixed-gender band that allowed them to bypass 'women in rock' restrictions. The 1990s saw super-grunge queens L7 come out of LA, and a female Pearl Jam emerged from Boston in the shape of Stone Zoo. Their guitarist Cathy Capozzi played Hendrix-style riffs with a ferocious virtuosity, regularly astounding audiences packed out with Bud drinkers. 'They're always saying, "Gee, you play just like a man!"' she wailed.[26] Stone Zoo were operating at the harder end of rock where, even in the heavy-metal explosion of the 1980s, female bands were not taken seriously. Girlschool, for instance, were considered by many in the industry to be just as good as their male peers Motorhead, but they never became a big stadium band. Other girl acts like Wendy O. Williams and Vixen were just seen as freakish. A strange record, taking into account the market for heavy metal: 'At metal gigs, believe it or not, there's usually a 50/50 split between men and women,' says rock journalist Neil Perry. 'Although the music – loud, nasty, obnoxious, screaming – is much more male-based than punk, gigs by bands like Skid Row, Megadeth and Metallica can be a real couples thing. Also a third of the readership of *Kerrang* (UK's top-selling heavy-metal magazine) is female.'[27]

Whether or not lack of support among women for all-girl heavy-metal bands is a kind of internalized misogyny, female acts often end up ditching the heavy riffs for something more 'acceptable'. The Bangles let go of their roots in the heavy rock bands of LA to make less threatening, chart-friendly post-Beatles pop. In 1986 Susannah Hoffs, Michael (Micki) Steele, and Vicki and Debbie Peterson were rewarded for 'defection' when their Prince song 'Manic Monday' reached No. 2 in the US and UK charts, and they had a rush of hit singles, from 'Walk Like An Egyptian' to the rousing ballad 'Eternal Flame'. The novelty tag dogged them, however, leading to their split in 1989. Women intent on rock credibility find that there are no short cuts.

For Bonnie Raitt, a lone woman singer and slide guitarist who at twenty years old was playing with blues greats such as Buddy Guy, Junior Wells and Sippie Wallace, her career took longer to get off the ground. With her red hair, round face and resolutely 'normal' presentation, Raitt could never be marketed as a cartoon chick. 'I think women like me because I'm one of them, you know,' she once said. One of the few female rock musicians to command respect from her male peers, Raitt was a serious player and key 'guest artist' for years, desperate for the mainstream success that eluded her. Throughout the 1970s she released a series of highly acclaimed albums such as *Takin' My Time* (1973) and *Sweet Forgiveness* (1977), intelligent interpretations of country, rock and blues that were not given due promotion by her label Warners.

Lack of recognition was exacerbated by her drink problem. Like Janis Joplin, Raitt partied hard to keep up with the guys:

'I wanted to be the female version of Muddy Waters. There was a romance about drinking and doing blues. Those blues guys had been professional drinkers for years, and I wanted to prove that I could hold my liquor with them. I bought into that whole lifestyle. I thought Keith Richards was cool, that he was really dangerous.'[28]

After being dropped by Warners in the mid-1980s, she spent several years in obscurity before sobering up and releasing the album that relaunched her career. In 1989 the aptly named album *Nick Of Time* sold over three million copies and yielded three Grammy Awards, including Best Female Rock Vocal Performance. Major success didn't come till she was nearly forty. It had taken a long time for her to pay her dues.

Despite its radical beginnings, the codes of mainstream rock are maybe too conservative, too rigorously male-defined for a woman to find a comfortable place. Artists as varied as Janis Joplin, Patti Smith, Joan Jett and Bonnie Raitt tried to push back gender boundaries throughout the 1960s and 1970s in the face of crushing supergroup 'superiority'. By the late 1970s an unexpected space opened up within which women could discard rock's 'language' altogether. It was punk that proved to be both their inspiration and their nemesis.

# 5 Final Girls

PUNK, PERFORMANCE ART AND PMT POP

A FINAL GIRL is the heroine left at the end of the movie. When everyone around her has been killed off, she survives.

## Tear It Up, Tear It Up

Seventies' pop became a bloated beast as the record industry feasted on a few high-profile supergroups such as Pink Floyd, The Carpenters and The Eagles. Erupting from the club and pub scene in the US and UK was a deliberately discordant note that by the middle of the decade centred around New York (club CBGBs iconoclasts such as The New York Dolls, Richard Hell, Tom Petty and The Ramones) and London (Sex Pistols, The Clash, The Damned).

Despite the influence of US 1960s garage-rock groups and the 1970s New York underground, punk as a major pop cult first took off in Britain. A small, overcrowded island with a bush-telegraph network of music papers and subcultures jostling for attention, it was ripe for a maverick entrepreneur like Malcolm McLaren to exploit, launching his anti-hero speed rock 'n' roll outfit the Sex Pistols to a curious and eager public. The original impact, as conceived by McLaren and his partner, designer Vivienne Westwood, was as theatrical spectacle or choreographed revolt. Their fashion shock tactics were within ritual limits, such as taking elements of SIM bondage gear and customizing them with the parody of tartan bondage trousers, skew-whiff torn T-shirts, safety pins as jewellery, black bin-liners, and nihilist black lipstick. 'It was optimistic and visually exciting,' says Chrissie Hynde, whose band The Pretenders became one of the coolest exponents of punk and later of New

Wave. 'We were blessed here in England in having Vivienne Westwood and Malcolm McLaren to give us some fashion tips.'[1]

Punk soon transmuted into far more than a sartorial spectacle. In registering disillusionment with the major 'fat cat' labels, DIY independents were set up, releasing the thrash chords and experimentation of countless new bands. The resistance became political, with campaigns such as Rock Against Racism (RAR) and Rock Against Sexism (RAS), and the (later derided) notion of 'street cred'. The more proletariat your roots, the harder your struggle, the more 'real' you were. As well as celebrating a vague anti-social anarchy, punk values were about identification with the disadvantaged, the dispossessed, the subcultural – and within this scene women formed their own kind of subculture. 'We were trying to find a new vocabulary,' says Linder Sterling, or Linder, art terrorist and former lead singer with avant-garde punk Manchester group Ludus, who once sang on stage covered in pigs' entrails and wearing a large black dildo.[2]

Punk gave women permission to explore gender boundaries, to investigate their own power, anger, aggression – even nastiness. 'I dressed like a wild teddy girl gone mad,' recalls Jordan, who worked with Westwood and McLaren at their Sex shop. Dubbed 'the first Sex Pistol', she was the Face of early British punk. 'I stole my eye make-up from Cleopatra, and my hair was a big, sweeping adaptation of '60s beehives. I'd buy everything in second-hand shops. I used to commute to London from Seaford, which is a very sleepy seaside town. I'd leave home sometimes just wearing Let It Rock black knickers with Buddy Holly on them, ripped fishnets, stilettos and a padded mohair jumper. I'd get hassled a lot. I'd have run-ins with people who thought I was offending public decency, but there were also some commuters turned on by it. I felt comfortable with the way I looked, it didn't take guts. Punk wasn't about hanging around being the weaker sex. As a woman I felt in control and invincible.'[3]

According to Linder: 'There were a lot of big lumpy women

punks around. They weren't "ideal" prizes, but they had small skirts on if they wanted. Punk was about being looked at, creating a temporary celebrity. There was something glorious about all those shapes and sizes on show.' Women felt free to express difference. Liz Naylor, co-editor of Manchester punk fanzine City Fun and later Riot Grrrl, asserts that punk in the 1970s was a visible threat. 'You were seen as deviant. There was a lot of anger and self-mutilation. In a asymbolic sense, women were destroying the established image of femininity, aggressively tearing it down.'[4]

Punk, then, offered women a chance to reject the 1970s pastel femininity of blue eyeshadow, flared jeans and flouncy tiered dresses that had been *de rigueur*, and consequently many entered the ranks of punk bands via a fashion route. 'I ran a small boutique in World's End with the designer Sophia Hallburn,' says Poly Styrene, one of the first women in punk to make a record, with her band X-Ray Spex. 'We started that whole bright colours, plasticky, whacky fashion as opposed to the black bondage stuff. McLaren and Westwood were older than us and we wanted to do our own younger fun thing, without the sexual connotations of their shop. Our stuff was much more asexual.'[5]

Born Marion Elliot in Bromley, Kent, to a British mother and an Islamic Somalian father, Poly left school at fifteen to work in Woolworths. Soon bored by that, she travelled around hippy festivals and fringe theatre before coming back to London to train as a clothes buyer, writing songs in her spare time. At eighteen she formed a band – 'It was just that time when anybody could' – and after advertising in the music press ('Young punx who want to stick it together'), assembled a line-up that included fifteen-year-old saxophone player Susan Whitby, or Lora Logic. Released in October 1977, their first single, 'Oh Bondage, Up Yours!', a frank retort to the objectification of women, featured Logic's vibrant sax and the raucous tension of Poly's gloriously controlled shriek. Banned by the BBC, it became an instant cult hit. In tune with X-Ray Spex punk resistance, Poly made few concessions to looking 'sexy', wearing her hair short, braces on her teeth and outlandish day-glo clothes.

'I wasn't one of the pretty punkettes. I was very conscious of wearing a brace. I was very conscious of wearing train tracks, but I wasn't going to hide it. I think it helped a lot of other young women who also had braces. I felt that if I made myself pretty people would treat me like a blow-up doll without a brain. I wouldn't have been so effective. When I listen to my old vocal style it personally grates a little, but then I wanted to be like that, I was rebelling. Although I could actually sing – I'd had opera training – I didn't want to sing. I wanted to be an anti-singer.'

Her stance initially upset male crowds: 'There was hostility in strange areas like Wales, where real macho guys would come up and create aggro, throwing beer over me. At that time I needed to be aggressive, they were all heavy kids out there. That was in the early days – but then we attracted a more arty audience.' Poly felt that punk did change women's position in the business: 'It paved the way for women to become not just sex objects. However, we can still be exploited. I used to say being a woman was no different to being a man in rock music, but you have to develop a hard attitude. Because we're feminine we tend to be softer-hearted, so people try and walk over us.'

Her views on gender were refracted through ten years of living as a Hare Krishna. I first met her when she released the EP *Gods And Goddesses*, a swirling, ethereal mixture of Eastern and Western melody. Wearing a floral dress, her hair curling softly round her ears, she was the antithesis of the smart, self-contained punk in the soldier-girl outfit who sang 'Germ-Free Adolescence' on *Top of the Pops* in 1978. Moving some distance from the cultural anarchy that spawned her, Poly's response to what she saw as the chaos of punk was to create a pristine world of ordered Krishna spirituality. 'Cleanliness is next to godliness,' she giggled.

Poly's bandmate Lora Logic remembers punk as a time of great opportunity. Only fifteen when she joined X-Ray Spex, Lora says: 'It was the best thing that happened to me at that age, I loved every minute of it. Poly was a really magical person, and we worked well together. We were both anti-fashion, anti-establishment. But after we'd had success, Poly felt threatened by my presence. My riffs were getting a lot of attention. They replaced me, and my little world was shattered.'[6] Lora went on to form her own band, Essential Logic, but in the early 1980s she, too, gave it up to join the Krishna movement. 'I grew up too quickly. People always said I was too serious for my years. I was taking drugs and living in squats. Krishna and the spiritual life made sense to me. I had to do it for my sanity and I never looked back.'

Punk was not an easy place to be if you were a woman. Though much has been made since of its liberating force, men were often unreconstructed when it came to girlfriends, expecting women to be 'seen and not heard'. As a result the girls who broke through were the toughest: they survived by adopting the cool veneer of cynicism, yet at the same time were open to contradiction. Siouxsie Sioux, for instance, the inflammatory Ice Queen of Punk, soon learned the dubious shock value of wearing a Nazi swastika armband.

**Siouxsie Sioux** at Polydor Records, 1979: punk's Ice Queen. (Pennie Smith)

'It was a shot of adrenalin to open people's pupils a bit, and in a way the people who were offended were offended by themselves,' she tried to justify to feminist monthly *Spare Rib* in 1979. 'Because of the Second World War, it's considered a symbol of injustice, a huge inhumanity, and people are deluded into thinking that's where it started and that's where it ended. It didn't. It's been going on right from the Middle Ages. Religion and witch-hunts were as powerful as the swastika.'[7]

Wearing a Fascist symbol and at the same time denouncing it soon became untenable. 'It was damaging to us. I saw no reason to wear it any more because it was being used as decoration and fashion . . . When I wanted to shock people then I had nothing formulated so it was just blatant and crude.'[8] In 1980 she and The Banshees released 'Israel' by way of atonement, but the stigma remained.

Despite this, in the late 1970s she was enigma itself, stark and stylish with her jet black hair, brooding eyes, wheeling arms and legs, and nonchalant defiance. At the epicentre of punk, Siouxsie was born Susan Ballion in Kent, Queen of the 'Bromley Contingent', a group of fans that followed the Sex Pistols from gig to gig. She was even present at a classic pop moment, on the set of the Thames TV *Today* programme when Steve Jones called presenter Bill Grundy a 'dirty fucker' and punk, until then an underground movement, hit the headlines.

Inspired by the 'have a go' spontaneity surrounding the band, Siouxsie decided to form one herself, playing her first gig rehearsal free at London's 100 Club Punk Festival in 1976, with Sid Vicious on drums. This early line-up, including Mark Pirroni and Steve Severin, thrashed through a bastardized twenty-minute version of 'The Lord's Prayer', 'Twist And Shout' and 'Knocking On Heaven's Door'. The general consensus was that it was awful. Two years later, though, after several line-up changes and a huge A&R bidding war, she secured a deal with Polydor. Marked by Siouxsie's distinctive, diamond-hard vocals, The Banshees' first single 'Hong Kong Garden' was a surprise British hit, reaching the Top Ten in 1978. 'Whenever the Banshees had a hit I'd think, "Ooh, we sneaked in that one." In the beginning I felt like we'd gatecrashed someone else's party. I'm proud of being part of something that was so innocent, a spontaneous combustion,' she recalls.[9] With songs on the album *The Scream* exploring everything from suicide in suburbia to the cult of Charles Manson to a butcher falling in love with a slab of meat, Siouxsie spoke of a thousand nervous breakdowns. By 1980 she had become tingling and subtly anthemic with *Kaleidoscope*, then psychedelic on *A Kiss In The Dreamhouse* (1982).

Although punk was about sartorial confrontation, Siouxsie cut a figure of strange elegance. I remember meeting her backstage after a gig at Leeds University in 1980. She was sitting at a table autographing photos, exuding mystique. Nervously, I went up to interview her for the student paper, fully expecting to be knocked back, but she turned out to be a regular gal, fond of film, music and clothes. We remained for an hour behind that trestle table while she talked quietly of her loneliness being the only woman on the road with an all-male band. Despite her vulnerability there was a spark in her eyes, an enthusiasm and dedication.

Seven years later that light was gone. I ran into her again at the Newcastle studios for the ground-breaking 'yoof' TV pop show *The Tube*. She had become a self-parody, hair black and jagged, face coated with orange foundation and eyes painted dark out of habit rather than theatrical celebration. She spoke through gritted teeth, looking as if any minute she might collapse. Then, as if she had sloughed off dead skin, two years later a new Siouxsie emerged: sleek, streamlined, her hair cut, her expression bouncy. Later she said, 'I needed time to pause and take a new direction.' Like many women in punk, she had to lay that aggressive defended self to rest. 'I feel more confident now. My voice has changed: in the beginning it was a protest voice, shouting as loud as possible over other people. I feel I can be more playful now. Everything felt so uptight, tense and abrasive then. Every time you went out on stage you put your head on the block; you'd get missiles thrown at you, you had to be hard to survive within that.'[10]

In the late 1990s, after 20 years and 12 albums, the Banshees decided to call it a day. Siouxsie and her partner, Banshee drummer Budgie, recaptured the spirit of punk with their percussive duo The Creatures. 'It was scary, but unless something feels a bit scary, maybe it's not worth doing. I realized that money and security doesn't sit well with the creative process,' she says. They moved to rural France because London felt like 'a rat run, very confined and village-y. Out here my head works differently. You can relax into ideas, let them *unfold*. It's an extreme contrast. But I like extremes, I'm not good at the middle ground.'

## I'm Always Touched by Your Presence Dear

On the other side of cathartic noise was subversive bubblegum. Blondie set the trend Stateside for cute harmonic pop songs with a blistering edge, a sound that echoed later through muscular pop outfits like The Go-Go's. The foundation for this sound centred in the 1970s architect of sardonic bleached bombshell, Debbie Harry. Happy to play a cartoon, Harry kept her hair white, her lips red and her skirts short. Though she came on like pop's ultimate blow-up doll, she sniggered underneath, fooling middle America, nay the world, into thinking she was the fantasy, a shiny modern Marilyn Monroe. Blondie, it seemed, were the ultimate Warholian mix of art and commerce.

Despite the sheen, Harry's roots were resolutely dark, bohemian and Lower East Side. The adopted child of middle-class philistine New Jersey suburbia, she escaped early into the creative, drug-addled sleaze of Warhol's Manhattan, working as a bunny-girl and waitress, taking tips and performing in bands such as all-female trio The Stilettos. Former art student Chris Stein joined them as a guitarist in 1974, and before long she and Stein created a different band altogether, with bassist Gary Valentine, James Destri (keyboards) and drummer Clem Burke.

In the New York alternative renaissance of the mid-1970s legions of painters, photographers and musicians would coalesce and separate in various permutations of 'performance art', while bands like the glam punk New York Dolls and mixed-

**Debbie Harry** at Isleworth Video Studios, early 1980s: 'Always Touched By Your Presence Dear'. (Pennie Smith)

gender psychobilly mutants The Cramps would play dives and rock joints on the Lower East Side. Blondie rose, phoenix-like, from CBGBs with a power pop barbed by punk mores. Despite a record deal in 1976 with Private Stock, the band were initially subject to an unofficial radio boycott. 'It was pop that was very aggressive, with a female front-person, and an aggressive female front-person had never really been done in pop,' said Harry. 'It was very difficult to be in that position at the time – it's hard to be a ground-breaker.'[11]

Their appeal spread overseas to Europe and Australia, with Britain in particular buying hit after hit. It wasn't until they moved to Chrysalis and released the Mike Chapman-produced album *Parallel Lines* that Blondie took off in the States, their single 'Heart Of Glass' going to No. 1, the album selling seven million copies in two years. With her punk attack and platinum 'dumbe blonde' hair, Harry had, however, created a double-edged sword. Promotional posters for the single 'Rip Her To Shreds' read, 'Wouldn't You Like To Rip Her To Shreds?' – an offensive headline, especially combined with the 'Blondie Is A Group' slogan that had the kickback effect of emphasizing her sex-symbol role rather than the music. Rock critic Lester Bangs brutally pinpointed this dilemma when he wrote:

'If most guys in America could somehow get their fave-rave poster girl in bed and have total licence to do whatever they wanted with this legendary body for one afternoon, at least 75 per cent . . . would elect to beat her up. She may be up there all high and mighty on TV, but everybody knows that underneath all that fashion plating she's just a piece of meat like all the rest of them.'[12]

Harry's provocative pose was very conscious. 'I wanted to inject film-star glamour. And I didn't want to be portrayed as a victim . . . It seemed, especially since I was in front of a rock band, and a rock band of all men, like the perfect opportunity to sing songs that were a little more playful about . . . the war between the sexes.[13]

Though she was convinced of her rebel status, Harry's irony fell flat. She was accused of being a 'publicity hooker' and a

'hypocrite' by other female punk performers. 'Blondie was easy
... a compact theatricality that was easy to understand,' she said
in 1993. 'I made my own image, then I was trapped in it.'[14] She
had a one-off hit in 1986 with 'French Kissin' In The USA', but
by then, she says, 'Warners were too busy pushing some other
blonde. I felt overshadowed by their commitment to Madonna,
and this feeling that I was being viewed as some competitive
thing that they couldn't devote much time or energy to.'[15] As the
hits faded, Harry retreated to nurse her partner and mentor
Chris Stein, who had fallen ill with a rare wasting disease called
pemphigus. In 1993, at the age of forty-seven, Harry came back
with a solo album *Debravation* that, despite competent dance
tunes, lacked the crystal sheen of the Blondie pop she was trying
to recapture. Wearing executive suits, with brown hair, she
looked oddly frumpy, yet still exuded a slight air of depravity,
like old perfume. I saw her perform at a gay nightclub in the West
End, in a blond wig and a black Lycra minidress far too small for
her ample size. Swaying on stage to old hits, Harry made an
uneasy survivor.

Years after Blondie, she was to look at Madonna and moan: 'I
wish it had been me!' The difference between them, though, is
that Harry believed 'You don't have to be tough to survive, you
have to be vulnerable . . . it's that sensitivity that makes you know
how other people feel . . . to reach them.'[16] Madonna, sinewy to
the last, would never have sacrificed worldwide adulation for
such apparent fallibility. By 1999, however, Harry was back with
a reformed Blondie and new album *No Exit*. They did a reunion
tour and enjoyed renewed critical appreciation. People, it
seemed, 'got' the joke this time. 'It's great to be back in the hot
seat,' Harry said, 'It keeps your ass warm.'

While characters like Harry and Siouxsie gave face and voice
to punk, Ohio-born Chrissie Hynde, a female fop who wore
ruffled shirts with her leather jackets, was serious about being a
rock star instrumentalist. At sixteen she had travelled hundreds
of miles to study her idols in concert. One night at a Rolling
Stones gig, for instance, Hynde was amazed by the way Bill
Wyman caught a note thrown to him by a female fan. 'With his

**Chrissie Hynde** in the WEA Records UK gym, early 1980s: rock heroine and role model. 'I was pissed off one night at the Vortex, when they cheered Elvis dying. Respect is very important.' (Pennie Smith)

left hand he reached up, plucked this note out of the air, put it in his pocket and kept on playing, which I thought was well cool.'[17] She was infatuated too with Keith Richards, the symbol of an outlaw freedom. 'Bourbon in hand, switchblade in his boot, guitar across his back, and the law at his heels – Keith Richards *is* rock 'n' roll,' 1960s icon Marianne Faithfull once said.[18]

As a teenager longing to be part of this world Hynde waited for hours once after a Kinks gig just to catch sight of Ray Davies, little knowing that fifteen years later she would have his child. From understudying male rock stars, she became a rock star herself. It was a long process, though, and Hynde 'did her time', moving to the UK in the early 1970s, latching on to the punk scene, writing briefly for *NME* and working in McLaren and Westwood's 'Sex' shop. After playing in different bands, including a stint with Mick Jones who later joined The Clash, Hynde assembled her own outfit, The Pretenders, with guitarist James Honeyman-Scott, Pete Farndon on bass, drummer Gerry Mackleduff and Hynde herself on rhythm guitar. Because so many musicians found her threatening Hynde had to fight to get a good band together. 'I had a vision. I held out and found the right guys,' Hynde told me in 1999. 'I'd been round the block so many times looking for this band, I was for *real.*'[19] Some mistook her determination for brash attitude. As The Damned founder-member Chris Millar remarked, 'I thought she was a loud-mouthed American boiler.'[20]

Gradually acknowledged with grudging acceptance by the London boy muso mafia, Hynde went on to become a pivotal Woman in Rock role model, crafting her own tasteful sound from speed punk and pop melody with hits such as 'Kid' and 'Brass In Pocket' standing out as major songwriting achieve-ments. Tall, pale and clad in black leather, she was both defiant and accessible, a quality producer Nick Lowe picked up on while working on the debut eponymously titled *Pretenders* album: 'Her voice sounded like the girls you see working on Woolworth's check-out counter . . . tough, but feminine . . . dodgy on the pitching [yet] sexy as hell.'[21]

Despite the enormous bad luck that dogged The Pretenders (Honeyman-Scott and Farndon both died of drug overdoses within a year of each other), plus incidents in the early 1980s where she displayed a penchant for vodka and getting into scuffles, Hynde seemed to keep her cool. She didn't let motherhood stop her touring or writing hits. From The Pretenders' debut single 'Stop Your Sobbing' to 1986's 'Hymn To Her' and the UB40 duet 'I Got You Babe', Hynde has always been a long-ball player.

At base, Hynde is a straightforward rock 'n' roller. For a while she was reluctant to be seen as a feminist, and even her environ-mental fights of the late 1980s were tempered. Her call to 'firebomb McDonald's' in the heady atmosphere of post-Live

Aid political pop was just as swiftly retracted in the moral music-business panic that ensued, while in 1994 when she released one of her most highly acclaimed albums *Last Of The Independents*, with a fresh Pretenders' line-up, Hynde snapped that she was through with animals and the environment. 'As far as I'm concerned you can bathe in blood. All the information's out there. People can make up their own mind now. It's nothing to do with me. I'm a rock singer.'[22]

Hynde had used the punk media axis sensibly to gain exposure, experience and a band. Chaos may have roared around her, but on her personal patch Hynde was still wholesome middle America, looking up to and learning from her rock idols: 'I was pissed off one night at the Vortex, when they cheered Elvis dying. Respect is very important,' she once said. Once Ray Davies's lover, then married to Simple Minds' Jim Kerr, then romantically connected with Nash Kato from 1990s grunge band Urge Overkill, Hynde sought union with her rock heroes, becoming a staple of the international music industry. Commanding on stage, even in her early forties, she transmitted a rare passion and commitment to her role as female guitar hero. There was one night at the Brixton Academy on the 1994 tour when Hynde began a song standing quietly at the back of the stage, only to run to the front and leap in the air with her guitar just as the melody took off – an inspired act. 'I *bet* she's seen some things in her time,' said one admiring fan. Though often confident to the point of truculence, by the year 2000 Hynde had mellowed. She was happier to discuss the subject of women in rock, from her own honest perspective.

'I'd been thinking about my band since I was fourteen. I wasn't inspired by females particularly. But that's the beauty of rock – it's androgynous, and I was a very androgynous kid. I didn't particularly want to be a female anyway, I just wanted to play guitar in a band. That punk moment in pop history let me slip in there very nicely because no one was allowed to say, "She's good for a girl".'[23]

Punk threw up a number of female bands who wrestled with the marshalled might of rock, but underneath the brittle bravado lay a lack of confidence. Although punk celebrated assertiveness, women were still aware of their position as relative newcomers on the rock scene. 'Some early rock was very macho. Maybe the guitar is the extension of the phallus, and holding a guitar made women feel uncomfortable. Also women during the 1970s were probably too busy with sexual liberation, working on priorities like the abortion campaign. Once they'd won a few political victories they could say, aha, now it's time to form a rock 'n' roll band,' says Karin Berg, head of A&R for Warners East Coast who was instrumental in signing several punk acts, including the B-52s, Television, The Cars and Hüsker Dü.[24]

This uncertainty revealed itself when in 1980 women from the main British girl bands – The Passions, The Au Pairs, The Raincoats, The Mo-Dettes, The Slits and Girlschool – assembled for a group *NME* 'Women in Rock' photo. 'Barbara [Grogan, from The Passions] suggests a picture with us all doing the clenched fist salute – "for a laugh". But would everyone see the joke? We decided not to,' wrote journalist Deanne Pearson.[25] Iggy Pop or Public Enemy would never have been so self-effacing.

That tension between tentativeness and anger meant these bands made an important contribution to rock in the early 1980s, investing it with an eerie, scratchy femininity. Less about shock tactics, guts and confrontation, their music was more a resolute expression of what it meant to be a woman at that time, in that particular culture. The Slits, for instance, wore knickers outside their trousers, wound reggae rhythms around a speed feminine sound and ridiculed 'Typical Girls'. Their punk burlesque reached its height for the cover of their 1979 Island debut *Cut*, where they were pictured topless, wearing loincloths and daubed in mud. Their anarchic energy unnerved people. 'We'd be dressed half in bondage fetish gear, half in Doc Martens, hair all out there, scowling at everybody. It freaked people out, particularly middle-aged men,' recalls their guitarist Viv Albertine. For her, the subversion of fashion codes was part of a general change. 'The whole scene meant a rigorous rethink of everything I'd ever thought before,' she states.[26]

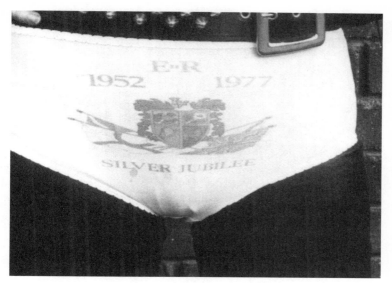

**Ari Up**
of The Slits in her
Silver Jubilee briefs,
shocking the nation
on the 'White Riot'
tour, 1977.
(Caroline Coon)

Rough Trade band The Raincoats were more introverted, creating a sense of fire and unpredictability with their violinist Vicky Aspinall and Ana da Silva's skittish vocals. Lack of musical expertise made them inventive. 'When I saw The Slits play it inspired me to think I could do it,' recalls founder member Gina Birch. 'I went out one day, bought the cheapest bass I could find, and sprayed it sparkly blue. Little by little I plonked away. It never occurred to me to get any lessons, I just picked it up myself.' She admits that at first the band had a struggle with their instruments, learning to play on stage.' 'But we brought an element of surprise, discovery and discomfort. We were an art-school band, trying to find a way of looking at the world that was personal and different, rather than deliberately oblique.'[27] Regulars at the Roxy in 1976, the club that spawned The Slits, X-Ray Spex and The Clash, they probably went further than their peers in dismantling rock 'n' roll time, constructing songs to reflect the constant variables of 'femaleness', with mercurial beats and flexible rhythms. It was never really commercial (celebrity DJ Danny Baker once said: 'They are so bad that every time a waiter drops a tray we'd all get up and dance') but

**The Slits**:
out-take from the
cover of their 1979
album *Cut*.
(Pennie Smith)

during punk days credibility lay in experimentation rather than
hits. 'There was a sense of occasion, a spirit. People compared it
to Dada,' said Birch. 'I felt like something was happening, that
the world was going to change and explode.'

Even though they didn't change the world, the complexity of
The Raincoats' work was later recognized as a major influence

on early-1990s girl bands. Dubbed the 'Godmothers of Grunge', they were said by Kurt Cobain from Nirvana to have played a crucial part in his musical history. 'Rather than listening to them I feel like I'm listening in on them. We're together in the same old house and I have to be completely still or they will hear me spying from above and, if I get caught – everything will be ruined because it's their thing,' he wrote on the sleevenotes for the reissue of their self-titled 1979 debut. Although he committed suicide just before The Raincoats were due to support Nirvana on their 1994 British tour, his tribute lives on.

With their song 'Off Duty Trip', about the true story of a soldier tried for raping a young girl and acquitted so he could continue with his army career, The Raincoats echoed many female punk bands in the way they tackled feminist issues directly. There were initiatives like Rock Against Sexism, for instance, a benefit network set up as a sister to Rock Against Racism, with money going to organizations like Women's Aid or Rape Crisis. One of the most overtly political groups of the era were The Au Pairs, a mixed band from Birmingham with a hard, funky edge, who sang about the British occupation of Northern Ireland and the tortures of patriarchy, their song 'Come Again', about faking orgasm and male definitions of female sexuality, earning the ultimate accolade of a BBC ban. Guitarist Lesley Woods and bassist Jane Munro were central figures in a band where lyrics, beat and instrumentation were all tightly honed, and their album *Playing With A Different Sex*, released in 1981 on Human Records, stood as a gender-clash classic .

## Our Lips Are Sealed

By going against the grain of rock 'n' roll most British female punk bands remained of cult-level status. In the States, however, where punk was more closely allied to harmonic pop, commercial success was possible. The B-52s, for example, a band from Athens, Georgia, who had two female leads and a fine line in raw surf music, got their name from a camp slang term for a bouffant hairdo. 'There was a rumour in New York when we first started that Cindy and I were drag queens,' said Kate Pierson about their 'trashy but intellectual' image of two-foot-high wigs and outrageous femininity. 'It was also a wonderful accident that our voices overlapped so uniquely with such strange harmonies.'[28]

Drawing from that vivid mondo pop, ground-breaking girl group The Go-Go's polished up its kitsch, aggressive harmonies and took the sound into the charts. 'We started the band just for fun and at first were seen as a joke or some kind of novelty act. There was, however, some genuine talent in the band, and we picked up quite a following,' says Belinda Carlisle, former lead singer with the group. Just after the release of her third solo album *Runaway Horses* in 1990, her hair scraped back into a respectable pony tail, her eyes a wide bright blue, Carlisle was the perfect pop star. 'I'm a compulsive, addictive personality,' she said, clipped and precise. 'I have to watch myself. To keep myself calm I meditate twice each day, for twenty minutes at a time.'[29] It seemed that only through dieting, exercise regime, and stints with Alcoholics and Narcotics Anonymous could she banish the Go-Go's of the past and properly launch a solo career.

In 1982 The Go-Go's were the No. 1 girl group in America. They topped the album charts with *Beauty And The Beat*, and had two hit singles 'Our Lips Are Sealed' and 'We Got The Beat', the latter reaching No. 2. It was a major achievement, especially considering the minimal success of previous all-girl bands like Fanny and The Runaways. While girl vocal groups had scored in the charts from the mid-1950s, female instrumentalists were still treated as a joke. The Go-Go's were the first women's band emerging from punk to achieve commercial hits. Drummer Gina Schock, for instance, was a baltimore teenager who played in a punk band called Edie & The Eggs, and worshipped local cult movie-maker John Waters. 'He made such bizarre films I always wanted to know him, but my mum and dad said if ever I was in any of his movies they'd throw me out. I wanted to be BAD!,' she says.[30]

Carlisle fondly remembers the wacky, colourful thrift-store clothes she wore around her home-town in northern LA in the late 1970s. 'I read about the Sex Pistols in British magazines and got into punk. In America it was more of an artistic, poppy fun thing, but we were still considered total freaks and treated with prejudice.' She would hang out with fellow punk Jane Wiedlin at LA clubs like the Masque and the Starwood, and after seeing the Sex Pistols' final performance in San Francisco, they decided to form their own band. After several line-up changes the group had Carlisle and Wiedlin at its core, with Charlotte Caffey on guitar, bassist Margot Olaverra (who was later replaced by ex-Girlschool Kathy Valentine) and drummer Gina Schock, a tough Baltimore veteran who was sceptical at first of the band's abilities. They soon tightened up on their instruments, constructing a catchy all-girl power pop in the tradition of the B-52s and Blondie.

A support slot for Madness at LA's Whiskey A Go Go led to a complete tour of England in 1980. It was a special time, not just because of the multi-racial post-punk Two-Tone fever that had gripped Britain, with Madness and The Specials at the helm, but an all-girl 'sister' group had started up in the UK, the seven-strong ska-based Bodysnatchers. Lead singer Rhoda Dakar clearly remembers it as an exciting period:

'We did a "Seaside Tour" – The Specials, The Go-Go's and The Bodysnatchers. It was a brilliant experience as regards being a woman in the music business. Including the roadies and crew, it was the only time there were equal amounts of men and women on tour. It felt like a normal job, we weren't marginalized, and in fact, as regards artists, women were the majority.'[31]

Like The Go-Go's, The Bodysnatchers were carving out new ground as they went along. 'We'd all never done it before,' recalls Dakar. 'We all had the same sense of innocence. If someone said, This can't be done, we'd ask why. As seven women we had a pack mentality – if we couldn't get what we wanted, like, say, a proper soundcheck, we'd all shout at once and get it. We all supported each other.'

After The Bodysnatchers split in 1981, transmuting into The Belle Stars, Dakar recorded a solo single 'The Boiler' on the

Coventry-based indie label 2-Tone. A stark, nail-biting narrative of a rape attack, related over The Specials AKA's light, jazzy backing, the record ends with Dakar's terrified screaming. 'It used to stun the audience,' she says. 'It is freaky if someone's standing there screaming at you very loudly.' Despite the harrowing subject-matter, it was a top thirty hit in the British charts.

Dakar and The Bodysnatchers were doing what countless male bands have the opportunity to do – learning and networking from each other. Touring with The Go-Go's taught them a lot about music-business professionalism. 'They were so slick!' Dakar says of the LA foursome. 'They'd been playing for some time, and their harmonies were really polished. We thought, wow, they can play really well. We were blagging it, basically, whereas they could actually do what they did.'

Doing what they did meant rapid success for The Go-Go's. The first signing to Miles Copeland's indie label IRS to have major chart hits, company and band went into promotional overdrive, burning out within two years. 'When we came back from England we told everyone that we were really big there. That made us cool,' says Carlisle. 'Success snowballed from there and we were at the top of the charts. We couldn't handle the pressure. We started to crack up under the strain, having a real wild time, taking drugs, drinking. We weren't happy. Everyone in the band wanted to do something else.' The band split after their third album release *Talk Show* in 1984 and Carlisle, bloated-out and drug-worn, struggled to establish herself as a solo singer. 'I started again with zero confidence. I'd only just got sober, just got married, and was feeling vulnerable. I had to tour with people like Robert Palmer.'

In 1987 she re-emerged streamlined and wholesomely sexy with the No. 1 hit, 'Heaven Is A Place On Earth'. 'My first album went gold, and that was great. Success now takes the edge off things, it cushions me,' she says. The ex-Go-Go's matured gracefully as individuals, with Jane Wiedlin following her own solo career and Charlotte Caffey forming late-1980s all-girl band The Graces, but the pressures riding on them being the first No. 1 commercial girl band meant that they combusted from within.

Like Bananarama in Britain, the effervescent, tomboyish vocal trio who had nearly as many hits there as The Supremes, The Go-Go's achieved success by being 'pretty punks'. Those who used the stage in a more defiant way found themselves largely ignored by major labels. In 1980 Barbara Grogan issued a cheerful challenge: 'A lot of the motivation for doing what I do comes from being a woman. There's nothing I enjoy more than being on stage and slagging off men.'[32] That sentiment was soon buried as the self-consciously styled MTV 1980s took hold, an era where political and feminist debates were condemned as moribund, and women's eccentricity was effectively silenced.

## Revenge as Art

'Rock music is a very aggressive and insecure means of expression,' The Slits' Viv Albertine once said, so why would women want to get involved with it? Performance artist Lydia Lunch was scathing about the genre: 'Get rid of the fucking raunchy bad rock 'n' roll! That's where girls should wake up instead of trying to cop second, third and fourth generation rock 'n' roll licks that were terrible in the first place. Why don't they just trade in their guitars for fuckin' Uzis?'[33]

When punk dissolved in the early 1980s, many women focused their sense of dissonance and difference on to the underground, carving out areas in avant-garde and performance art. The exploration of taboo and what it means to be a woman *in extremis* has long been a tradition, from the rough-cut 1950s Beat movement to the 'Happenings' of the 1960s and the ground-breaking charge of 1970s all-female German group Malaria. Mostly this music exists, by its very nature, on the margins. Laurie Anderson is one of the few examples of a woman from such a background who made a connection with pop.

Her approach is abstract, intuitive, non-linear and typically 'feminine'. Her 1981 smash British hit 'O Superman' was eight minutes of echoing tape-loop whisper, a synthesized classic and unexpected success. The lack of a build-up and explosive rock release led to musicologist Susan McClary hailing it as a subversion of 'phallo-centric, triumphalist structures of Western classical music'.

In 1992, Anderson said,

'I've never been interested in plot. I think plot is something that takes all the boring days out and leaves the exciting ones in. Most real things unravel in a much more textured way. But that's not particularly feminine or masculine, I think. Maybe you could make a case for action-oriented being male, detail-oriented being female. But I've never been interested in these clichés, I don't find it helpful to put that grid on what I do.'[34]

'O Superman' was one part of a huge work-in-progress, an eight-hour-long multi-media 'solo opera' called 'United States I-IV'. She was trying to write the entire cultural history of the US: an ambitious project that was astonishing, not just in what it encompassed – special effects, slides, films, stand-up comedy, off-the-wall soliloquies, performance – but in the fact that Anderson did not feel the need to limit herself, keep to the safe surround of 'womanly' expression. Stepping out of that comfort zone meant that Anderson was unafraid of technology, using, abusing and fooling with it. Only through this process could she have invented her famous tape bow, where a tape loop is bowed across a violin with cassette heads instead of strings. Her 1986 single 'Language Is A Virus From Outer Space' (the title taken from a William Burroughs novel) showed her sense of moving beyond the traditional narrative of rock 'n' roll to decode some of its associations. Rock was not important to her, just one more tool to express her 'vision'.

Resident of the lower Manhattan loft scene of the early 1970s, Anderson has a background in visual art, and moved from sculpture into music with a twelve-hour-long audio-visual experience 'The Life And Times Of Joseph Stalin' at the Brooklyn Academy of Music in 1973. Her first LP releases – *Big Science* (1982) and *Mr Heartbreak* (1983) – were abstract, conceptual offerings, while *Home Of The Brave* (1986) delved into more traditional songwriting territory, co-produced by disco-dance king

Nile Rodgers. 'She had an evolved consciousness – maybe post-feminist. She'd gone all the steps and one further,' recalls A&R Karin Berg, who signed Anderson to Warners on the strength of 'O Superman'. 'She saw the world: whatever her eye turned to – the desk, the plant, the relations between people – she had a way of expressing it in breathtaking simplicity and intelligence.'

Anderson, however, had a whimsical relationship with pop. As writer Robin Denselow once remarked: 'There are numerous themes in Anderson's work but no arguments.' By the early 1990s, she was becoming more explicitly political, as if, having established freedom through the abstract, she felt confident with arguments rooted in everyday life. Hence her work in the 1990s with the Women's Action Coalition, and child-abuse survivors. As well as plugging into the Internet, she was punctuating 'the membrane between personal and political'. She even began to see her music as typical 'women's work', as 'little islands that relate to each other. Women are more attuned to helping relate and less to [singleminded] breakneck change.'[35]

Also coming from a performance art world was Yoko Ono, who by the 1990s was being cited as an influence for female punk and hardcore girl acts such as Hole. Courtney Love adopted her as a heroine not just through her identification with Ono's role as vilified rock wife, but also in terms of music. The daughter of a Japanese banker, Ono established herself as part of the New York avant-garde art world from the early 1960s. Christened 'High Priestess of the Happening' in the 1960s, she performed musical pieces, presented art 'events' like 'Cut Piece', where she invited an audience to cut off her clothing with scissors, and made films such as the infamous *Bottoms*, a feature of 365 human bottoms which was initially refused a certificate from the British Board of Film Censors. Her music career did not really develop until she became romantically involved with John Lennon in 1968, and the two formed the Plastic Ono Band, also sparking off situationist peace initiatives such as 'Bed-Ins'.

With Lennon she made a series of experimental albums, such as *Unfinished Music No. 1: Two Virgins* and *The Wedding Album*. Beatles fans were mystified by her caterwaulings, but there was method in her screaming. By the early 1970s Ono was emerging as a strong feminist artist, songs such as 'Woman Is The Nigger Of The World' earning her a place in the female rock canon. Ono has always been dogged by accusations of dilettantism, however, and though her contribution to 1980's *Double Fantasy* album with Lennon was critically acclaimed, particularly the sharply evocative single 'Walking On Thin Ice' (released after his death), her subsequent albums released throughout the 1980s failed to make an impact. Some have claimed, like Lennon, that she was 'twenty years ahead of her time'.

By the late 1990s, Ono's work was being re-evaluated in the light of punk-inspired bands like Sonic Youth and Nirvana. 'It's almost as if Yoko's music really belongs to the 1990s,' said her son Sean Ono Lennon. What had once sounded like unlistenable catharsis was embraced as avant garde. In 2001, at the age of 68, she was still intensely creative, releasing a new studio album, *Blueprint For A Sunrise*, and taking her retrospective art exhibition 'Herstory' around the world. Both the album and the show highlighted her outrage at violence against women, and anyone interested was invited to contribute to a range of women's charities. It had taken decades for Ono to be acknowledged as a feminist performer with a singular vision. She once said drily that being blamed for the break-up of the Beatles probably did little to help her reputation. 'It was like the English fighting the Japs again . . . like what is this – she's going to cut your throat while you're asleep or something,' Ono recalls.

What of those female artists who have gone further than Ono or Anderson in rejecting the music industry – commenting on rather than being of it? Though representing a challenge, their disdain of rock music can make them less authoritative as commentators.

Karen Finley, for example, a San Francisco Art Institute graduate who moved to New York in the early 1980s to 'get press', has been reduced to the yams debate. Never mind her impassioned feminist work on male violence as a multi-media artist – everything boils down to the canned yams she smeared on her backside during a performance on female sexuality.

Against a crude background of attack and censure from the National Endowment for the Arts (NEA), *Village Voice* writers C. Carr and Pete Hamill engaged in an intellectual pro/anti slanging match, while right-wing senator Jesse Helms denounced Finley's sexual satire as obscene and pornographic. 'They were never interested in my intellectual abilities,' Finley said. She got press, but not necessarily in a way she had anticipated.

Sex as shock tactic has long been a pop-culture preoccupation, particularly in the States, where fundamentalist Christianity exerts a strong influence, but its effectiveness is defused when people see no further than the knee-jerk image. Far more revolutionary was Finley's public sculpture, a poem called 'The Black Sheep' cast in bronze and set in a concrete monolith in a homeless area of the Lower East Side. A moving paean to society's outsiders and disaffected, it conveyed a sense of humanity, and was visited regularly.

Musically she was unforgiving, creating it for 'a political reason' and meeting pain with pain. Finley's 'The Truth Is Hard To Swallow', in which men list the sexual activities they enjoy, became a cult record, while her collaboration with Sinead O'Connor, 'Jump In The River', which ends with Finley's distended, cathartic shrieking, stands as a forthright female anti-pop track. Though she wasn't as strong a musician as she was an artist, Finley appreciates that music is cheap and therefore more accessible to a mass audience than the best installation.

British independent 1980s artist Danielle Dax used painting on the body to make her statement. A beautiful singer with huge cat-like eyes, she pottered along for years creating her own experimental solo albums with titles like *Pop Eyes* (1983) and *Jesus Egg That Wept* (1984) — an amalgam of Captain Beefheart, Indian ragga, vaudeville and soft-centred pop – garnering critical acclaim and minimal sales. The daughter of a Southend dress designer, Dax first performed naked and daubed in paint with her band The Lemon Kittens, then in mixed outfit The Shockheaded Peters, before going solo, working with loop tapes and sampling long before they became common currency.

Treading the indie road was hard for her, but she felt secure in her music being a complete expression of self:

'With music I'm competing mainly against men, so for a long time I never built up those relationships you can have with women, I felt quite isolated. I'd go to studios and they'd say, "Who played this?" And I'd answer, "I played it all", and every time there'd be an incredulous look. Obviously sexism goes on all the time and I get extremely annoyed about it but I have to stop thinking along those lines because it makes me so angry it almost stops me functioning. All I've done is had goals and tried to see them through.'[37]

## Cheap Tricks

A graduate of the US hardcore scene, multi-media 'confrontationalist' Lydia Lunch was more directly involved with the music business at the start of her career as shrieker/guitarist for punk band Teenage Jesus and The Jerks. In 1984, the year she launched Widowspeak Productions to release her work with a range of collaborators including musicians Nick Cave, Rowland S. Howard, Sonic Youth and Einsturzende Neubauten she was a fiendishly articulate, diminutive spitfire with full, red lips. She didn't always make sense, but in that Camille Paglia school of thought – throw enough concepts at the wall, one's bound to stick.

Fellow writer Amanda Lipman and I interviewed her for *Spare Rib* in singer Marc Almond's Soho apartment, which she had borrowed for the occasion, surrounded by icons and religious paraphernalia. Considering the Long Island working-class Italian Catholic background that spawned Lunch to a lifetime of fighting 'the fundamentals of fear, guilt, suppression and oppression', the religious theme was fitting. She had exorcized her experience of incest and abuse in the pain games and candid brutalization of 'Daddy Dearest' on her 1983 *Uncensored Lydia Lunch* collection. Talking of fear as a desirable emotion, Lunch said, 'Sometimes when you can't feel anything you'd rather feel pain than nothing.' An early Super-8 film she shot with hardcore's stand-up comedian Henry Rollins depicts

Lunch as a girl whose house is broken into one night by a man who rapes her. The punch-line is that having confronted her fears, she asks him to stay.

Not surprisingly, the *Spare Rib* collective were unimpressed when we reported back. ('I can't see the difference between her and Erin Pizzey, except this is dressed up to look streetwise,' said one. 'Sensationalized, upsetting, unacceptable,' remarked another.) They all had a point: I, too, was taken aback when I suggested that her Super-8 was a male fantasy and Lunch spat at me, 'Some women like to be fucked hard up the ass and slapped across the face, OK?'

While Lunch began as an isolated, determined individualist, within ten years her world-view had rounded to include the concept of a Conspiracy of Women: a political party run by women for women. 'I'd like to encourage other women to become more political, to bond together, and spread communication outside of their small circles,' she stated in *Angry Women*, the impressive 1991 Re/Search publication that has become a feminist pop-culture set text.[38] Rock music was no longer her art form. Even as early as 1984 she had asserted,

'Music is too contrived. Music at first felt like the easiest way of expressing myself, but in the end I found the girl rock singer, Miss Trendy-about-town, a ridiculous concept.'[39]

Rock was never her driving force (her *In Limbo* LP was rather vapid Goth doomspiel), although she used its codes. Another Angry Woman, Diamanda Galas, operated right within musical textures: 'Sometimes my performances feel to me like a ripping of the flesh, like a blood-letting,' she once said. Taking on the role of shaman, Galas has rich ancestry to draw on; digging into her strict San Diego Greek Orthodox background, she resurrected in performance the power of the ancient Maniates, Greek butcherwomen who decapitated their enemies and sang the *Miroloyia*, a keening Ritual Death Lament. Like a latter-day Clytemnestra, she uses music as catharsis, flexing her voice and several mikes to create everything from deep bass blues to a 'blood-shrieking' cacophony. Galas is a warning. Lunch is a griper by comparison.

Galas grew up playing piano with her father, a jazz musician and gospel-choir leader. After a stint with the San Diego Symphony, she performed in European avant-garde opera before returning to the States in 1982. Her Mute LP trilogy, *The Masque Of The Red Death*, incorporates parts of the Old Testament, readings from French visionary poets like Baudelaire and Gérard de Nerval, and an apocalyptic vision.

Resolutely self-reliant, Galas carried a .38 Special and trained herself to use her voice 'like a gun'. A former prostitute protected by drag queens, Galas, like the French philosopher Foucault, gives a sense of living life as resistance while romanticizing street life and pain as a source of 'truth'. 'I learned a lot about being a woman from these black drag queens,' she said. 'The power behind the role and how you can use it. Very important – I learned how to walk down the street without fear.'[40]

Although she has appeared on mainstream TV, and has a devoted fan following, Galas dismisses pop music as purely descriptive, saying she's a 'real' musician rather than a rock musician. 'Rock singing is something men do to get laid or get their cock sucked after a gig – you can smell it. All rock singers are just singing to their dick! Well, I'm not singing to my dick!' she said in 1991.[41] Three years later she recorded an album with John Paul Jones, former bassist in one of the biggest cock rocker groups of all time, Led Zeppelin. And who's to say we don't believe in irony?

## And She's Not Even Pretty: Riot Grrrl Warriors

Though the first wave of punk rose like a flare, it heralded less a grassroots change for women than the scene's submission to a few high-profile and extremely determined individuals. Potential long-term acts such as The Slits and The Raincoats disappeared after all-too-brief careers, damaged by the need to have male approval within the business. 'The whole climate changed in the

'80s – music reverted back to a careerist option,' says Viv Albertine. 'It gets hard for a woman to be the object year after year. But we were amazed that there was this void, with no one taking up the baton. There was a ten-year gap until Riot Grrrl and Elastica came along.'[42] By the early 1990s, however, a new generation of girl bands was excavating their history, chancing upon groups like Delta 5 or X-Ray Spex as if they were Virago Classics.

The 1990s hardcore girl groups took their success for granted, refusing to accept that they were 'in' on male sufferance. Key feminist bestsellers such as Naomi Wolf's *The Beauty Myth* and Susan Faludi's *Backlash* ('I met Susan Faludi, and that's as close as it gets to Elvis,' said grunge queen Courtney Love) reflected a rejuvenation in ideas, a sense of feminism refracted through a younger generation put off by their mothers' acoustic separatist protest. From college campuses to benefit concerts and direct-action groups such as Women's Action Coalition (WAC), Women's Health Action and Mobilization! (WHAM!) and ACT UP, girls began to hone their own feminism, working alongside men at college radio stations, small record labels, in street theatre and in bands.

As women started to realize the gains they thought had been made weren't so concrete after all, they 'got political'. 'For girls to pick up guitars and scream their heads off in a totally oppressive, fucked-up male-dominated culture is to seize power . . . we recognize this as a political act,' said Tobi Vail, drummer in the US band Bikini Kill.[43] To them, women playing rock was a form of direct action, Riot Grrrl the agent of revolution. Much of the impetus for this revolt came from punk, a metaphorical shrine built to the punk 'grandmothers'. According to Rachael, guitarist/singer in UK girl band Pixie Meat: 'What Riot Grrrl did for me was to help fill in my missing history (by "my" I mean women's). It helped me discover amazing bands practically ignored by the music magazines and rock family trees. Bands like X-Ray Spex, The Au Pairs, Patti Smith, The Slits and The Raincoats filled in those missing gaps and sang punk/rock 'n' roll from a female perspective. Suddenly it all made much more sense, it put me as a female into the scene'.[44]

Meanwhile, Anjali, vocalist and guitarist with defiant 1990s girl band The Voodoo Queens, said, 'I was a big Chrissie Hynde fan. Apparently she stood outside the guitar shop looking at guitars whilst her girlfriends were out chasing boys. Wow, I thought, this woman's cool.'[45]

While disaffected 1980s artists like Finley and Galas drew on the avant-garde, by the early 1990s, a movement more central to rock was needed and Riot Grrrl filled the space. It began as a fervent spark between individuals. Inspired by the Mount Pleasant riots in Olympia, Washington in 1991, a girl named Jennifer Smith wrote to her friend Allison Wolfe, singer and bassist in Bratmobile, one of a few angry and active girl bands on the underground circuit, saying she wanted a similar 'girl riot' to disrupt the local music scene. Over Independence Day weekend in 1991, the girls got together in guitarist Erin Smith's bedroom and created the first Riot Grrrl fanzine. Feeling that some kind of organized female network was needed, other all-girl bands like Mecca Normal and Bikini Kill also became involved. Riot

**The Raincoats** at home in London, early 1980s: 'godmothers of grunge', and Kurt Cobain's favourite band. (Pennie Smith)

Grrrl took off with a series of meetings at its Washington HQ and a landmark 'Girl Day' at the International Pop Underground Festival in Olympia the following summer. Fanzines such as *Girl Germs* and Bikini Kill's own text enabled girls to link up in towns throughout the States, writing their own 'zines, compiling addresses and encouraging each other to form bands.

It was a teenage revolt that sprang up against a backdrop of fevered 'PC' (Politically Correct) debate in America on issues such as date rape (with polemicists like Naomi Wolf and Camille Paglia slugging it out in public), abortion and the Anita Hill–Clarence Thomas sexual harassment case. In a country where women still earned roughly seventy cents to every man's dollar, Riot Grrrl attracted women from varying backgrounds, not just the underground music scene – though music has been its base.

'Music is an integral part of youth culture that makes it possible for girls to infiltrate male-dominated society,' said Riot Grrrl Chia Pet. 'You're expressing something by your presence and it's communal. Everyone's right there with you.'[46] A prime mover within Riot Grrrl New York, spoken-word performer Juliana Luecking told me,

'[It is important as a] first expression of art or music. It is most effective in sparking excitement, making alliances. So what if there is no definitive statement – when you're young your ideas change every day, whether you're gonna be a writer, a musician, a pizza maker. It's about women yelling and expressing anger. They say love brings people together, but anger brings them together a lot quicker.'[47]

This revolution by Xerox spread like wildfire in the States at a serious grassroots level, with enthusiasm spilling over to Britain with the help of Riot Grrrl-identified bands like Huggy Bear. It was as much about speaking out – decoding verbal expression and manipulating visual images – as it was about playing in bands. From Surrealism to 1970s punk to 1980s hip hop sampling, there has always been a tradition of the powerless appropriating the language of those in power in an attempt to subvert it. Though Riot Grrrl seemed to be predominantly white

and middle class, it still spoke to girls isolated in angry resistance. Much of this was centred on the tyranny of the beauty
myth. Teenage years, like rock 'n' roll, are about getting laid. Am
I attractive enough? cool enough? sexy enough? When an inner
identity has yet to evolve and mature, image is all. Naomi Wolf
wrote:

'It's dead easy to become anorexic. There were many starving girls in my
junior high school, and every one was a teacher's paragon. We were
allowed to come and go, racking up gold stars, as our hair fell out in
fistfuls and the pads flattened behind the sockets of our eyes . . . An alien
voice took mine over. I have never been so soft-spoken. It lost expression
and timbre and sank to a monotone, a dull murmur the opposite of
strident. My teachers approved of me.'[48]

Fanzines were an alternative to the busy, chattering collusion of
women's magazines, pinpointing oppression through irony – the
word-games, the cut-up sentences, 'Cindy Crawford's diet: she's
got the body, she's got the man', 'Attractiveness is a courtesy',
'Are there any "special" aids that will ease the strain on hands
when crafting or sewing?' One of the best fanzines, the Pitts-
burgh *Pawholes*, was like a sampled record – a collection of
comments and cartoons that went beyond inter-band bitching
to discuss solid ideas. There was an investigative piece on the
international make-up network Mary Kay ('My worst nightmare has come true. My mother has become a cosmetics
salesperson'), and a picture of Glenn Close in *Dangerous
Liaisons*, all heaving, hemmed-in bosom, over two stark
sentences: 'Décolletage is high fashion in the court of Charles II.
Breasts are bared to the nipple and forcibly swollen with iron
corsets.' It showed the beauty myth in brutal relief.

It also echoed the work of 1970s punk musician Linder.
Inspired by fanzine culture and the way anti-fascist artist John
Heartfield used montage, the former Manchester art student
assembled pictures from porn mags, shopping catalogues and
pictures of household appliances as a disturbing comment on
the sex roles. Her cover design for The Buzzcocks' 1979 single
'Orgasm Addict', for instance, was a cut-up collage featuring a
naked woman with an iron for a head, and teeth where her

nipples should be. From her raw graphics to Barbara Kruger's late 1980s ProChoice slogan 'Your Body is a Battleground', women have understood the need for a visual vocabulary, and the need to tear it down.

Many hardcore girl bands made a comment on beauty that in some ways was more disturbing than 1970s punk – paedophiliac, perverse and schizophrenic. They would go out on stage

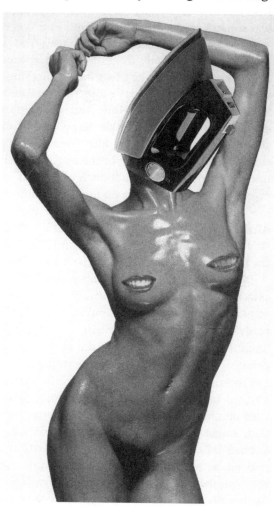

**Linder Sterling's** classic montage cover for The Buzzcocks' 1977 'Orgasm Addict' single. (Linder Sterling)

in sheer slips and baby-doll dresses, with a slash of 'fuck-me' ruby red lipstick, flower tattoos, and the words 'SLUT' and 'BITCH' scrawled on their arms and stomachs. Cut in as defiant self-mutilation, the words were a celebration of victim in a way that punk never dared to be. It was as if they had come up with a neurotic amalgam of all the hot 1990s roles for girls, from super-model to bitchin' babe to pliant waif to grunge Generation X. And because their music expressed anger and female violence it was sometimes dubbed 'PMT Pop'.

A common code among the bands was the obscene lyric coupled with the frilly frock. Babes In Toyland's Kat Bjelland, for instance, looking like a five-foot-something porcelain blonde, spat out songs about 'dirty motherfuckers' and potential rapists, while Daisy Chainsaw's Katie Jane Garside used the stage as a site for her bloodied female angst and Courtney Love sang shock-songs of arch irony like 'Teenage Whore', writhing on stage in a torn slip. One night she stage-dived into the crowd, her underwear pulled off by a 'bunch of football guys' hostile to her projection of aggressive sexuality. Both vilified and deified in the press, Love and her band Hole (named after a line in Euripides' *Medea*, where the protagonist talks of a hole piercing her soul – 'It's about the abyss that's inside,' said Love, simply) represented the muddle of contradiction at the heart of the new girl rock.

But it was the tension of those conflicting signals, the sheer velocity of these women turning themselves inside out, that attracted attention and admiration. 'I wouldn't be in a band if I really cared what people thought of me,' said Love, whose frank, feminist boxing matches with the press ensured that the gender debate was kept alive. Treating everything as a huge, horrible joke, LA rockers L7, too, disarmed with disdain. On stage at Reading Festival in 1992, singer/guitarist Donita Sparks pulled out her used tampon and flung it into the audience; then while performing their single 'Pretend You're Dead' live on Channel 4's *The Word*, another L7 dropped her shorts and flashed her crotch. Their 1992 major label debut album *Bricks Are Heavy* may have revelled in rebel insolence, but the follow-up *Hungry For Stink* pushed even further that dividing line between sarcasm and self-loathing.

L7 said, 'Our fans couldn't give a shit if we're women', but, angry at US women's diminishing right to control their own bodies, they founded the pro-abortion coalition Rock For Choice. Few women's bands opt for consistency in their presentation. Bikini Kill started out by paying for their instruments through stripping, and early stage shows had them peeling off to their bra tops. Courtney Love once pulled a breast out on stage: 'See, I've got my tit out!' All this is the girls' version of cock rock: crude, spirited and, in their eyes, revolutionary. The message passed down via punk is that nothing succeeds like excess.

**Linder Sterling's** feminist photomontage for *The Secret Public*, a one-off 1970s punk fanzine. (Courtesy Linder Sterling)

It's one that is easily misconstrued. In Britain particularly the media picked up and skimmed the top from the movement before it had a chance to breathe and grow. Its main proponents, Huggy Bear, a raucous, mixed band from Brighton, propelled Riot Grrrl into the limelight in 1993 when they were thrown off *The Word* after performing their single 'Her Jazz' and causing a kerfuffle in the audience. 'It was a great moment of youth against youth TV,' says Liz Naylor, who launched her Catcall label with the Huggy Bear/Bikini Kill compilation *Our Troubled Youth*.[49] On the ensuing tour, they would struggle to separate audiences, drawing girls into the usually hallowed male-bonding sanctuary of the 'mosh pit' at the front of the stage, in order to create a degree of female solidarity. Huggy Bear concerts became war zones. Naylor recalls,

'Gigs were like political rallies. There were occasions with a palpable atmosphere, a tension in the air, like guys had paid £4 to come in and look at the enemy. Our constant saying was, "Let's go out there and do it." Guys would heckle, and there was one incident at Derby when Jo from Huggy Bear got hit, the gig was called off and there was a riot. We'd tapped into that part of the male psyche that likes to get pissed with mates and go into queer clubs. It was like playing to an audience of London cabbies.'

Huggy Bear's retort to the harassment, through their own newsletter network, was unequivocal: 'Queer-kid punk rockers give off an organized and tactical aura known as Lad Repellent . . . remember this as you male-bond in your hardcore scrum.'

As Riot Grrrls began to infiltrate the mainstream music media, they faced new kinds of challenges. London fanzine editor Bidisha was fifteen when she wrote her first review for *NME* in 1993.

'I reviewed Nirvana without listening to the album and sent if off to twelve places for a laugh. I then got a call from *NME* asking me to do a review. The editor wanted to meet me, but I'm adamant I don't want them to know what I look like. I don't want to be controlled. I don't want to respect somebody I don't have to respect.'[50]

Within six months she was a regular contributor to the Live review pages.

Though Riot Grrrls were certain they stood on a firm ground of angst and outrage, older women were confused. Unconvinced about Riot Grrrl, Moe Tucker, drummer of The Velvet Underground, asked me, 'Girls who write "SLAG" across their stomachs, that's bullshit – what's that about? It's demeaning to females; you have a right to play music without calling yourself names.'[51] Kim Gordon, meanwhile, from cult superstar heroes Sonic Youth, saw it as a positive force: 'It'll get corrupted and lose its potency,' she said. 'But ideologies do serve their purpose for a period of time and then they don't work any more because they become closed. But that's OK, because something else comes along. It's all about empowerment and confidence.'[52]

Riot Grrrl was essentially about empowerment but, wary of the bad press, the 'Riot Frrrumps' and 'Feminazi' tags, many women in bands distanced themselves from it in droves. Riot Grrrl ultimately was a fanzine-led flashpoint, a media rocket supporting the key issue – a woman's place in art and rock culture.

The most powerful impetus for what was variously dubbed 'foxcore' and 'female grunge' initially came from the US, where there has long been a tradition of vast, 'shitkickin'' rock. Having been together since 1988, by the early 1990s all-girl Minneapolis outfit Babes In Toyland were comparatively old hands. Their 1990 debut album on Minneapolis Twin/Tone label, *Spanking Machine*, caught the attention of Sonic Youth's Thurston Moore, who invited the band to support them on their European tour. The follow-up, *To Mother*, became one of the ten best independent albums of 1991, while their third, *Fontanelle*, was hailed as ground-breaking. With their cathartic rush of psychotic rock, Kat Bjelland, Lori Barbero and Maureen Herman went beyond the novelty all-girl-band status to credibility as a headlining 'alternative' act.

'Rock 'n' roll has been run by men, but that's changing,' Barbero said in 1993. 'Always women were just there as a front, but now we're playing the music and writing it too.' She's cheered that the number of women in their audiences has grown. 'It used to be 80 per cent men, now it's nearer 50 to 60 per cent. We get a lot of mail from women inspired to form their own bands, learning to be aggressive instead of oppressed. Like the empty dance-floor metaphor, it always takes one to go out and start the dancing.'[53]

A major feature of the Babes' sound was Barbero's relentless power drumming. Taking the one instrument that has been hallowed and jealously guarded male rock 'n' roll territory, she made it her muse.

'When I went to see concerts as a kid I'd always watch the drummer. I thought that was awesome, the most physical thing you could do. There was a woman in Minneapolis called Cindy who played in a band called NNB in 1980 – she was the first female drummer I ever saw apart from a cartoon. She was hot. I was gonna grow up to be hot. Women play drums just as powerfully as men, but with a different rhythmic pattern. I always hit 'em hard. I pound. It's therapeutic. It's made me strong – I like going to the gym and I'm always moving equipment.'

Another player who vigorously crushed her drums into submission was Patti Schemel from Hole. With her long hair flying out, she looked as if she was playing somewhere in mid-air, in another world. While most attention was focused on frontwoman Courtney Love, Schemel nevertheless had a captivating beauty that she seemed to be unaware of. During a London gig in 1993 a man in the crowd yelled out in gasping appreciation: 'The drummer is so horny!' For a second Schemel paused in abashment, blushing red, touched by the observation. This was a woman's sexuality unadorned. No theatrics, no device, no defensive irony – using red lipstick (colour sticks to the lips) like a scar, showing a breast the way one would throw down a gauntlet. No, the drummer was the baseline, the heartbeat, the engine-room of the band, and because she felt that no one was looking, the woman was truly able to come into her own power.

The sexuality of Courtney Love was a witch's parody. Deliberately clumpy, her baby-blond hair a mass of split ends, Love also had an odd grace. Like movie star Ellen Barkin's lopsided grin, Love is quintessentially asymmetrical. I first met her on the Spanish film set for Alex Cox's 1986 cult flop *Straight to Hell*, a mock spaghetti western starring The Pogues, Joe Strummer and Elvis Costello. Love was a co-star, at first aloof and disdainful. I was a budding *NME* writer on my first assignment, overawed by the rock heroes cluttering the set. While I was sitting forlornly on a rock watching the shoot, Love came over, plonked herself next to me and said, 'I've been watching you, and I've decided you're cool.'

There followed three days of hilarity, laughing by the pool, hanging out in old cars on the set, getting drunk. She had a talent for exaggeration, and a wicked unfettered sense of humour that honed in skilfully on target – the equivalent of an exploding direct hit. Grace Jones had come for a day to perform a bit part. 'She was psychotic with her stardom,' said Love. 'Her make-up artists worked with a pair of binoculars and took eight hours to do her face. It was scummy stage make-up, tacky as hell.' A running mate with Lydia Lunch while they were living in Los Angeles, Love recalled, 'She never did the dishes and would lie on her bed sometimes screeching, Let's go beat up some *girls*! So we'd go downtown and beat up some girls. I feel a bit ashamed of that now . . .' As for herself: 'I'm not upper-middle-class and I was never popular at high school. I have a tattoo and I'm subculture, a teenage bag lady.'[54]

At that point Love was a nascent movie star, formerly in Cox's punk biopic *Sid and Nancy*, her eyes set on Hollywood. Apart from a few choice reminiscences of her time living in Liverpool with Julian Cope, she made little reference to playing in a rock 'n' roll band. A few months later, one grimy, rainy autumn afternoon she sat in a café near the *NME* office. Love was wearing a faded pink synthetic furry 1970s bomber jacket and seemed fazed. She'd been staying with Cait and Elvis Costello, and the couple found her an undisciplined house guest. But it was then that Love confessed to me, half wondering what I'd say, that she would like to play in a band. Yeah, go for it, I said, thinking it was just her fantasy. Four years later, with some serious application and canny songwriting, she had made her own myth come true.

**Courtney Love**
at Reading Festival,
1994: rock widow
and reluctant
Riot Grrrl.
(Mick Hutson/
Redferns)

After *Vanity Fair* had done a hatchet job on her and she was at the centre of controversy as a Nirvana wife and token Riot Grrrl, she wrote to me:

'I WORKED from the moment you met me to be competitive with the boys. We would like girls all over to form bands, indeed it's my fondest desire. But if you're going to pick up a wooden spoon and a saucepan and put out a bunch of crap, well, that's fine too – but I don't have to go down there with you and beat on that pot. I don't feel musically competitive with the Babes In Toyland, or The Raincoats, or with anyone who doesn't understand the power of a GOOD SONG. Whether it's "Chelsea Hotel", "Temptation", fucking "Pretty In Pink" – I don't care. A good song's a good song. That's my politics. Please don't slice PJ Harvey in half – her assimilationist compromise has done more for us than 30 Grrrrrls banging on a pot and spoon. I'm not trying to hurt other women. I'm just pissed that they pick on PJ.'[55]

This was written a year before the double tragedy of her husband Kurt Cobain's suicide and the death of her bass player Kristin Pfaff from a heroin overdose. The reality of being a rock queen living in the headlines was becoming too hard to bear.

By 1996, Love had bounced back, returning to the movies with a critically acclaimed performance in *The People vs. Larry Flynt*. She was never far from the headlines. After the release of another Hole album, Celebrity Skin, Love took on the might of the record industry in 2001. In protest at a corporate takeover that resulted in her label Geffen being swallowed up into the huge Universal Music Group, she sued the latter, to release her from a restrictive contract. 'I could be the music industry's worst nightmare,' she blazed, 'a smart gal with a fat bank account unafraid to fight for a principle.'[56]

PJ Harvey dealt with media approbation by ignoring it, holing up on the Dorset farm where she was raised, like a remote, scalding latter-day Tess of the D'Urbervilles. Her songs were an earthy kind of blues informed by childhood experience wringing chickens' necks and delivering still-born lambs bloodied and in bits. Polly Harvey, knock-kneed Queenie towering in her platform slingbacks, wardrobe feather boa and glitzy pop-star shades, was the nearest thing in the 1990s to Patti Smith's authoritative androgyny. She played a trawling, bowdlerized version of swamp blues with an all-male band and her audiences were half-and-half men and women. Her 1993 hit album *Rid Of Me* covered everything from vaginal aridity to sodomy while 1995's *To Bring You My Love* ached with earthy female desire. Harvey, however, had no truck with Riot Grrrl feminism:

'I saw Huggy Bear once and they were inviting people to have debates about feminism between every song. I just thought, What is all this fuss about? Why are they trying to separate men and women so much? I felt like getting up on stage and saying in a ridiculous accent, men and vimmen, men and vimmen . . . We're pretty much the same really. I feel very similar to a lot of men – I don't feel particularly different to them. What's the problem?'[57]

**Polly Harvey**
in Pennie Smith's
Osterley studio,
1993: her lyrics
covered everything
from vaginal aridity
to sodomy.
(Pennie Smith)

The 1990s girl bands began to readdress gender issues where 1970s punk had left off. De-emphasizing difference has a particular kind of power. Sometimes this means assimilation, a buckling of the self to be 'one of the lads'. At other times it is an unconscious living out of power, a superlative state in which no particular gender has appropriation of certain kinds of behaviour. 'Shitkickin' rock' comes with a male-code label; eradicate that – no one owns those codes after all – and there is a sound, like Harvey, that speaks beyond gender, in some kind of mutant individualized territory.

Entering that, though, requires an insouciance and inner belief. Most women learn that sex is their currency, both their prison and source of power. On an everyday level in pop music a range of defensive weapons are employed. Some female acts rely

more on the sly subversion of quirky lyrics than on the confrontation of obscenity. Humour has often been used by women
to deflate male rock conventions. The Voodoo Queens made it
the centre of their set, eating chocolate on stage and ridiculing
the rock-star adage that a woman in the limelight must always be
a sexy size 10, with their song 'Supermodel Superficial'. Whimsy
can be used as a tool when women feel insecure about their
music. Just as men take refuge in loud power chords when they
feel unconfident, so women can lose focus and lapse into the 'oh
gosh, I just dropped my guitar' shield of winsome chaos. This
was something UK Riot Grrrl band Mambo Taxi learned gig by
gig, for instance, building a power-base by becoming increasingly proficient on their instruments.

Huggy Bear turned 'in yer face' guitar into a political act,
while Daisy Chainsaw's Katie Jane Garside made her stage a site
of terrorist female angst, and Silverfish front-woman Lesley
outdid the men in her band with fearless lass-talk.

'Someone said I go for things like a man. Maybe that's
because I'm more aggressive and assertive – traditional male
qualities,' Lesley said to me once in her tough Glasgow accent. 'I
think women are just as aggressive as men but it's suppressed in
us. With men it's totally out of proportion.'[58] Aware of the power
of a good rock slogan, her 'HIPS, LIPS, TITS, POWER!' sold
many a T-shirt and became a Riot Grrrl catchphrase. She
dispelled the beauty myth in early days with a defiantly asexual
shaved head and Doc Martens image. Later she moved away
from having to prove she was louder and harder than the next
man by experimenting with her feminine side. 'Men react to you
completely differently if you're wearing lipstick and a dress. But
if they can't take you seriously in a frilly frock, then fuck 'em,
basically.'

## I Have No Idols

'Right now popular music is so out of balance – it's weighted to the
masculine. We need very female things but they don't get played on the
radio. Female music is also much more difficult to play. Crazy timings, crazy

chords and millions of notes all crammed in. All the little details have to be perfect.'

KRISTIN HERSH of The Throwing Muses, author interview, London, 1994

'Feminine chord progressions? I don't think so, that's The Beach Boys. Masculine chord progressions? That's L7. Feminine and masculine don't exist in music . . . It's like a masculine and feminine cigarette; it's all tobacco.'

KIM DEAL of The Breeders, quoted in *NME* by Stephen Dalton, 1993

The three main British summer festivals in 1993 were a good indicator of how, in the year of the Riot Grrrl and the frenzied gender debate, women were progressing. Out of 103 bands at the Phoenix event in Stratford-upon-Avon, there was a total of four female acts – five, counting the two women in Abba revivalists Bjorn Again; Reading had six out of sixty and Glastonbury had the edge with ten out of eighty acts on the three main rock/acoustic stages. Overall, female acts made up less than ten per cent of the artists on the bill.

While the career of an all-girl band or the solo female artist was fraught with particular problems, most progress for 'women in rock' seemed to have been made within mixed-gender rock bands such as The Throwing Muses, The Pixies, Sonic Youth and The Breeders. Although 1970s punk trumpeted a frontier-crashing musical mix, the mixed-gender line-ups were usually at the conservative level of girl singer plus three guys, whether it was Exene Cervenka in LA rockabilly hardcore unit X, or Debbie Harry in Blondie. Later bands created a more compulsive alliance of male and female energy, incorporating traditionally female freewheeling, flowing sounds with straight-ahead, solid rhythmic 'male' power. In the late 1980s and 1990s this sound became one of the most commercially successful on the American alternative scene, a style pioneered in the mid-1980s by Boston-based band The Throwing Muses, whose 1986 self-titled debut was a wall of religious cacophony with potential rhythmic sense buried inside. Kristin Hersh, Tanya Donnelly and Leslie Langston, along with honorary man David Narcizo on drums, offered up their sensitivities to the college circuit and attracted a huge cult following through five albums, before

Donnelly left to form her own project, Belly, and Hersh took time off to have a baby before going solo.

The Throwing Muses are a good example of how women use the space of the independent scene to express directly their emotional territory – the chaos, the insecurity, the search for identity, the determined self-sufficiency. As they became more confident as performers, the Muses moved on to the bolder lines of mainstream melodic rock. 'It became easier as we got more masculine,' Hersh said two years after the release of the Muses' sixth album, *Red Heaven*. 'If your power comes from drums or 4/4 time it's easier to shut down and relax into the music. It also probably helps the listener. People used to say we were all playing different songs at once, now it feels like there's some kind of solidity.'[59]

By 1994 she had released the bare, stunning acoustic solo debut *Hips And Makers*, a collection of songs that moved from chilling swing to rhythmic angst. To her it illustrated the power of charms.

'Women have these charms, these behavioural patterns, outfits, little pieces to attract and work people. They don't push people around, they actually use their bodies. It's a really physical thing to do. You can't really own anything, you can't really own property. It's all bits and pieces and lucky charms and little handbags and suitcases. If you try to use them as weapons or depend on them too much they can be stripped of all their power by other people. As soon as that happens, bang! they're old, called "over the hill". So, charms, charms, charms, charms – wrinkle, bang! they're gone. If you don't use them as your strength they're not gonna make you healthy.'

A former member of Throwing Muses labelmate band The Pixies, vocalist/guitarist Kim Deal didn't believe in a magical emotional gender difference. She felt that there was no longer a need for contest with male musicians: 'Why do we even need to take away their thing?' she once asked. 'Why don't we just ignore it and create this much cooler thing?' Her outfit The Breeders came up with one of the coolest rock singles of 1993, 'Cannonball' – a lush vocal refrain swinging with a spot-on iron-clad guitar riff. After an acclaimed debut, *Pod*, in 1990, and an assured follow-up, *The Last Splash*, they were part of a 1990s mixed-band vanguard on the way to stadium status.

The attraction of mixed gender is that when it works at its fullest, a woman is paradoxically freer to be herself: attention is less on the 'novelty' tag, there isn't the constant need to prove she can play an instrument. She can negotiate for equal space with the boys: Miki Berenyi and Emma Anderson from Lush, Lesley Silverfish from UK rockers Silverfish, and Kim Gordon in Sonic Youth – all enjoyed the respect of their male co-players, burying gender difference in a unified sound.

One of the most promising stars to emerge as a 'boy boss' in the Patti Smith tradition was 'rock babe' Juliana Hatfield. Through touring with a variety of bands, including Blake Babies, and collaborating closely with former partner Evan Dando from The Lemonheads, Hatfield honed her own distinctive style. While her debut *Hey Babe* was marred by intense, girlish personal meanderings, her 1993 follow-up *Become What You Are* ached with a fresh confidence. She had an unusual image as the Sensible Woman of Rock. Sensible women don't sell – surely they have to have a cleavage, a gimmick, a kooky quality, a penchant for self-mutilation or errant PMT? But Hatfield's power was in being simply and directly herself. The sense of her world-view, anchored by strong, eloquent guitar rock, came through with a new kind of songwriting – from the devastating clarity of 'Supermodel', scathing in its attack of 'five thousand dollars a day' vacuity, to the declarative disruption of 'I Got No Idols'.

The Final Girls of punk and its offshoots found that in order to be noticed and be counted, they had to express rage. Like Sigourney Weaver in *Alien*, they killed off the psychological enemy of patriarchy and 1970s supergroups with shock tactics. While punk was their impetus to untangle the language of rock to suit themselves, in another area women were advancing softly-softly, quietly colonizing the powerful intimacy of the singer/songwriter genre. In the late 1960s, when women were overlooked by the 'serious rock' scene, Joni Mitchell was the only way out.

# Ladies of the Canyon

## FEMALE SINGER/SONGWRITERS OF THE GRAND HOTEL

# 6

**Frailty** (see **fragile**): Insubstantiality . . . nothingness . . . illusion . . . fallacy . . . weak thing . . . trifle . . . folly . . . fantasy . . . empty talk . . . brittle . . . chimera
> *Roget's Thesaurus*

'Frailty, thy name is woman!'
> SHAKESPEARE, *Hamlet*

'Young Woman her name was Dull.'
> BUNYAN, *Pilgrim's Progress*

'Wommen desiren to have sovereynetee.'
> CHAUCER, *The House of Fame*

IN 1928 VIRGINIA WOOLF wrote that an aspiring woman writer who wanted to speak her mind needed 'A room of her own and five hundred a year'.[1] From the early nineteenth century women made a major contribution to literature, partly because their modestly growing economic independence could stretch to a desk, a chair and a piece of paper. The tools of the trade were inexpensive and easily available, unlike, say, the materials and team work it would have needed to stage a play, paint an epic portrait, or compose for a symphony orchestra. With writing a woman was less reliant on patronage or established institutions to get her work done.

Women excel at singer/songwriting for the same reason that they are good novelists, because it is an easily accessible medium. In folk music all a female songwriter needed was an acoustic guitar (if that) and a voice. The lullabies and ballads women sang to lull babies to sleep became a part of folk history, as did the songs they sang at work, brewing, baking, seamstressing, weaving, fish-gutting – music created by 'ordinary' people with songs and trades that had been handed down through generations.

Pure economics has meant that women have often taken simple instrumentation as their resource, opting for solo expression as a way of not having to negotiate the male network of band politics, other musicians' egos or complicated tour arrangements that interfere with childcare. Although the word 'genius' has been used unreservedly to describe male artists such as Bob Dylan and Leonard Cohen, women have turned out consistent quality writing in far greater quantity than male solo singer/songwriters, their material ranging from the autobiographical to the poetic and the perverse.

Women have always written to make sense of their world, to clear an inviolable space that is theirs rather than the possession of a man. Folk singer and archivist Peggy Seeger says,

'A lot of folk music expressed feminist opinions and reflected women's lives. There were ballads outlining women's social positions and rights, talking about ownership of women by fathers, sons, families. There were revenge songs in code showing women to be smarter than men, or dressed as men, proving themselves just as good in certain situations.'[2]

Until 1880 in England, a married woman was not allowed by law to own property. Man was a creature of substance, while woman was insubstantial – there to look decorous or work the horses, depending on her social class. As her experience did not reflect the outer world of war, politics and finance, it was not deemed relevant. But swaddled in her domestic interior, giving birth to, raising and cooking for the men of the future, she wrote down copious observations in diaries and letters, most of which, like countless songs spontaneously made up in farms or parlours, didn't survive. Until the nineteenth century, when women's writing began to be published in a significant sense, the female view was cruelly private.

Through that private self-expression, uninvestigated by the 'public' world, women gave their sex substance. Two hundred years later women excluded from male rock and jazz traditions undertook a quiet revolution, creating a powerful area for themselves, subversive in its personal concerns (love, loss, children) and its firm, reflective attention to detail rather than the broad brushstrokes of rock.

## Reckless Daughters

In the 1950s, while dream babes and jazz-age swing beauties were glamorizing a male-defined view of pop, artists such as Peggy Seeger and the McGarrigle Sisters were paving a more idiosyncratic and personal path through folk music.

The wife of the late Scottish folk singer Ewan MacColl and sister of US folk heroes Mike and Pete Seeger, Peggy was one of the first women prominent on the folk scene of the 1950s and 1960s, specializing in ballads sung from a feminist perspective. Born in New York in 1935, she settled in England in the mid-1950s and released more than thirty solo albums throughout her career. 'I prefer the term songmaker. Songwriter suggests literacy,' she says, most interested in folk in its pure form. Praising its versatility she emphasizes: 'With folk, most instruments are portable, not big or electric. The essence of folk song is that you take it with you.' By the 1980s her stepdaughter Kirsty MacColl had taken on the family mantle, but fused folk with her own solo pop ballads or worked with melodic punk acts like The Pogues. MacColl later brought Latin rhythms into her work, but her career was tragically cut short in 2000 when she was killed in a boating accident off the coast of Mexico. After her death, many acknowledged MacColl's contribution to UK pop songwriting.

Staying close to folk traditions were the French-Canadian McGarrigle Sisters, Kate and Anna, who started performing on the late 1950s Montreal coffee-bar circuit, before moving to the States and fusing their folk rhythms with Louisiana cajun and country and western. Although eclectic, they always kept their Celtic edge. Prolific songwriters, their material has been recorded by such artists as Linda Ronstadt, Emmylou Harris and Marianne Faithfull, but it wasn't until 1976 that they recorded their debut album, *Kate And Anna McGarrigle*. Their releases may have been sporadic over the years, but they have still been a reference point for countless acoustic-based artists.

Rising on the crest of the 1960s grassroots revolution, where the notion of 'authenticity' first became pop, the folk scene inevitably threw up a female star who sparkled across music categories. Described, somewhat misguidedly, by Linda Ronstadt as 'the first woman to match a man on his own terms as songwriter, guitar player and incredibly magnetic human being', Joni Mitchell set the tone for decades of songwriters to come, influencing everyone from Prince to Seal to Suzanne Vega and Annie Lennox. An intellectual songwriter, she disproves the theory of musicologist Wilfrid Mellers that women are successful with folk/pop because it is about 'instinct, as contrasted with the dominance of intellect and will'.[3] Many female artists write from a root instinct, but structuring a song from that relies as much on intellect as it does on gut hunch-work.

Mitchell's music, from her debut *Songs To A Seagull* to her 1994 album *Turbulent Indigo*, is highly cerebral. Working in minor keys as much as major, experimenting with cadence and inflection, layering her songs with deft touches of jazz, rock and folk, Mitchell thrives on difference, on the unpredictable. Although her impact has been legendary, she has had few pop hits apart from 'Big Yellow Taxi' in 1970 and 'Help Me' in 1974. Every line is carefully wrought to create a precise expression of feeling, which makes her music at times curiously difficult to listen to – she doesn't opt for easy melody or satisfying conclusions. 'My music is not designed to grab instantly. It's designed to wear for a lifetime, to hold up like a fine cloth,' she said in 1994.[4]

*The Hissing Of Summer Lawns*, a complex, jazz-orientated album released in 1975, was widely considered to be her best. On that she was scathing about California mores and commercialism, consolidating her role as the 'difficult artist'. Born in Alberta, Canada, in 1943, she trained as a commercial artist before taking up music as a career, singing in Toronto coffee houses. A young marriage to performer Chuck Mitchell lasted barely two years, and after its demise she moved to New York

City, in demand as a major new songwriter for such artists as Judy Collins, Johnny Cash and Fairport Convention. Signing to Reprise in 1967, she worked with ex-Byrd David Crosby as a producer of *Songs To A Seagull*.

After cutting her teeth on folk basics she moved quickly from acoustic, melodic work to 1970's more sophisticated *Ladies Of The Canyon*, her breakthrough album. Throughout the 1970s her work became more dense, reflected in such layered albums as *Don Juan's Reckless Daughter* and *Mingus*, where excursions into jazz alienated her core rock audience. Jazz buffs did not take her seriously either, 'who's this white chick?' being the general sentiment, but what was significant was the confidence with which Mitchell crossed genre boundaries, without feeling the need to explain herself. 'The whole unfolded like a mystery. It is not my intention to unravel that mystery for anyone, but, rather, to offer some additional clues,' she wrote on the sleeve of her album *The Hissing Of Summer Lawns*.

Despite a solid musical reputation Mitchell didn't escape continual speculation on her private life and a series of broken relationships. After *Rolling Stone* magazine published a diagram of her alleged love affairs, giving her an award as 'Old Lady of the Year', she didn't speak to the magazine for eight years. Mitchell rode out the stereotyping, and showed how women can achieve longevity within the music business. Once dubbed by Crosby as 'about as modest as Mussolini', Mitchell is forthright about her talent, claiming a sense of 'greatness' and originality in a way that is usually reserved for men. This hasn't always endeared her to critics, who found some albums impenetrable. 'The final insult is to watch my imitators elevated while I'm still being trashed,' she said. By 1991's *Night Ride Home* and *Turbulent Indigo* (1994), though, Mitchell was getting due recognition. Relying less on hit singles, she built up album sales over a period of time and, without the pressure of having to follow chart trends, achieved a rare position of independence.

In 1997, however, she had a surprise hit when Janet Jackson sampled 'Big Yellow Taxi' for her single 'Got 'Til It's Gone'. The previous year she compiled two (ironically titled) *Hits* and *Misses* anthologies. She continued to be prolific, releasing *Taming the Tiger* in 1998, and *Both Sides Now* (2000), a moving collection of standards recorded with a 70-piece orchestra. Though she never sold as much as peers Carole King, Janis Joplin and Aretha Franklin, Mitchell has always been hugely influential, considered a 'musician's musician'.

A songwriter even more hit-free than Mitchell was Laura Nyro, the Bronx-born singer and poetess who was booed off stage at the Monterey Pop Festival. Signed by David Geffen to Columbia, she wilfully followed an anti-commercial route, composing beautiful songs such as 'Wedding Bell Blues', 'And When I Die' and 'Eli's Coming' that became Top Ten hits for other acts (5th Dimension, Blood, Sweat and Tears and Three

Dog Night respectively). Her own interpretation was an eccentric fusion of rock, jazz and unpredictable vocals that appealed to a cult audience long past her unofficial 'retirement' in the late 1970s. By the time of her death from ovarian cancer in 1997, a younger generation of songwriters, from Kate Bush to Suzanne Vega, were paying tribute. Her 2001 posthumous album *Angel In The Dark* was a critically acclaimed collection of ballads and off-kilter soul music that sealed her reputation as one of rock's quiet heroines.

Another lone voice was that of teen star Janis Ian, who had a No. 14 hit in 1967 at the age of sixteen with 'Society's Child (Baby I've Been Thinking)', a controversial song about an inter-racial love affair. Although she released a second pop anthem in 1975, the mournful tribute to teenage angst 'At Seventeen', and her albums sold respectably throughout the 1970s, her songs lacked the drive to sustain an impact in the pop world. She had renewed success, however, in the 1990s with albums like *Breaking Silence* and *God And The FBI*, the latter a biting, ballsy take on everything from religion and the state to the commer-cialized gals of 'New Country' pop.

Like Mitchell, many female singer/songwriters (who are essen-tially publicity-shy poets) have had an uneasy relationship with the pop charts. Rickie Lee Jones, the Chicago-born tomboy who had an international hit in 1979 with 'Chuck E.'s In Love', began her career as a minimalist beat poet. Despite the massive success of her late 1970s debut, the 1980s were marked by a jazz-tinged emotional limbo, as her albums became increasingly introspective. Pop needs bolder strokes and a willingness to risk being crass.

## I Feel the Earth Move

While the success of Joni Mitchell, and to some extent Laura Nyro, encouraged women to follow their muse in a highly indi-vidualistic style, it was Carole King who showed how the discipline of pop commercialism could be inspiration itself. From 1961, when she wrote The Shirelles' 'Will You Still Love Me Tomorrow' with husband Gerry Goffin, King showed an

ability to encapsulate what women were thinking. 'That definitely spoke for young women all over who were wondering if
they should "do it" or, will you respect me in the morning?' she
said of the Shirelles' hit.[5] Her early 1960s New York Brill
Building experience churning out songs for girl groups such as
The Chiffons and The Shirelles, coupled with her later laid-back
living-in-LA mindset, was reflected in a new sound. The phenomenal success of her 1971 album *Tapestry* plugged into a
female *Zeitgeist*. In New York, King was an enthusiastic self-
starter, happily married and riding high on the youthful
excitement of the R&B explosion. The beginning of the 1970s
saw her in a contemplative mode, newly divorced and bringing
up two small children on the West Coast. Her songwriting
became more introspective, more adult than 1960s hits such as
'Will You Still Love Me Tomorrow' and 'The Loco-Motion', yet
it was still as direct and vigorous. In a different way to Mitchell,
King set the tone for a whole generation of female singer/
songwriters: she created a sound that perfectly captured the
post-1960s party hangover, a 1970s era of getting sober, and,
particularly for women, evaluating relationships. Who was that
man I married on the Vietnam march? How come I've ended up
in suburbia just like my mother? Why don't we talk any more?

*Tapestry*, from the clear, confident piano chords of 'I Feel The
Earth Move' to 'You've Got A Friend', with its gentle sense of
hope, to the devastating perception of 'It's Too Late', articulated
thirtysomething America, and as a consequence sold over
thirteen million copies (making it one of the biggest bestsellers
of all time), won four Grammys and remained in the album
charts for five years. Although King released many more albums,
she was not fond of touring or high-profile promotion, preferring to stay in semi-retirement on her Idaho ranch. *Tapestry* was
her peak – a woman's personal statement that stretched the
boundaries of pop, sealing style that infused the work of many
other artists, from Carly Simon and Cher to Martika in the early
1990s. Mitchell's wayward experimentalism may have been
more hip, more self-consciously artistic, but King's assured and
seamless manipulation of pop's language has been just as influ-

ential. This was apparent on her 2001 album *Love Makes The World Today*, which included guest spots by stars ranging from Wynton Marsalis to Celine Dion.

The other major presence among early-1970s female singers was Carly Simon, a less consistent songwriter who nevertheless was an arch manipulator of image. Daughter of the co-founder of the publishing empire Simon & Schuster, Simon first 'played out' with her sister Lucy in New York folk bars while attending the exclusive Sarah Lawrence College. Bob Dylan's manager Albert Grossman came into contact with Simon and tried to groom her as the 'female Dylan'. Like Joan Baez, she was to be the 'yin' to his 'yang'. Less successful than Bob, Simon met her perfect partner in James Taylor.

Both were 'poor little rich kids' from moneyed backgrounds, though Simon was more adept at coping with talent and success, sliding wit into a few seminal pop songs. Her 1972 classic 'You're So Vain', for instance, was a frank poke in the eye for an unnamed lover: speculation centred around Warren Beatty, Mick Jagger and James Taylor, but Simon, archly playing the media game, refused to tell. She was already a society star, having won a Grammy Award the previous year as Best New Artist for her debut *Carly Simon*, which included the huge hit 'That's The Way I've Always Heard It Should Be'.

Simon always had a racier image than her contemporaries, a tougher, more knowing, even cynical edge that set her apart from the vulnerable circumspection of other folk/pop singers. Women in this genre have often been perceived as loners, writing songs in self-imposed solitary confinement only to emerge every so often to take a lover – but Simon broke the rules with her very public marriage to James Taylor. Though he received greater accolades, Taylor was actually a frailer talent than Simon, plagued by self-doubt and a moody introspection.

When the couple wed in 1972 they were part of the rock aristocracy, kingpins of the new breed of singer/songwriters. Marriage, particularly for Simon, seemed to stifle creativity. She had sporadic hits up to the end of the 1970s, including the 1977 *James Bond* theme 'Nobody Does It Better', but it wasn't until she split up with Taylor in the early 1980s that she took musical chances again – particularly with 'Why', the glistening disco-ballad she recorded with Chic. Staying the celebrity course, Simon returned to the fray in 1987 with the album *Coming Round Again*. At ease with pop industry whirl, she became singer/songwriter as entertainer – associating with pop culture's well-connected right up to the 1990s, particularly as a public friend of 'baby-boomer' President Clinton.

In stark contrast the story of Joan Armatrading, the Queen of acoustic-based pop songwriters, is one of a struggle out of grey obscurity and isolation. When she was signed to A&M America in 1974, Derek Green, then head of the company's British arm, was less than enthusiastic, thinking that she was uncommercial and had no image. What's more, she was black, female and a poor investment. 'Don't spend too much money,' he warned her first producer Pete Gage.[6]

Although she was dubbed humourless, becoming a national British institution with the nickname Joan Armaplating, Gage noticed early on that Armatrading's smile when it appeared, 'was like a ray of sunshine hitting a completely iced planet'.[7] Her aloofness was less a result of arrogance than of being scared stiff. As a black woman in the early 1970s working with male musicians and producers in the rock sphere, she was a complete anomaly. When hiring musicians for the Joan Armatrading album sessions, the confident, briskly male producer Glyn Johns, who'd already had major success with Joe Cocker, Led Zeppelin, Steve Miller and Traffic, said, 'I've got this session with this young girl who doesn't really know what she's doing.' Others' doubt in her ability must have been a destabilizing experience. Recording the early albums she had a major problem communicating, just telling musicians what she wanted. Acutely shy, she built herself a little hut of screens and soundboards in the centre of the studio where, in utter privacy, she created that startling intimacy of some of her best songs.

Armatrading has always been out of place, in the sense of having no place. She was born in 1950 in a small house in Basseterre, the capital of St Kitts, and her parents and two older

**Joan Armatrading** on Wandsworth Common, South London, 1974: an early publicity photo with the smile that 'was like a ray of sunshine hitting a completely iced planet'. (Val Wilmer/ Redferns)

brothers left her when she was three to start a new life in England. Brought up by her grandparents until she was seven, Armatrading was then sent off to Britain with her name on a string round her neck. She rejoined her parents Amos and Beryl Armatrading who by then were living a quiet life in a white district of Birmingham – 'one of the most meaningless places in Britain,' Joan said later. Coming from the bright warmth of the West Indies to a draughty concrete slab in the Midlands must have been a traumatic experience. Armatrading's response was retreat into songwriting, taking up guitar and pouring her emotions out in a chilly back bedroom.

After leaving school she performed in various Birmingham bands and a regional version of the musical *Hair*. Early songwriting collaborations with extrovert actress/singer Pam Nestor ended up on the shelf at Essex Music Publishing to be discovered in 1971 by Elton John's producer Gus Dudgeon, who decided to take a chance on Armatrading's strange, raw talent. Teaching herself in isolation meant that Armatrading had developed a distinctive, but erratic style, and her problem lay in having to relearn enough in order to work with other musicians. It took a succession of top producers – Dudgeon, Johns and Blondie's Richard Gottehrer, who nurtured her through the triumphs of albums like *Joan Armatrading* and *Me, Myself, I* – before she felt confident enough to produce herself.

Armatrading's success lies in the peculiar vision that informs her work. Her 1976 hit 'Love And Affection' on her historic self-titled debut conveys tension, vulnerability, pride and loneliness, all in one song. Her words resonate with unusual inflexion, from the cool phrasing of the lonely but determined wallflower heroine of 'Love and Affection', to the full-tilt rollercoaster despondency of 'Down To The Ground', a masterly analysis of rejection.

*Me, Myself, I* in 1980 and *Walk Under Ladders* in 1981 were two more creative peaks, but her only other UK hit was 1983's 'Drop The Pilot', and she never achieved the superstar status she was capable of in the States. 'In America, to be black and English is weird,' she said.

Armatrading downplays her public persona. 'I wouldn't even begin to attempt all that Madonna showy, glitzy, glamorous stuff,' she said in 1992. 'It's just not me. I'd look ridiculous. You've got to do what you feel comfortable with.'[8] I spoke to her when she was promoting her last A&M album *Hearts And Flowers*, her most declarative in years. Though relaxed and humorous, she was still expert at fielding personal questions. Armatrading's reticence has made her boring to the showbiz world in a way that belies the sharp perception of her lyrics. More than Carly Simon or 'corporate artists' like Madonna, Armatrading shows a stark contrast within the star role, how talent and fame can sit so uneasily together, particularly as the singer/songwriter, a role that demands both introspection and personal exposure.

It seems as if each decade could allow one black token woman to 'break rank' and play acoustic rather than dance music. In the 1950s and 1960s it was folk/gospel singer Odetta, in the 1970s it was Armatrading, while in the 1980s Tracy Chapman emerged. 'People make comparisons, but I don't sound or write like Joan Armatrading,' Chapman said. 'I like her music and respect her as an artist, but I haven't moulded myself on her. I think what I'm doing is neat. I'm breaking new ground: there aren't too many black women who play acoustic guitar and sing of the things I do.'[9] With her dreadlocks, combat trousers, guitar and a set of devastatingly simple songs, Chapman was beamed by satellite from the 1988 Nelson Mandela 70th Birthday Tribute concert to catch the international heart. A busker on the Cambridge coffee-house circuit before she was signed to Elektra, her self-titled debut went platinum soon after its release.

Like Armatrading's and Odetta's before her, Chapman's achievement was considerable in the fact that she was one of the first black female singer/songwriters to become a star. Though by the 1970s women had established themselves within the genre, it had become the salubrious ghetto of the white Western educated female, with artists like Joni Mitchell and Rickie Lee Jones afforded serious study in the rock press. This trend was to continue in the 1980s, when most female performers (particularly black) were written about with constant reference to collaborators or producers, as if they couldn't possibly be prime authors of their work. The select few, however, true to definitions of High Art, were treated like sisterly seers, the caryatids on a Parthenon headed by Bob Dylan, Leonard Cohen, Lou Reed and Iggy Pop. Academic commentator Jim Collins refers to such cultural elitism as the 'Grand Hotel', a theoretical place where production is orchestrated around a fossilized master system.'[10]

Within rock music male singer/songwriters are the revered canon of (nearly) Dead White Males, whereas women, despite their prodigious output, are rarely granted that status.

One woman who broke through to the stratosphere of Top Bohemian Artist was Kate Bush, riding the wave of 1970s progressive rock and 1980s pop with an errant individualism. Although she wasn't predominantly an acoustic artist, Bush elevated songwriting to an almost messianic level. 'I'm not after money or power but the creative power,' she once said. 'I'm fascinated by the whole creative process – I think you could probably say I was obsessed by it. It's not that I'm running away into my work, it's more that my work moves headlong into my life.'[11]

### 'How Many Dancing Songwriters Can You Count on One Hand?'

So wrote *NME* journalist Jane Solanas (formerly Suck) in 1983, in an appreciative piece that made links with Bush's wholly sensual world.'[12] Bush had burst on to the scene in 1977 with wondrous, almost mythical impact. Her No. 1 debut single 'Wuthering Heights', an offering to the lost love of Cathy and Heathcliff, was a brittle, shivering pop song with a folk base incorporating strings, piano and mournful echo. Nothing like it had been heard before: especially the voice – a high-pitched wander through octaves that pierced through the banality of daytime radio.

Though its impact was immediate, the single had taken a long time to gestate. EMI had signed her in the glory days of the mid-1970s when the music industry was running at a profit and there was money to slosh around on new artists. Introduced to an EMI executive by a supergroup musician – Pink Floyd's Dave Gilmour, her brother's former schoolfriend – Bush was signed up at sixteen for a £3,500 advance, on the strength of a rough demo of 'The Man With The Child In His Eyes'. 'We gave her some money to grow up with,' said EMI executive Bob Mercer. 'EMI was like another family for her . . . she was the company's daughter for a few years.'[13]

**Kate Bush**
on BBC programme
*Blue Peter*, 1979:
sexy theatrical
artifice.
(David Redfern/
Redferns)

Bush came from a close-knit, musical family in the Kent countryside; Gilmour, the 'Great White Male' patron, gave Bush her entrée, while the happy accident of an industry in the black gave her time to develop as an 'artist' – but it's what Bush fashioned out of those advantages that made her remarkable. I was aware that things wouldn't be how I wanted them unless I was willing to fight,' she said. After taking dance classes with mime maestro Lindsay Kemp, and gigging around South London pubs with her KT Bush band, she was finally allowed into the studio to work on her debut *The Kick Inside*.

Though dismissed as 'erotic trivia' when it came out in 1978, this hit album was the foundation stone of her success – its pop melodies opened her up to the public, yet there was enough experimentation to provide space for future eccentricity. Through seven hit albums, up to the late 1990s and beyond,

Bush always retained a special bargaining place in her major record company. One of the few artists who refused to do promotional tours, her only foray into live concerts was on her critically acclaimed 1979 Tour Of Life. For Bush the road was too stressful, and she kept her creativity to the safety of the studio and videoland. Rarely granting interviews, she maintained that art should 'speak for itself'. Luckily, her art sells. In volumes. Hence EMI's paternalistic, patient approach. 'She can't really conceive of being crossed – only opposed. Which opposition will always give in to her reasonable demands,' said another EMI executive.[14]

Bush's music is like Innocent Art – childlike rather than childish – painted in bright colours and deeply felt emotional hues. She is a very shy woman. Although she gradually grew more comfortable with the media world, to the extent that celebrities such as Eric Clapton, Prince, Nigel Kennedy and comedian Lenny Henry had guest spots on her 1993 album *The Red Shoes*, Bush managed to keep her artistic self hermetically sealed.

Taking a literary approach to songwriting, she has drawn from novelists as varied as Emily Brontë, Tolkien and Stephen King. Her songs are mini-dramas, whether mystic ('The Dreaming'), aggressive and decisive ('Sat In Your Lap') or fanciful and dynamic ('Running Up That Hill'), incorporating elements of science fiction, horror, fairy tale and women's pulp erotica. 'The English vibe is very appealing,' she says. Terry Slater, who signed the Sex Pistols a year after Bush, remarked 'She's from the roots of Great Britain. It's not a gimmick or produced. She's the first really English girl singer for a long time.'[15]

## A Little Bit Country

While artists like Joni Mitchell and Kate Bush stretched the boundaries of 1970s folk/pop, women made great strides in country music. A powerful and autonomous section of the music business as a whole, country has often influenced and crossed over into pop, creating performers who straddle both spheres, such as Dolly Parton, Tammy Wynette and 'Little Miss Dynamite' Brenda Lee, who made No. 1 in the pop charts in 1960 with the ten-million seller 'I'm Sorry'. Unlike Mitchell and Bush in their rarefied lyrical worlds, women country artists operated on a more prosaic level, singing downhome songs of romance, love, loss and divorce.

Up to the 1970s a religious fundamentalism dominated country music, and Nashville was intensely conservative. Fifties female country star Patsy Cline literally broke her neck trying to keep her marriages together, cooking whenever she was home, exhausting herself trying to meet each husband's demands while tearing around promoting her records. Once, after a car accident, she went into the recording studio with her broken ribs barely healed. The brassy, braided cowgirl from Shenandoah Valley, Virginia, was killed aged thirty in a plane crash in 1963, in a mad hurry to get home through thick wintry fog. Her life was an untenable wrestling match with the desire to be a star and a moral imperative that expected her to be at home tending to her man. Although Tammy Wynette upheld the latter sentiment in the late 1960s with the unquestioning faithfulness of 'Stand By Your Man', the smash hit 1975 re-release of the song, followed by 'D.I.V.O.R.C.E.', pulsated with an element of high camp. 'Stand By Your Man' turned out to be the biggest-selling single ever recorded by a female country singer. Though it was snapped up by many young married women who found her sentiments rousing, her record also became a kind of alternative gay anthem. No mistress of convention herself, having been through a catalogue of public addictions and messy marriages, Wynette actively welcomed her status as a gay icon.

Her story has a sad ending, however. Despite earning a fortune throughout her career, she was declared bankrupt in 1988, and felt compelled to work right up to the end. Shortly before her death, Nashville journalist Andrew Vaughan caught a show at a cabaret club in the suburban sprawl near Disneyland. 'It was like watching someone who'd been embalmed,' he says, 'Her face looked like she was dead already. It was sad to see her.

I couldn't bear to watch. Her voice was thin and croaky, and she couldn't hit the high notes. She was a really sick woman.'[16] By this time she deferred everything to her producer husband George Richey. With him, she said, she felt as contented as a little girl, 'when Daddy was always there to take care of me.'[17]

When she died aged 55 in 1998 after years of severe stomach ailments and an addiction to painkillers, three of her four daughters, Jackie Daly, Tina Jones and Georgette Smith filed a $50 million wrongful death suit against Richey, and James Wallis Marsh, the Pittsburgh doctor who had treated Wynette. While some say that Richey devoted himself to her, others, such as Wynette's friend Martha Dettwiller, have denounced him as 'an ugly gatekeeper' who 'controlled Wynette's life'. Spokespeople for Richey counter that 'the loving care' Wynette received 'extended her life and permitted her to do what she loved'.[18] Whatever the truth, Wynette was like one of those beleaguered women in a tragic country and western ballad, seemingly at the mercy of the men in her life.

Meanwhile her peer Dolly Parton felt free to launch a feisty attack on sexual double standards, combining straightahead tales of small-town life with the pop-cartoon blonde. A kind of female talisman, Parton was an example of exaggerated womanhood, with her wasp waist, blond bouffant hair piled high and balloon-shaped bust. Born in 1946 in a poor area of the East Tennessee mountains, she began playing guitar at six years old. Brought up singing in the Church of God, she came to Nashville at the age of eighteen with a notebook of songs, within two weeks landing a deal with the Monument label. One of her early country releases 'Dumb Blonde' (1967) broke the stereotypes of both the dumb blonde and the patient, long-suffering wife. Parton sang of a woman learning to survive through her own resourcefulness. A shrewd businesswoman, Parton later built up a career in Hollywood as well as Nashville – starring in such early 1980s films as *Best Little Whorehouse in Texas* and *Nine to Five* – but it is her songwriting that has proved most lucrative. Her song 'I Will Always Love You', for instance, was a massive hit for Whitney Houston, one of the biggest-selling singles of 1993 .

## Solitude Standing

Although the ladies of the Grand Hotel were eclipsed by late 1970s punk, designer pop and the awful boys' pop rock of the mid-1980s, they re-emerged in 1987 when a slip of a girl with a long face from New York City made female acoustic songwriting Big News again.

I first met Suzanne Vega in 1992 in an impersonal record-company office. MTV flickered on a screen in the background, while she sat almost demure, dressed in loose, beige clothing – very calm, very Buddhist, very yin-and-yang. Her image seemed to be reflected in her music: considered, precise, lyrical, literary, but with a smart pop sensibility. A year later she inadvertently admonished me for coming to conclusions about her supposed serenity. 'People don't bother to probe beneath the surface. Usually there's all kinds of things going on.'[19]

The second time we met it was a hot August afternoon in 1993. In the lull between touring and the next album, she was taking a break, holed up in a London flat, observing life and waiting for the muse to overtake her. We arranged to meet in Kew Gardens. The trains had been delayed and I was half an hour late; as I rushed up to this impatient sylph-like figure, I was struck by her incongruity amid the lazy, bright, bee-crammed flowerbeds of Kew. Fully made up, dressed in a black designer suit, Filo-fax in hand, she looked very New York, very profes-sional. It reminded me of something she'd said before: 'I went about my career like a business.'

Sitting in the shade of a secluded summerhouse, Vega tackled this thorny question of 'women in rock'. In many ways Vega is a good spokeswoman. Articulate and imaginative, she is an intel-lectual with a keen appreciation of 'the street'. She came to prominence in 1985 with the hit single 'Marlene On The Wall' and self-titled debut album, her success ushering in a new wave of record-company investment in women singer/songwriters. This was a Good Thing, especially considering the low point women performers reached in the early 1980s, when after the collapse of punk, the vacuum was filled with commercialized video-friendly pop/rock acts such as Pat Benatar or Madonna. Vega offered new hope for women who wanted to express themselves through the integrity of a new kind of urban folk.

Growing up in New York City with her mother and Puerto Rican stepfather, Vega saw herself as half Puerto Rican, imbibing the rich, frenetic multicultural vibes of the city, yet creating in the midst of that an oasis of calm for herself. A former dance student, she went on to Columbia University and majored in English. She could have carved a path as a straight writer, but chose instead to channel her talent in songwriting. Vega's musical career began when, as a child, she was picked to sing at Pete Seeger's knee in Carnegie Hall. By sixteen she was playing downtown coffee houses, establishing herself on the early-1980s New York Village folk circuit. Acknowledging the generational influence, she recalls her grandmother, the late Helen Grant, who played drums in a 1930s all-female boogie-woogie band that was described on posters as 'the hottest band this side of Hades'. 'I never knew her,' says Vega. 'But it's ironic that I picked her way of life without meaning to. I thought I was being original and clever picking this lifestyle for myself – then I found out that she did it fifty years before.'

In her determined way the teenage Vega sought out the best venues to play, and secured regular dates at Folk City in the Village. She became part of a scene that was then small but vibrant. 'To us it'd never gone away. The real world wasn't paying any attention, it was into punk and New Wave – but we were all thrilled, writing a lot, influencing each other.' After associating with prime movers like Jack Hardy, Vega came to the attention of A&R woman Nancy Jeffries, then at A&M. It took a woman to realize the potential of a female singer/songwriter, flying in the face of fashion and signing Vega to widespread record-label opposition. She effectively launched the next wave of the genre. 'I wasn't sure at first; I'd been sent a tape through a friend in the company and thought she was just another folk singer,' recalls Jeffries. 'Then I went down to see her and realized that there was something different about her, something interesting.'[20]

Vega's downbeat, street-level approach won her a deal. 'Nancy really took a chance on me,' she says. 'She felt it was too good to pass up. I owe her a lot. She was great at seeing me through the whole thing. 'Sfunny, when I heard an A&R person was coming to see me, I was expecting a big fat guy with a cigar, and here was this long, skinny woman with a delicate stomach. She was fascinating – a real kinship there.'

**Suzanne Vega** at the Cambridge Folk Festival, 1991: leading in the new breed of late-1990s singer/songwriters. (Steve Gillet/Redferns)

Despite record-label scepticism ('maybe she'll sell 30,000'), Vega's debut album sold over a million, and her second, *Solitude Standing*, sold three million, with follow-up album 1990's *Days Of Open Hand* also charting well. Despite unlikely singles success with 'Luka' in 1987, a subtle song about child abuse, and the dance-floor rap of 1990's 'Tom's Diner', Vega is more the archetypal album artist. Working in a field where women are encouraged to explore their emotional range, she covers every topic from transsexualism to love in Liverpool. Vega's success showed how female singer/songwriters could reinvent themselves. Although their relative disappearance after punk gave the impression that they went away and came back, they had been there all the time, writing, constructing and commenting on their lives, regardless of music-industry hype. Vega, for instance, refused to be boxed into the 'acoustic' corner, adding beat-driven, leftfield pop to her repertoire with 1990s albums like *99.9°F* (1992) and *Nine Objects Of Desire* (1997).

In the wake of Vega's success there was a flurry of signings, as each major record company raced to get a folkie female on its roster. The craze brought up significant questions about gender – in the same way that there has long been a literary debate about male and female writing, there have been questions about whether female singer/songwriters are equipped to be more than just 'The Other', addressing 'universal' as well as domestic or personal issues. Vega says,

'I don't like to think that women can't understand larger issues or express them. But if a woman did do a "larger" song, I don't know if it would be perceived in the same way. I've always felt like the character from *Notes from the Underground*, sitting in a small room, identifying in a Kafka-esque way with people who work in day jobs. I then realized that as a woman I am an anti-hero. There are no women heroes. The only one you really have is Joan of Arc, and she's a martyr, not a hero. I find this frustrating. How can I take my anti-hero stance if I'm already considered to be an anti-hero because I'm a woman? That's not fair. Once women learn how to write in that broad way without losing their individuality, it'd be a good thing for everyone. If you were to write a song called "Pride In The Name Of Love", it might not feel real to a woman singing it. Love to a woman means other things like sacrifice or caretaking, not necessarily pride.'

Thirty years earlier, Peggy Seeger had grappled with the same issue.

'A woman's territory is much smaller than a man's. Women seem satisfied with less, which is probably why we've gotten less. It was traditional for women to be involved with children and family – I see nothing wrong with that. What is more universal than love, than the domestic? As a Marxist, I saw that one of the purposes of [Marx's] philosophy was to decentralize. The concept of a "brotherhood of man" is highly centralized. I don't think universal is a good idea. Universal is what creates multinationals – pop music that's the same whether you're in Rio de Janeiro or Iceland. If that's universal who wants it?'

Aimee Mann, an intelligent singer from Boston who left her late-1980s MTV band 'Til Tuesday to go solo, got irate at the way her work was telescoped or tamed. 'I've been called "waif-like". I don't know why because I feel I'm aggressive,' she said. 'Someone saying "fuck you" in a higher voice seems to carry less impact, I guess.'[21] More constructively, she has been compared to a female Elvis Costello and her personal, harmonic pop 1993 debut *Whatever* on Imago certainly had that insightful edge. By 2000, her songs reached a wider audience with her award-winning soundtrack to the hit film *Magnolia*.

By the late 1980s, however, the success of female singer/songwriters had created its own kind of Grand Hotel ghetto. There was a cloying sense of spiralling inwards, drawing the listener into a private emotional space, one which the female artist refused to clarify, taking refuge in enigma. Though a cosy place to be, it was ultimately unliberating, lacking the forcefulness of being 'out in the world' – hence those dreaded epithets 'frail . . . fragile . . . winsome . . . whimsical'. By the early 1990s, as if in agreement with the strides made by women in rock, female singer/songwriters began responding to the challenge of placing their material into the declarative, public arena. After five albums, Canadian songwriter Jane Siberry finally acknowledged that she was no longer composing in her bedroom – there was a world out there of rap and rock, and this was reflected in her 1993 album *When I Was A Boy*.

Like Vega, Siberry suffered from the Joni Mitchell syndrome. As Mitchell was the most famous female singer/songwriter, any women coming after her had to be compared to her – regardless of the fact that Vega and Siberry created completely different music. Vega's acoustic-based, guitar-centred vignettes had one eye assiduously on the pop market, whereas Siberry meandered through her own secret garden of synthesized soundscapes for years, not motoring into the wide world until the early 1990s.

Until then she was the critics' darling, mentioned in the same breath as Mitchell, Kate Bush and Laurie Anderson as a woman who 'shattered the boundaries of pop music'. To Siberry words such as 'spellbinding . . . heartstopping . . . genius' were complimentary but relatively meaningless. Behind the hyperbole there was the sense of a genuine talent feeling her way by instinct and intelligence. By the early 1990s she had moved from monitoring her own moods to monitoring those of the times, incorporating dance rhythms into her ethereal rock sphere, and introducing 'universal' themes such as religion, mythology and symbolism.

'People have rejected formal religion and after years of looking for something that fits, they've come round full circle to valuing elements within religion, like symbols, that work on the same level as poetry and music – without taking on board the formal structure itself,' she said in 1993.[22] Siberry rose to prominence in the late 1980s when Vega's success gave the green light to A&R departments looking for the next big Consumer Thing. Album artists as diverse as Mary Margaret O'Hara, Syd Straw and Tanita Tikaram were launched, lauded and promoted, with varying degrees of success. After four best-selling albums in quick succession, Tikaram, for instance, had to take a break from a business that readily categorized her as the 'female Leonard Cohen'. She travelled and 'hung out' for three years until the release of *Lovers In The City* in 1995, a more mature and connected expression of her identity. She was part of late-1980s marketing which concentrated on 'quirkiness' or eccentricity, while by the early 1990s the focus was more on ironic blues stylists such as Sheryl Crow (see Chapter 14) and Brenda Kahn. While many women singer/songwriters focus on lyrics at the expense of their music, however, Siberry emerged as a major voice through the sheer brilliance of her technique, moulding music with words to invent shimmering sound poems.

At first she veered wildly between perceptive poignancy and obscure whimsy. An early track, for instance, called 'Mimi On The Beach' is a kind of Sylvia Plath poem set to music about a teenage girl looking out on to the world, tense with peer pressure and despising the 'jocks' on surf boards at the beach; the song is self-conscious, wordy, arch – coming across as a failed experiment. For later songs like 'Temple', the opening track on *When I Was A Boy*, Siberry jettisoned the verbiage, creating a darker, more brooding feel.

Siberry's journey reflects the path of many 1980s singer/song-writers. Born in suburban Canada (Etibicoke, near Toronto), she hung out on the late-1970s folk coffee-house circuit, did a college degree and was also influenced by punk, hence the element of dissonance, a deliberately surreal edge to her writing. Her self-titled debut LP was financed by a waitressing job, her next two were released by a small independent before she came to the attention of the major Reprise. Her album *The Walking* was the object of some well-targeted promotion and a key tour in Europe and the US. Siberry was sold as part of pop's High Art, but, as she says, 'I exist in no one's ghetto.'

Siberry did not find commercial success easy. 'My music is subtle. Air-placing [radio play] is a problem. The record company is missing a major tool. I'm always very respectful. When I gave them *When I Was A Boy*, they felt their hands were tied, there was nothing to work with. I said, I'll create a front door for this record, something you can be enthusiastic about. I didn't want it to go out and disappear.' Realizing that her escape was as much her responsibility as the record company's, Siberry wrote the declarative ballad 'Sail Across The Water'. 'That pattern of introverted songwriter is hard for women to break out of,' she said. 'The programming goes deep when you're told that you'll only be loved if you're nice and quiet, otherwise you're considered a fishwife or homosexual. Fortunately the louder voice is getting stronger, shrugging off that worry.'

Siberry exercised her louder voice with fellow countrywoman k.d. lang in the duet 'Calling All Angels', on the soundtrack to the Percy Adalon film *Salmonberries*. Robust and besuited, with a quiff and a legion of lesbian admirers, Kathy Dawn spearheaded a late-1980s resurgence in country music, in tandem with the singer/songwriter revival. Bands such as the Cowboy Junkies and Lone Justice were playing their own 'cowpunk' hybrid, a combination of country rhythms and post-punk attitude. Former lead singer with Lone Justice, Maria McKee recalls, laughing, 'We thought we'd be the first to change the face of country music, really shake it up. We wanted to make it more accessible to a younger, hipper audience – get it back to the rawness and punk energy it had in the beginning. Hank Williams was a punk, just as much as Tom Petty.'[23]

By 1987 she had left the band to go solo, and her eponymous debut, a collection of glorious, soaring gospel-flavoured songs, marked her move into a more dramatic pop territory. 'I was brought up in a white Baptist church close to fundamentalist; later my parents joined the Charismatic church, which is like the black Baptist church. I always sang in church as a child.' Like many country singers, McKee's roots were in a fundamentalist Christian tradition, but she was also brought up in the hippy counter-culture of 1960s LA. Her background has rich story-telling potential: her aunt and uncle were tightrope walkers who collected vaudevillian history books, and her elder brother was in the original 1960s hippy band Love ('I remember being taken to gigs on Sunset Strip at four years old'). McKee's songwriting mixed these different influences: 'I get inspiration anywhere, anytime – from observing life to reading Tennessee Williams plays.'

By the early 1990s a more alternative strand had grown up within country music, with female artists such as lang, The Indigo Girls, Mary Chapin Carpenter and Kathy Mattea singing songs that were less about nostalgia or camp, more directly related to living in the post-nuclear family age. Nanci Griffith was received as the torch bearer for this new generation. While Wynette was courted as the First Lady of Country, Griffith was named its First Woman.

She began playing guitar and singing in the honky-tonk bars of her native Austin, Texas, recording folksier material for inde-pendent labels before emerging in the 1980s with a series of albums (*Little Love Affairs*, *Storms* and *Late Night Grand Hotel*) that plugged directly into the heart of country music while at the same time determinedly pushing back its boundaries. Inter-viewed in *City Limits* in 1991, she said,

'Country has always been at my roots. Carolyn Hester, Loretta Lynn, these people flow through my veins. But so do The Everly Brothers, so does Frank Sinatra . . . Roy Orbison . . . Their appeal is hopefully the same as mine –

imaginative slices of small-town romance or dreams of escape. The only thing that sets them apart from, say, George Strait, is a ten-gallon Stetson.'[24]

Griffith's challenge to country conventions while at the same time working within them earned her the dubious privilege of an unspoken blanket ban by country radio. 'Country stations never play my records because I don't fit in with their narrow definitions of what a country singer should be.' Griffith sang about the diverse power of human relations, whether it was the plight of a dispossessed farmer, or the agony of alcoholic loneliness. 'I could write songs full of flowery romance, but I just don't feel I've got the time, and I'm pretty sure that my listeners wouldn't have the patience.

The flowering of the late-1980s female songwriting boom was both an insult and a boon, giving women more exposure while at the same time ironing out differences. 'The media has insisted on putting women together. No one thinks of male singer/songwriters. Women have different characters – there're huge differences between, say, me and Sinéad O'Connor. We have to stop being defined in terms of each other,' said Vega. This attitude was clearly displayed on the May 1994 cover of rock bible *Q* magazine, where under the coverline 'HIPS. LIPS. TITS. POWER' (a reference to Lesley Silverfish) three female stars in their glad rags crowded together. Scrawling blues terror PJ Harvey, Icelandic techno chick Björk and America's answer to Kate Bush, the shamanic piano-playing Tori Amos, all came from different musical backgrounds, but they were dealt with *en masse*, as rock's Three Faces of Eve. They spelled out sex, separation and novelty, rather than their status as respected musical figures.

If there was a link, it was that they were all songwriters, reflecting the explosion of influences in the 1990s. Though she has found the term feminism problematic ('It's like a stale old pussy, man. Your experience as a woman isn't compartmentalized under a heading', she said in 1998[25]), Amos is the most explicitly feminist of the three. The daughter of a Methodist minister from Maryland, Amos won a piano scholarship to the Peabody Conservatory in Baltimore at the age of five, but left at eleven, and by her teens was playing Gershwin in gay bars. Desperate to break into the business, she moved to LA and sang in an ill-advised metal band called Y Kant Tori Read, before throwing off her rock chick status for a more experimental approach. It paid off. She moved to London and kicked off her career in 1992 with the debut *Little Earthquakes*, which featured the song 'Me And A Gun', a devastating pared-down account of her experience of rape at gunpoint. Since then she has produced bestselling albums such as *Under The Pink* (1994) and *Boys For Pele* (1996) that combine complex rhythmic shifts and abstract lyrics with powerful pop melodies. She interweaves myth and fantasy into salty songs about womanhood, love and lust. And unlike the ladies who decorously tinkled parlour piano in the nineteenth century, Amos brings out the inherent feminine sensuality of the instrument, playing the piano in a way that is raw, ultimate and, at times, overtly sexual.

By 2001 she was directly interrogating what it meant to be a songwriter with *Strange Little Girls*, an album covering 'classic' songs by male songwriters, sung from the female point of view. Using the rhetoric of her Christian upbringing, Amos told me she was exploring 'how men say things and what a woman hears. You take a man's Word, you take his seed. The word became flesh in the wound of the voice of the woman.'[26]   In her hands, for instance, Slayer's 'Raining Blood' is about female fertility: 'I don't see Satan in this. I don't see blood as gross, demonic and wounding,' she says. 'Blood is healing and cleansing, it's our sacredness as women. A lot of religions shamed menstruating women. We shouldn't take on board that negativity anymore.'

She also took apart the sophistry of 10C.C.'s 'I'm Not In Love', a stalwart smooch classic from the 1970s. 'Lots of male journalists say, "It's the most wonderful rhetorical thing ever said, I'm not in love." You go – it is? I'm not in love so don't forget it? Even if it's to yourself? My gal says, Truly I'm not either. So are you ready for that? It's a very dangerous game when love is not involved. I'm taking it to a place where I think it really is.'

**Tori Amos**
live at London's
Union Chapel,
2001: 'You honour
the women before
you and after you.
There isn't a
copyright on this
story.'
(Tabitha Fireman/
Redferns)

In constructing the album, Amos interviewed a range of male listeners and was struck by the fact that none of them asked about the feelings of the woman in a song, whether it was the teenage protagonist of 'I Don't Like Mondays' or The Stranglers' 'Strange Little Girl'. With that she visualized these women: 'I call my songs girls, and these were strange ones. Some of them you might not wanna have coffee with, but I was able to hold their essence, because I was able to align with them in some way. All the women were in the background, wafting through with high-heeled shoes and pedicured feet.'

Most striking of all was her rendition of Eminem's ''97 Bonnie & Clyde', his No. 1 rap about murdering a troublesome wife and dumping her in the trunk of a car.

'It stared me right in the face: bloody irresistible. How could I not pick up that gauntlet? She had no voice. The women approved of that one. When I said, I'm doing this, they all applauded. They're so sick of the bitch in the truck and yo bitch this and bitch that. The ghost of this woman showed me, as she lay dying in songworld. She's hearing him say his version to 'their' daughter. She cannot protect her daughter, who'll be made an accomplice in a very . . . rhythmic way. It's all a little bit on the backbeat. It becomes very low rider groovy and seductive. Wait a minute, this girl will have this legacy for the rest of her life, her mother can do nothing to protect her now.

'No one takes away Eminem's power as a songwriter. Sometimes he can really hit it. He put his finger on the domestic violence issue and portrayed it from a point of view that's real. So we just turned the camera around and showed what's happening in the back of the trunk.' In response to the view that Eminem's song is satire, Amos is unimpressed. 'Eminem isn't John Cleese, he's not funny. There is a level of malice. Some say it's dark comedy. All that was workin' but, I wonder what she felt? No men I talked to asked that question. But the women in the back room screamed: "What about her?"'

The third woman on that *Q* front cover, Björk, hinted at a new technological direction for female songwriters, marrying a personal, narrative approach to writing with house beats, avant-garde indie rock and shades of jazz on her best-selling 1993 solo album *Debut*. She recorded this having moved to London, after singing with various Icelandic punk bands, including the anarchic Sugarcubes. 'I realised I could have an easy life in Iceland, just have a glass of Cognac and good books and two jobs and do my songs in the evening, but I would be such a consumer, taking it all in and not giving anything back. I thought: OK, I'm 27. If I don't go on a mission now and make some sacrifices, I will never forgive myself,' she told me in 1995.[27]

After establishing herself with *Debut* and its follow-up *Post* (1995), Björk began shrugging off the elfin 'little girl' image ('so as not to threaten people I pretended I was really stupid. It's a good little game to play'). She recorded *Homogenic* (1997), a bold, beautifully crystalline set that reflected her love of Iceland, and in 2001 delved even deeper into stark, electronic balladry with the icy soundscapes of *Vespertine*. I met her again in New York while she was recording *Vespertine*, and she recalled the photo shoot with PJ Harvey and Tori Amos. 'When we meet that connection is still there,' she says, 'We tell each other what we're going through, and understand in the way that no one else can. We're in the same jobs, seeing through the bullshit to how you really feel – but we're also very different. Tori is magical and euphoric, while Polly has a more earthy quality.[28]

Björk was also part of a new breed fully at home with video, using it as a tool of expression. A decade earlier video was an innovation that had a limiting effect on female artists; through MTV it dominated the 1980s to the extent that visual presentation was put squarely before musical worth. In this growing high-tech assembly of pop images, the field was ripe for someone to seize power, and MTV found its Goddess in Madonna.

# 7 Lipstick Traces

## MADONNA, MANIPULATION AND MTV

**Hips:** Projection of pelvis and upper part of thigh-bone on each side of body

**Lips:** One of the fleshy parts forming edges of opening of mouth (upper/lower/under lip) . . . redden one's lips . . . bite one's lip . . . curl . . . escape one's . . . hang . . . lick or smack . . . pass . . . stiff upper

**Tits:** (Vulg.) Nipple (esp. of woman), woman's breasts . . . two milk-secreting organs on upper front of woman's body . . . source of nourishment

**Power:** Ability to do or act . . . particular faculty of body or mind . . . vigour, energy

*Oxford English Dictionary*

'One manager we had was sleazy. We were watching a video of Debbie Harry and there was a shot of her lying down with a close-up of her face. He said, 'You should look like that when you're singing live.' Thing is, it didn't look pornographic, Debbie lying there singing, but his interpretation of it was.'

ALEX, lead singer with 1980s girl rock band The Shop Assistants, author interview, Aberdeen, 1987

IN 1975, QUEEN'S 'BOHEMIAN RHAPSODY' sat at the top of the British charts for nine weeks, a rock operatic *mélange* that was remarkable as much for the accompanying video promo (the first of its kind) as the song itself. This paved the way for pop as three-minute TV commercial. Until the early 1980s, the visual promotion of pop was not highly developed or co-ordinated, so in some ways many women could 'slip through the net' of image stereotyping.

Throughout history the female body has been objectified as a source of sexual arousal or suggestion. Women have always felt the pressure to look decorative or pleasing, but within pop and rock, when the star is the focus of a mass gaze, this expectation is increased tenfold. In the face of the pop orthodoxy that a woman is there first and foremost to look attractive, female artists have consistently had to negotiate the Image issue. 'There's always what we call the Cleavage Question,' said singer Suzanne Vega. 'How much to show, when to show it, if at all.'[1]

While Cleavage was the main sexual barometer of the 1980s, when pop was in its infancy with the 1920s vaudeville blueswomen and 1940s jazz swingers, focus was on the Leg. With 1950s dream babes the emphasis may have been on the *Derrière*, as opposed to the fetishizing of Hair in the 1960s. Whatever the focus, the acceptability of women in pop has rested on their ability to read and wear the codes, to promote whatever bodily part is fashionable at the time.

'One important function of clothing has been to promote erotic activity: to attract men and women to one another, thus ensuring the survival of the species,' writes fashion semiotician Alison Lurie.[2] This activity was first commercially exploited on a large scale with the rise of the Hollywood 'picture personality' and a star system constructed through studio publicity, films and fan magazines. Mass-media exposure gave actresses such as Grace Kelly and Marilyn Monroe a highly public, even mythic status. Monroe set the trend for bouncy, fluffy, blond seduction with her 'breathy voice, her "horizontal walk", her revealing dress, her half-closed eyes and half-open mouth.'[3] A glamour girl immortalized through Pop Art in Warhol's repetition of blurred images, Monroe became the talisman for commercial sexual desirability.

This Hollywood ideal was reflected in the growing 1950s music industry with stars such as Peggy Lee, Alma Cogan and Eartha Kitt projecting an image of high glamour. By the 1960s, however, the success of teen-girl groups ushered in a new look predicated on youth and freshness. Curves were out, wiggling sylph-like hips were in. Although women had always felt compelled to diet (jazz star Dinah Washington, for instance, was desperately addicted to diet pills), with the arrival of TV and even greater means of visual promotion, more and more female artists subjected themselves to tortuous slimming methods. Florence Ballard was sacked from The Supremes partly because of her weight problem. Along with Mama Cass Elliot, she became one of the first casualties of the burgeoning pop industry.

## Don't Call Me Mama Anymore

A dedicated artist with a warm, full voice perfectly suited to the golden pop that made The Mamas and The Papas world-famous, Cass Elliot fought a constant battle to be taken seriously. 'I felt that I was carrying the other three,' she said in 1972. 'I'd get out on stage and say to myself, "Why should I be doing all this work for the four of us when I could be earning more as a solo act?"'[4]

Elliot saw herself as the lynchpin of the band, a folk/rock-based vocal four-piece comprising Elliot, John Phillips, Michelle Phillips and Dennis Doherty. Their first hit, 'California Dreamin'', a late-1960s classic, was followed by a succession of others including 'Monday Monday' and 'Dedicated To The One I Love', but Elliot was itching to have a solo career. Her voice was the strongest, yet attention focused on her heavy image at the expense of her musical talent, and she was fed up with being stereotyped bubbly 'Mama' in contrast to Michelle Phillips, 'the pretty one'.

Preparing for a Las Vegas solo debut in 1968, Elliot went on a strict diet and lost 110 pounds, but halfway through the first show she went down with a throat haemorrhage. 'I couldn't sing,' she said. 'All I could do was cry.' Despite a faltering start, she went on to release five solo albums, touring top 'rooms' throughout the States. Her diet struggles caused damaging fluctuations in weight, and in 1974, at the age of thirty, she died of a heart attack. *Don't Call Me Mama Anymore* was the title of her last album.

Elliot found it impossible to live up to the 1960s angular ideal, but by the early 1970s the pop scene had begun to diversify, allowing room for differences. At one end of the spectrum was ABBA's bright, shiny kitsch, while at the other, a downbeat Joan Armatrading wouldn't let go of her woolly jumper. Taking advantage of the relaxation of sartorial rules that came in the wake of 'serious' 1960s rock acts such as Dylan or The Grateful Dead, where scuffed denim was *de rigueur*, Armatrading addressed the image game by refusing to play it. '[Once] I'd done an absolute miracle . . . I had actually got Joan to take off the Blue Sweater. She lived in a big, baggy, blue sweater. The first night at Ronnie Scott's she was going to wear the Blue Sweater, but I managed to persuade her into wearing a white blouse,' recalls her first producer Pete Gage.[5] This was a rare occurrence. Armatrading said,

'I've always worn clothes that I feel comfortable in. They kept saying things like, "Have you thought of wearing a dress or putting your hair up? At least stop wearing that little woolly hat on stage." I went right on doing what I wanted to do. You've got to be a bit stubborn because most of the record business is run by men, and men always have set ideas about how things should be. There's a lot of pressure on women to conform. If you want to survive you've got to be either strong or stubborn or deaf.'[6]

Pleased that she was able to sell millions without taking her clothes off, Armatrading later said sagely, 'You need all that showy, glitzy, glamorous stuff, and you need me. If you had one or the other it'd be boring. Also, being glam is just not me. I wouldn't even attempt it.'[7] There is an early shot of Armatrading and her songwriting partner Pam Nestor, self-effacing but subcultural, lolling in the latter's Notting Hill flat. Nestor has stripy socks up to her knees while Armatrading wears a pair of scruffy flared jeans and army boots, her Afro-style hair neatly clipped. Showing both an assertion of individuality and careful attention to detail, this image suited the rock songwriting genre Armatrading had chosen, an area where she had space to make a simple, yet powerful statement.

ABBA's prominence in mainstream pop, however, rested on a stylistic nightmare: two female singers Agnetha (Anna) Faltskog and Anni-Frid (Frida) Lyngstad who encapsulated the crude certainties of 1970s teen-girl culture with their luminous blue eyeshadow, shiny pants and platform shoes. The ABBA women linger in the mind because along with male partners Bjorn

Ulvaeus and Benny Andersson they riveted image to music, making the two interchangeable in the public imagination. The hit 'Mama Mia', for instance, was two pairs of their video lips in close-up; 'SOS' was platinum-haired Faltskog frowning and screwing up her face to sing; 'Fernando' was lip-gloss in the firelight; while 'Dancing Queen' had the women twirling their bodies in disco glare.

It was the band's judicious use of TV and print exposure that consolidated their image with record buyers. Even though they came from a relatively small country, rarely played live and had no major concert appearances in the US, by 1978 they had become Sweden's fastest-growing corporation, with a yearly gross of over $16 million. Anna and Frida cultivated the slick 'girl next door' pop image that ushered in the new video age, while Kate Bush took that polish one step further by turning herself into an erotic fantasy.

An early shot from Kate Bush's 1978 publicity campaign has her looking full-lipped, big-eyed and open-nostrilled to the camera, wearing a clinging vest, her nipples showing through. When asked about her image at the time, Bush insisted that she didn't feel exploited and answered matter-of-factly,

'I suppose the poster is reasonably sexy just 'cause you can see my tits. But I think the vibe from the face is there . . . Often you get pictures of females showing their legs with a very plastic face. I think that poster projects a mood . . . I'm going to have trouble because people tend to put the sexuality first. I hope they don't. I want to be recognized as an artist.'[8]

Some years later, at the time of her third or fourth album, the penny dropped. 'I was very naïve and I was very young,' she said of early photo sessions which led to her being one of the most popular 'wank' images to grace student bedrooms. 'It was all very new to me and, in the first year, I learned so many lessons about how people wanted to manipulate me.'

The tacky display of Bush's girlish femininity was replicated throughout the 1970s in a more anonymous form on record sleeves and publicity posters, from Roxy Music album covers to the 1976 advert for former Vinegar Joe singer/guitarist Robert

Palmer's solo album *Pressure Drop*. There, in cod-David Hockney style, the besuited male singer was foregrounded in a luxury apartment, while in the background a woman, stark naked except for a pair of extremely high heels, stood with her back to the camera. As the 1970s trundled on, the link between sex and selling records was becoming more and more explicit. The knock-on effect of this relentless focus on the female form had its most tragic impact on a young singer who internalized the terror of the world's gaze by starving herself.

## Top of the World

In 1974 The Carpenters were at the peak of their fame. The previous year had ended with 'Top Of The World' at the No. 1 slot, their tenth Top Ten US hit. Their album *The Singles 1969–73* became one of the all-time biggest sellers worldwide. And within five years of their first hit 'Close To You' (which went straight to No. 1), the duo had fifteen hit singles, six top-selling albums, and won three Grammy Awards. Their record sales were in excess of seventy-nine million copies. A symbol of what could be achieved in the record-company profit jamboree of the early 1970s, when the industry was in the black and throwing money at gigantic supergroups, The Carpenters were more than a corporate lynchpin. According to President Nixon, 'The Carpenters represent all that is true and best in America.' Their sound, aggressively homespun, eerily precise and vocally beautiful, was piped through airports and hotel lounges worldwide.

The Carpenters were the Sound of the 1970s. Their mass-market lush harmonic swathe penetrated global consciousness – from tots, teens and rednecks to cynical pre-punks dressed in black. 'No jive,' *NME*'s acerbic and cult 1970s writer Nick Kent wrote in 1973, '– ever since I picked up on The Carpenters, I've become less concerned with pressing issues like Watergate, Ulster and breast cancer. Already I'm sleeping better. Don't miss out on The Carpenters. Sterilized for your own protection.'[9]

The word 'sterilized' is used with uncanny precision. In 1974, amid consumerist plenty, Karen Carpenter began starving herself. 'This year it's Karen who's zonked out on stardom,' wrote journalist Andrew Tyler. At a Frankfurt concert he was disturbed by the fact that, 'The band are immaculate, Karen is immaculate and no one misses a stroke . . . her singing is resonant and deadly accurate . . . But it's not actually happening.'[10] Karen was notable by her absence.

When Karen first developed anorexia nervosa (self-starvation), her desire was simply to slim. As a child she had been quite heavy, tactfully described by her mother as 'hefty round the butt' and when The Carpenters first became famous she was dismayed by reviews that called her 'chubby'. 'How can anyone be too thin? Women are supposed to be thin. When the spotlight's on you they can see every pound. They don't just review our music, they review our hair, they review our clothes,' Karen says to her mother, standing in front of a mirror in the film *The Karen Carpenter Story*. Karen's obsession then gradually became a response to a world where, even with The Carpenters on top of the toppermost, she airbrushed herself out of existence.

Her insecurity went deep. Born in 1950 in New Haven, Connecticut, Karen was uprooted at twelve when the family moved to Downey, southern California, where young Richard felt he was better able to pursue a musical career. His father sacrificed security and pension rights after twenty-five years working as a printer to relocate the family in an area where the kids' talent would be noticed. A self-possessed young soul, Richard had a clear idea from the start how he wanted The Carpenters to develop musically. He persuaded Karen to come off the drums she loved playing to become a lead vocalist. 'She had a singing voice that was deep and powerful and very good,' he said. '[At first] it needed tutoring, but I realized that she could do something with it.'[11]

Karen may have acquiesced, but deep within was a rebel tomboy, the girl who preferred baseball to cookery or needlework; who watched her brother's band practise for hours before

**The Carpenters**
in London, 1973:
Richard and Karen,
'zonked out'
on 1970s
superstardom.
(David Redfern/
Redferns)

sneaking down to the drums one night and playing herself; who drummed in the school marching band and persuaded her parents to buy her a brand-new green and gold six-piece set. At sixteen Karen was playing with Richard and friend Wes Jacobs in The Carpenter Trio, desperately trying to look old enough to appear in local bars. Despite winning an RCA contract with the prestigious talent-spotting *Battle of the Bands* live contest, they recorded material which went unreleased, and it wasn't until their concentrated efforts as a duo that The Carpenters found success. It was the intensity of their relationship and their smooth, unified sound that attracted A&M boss Herb Alpert when he signed them in 1969. With her warm, generous voice Karen gave a fresh slant to established material, personalizing classics and eradicating triteness, making even 'Close To You', one of Bacharach & David's most innocuous songs, meaningful. Not surprisingly, soon after its release in 1970, the song shot to the top of the charts.

Working only with their own voices and continual studio overdubs, Richard and Karen achieved a trademark seamless quality. 'I guess you can't beat a better blend than with yourself,' he once remarked. The excitement of racking up hit after hit at first obscured Karen's anxieties, but by 1974, when singles such as 'We've Only Just Begun', 'Goodbye To Love' and 'Yesterday Once More' had entered international consciousness, Karen found herself in the pop stratosphere without an anchor. 'Zonked out' and continually on the road with six hair-driers and an array of smiles, she didn't know who she was.

'I suspected that something was drastically wrong, but she never looked ill. She just looked, well, thin,' Richard said, with classic understatement.[12] The clues are there not just in her prominent cheekbones and bulging eyes, but written into the grooves of the records. She sang of a tortuous world full of strangers on 'I Won't Last A Day Without You', of being a misfit on 'Rainy Days And Mondays Always Get Me Down', where everything is coloured by a vague shadow of unease. In the same way that Billie Holiday took schmaltz and made it her own, Karen infused a corny song with a rare intelligence and integrity. Like all the major interpreters she didn't sing a song so much as inhabit it, and despite the 'squeaky clean' epithet, crying out from many of the tracks was a genuine white suburban blues. It was as if Karen was channelling all her existential unease into songs like 'Superstar' and 'Solitaire'. Had she followed a solo path, she might well have ended up like Helen Reddy, singing strong narrative songs of women's experience.

As it was, Karen didn't let go of her internal strictures and never fully explored what it meant to be a woman. Protected by a close-knit family and jealous of Richard's affairs, she found it hard to form romantic relationships 'outside'. There were rumours of an engagement with Alan Osmond, another member of a squeaky-clean clan. 'There's really nothing in it,' she said, when asked about the affair. 'We're on the road so much there's not really much time for *that sort of thing*' (my italics). Apart from a few doomed suitors, Karen's only real public relationship was with property businessman Tom Burris. She married him in 1980, only to divorce him shortly before her death in 1983.

In an entertainment world where women were socialized to please, Karen, ever-polite and witty on the surface, showed alienation by developing a covertly hostile disorder. Analyst Susie Orbach writes of the similarities between anorectics and political prisoners who go on hunger strike, the suffragettes and IRA detainees who used starvation as the final means to fight for their cause.[13] In Karen's case, the cause was her own sense of self. In 1979 she made a last, decisive bid for independence when Richard was in drug rehabilitation for his addiction to Quaaludes. Moving back to the East Coast of her birth, she went to New York to record her solo album with producer Phil Ramone. Although scared at first ('I'm not real good at being away from home by myself'), Karen flourished in the studio. The record was weak, but Karen was beginning to discover a sense of her own musical identity.

Disappointed that she'd taken a step without him, Richard made it obvious when the album was later previewed with Herb Alpert and A&M co-founder Jerry Moss that he'd rather concentrate on new Carpenters material. The guys were not enthusiastic, and Karen's solo debut was never released. Although she put a brave face on her disappointment, Karen was clearly bewildered. 'Why is this happening?' she asked Phil Ramone at the time. 'What did I do wrong?' She always saw the hits more as Richard's achievement than her own. In the end, power over her own body, fuelled by the pressure to present a desirable pop image, became for her the only tangible achievement. 'She looked absolutely terrible, you could count her ribs, and every bone in her body was sticking out. The sad thing was that she thought she looked terrific, but still needed to lose "a little more",' said Richard.[14] Part of the nightmare was the fact that Karen began wearing revealing clothes because she believed the more weight she lost the better she looked.

When the illness took hold, at five foot four and a half inches tall and broad-shouldered, Karen weighed just five and a half stone (seventy-seven pounds), yet still felt over-exposed in the media glare, believing that too much fat was on display. Richard apparently said at one point before she developed anorexia that he didn't like 'chubby women'. While his influence was considerable, he was only voicing a truism that holds in the business. When a woman's body is sold as sexual product and slimness as the most desirable image a girl can have, female performers inevitably focus on their weight. International fame and feeling vulnerable in the spotlight can take this obsession to extremes.

In 1975, a year after the disease took hold, The Carpenters had to cancel a thirty-eight-date sold-out British tour because Karen was too weak to perform. In the next eight years she was in and out of hospital seemingly immune to recovery. She bought a new home where an eight-foot stuffed rabbit sat mournfully on a love-seat and the kitchen was full of sparkling pots, pans and cutlery that remained unused to her death. Shortly before she died in February 1983, though, it seemed as though Karen was beginning to put on weight again, making psychological headway with plans for a new album and tour. Cruelly, her body couldn't take the extra weight and she had a sudden cardiac arrest. Caught in the claustrophobic, rootless world of the 'conquer all territories' music business, Karen Carpenter literally made herself disappear.

## Material Girls?

In the late 1970s when Karen was wrestling with her weight, there was a counter-movement to image tyranny in the deliberate anti-exploitation stance of punk. Women used image as a weapon they could turn against the industry, either by ignoring it (e.g. The Raincoats' 'dressing down' and concentrating on the music) or amplifying it (e.g. Siouxsie Sioux's peephole bras and bondage gear). Both approaches were aggressive tactics that survived the brief explosion of punk, but which, in the 1980s video age, were completely marginalized.

As Gil Friesen, former president of US A&M Records, said, 'It was no longer a free-for-all expanding market. It was, going into the 1980s, an industry where there was tough competition for market share, with business principles that governed.'[15] The teen buyers who had fuelled industry expansion in the 1960s and 1970s thinned out by the end of the decade, leading to the 1979 'crash'. Singles sales slumped to 10 per cent of all record sales, and major record company CBS lost 46 per cent of annual profits, selling assets and stocks in order to survive.

The 1980s coincided with the rise of the corporate artist. CBS may have been releasing 150 albums a year from a roster of 200 artists, but their profits were made on the strength of two stars: Michael Jackson, whose 1984 album *Thriller* netted twenty-five million sales, and Bruce Springsteen, whose *Born In The USA* sold twenty million. Hit albums from acts such as U2, Lionel Richie, Phil Collins, Dire Straits, Prince and Madonna all helped pull the industry out of its five-year slump.

'The superstar is the giant bonanza. The big hit is to develop superstar careers. That is the biggest win you can have,' said CBS Records' Al Teller.[16] In an industry where of forty albums released a year by newcomers only a third are heard of again, it is inevitable that superstar success sets the standard. With an industry decline in the production of new albums, groups were signed and developed on a very tight leash. The demand for short-term profit throughout the 1980s and 1990s saw an industry playing safe with saleable images, and one of its most dependable agents was MTV.

Warner Communications' MTV opened for business on 1 August 1981, and within two years the first American cable music channel Music TeleVision became second in importance only to radio as a music-industry promotional vehicle. Pop images became crucial mass-marketing tools, creating a demand for slick sexual presentation, whether it was Laura Branigan succumbing to simulated rape by a masked intruder in her 1984

'Self Control' video or Olivia Newton John pumping out 'Let's Get Physical'. There was a growing place for performers *au fait* with the power of advertising and its shadow sister, the soft-porn industry. Into this gap jumped Madonna.

For a late-twentieth-century phenomenon, her entry was inauspicious. In 1983 she appeared on *Top of the Pops* with two backing dancers, singing 'Holiday'. The single went to No. 3 in the UK, No. 16 in the US, received as lightweight chart pop. Madonna began her career dancing with Patrick Hernandez's disco revue in Paris, and looking like an ambitious Europop *ingénue*; the tackiness showed. This didn't alter much with the release several months later of 'Like A Virgin' with its accompanying video that had her writhing on a Venetian gondola and gliding through marble rooms in a white wedding dress. Hindsight and masterful redefinition of that song in subsequent stage shows gave this early promo a gloss that it didn't necessarily deserve. Despite protestations by the academic Camille Paglia that 'Like A Virgin' had 'coruscating polarities of evil and innocence',[17] in 1985 it came across as cheap tack promoting well-worn pictures of madonna/whore stereotypes.

'She can offend people . . . yet, if you look at what she's saying, it's no big deal – it's just a tease . . . she can seem so outrageous when she's really the girl next door. That's a very unique mix,' said her former co-writer and musical director Patrick Leonard.[18] True to the capitalist ethic of tantalization without real satisfaction Madonna has always promised more than she actually delivers, with an instructive understanding about how much business is about manufacturing pleasure and stimulating desire. It seems right that she was born near Detroit, home of that dependable metaphor, the Ford production line. Her follow-up hit to 'Like A Virgin' was a two-dimensional, jokey celebration of that very ethic – imitating Marilyn Monroe in 'Material Girl', yet adding the neat catchline, 1980s-style, that, unlike Monroe, Madonna was In Control, Not a Victim.

Because she became so famous, she also became the media hold-all for post-modern academic theories on pop culture, sexuality and capitalism. She was looked at as a phenomenon rather than a person, and became a 'metatextual girl', an example of 'female spectatorship and agency', 'the staging of the body' and the 'heat of surface desire'. However, these disconcertingly vague buzz phrases do nothing to illuminate the process that led to Madonna's domination of pop. She did not ascend into the firmament like a self-contained pop miracle. A product of the industry that made the scaffolding to put her up there, she had an ability to pick up underground trends (club dance music, Vogue-ing, androgyny) just before they hit the mainstream, riding the wavecrest with deceptive ease. Working with muscle and acumen, she moved quickly, making sure she was in place before competitors. Madonna may not have the originality, the wallowing messiness of the artistic muse, but her gift is in packaging the results, with soundbites.

Canny about the prime movers in any scene, in 1982 she persuaded Michael Jackson's manager Freddy DeMann to represent her and she drew to herself designers, producers, photographers, dancers and directors such as Jean-Paul Gaultier, Jellybean, Shep Pettibone, Steven Meisel, Herb Ritts, Mary Lambert, and Alex Keshishian to mastermind images for her. Pouring money into visuals, she was the first female artist to fully exploit video. She also had a clear idea about the music to go with those images. Musical director Patrick Leonard recalled how Madonna secured him for her 'Like A Virgin' tour. When her manager first approached, he turned her down flat, unimpressed with the album. 'It was too poppy for me.' The phone then rang again, this time with Madonna on the line. 'I've never known anyone so direct in my life. She knew exactly what she wanted and what she expected. She was so clear in her thinking. She told me that I could have *carte blanche* putting a band together, sorting out the songs, everything to do with the music. It typified Madonna.'[19] Leonard accepted the offer, eventually making well over $5 million from that association.

This business sense reached a peak in 1991 when she formed a joint company with Time-Warner, receiving a $60 million advance for the multi-media Maverick and renegotiating her recording contract with a $5 million advance for each of her next seven albums, along with a 20 per cent royalty rate. Rivalling Michael Jackson as the ultimate corporate artist, Madonna generated sales for Warners of over $1.2 billion in the first decade of her career shifting seventy million albums. She envisaged Maverick as capitalizing on the talented people she had gathered along the way. 'It started as a desire to have more control,' she said, 'and became a kind of artistic think-tank.'

If Madonna was just about putting a lucrative sheen on mediocrity, however, countless dancing-revue girls would be up there with her. Back in 1985 something interesting was happening.

First there was the 'Like A Virgin' tour, where her raw girl energy pulsated through a set of superlative dance routines. This was the fuller-figure Madonna with the flashing smile, her charm deepening and radiating out. It was a persona consolidated by Susan Seidelman's film *Desperately Seeking Susan*, in which Madonna played an amplified version of herself, an enjoyable hustler with fiery lipstick and a customized leather jacket. She was the insouciant gum-chewing leader of the girl gang who roused millions worldwide at Live Aid when, with bare, bold reference to *Playboy*'s publishing of early nude shots, she shouted, 'I ain't gonna take shit off today.'

Within the space of a momentous first year, Madonna turned from being a female sell-out to a feminist icon. But because it was success driven by sex appeal, a tricky package at the best of times, she has regularly shifted in and out of favour ever since. Artistically, too, it was never plain sailing. Marriage in 1986 to celebrity brat-packer Sean Penn and the release of a sophisticated finely tuned pop album *True Blue* did nothing to ameliorate the loss of face she must have suffered in trying to negotiate Hollywood. For the first time there was a desperate edge to her determination as she played one duff role after another in *Shanghai Surprise*, *Who's That Girl* then *Bloodhounds on Broadway*. Even in 1990's big budget *Dick Tracy*, she had a wooden, self-conscious air.

Unable to let go of 'Madonna', the star has had difficulty making it as a film actress. By 1989 the strain was telling. After a traumatic violent divorce with Penn, she went underground and came up with what could have been a major turning point – her fourth album, *Like A Prayer*. 'She was upset and in tears a lot of the time. Normally she's a very fast worker, but it took maybe three or four times as long to make the record because she kept breaking down,' recalled Leonard. 'We called it her divorce album.'[20]

The new colour of her hair spoke volumes; growing out the blond to become dark reflected an inner tension and the surfacing of brooding emotion. The break-up with Penn devastated her, but from that trough and loss of control there emerged a nascent, human, artistic self. On reaching her thirtieth birthday she was re-evaluating her childhood, expressing pain, delving deep into anger, grief and a visionary sense of joy. The title track was pure devotional pop while the accompanying video, with the tableaux of gospel choir and Madonna kissing a sorrowful black Christ, was pure inspiration. Never mind that it was condemned by religious groups, never mind that Pepsi halted the campaign to go with the album's release, and it shot to the top of the charts in the wake of controversy – the album was genuinely moving, from the ebullient call to arms of 'Express Yourself' to the semi-autobiographical 'Oh Father' and the tender 'Promise To Try', a song dedicated to the mother who died when she was a child.

One of the biggest challenges for a woman in pop is to express herself from the core. Creative art is as much about encountering the uncontrolled self as it is about selling the capable side to the world. For once, Madonna had allowed herself to let go. 'The "Like A Prayer" video was about overcoming racism and overcoming the fear of telling the truth. I had my own ideas about God and then I had the ideas that I thought were imposed on me . . . I believe in the innate goodness of people,' she said.[21] Madonna could have gone on developing this new adult potential, but she was offered the chance to play gangster's moll Breathless Mahoney in *Dick Tracy* on the condition that she retrieve one of her most saleable assets, her blond hair. 'Along with the album, which was much more personal, I felt great having my own hair colour for the first time in years . . . that was the avenue I was going down – and then all of a sudden I had to change it.'[22]

As if scared by the introspective road she had started to go down, Madonna acquiesced to director (and celebrity lover) Warren Beatty for the film, and dyed her hair blond again. With that she had switched back on to the baubled Gentleman Prefer Blondes show circuit, reviving the 'show pony' routine. Blond became a habit that would be harder and harder to break.

The 1990 'Blond Ambition' tour to promote her *Like A Prayer* album was a triumphant spiritual journey through masturbation,

**Madonna**
in 1990: cool and
sculpted for her
'Blond Ambition'
tour.
(Michel Linssen/
Redferns)

Catholicism and Gaultier-designed pop. It also marked
Madonna's changing body. Aware that her physique was a prime
commodity she rigorously worked off the puppy fat that made
her 'Like A Virgin' tour so endearing, and re-emerged with
sculpted muscles for the high-octane vision of 'Blond Ambition'.
It's no accident that many female performers dramatically lose
weight when they reach a certain point of fame. As Madonna's
fat disappeared, in its place came rituals, special diets, frantic
exercise regimes and a sense of regimented control. As with
Karen Carpenter ten years before, physical fat for her had
become a metaphor for weakness and lack of control. It was a

hard look, in tune with the new toughness of her videos, and the tour documentary *In Bed With Madonna*, a 'frank' behind-the-scenes film that gave her the box-office cred she so badly needed. The downside was a growing sense of cold commercialism.

While Madonna set her stamp through a kind of video situationism, her first major competitor, Cyndi Lauper, found the process less easy. Also from an Italian-American lower-middle-class background, with a keen knowledge of pop and therefore an ability to subvert it, but with a more erratic temperament, Lauper is arguably the more musically talented of the two. Arriving a year earlier than her soul sister, Lauper hit the charts in 1984 with her unashamed feminist anthem 'Girls Just Want To Have Fun'. Voted 'Woman of the Year' in 1985 by *Ms* magazine, she continued to pepper the pop scene with her sparky personality, whether it was lighting up the dreary Live Aid video when she leaped at the microphone like a raw, multicoloured terrier, or yelling out 'I Drove All Night' at the top of her lungs in 1989. 'I dyed my hair at nine with green food colour on St Patrick's Day,' she recalled. 'My mom was modern, she let me go with it. I had that sense of fashion. My Barbie dolls looked great! I just extended that in the 1980s.'[23]

She wore thrift-store clothing and sang accessible dance music in a helium voice, just as Madonna did later with the tattered tulle, lace and crucifixes. She sang of female masturbation in the Top Ten hit 'She Bop' six years before Madonna writhed on a stage bed in an orgy of self-consummation. Interviewed in 1994, she said,

'I wanted success out of anger. People would give me grief about the way I dressed, then Boy George's success opened the door for me. At the time of "Girls Just Want To Have Fun" I was shocked at the reaction. I'd go out on stage and the audience would be filled with girls screaming, ripping at my clothes. I'd never heard girls screaming over a woman before, and at first I thought, They think I'm gay. The only bad thing is I wasn't! You can't live in that sort of atmosphere as a meteoric phenomenon, it doesn't go with being creative.'

**Cyndi Lauper**
live in the mid-
1990s: 'I wanted
success out of
anger.'
(Steve Gillett/
Redferns)

Both were hard-working products of the New York club scene but where Lauper, alienated by the constant pressure to be 'commercial', lost momentum and direction after her initial huge success (her first solo album *She's So Unusual* sold more than four and a half million copies, yielding four Top Ten singles in 1984), Madonna made a point of restlessly building on every achievement. 'It's always been a struggle for me to sell myself,' said Lauper.

Her motivations are different, this much was apparent during her London shows at the end of 1994, when she did heart-rending scat and played an array of different instruments. Considering the dichotomy between her mainstream career and her artistic credentials, in a strange way Lauper is pop's Biggest Secret. She took a cool appraisal of Madonna's success:

'I actually passed her one evening coming out of a studio. I was dressed like a nut, a bag lady. I said hello to her, but I don't think she recognized me. She seemed kind of alone, with all her bodyguards. I hailed a cab and went home where the light was on and my husband and cats were waiting for me. I felt like I had the charmed life. As a writer I need that. Madonna's a terrific businesswoman and entertainer, but I don't know if her dream is to sing that great song, or hit that perfect note. I don't know if moving people is important to her. I wouldn't compromise that.'

Later Lauper adjusted her view, looking at Madonna with a fond, almost sisterly air. 'I think God put us on the earth at the same time, and it's so strange. Sometimes I see a picture of her and I think it's me. I look, think, Hey I didn't wear that – then I see her face. Her face looks like mine and it's *her*,' she said when her 1994 Greatest Hits compilation *Twelve Deadly Cyns . . . And Then Some* came out. She went on,

'We like a lot of the same things but are very different. When she approaches the rhythm she comes from that dancer place. It's almost like Eartha Kitt. She was going to see Eartha Kitt for a while . . . She certainly presses buttons on everybody. I think every woman has a sexuality and shouldn't be castrated.

'They always compare us – but they do that to women. It's like, no matter what I said or she said it would always come out like a cat fight. It's silly.'[24]

Lauper displayed a girl-pop solidarity that was rare in the mid-1980s. While Madonna encapsulated the image of modern competitive sexual female, another image dominating the decade was that of Prince's Women, glamorous acts tending towards the basque/suspender school of video like Vanity/ Apollonia 6 and Sheena Easton, who earned a reputation of being His Purpleness's appendages. As a stylist once remarked to me, 'Basically they have no choice. They're his walking fantasy. He's outrageously rude: "I want to lick your cherry", "twenty-two positions in a one-night stand" – it's grit sex, no bullshitting. He's saying, "This is who I am, these are the women I like and this is what I write my songs about." Good on him, at least he's honest about it.'

Though Sheena Easton admitted that she was playing a role, slapping on the ham, even she got touchy when I suggested that the Prince connection overpowered her, compromising any sense of being an artist in her own right. 'I'm sick of being asked whether I had a relationship with Prince. It's boring having to answer the same question twenty-five million times. I think it's a sexist attitude, assuming that if a man and a woman work together they've gotta be sleeping together. It's very narrow to assume they can't have a friendship and mutual respect.'[25]

After leaving her working-class Glasgow roots to set up home in LA, Easton became a million-seller in the States as well as a successful health and fitness expert and celebrity actress, appearing alongside Don Johnson in *Miami Vice*. In 1984 parental watchdog PMRC tried to ban her Top Ten hit 'Sugar Walls', a saucy song penned by Prince in his monumental *Purple Rain* period. After the court-case controversy with PMRC it took Easton a long time to shake off the Prince Connection.

It became an industry truism that if you were a woman and Prince wrote you a song, he was making a move. On a personal level that may have been the case, but professionally it was more to do with business acumen and ego. A prolific songwriter, his songs were the equivalent of a product stamp. For a woman to be bequeathed a Prince song for her new album meant instant credibility: in pop terms she had arrived. Martika was a purveyor of trite pop and soufflé cover versions until Prince got hold of her and gave her 'depth' with 'Martika's Kitchen'; ditto Lisa Stansfield; even Mica Paris's career took a boost when he noticed her singing at his party after a London show.

Attention from Prince meant immediate access to top players in the industry. Because of the widespread respect Prince had within the business, his approval and patronage acted like a calling card. He preferred working with women, and empowered many in his career: Meli'sa Morgan consolidated her early success with a song from his *Controversy* album, Chaka Khan had phenomenal attention with her classic version of his 'I Feel For You'. 'Any artist working with Prince has to come away enriched. His spontaneity is so infectious, as is his courage and belief in his music,' said Easton. 'He's always given great respect to women – he's worked a lot with women engineers in a generally male-dominated field. He doesn't pigeon-hole and label.'

Easton's is a positive view, but Prince's influence worked like a double-edged sword. He was pro-women to the exclusion of men, maybe because he is less afraid of dealing with them. Prince's bass player Mark Brown once said: 'He knew them better than he knew us [the men]. He would open up to the women. They would hang out with him, go shopping with him, and he'd spend money on 'em. But with us, it was never like that.'[26]

In his biography *Prince: A Pop Life* Dave Hill suggests that the star focuses on women to fuel a passionate kind of narcissism, 'gazing at his own reflection and seeing a girl look back'. Prince has cultivated a charming effeminacy to counteract his masculine poise. His is a flattering, intense gaze. One memorable day in 1988, I inveigled my way with another journalist into his studio at Paisley Park, hoping to stumble on an interview. I was sitting looking at a yellow pad with the words to 'Lovesexy' scrawled on it in a purple pen when His Highness walked in and sat quietly in the corner, exuding a palpable charisma. 'Oh my God,' I said, involuntarily. He wore a silk Paisley shirt, and even though it was the middle of the day, was clean, coiffured and scented. There was a smile, a short 'Hi', and it wasn't until after we had been diplomatically ejected that I remembered his appraising, assessing look, from the top of my peroxide-blond hair to my black shoes. It felt flattering, yet at the same time disquietingly direct, as if mixed in with the sense of mentor/protégée potential was a business brain fast at work, totting up a prospective product.

If I could sense that from a single look, working with him as a woman could be an overpowering experience. In many ways he is a symbol of what any woman confronts in getting her art out into the world – an inevitable wrestle over who controls image and musical interpretation. More malleable personalities have lost out. Vanity/Apollonia 6, for instance, one of Prince's first girl groups specializing in lingerie, high heels and soft-porn references, never rose above being a smutty, shock-tactic joke. Their name was linked to what tabloid editors describe as a 'nipple count', a connotation worsened by the knowledge that Prince originally planned to call the girls The Hookers.

Among the Ones That Got Away, Sheila E., daughter of Santana percussionist Pete Escovedo, escaped the titillation ghetto by emphasizing her role as a vibrant drummer and instrumentalist. Likewise Wendy & Lisa, who always maintained an ironic muso detachment when playing in his band The Revolution (witness Wendy Melvoin's self-possessed guitar strumming on the 'Kiss' video; in a neat reversal of roles she is the one 'doing stuff' while Prince flits around as the decoration. Only a man with such power can play around with that role of powerlessness). Virtuosos in their own right, Wendy & Lisa had to leave The Revolution to establish themselves as independent artists.

Capitalizing on gender confusion and male fantasy, Prince encouraged women to 'get sexy' in a very traditional decorative manner, yet somehow stretch their artistic potential. His peculiar message sums up the contradiction that lies at the heart of women's image in pop.

## Cleavage City

As the 1980s progressed into the 1990s, the music industry became increasingly corporate, with multinational takeover of not just independents, but middle-ranking majors. Sony bought CBS, while EMI took over Chrysalis and Virgin. BMG snapped up RCA and Arista, while Polygram incorporated Island and A&M, and the Japanese giant Matsushita became 'passive' owner of MCA. George Michael took Sony to court in 1993 in an attempt to get out of a contract binding him to a company that treated him as mere software for their hardware. Although he was arguing that he had grown up since Wham! and wished to be treated like a serious artist rather than a number-crunching sex symbol, the irony was that in his videos women still played an unreconstructed (albeit 'tasteful') role as erotic decoration. 'Freedom 'go', for instance, featured the supermodels *à go go* – Naomi, Linda *et al.*, while 'I Want Your Sex' became famous for its focus on female erogenous zones.

Michael occupied one end of a spectrum in which women had become increasingly commodified, with the use of models in videos a sign of a male artist's virility. The better-looking the model/dancer, the greater the rock star's supposed pulling power. In 1986, for instance, the besuited rock lounge lizard Robert Palmer sang 'Addicted To Love' with a collection of mannikin models playing guitars behind him. All wearing identical little black dresses, ruby-red lipstick and blank automaton stares, they were the MTV equivalent of the Stepford Wives. 'Intuitively I know that's about as misogynist as it gets,' singer/songwriter Michelle Shocked said in 1989, shortly before she mimicked that transgression, with a succession of Schwarzenegger beefcake types performing in the background to her video for the song 'On The Greener Side'.

At the more low-budget end of the scale there were standard heavy metal images such as Mötley Crüe's 'Girls, Girls, Girls' 1987 video where women in bikinis danced in a sleazy club, wrapping themselves around poles Thai-butterfly style. And hip hop outfit 2 Live Crew picked up on soft-porn imagery with their 1990 *As Nasty As They Wanna Be* record sleeve depicting a row of barely bikini-clad butts so obviously sexist that many shops refused to stock it. George Michael's lingerie may have been more expensive, but the impulse came from the same source.

'Shit, she's a major babe. Do you know what it feels like, on a rudimentary level, to watch a girl dance like that to a record you've made? Fuck world peace, man,' self-stylized 'sex-on-a-stick' soul rocker Terence Trent D'Arby told journalist Dylan Jones at his home in Hollywood Hills. D'Arby was watching a video casting of semi-clad girls auditioning for his next promo. Pressing the pause button he said to the dancing model on the screen: 'You should never trust a mystic without a dick. Never.'[27]

Madonna tried to turn these erotic codes on their head with satirical humour – the starkest expression of this being her 'Open Your Heart' video where, clad in a black bustier, she performed to a line of sad male voyeurs. With a complete understanding of the camera she turned it into a fetishistic gaze. The exuberance of her control, together with the fact that she was the highest-earning woman in pop, meant that Madonna became the yardstick for executive decisions on marketing. From the mid-1980s onwards there was a proliferation of blonde wannabes in the charts, from Vanessa Paradis to Patsy Kensit, all shedding clothes and spouting a contradictory message about 'control'.

Reservations about Madonna's blatant selling of sex were legion, with many women artists feeling the pressure to follow her agenda. Upcoming stars such as Kylie Minogue and Lisa Stansfield underwent the transformation from girl-next-door to sex siren, with varying degrees of success or credibility. Stansfield's make-over for her second album *Real Love* in 1991 entailed a concerted effort to make the northern Rochdale lass 'get sexy'. Instead she just looked staged and lit, a kind of middle-of-the-road Housewives' Choice, even when cavorting naked in a pile of flowers. When I interviewed her in 1990, she had a firm handshake, on-the-edge soul and an exuberance that were later smoothed down – visually at least. 'I want to stay self-contained in Rochdale,' she said. 'The streets in London are not paved with gold, and even with success things are totally normal. Even limos don't make a difference.'[28] This was before the international marketing team really took over.

By the early 1990s a heated public debate about what was acceptable and what let the side down raged among performers, audience and critics. Miki Berenyi from top indie rock band Lush voiced the reservations of many women in her analysis of the diminutive Australian singer Kylie Minogue and her dramatic change of image in the late 1980s:

'I have a massive problem with her because she epitomizes the acceptable role. She makes records for men. Loads of blokes like the Manic Street Preachers and Bobby Gillespie [of Primal Scream] go on about her being a great pop star, but can you remember the words? It's a shame she gets so much credibility when there are so many women worth a hundred times that; it annoys me that Sinéad O'Connor has a great voice but people slag her. As a woman going on stage you have to have a degree of responsibility. It's war; you shouldn't stick up for Kylie, she should be fought at every turn.'[29]

Labelled Gender Traitors, these blonde bimbos and 'men's women' brought to the surface female anxiety about power and exploitation, along with the questions of who owns the pop sex fantasy? and who is the fantasy for? In 1987 I saw hungry, rising young rap stars Salt 'N' Pepa posing for a magazine cover in a New York SoHo loft lying on the ground at the feet of their producer Hurby 'Luv Bug' Azor while the photographer pointed his camera down and someone showered them with dollars. At this, their normally taciturn British record-company representative intervened. 'No,' he said. 'Not that.' The girls had begun the shoot standing proud in their trainers; by the end they were literally reduced to the floor, Luv Bug imitating a pimp.

Even Chaka Khan, one of the most respected and influential soul artists in the business, has never been free from the pressure. She once turned up for an *NME* photo shoot in the late 1980s wearing a flouncy, off-the-shoulder cotton dress, announcing,

'For this interview I've put on a dress. I don't feel like wearing a dress. I would have preferred something more comfortable, less contrived, less , constricting. My manager asked me to wear it. It's part of business and reluctantly I have to go along with it. There are some things I won't forfeit but I have to be realistic and go along with the dress. It's supposed to make me look pretty, show me off: cleavage city.'[30]

Young female video director Tamsin Haughton told me that it's not simply a case of men pushing women into being sex objects:

'I worked with a singer who's an intelligent songwriter. The band didn't want to bother with styling, apart from her. She was the only one with make-up, and beforehand she said to me she wanted to look glamorous, to bewitch. She was wearing a white dress, and as there was water in the video, of course it got wet. "Is my body showing through?" she asked. Yes, it looks sexy. "I don't want to project that image." The girl didn't want to project that, but all the messages were that she wanted to be fancied.

'Women have a lot of problems understanding their sexuality – if you're intelligent you're not meant to be part of that scene, you're meant to be appreciated for your mind. But women also like dressing up, enjoying their sexuality. I get women saying to me, "If I wear that my tits will stick right over the top and it'll look sexy." Image is so important, a woman will do better if she's got a great body and a great face: it's a world people want to be part of. People buy a reflection of what they want. Also, a singer won't wear anything she doesn't want to. It's her video, her money. If she argues long enough, she'll get what she wants.'[31]

Women may describe it as control, but there is usually a degree of acquiescence to the sexual norm, if only because it's good for business. Haughton, who has also worked as a model and appeared in pop promos, unconsciously highlighted the nub of the problem. 'It's intriguing, fascinating to play with an image of who you can be. I like to see *how people express me*' (my italics). When an artist no longer expresses herself, what is she compromising?

She may get what she wants, but at a price. Pamela Hunter, former creative director at Virgin Records, recalled a campaign in the early 1990s for acid-pop duo Kiss Of Life, when for the visuals on the first single (CD sleeve and promotional shots) singer Victoria Maxwell wore a loose, low-key dress she felt comfortable in. 'When the record didn't sell that well, the whole campaign then revolved around the state of her dress. The head of marketing said to me, "There's a problem with styling, someone will have to take control of that girl, put on clothes that'll sell her".'[32]

For Hunter there was always a nail-biting moment when she would try and sell a video to 'the salesmen on the road' before it went out to the public. 'We'd all watch the video in a marketing meeting and wait for everyone's response. There'd be silence,

then, "Fantastic . . . but where's the sex?" The head of the
company would be saying, "Can we put the girls in sex outfits
upfront?"' Referring to a video she had once seen of Alice
Cooper on tour playing with a blow-up doll in fish-net stockings,
a hose pipe strangling its neck, Hunter said, 'Music is meant to
be revolutionary, making you look at things in a fresh way, but
people are still voyeurs, sexually aroused by images of women
being strapped or locked up. Men are more susceptible to
putting those images in video treatments, they'll push further for
them.'

Photographer Kevin Davies, who works in fashion editorial as
well as music-industry visuals, said frankly, 'People say, "Make
her look gorgeous." Make her look fuckable, that's what they
really mean. When male photographers shoot women, it is about
their fantasy, that old 1960s thing of "Burn that lens, baby, lick
the camera." A lot of them do fashion because they want to fuck
women, it's as simple as that.'[33]

Creating the fuckable fantasy woman has long been a preoccupation of pop music, especially now the medium has
become so visual. While a woman rightfully takes pleasure in
looking beautiful or exploring her sexual power, too often this is
marketed as homogenized youth erotica, a mass-market version
of beauty that, like dicing with the tabloid press, is for many too
powerful to take on and win. MTV's executive vice-president
Judy McGrath was fully aware of the Frankenstein's monster
that had been created in the 1980s when women often became a
superfluous sexual presence, playing no instrument, having no
say in the music and just providing the 'horny' factor.

'I think we hit a real low spot in the mid- to late '80s, when there appeared
to be a preponderance of videos where women were relegated to the
background . . . The pinnacle of that was the Sam Kinison video with
Jessica Hahn, with lots of rock gods surrounding Jessica writhing. Someone
said to me around that time, "I understand you had to play it, but did you
have to make it a hit?" And that's when I realized that we could be more
than just passive programmers here, and how we play it is up to us . . . it
was too easy to just sit back and say, "Hey, we don't make the videos."'[34]

Block video-watching would reveal a simple visual language in which women were just ciphers or body parts. By the early 1990s McGrath was championing many female artists and mixed-sex groups where 'girls are not just sitting there for visual appeal'.

'You have to get your image sorted out from the word go,' said stylist Tanya Haughton (sister of Tamsin), who in the early 1990s worked with New Order, The Shamen and a host of young dance bands. 'People always remember you from your first hit, and it's difficult to shake off that first image.'[35] Madonna has played it with a strong mixture of suggestion and aggression, a combination that rap/singer Neneh Cherry also tried, wearing girlie Lycra shorts but keeping her hands wrapped like a boxer for the cover of her 1989 debut *Raw Like Sushi*. 'They'd love to stereotype you as a bimbo if they could,' she told me shortly before its release. 'That's why you have to try and keep one step ahead, be provocative.' Her stylist Judy Blame, a gay man who has the knack of bringing out a woman's individuality, added, 'She wanted a strong, sexy image – one that said, "I know I'm good-looking, but keep away."'[36] Cherry then found that when she let go of her raunchy image for her second album *Homebrew* in 1992, she met with widespread record-company disapproval. Blame explained,

'She'd made it at home, with a very homey vibe, and said to me, "No bra and panties this time, Judy, I'm sick of seeing Madonna in it." So we did shots in Sweden and came up with a very homey image. When I took it to the record company [Circa, part of Virgin, and now of the EMI empire], they said, "Oh shit, it's not bra and panties." They'd prefer her stomping around in a leather miniskirt. At one point, when the album wasn't selling, they blamed it on the visuals, saying she didn't look sexy enough. I thought she looked relaxed and gorgeous, but because it wasn't obvious, marketing men were moaning, "Oh my God, is Neneh a hippy now?" They couldn't categorize it – but on a fashion tip, it was actually pre-1990s grunge. It's good to be subtle sometimes.'

Blame, who started out styling Boy George and who now operates at a high level in fashion and music, feels that women like working with him because he is not a threat. 'It's always a problem for women that the music industry manufactures them to a male fantasy rather than a woman's point of view. I like to feel I'm breaking that up with artists like Björk, who does it on her own terms.' To a certain extent, being on the margins himself makes him more sympathetic:

'The business is very homophobic. Most people see me as a Queen Bitch, don't mess with him. I promote that image, otherwise they just think you're a nancy, and a lot of men feel intimidated. Especially if you're dressing a band: two of them might be queens, but the other two that aren't are really jumpy. I don't get that with women because there's no threat from me sexually.'

Even in the year 2000, women were still struggling with the pressure to be sylph-like and sexy. Spice Girl Mel C admitted that at the height of their fame, she had got into the trap of thinking: 'I've got to be thin, I've got to be thin.' She exercised to the point of obsession, escaping to the gym as a way of avoiding stress. 'I feel safe in the gym. When I'm working out, it's just me and the weights. No one can get to me,' she said at the time.[37] She became whippet-thin, but it was an image that demanded tortuous levels of self-denial to keep up. 'I never thought I was good enough to be a Spice Girl, so I had to make myself as perfect as I could' she said in 2000, after the band had peaked. 'Then I just thought, "Wait a minute, I'm not a robot," so I stopped. I was too thin, but it's hard when you've come from the extreme to accept your natural figure.'[38] When she stopped working out and put on weight, the tabloids mocked her as 'butch' and 'beefy'. The comments hurt, but she deflected them with a wry joke. At a photo session she pointed to her full cleavage saying, 'These cost me thousands of pounds . . . in food and beer.'

Many pop girls opted for cosmetic surgery to give their careers a Pamela Anderson-style lift. This led to rocker Chrissie Hynde saying in disgust: 'Fake tits . . . when did mutilation become so popular?'[39] Some artists did find it possible to resist, however. Justine Frischmann, lead singer with Elastica and a cool-headed female musician who has no intention of being sold as a rock 'n' roll trinket, was asked by a music glossy to pose naked, Christine Keeler style, with her legs astride a 1960s chair. Not surprisingly, she refused. Gorgeous US singer/songwriter Jewel, meanwhile, did a photo shoot for *Rolling Stone* magazine, and was asked to appear naked on a horse. 'A dress is fine,' she said politely.

When teenage UK pop star Billie went to a photo shoot for a men's magazine she requested beforehand that there were to be 'no bikinis'. Upon arrival at the studio, the only items on the stylist's garment rail were bras, knickers and hot pants. She refused to go semi-clad, and as a result, lost the magazine cover. 'I didn't get a front cover because I wouldn't get my tits out, basically,' she told me. 'At the time I was disappointed, thinking Oh man, I should've done that. But when I got home and thought about it I realised you have to stick by your principles. I don't think a woman needs to show all her flesh to be beautiful.'[40] Unfortunately by 2000, she had succumbed to the pressure to 'broaden her audience', being photographed in skimpy clothes, or nothing at all save for a strategically placed leaf.

In the late 1990s every young woman in the public eye, whether a TV presenter, classical soprano or rocket scientist, was aware of the expectations of the burgeoning 'lad mag' market, with titles such as *Loaded* and *GQ* providing a new kind of soft porn. Female musicians, in particular, felt that their talent was overlooked at the expense of image. Saffron, the striking lead singer from techno pop band Republica, complained that women in bands were often passed over for 'someone who'll wear nothing but a fur-lined sporran.'[41]

No matter how long they have been in the business, women still have to deal with the sex imperative. Even when she was approaching fifty, Cher seemed to be a female Dorian Gray, getting younger as she became older. Buying cosmetic surgery as a way of maintaining the illusion, she would display the results in skin-tight rubber and leather, and show her famous butt tattoo at every opportunity. Spokesperson for a US health and fitness chain and the 'step' aerobics workout, she needed to spend a lot of time and energy to keep up her image. One night before a

concert, a *Newsweek* journalist saw her sitting on the floor of her dressing room staring at a mountain of cosmetics. 'My body's just going to shut down soon, and I'll have to stop,' she said. 'I don't know how many more times I can beat this face into submission.' But the show must go on, and according to her sister Georganne LaPierre, 'She loves the glamour of who she is.'[42]

The fiftysomething singer screamed out almost cartoon-style the extremes that women can go to in the image business. Allegedly nipped and tucked more drastically than Michael Jackson, Cher adheres to the American dream of reinvention of self: 'Getting old doesn't have to mean getting obsolete . . . If you really want something badly enough, you can figure out a way to make it happen. I mean, in America, you can grow up to be President.' With an estimated annual earnings in 1991 of $10 million, it may have paid off financially, but at forty-five, after innumerable best-selling albums and Oscar-winning Hollywood success, she still said 'Sometimes I just don't feel proud of what I've achieved . . . I think, "Someday soon you'll do something worthwhile, something that's really great."'[43]

Manufacturing herself as a male fantasy meant that she encountered a split between Cher, the glitzy character ('Sometimes I'm not even sure what being Cher is'), and Cherilyn, the woman who'd sooner appear on stage in sweatpants and a T-shirt singing songs by Bonnie Raitt and Bob Seeger. Once, when she had a reunion with late partner Sonny, she suddenly wanted to 'cover up my arms, my legs, everything'. As if she was trying to reclaim her body for herself.

## Nice Record, Shame about the Face

Considering that the pop ideal is slimness, youth and health, what of talented women who are old, overweight or disabled? It sounds unsexy as hell, but women like Tina Turner, Alison Moyet, Etta James and Martha Wash (former Weather Girl) have ignored the pop prescription for success. 'If someone handed you a brief, "There's this 45-year-old black woman, she once made it in the business as someone's sidekick, but she's going to be a megastar," you'd be like, fuck off, no way,' says stylist Tanya Haughton. 'But if you're confident, you can wear anything, be anybody. Because she's older Tina Turner has depth. Yeah, she looks good, she's this age, she's been through these traumas; listen to that voice, see that figure. It's an honest role rather than a con.'

Deborah Harry found it difficult to let go of the blonde, slim image that characterized her in Blondie, but in getting older and letting her brown hair grow through, she found new freedom of expression.

'Sexuality comes from within. It was scary at first, confronting the world with my own hair, but now I can say, "Well, you're not getting any younger, are you?" I don't care, I really love it, because I was trapped for so long. I used to have a compulsion to be as thin as possible. I'll never be that way again because I've got used to my body type and I know what it can and cannot do . . . Actually, I always felt I could sing better when there was more meat on me.'[44]

One artist who has never tried to reconstruct her body for a commercial image is Alison Moyet, the British vocalist who rose to success in the early 1980s as one half of Vince Clark's whizz-kid pop duo Yazoo (Yaz in the States). Although she has always been heavy, it's never been a simple case of sounding the trumpet for weightier women. Sanguine about the 'fat girl made good' image perpetuated by the tabloids, Moyet says, 'I don't think I've ever sold a record for the way I look. But in that sense it's easier for me than for a girl whose whole image and marketing is based on the way she looks. I mean, she's got a lot to worry about.'[45]

It is often argued that a sexy image is there to distract the audience from limited talent or average material. Moyet, the spiky ex-punk from Essex with a blue-eyed stare, has an arresting, pulsating voice in any medium. In a way, she received the ultimate accolade: being respected for her voice and song-writing talents first, her looks second. She sees this as a double-edged sword: 'It's never fun to be publicly humiliated. When I was twenty-two I sold loads of records and no one wanted to shag me then. Your size determines how people perceive you. If you're a fat bird you're weak, unsexual and self-indulgent.' Moyet went through an air-brushed period during the mid-1980s when Yazoo split and she recorded two best-selling MOR pop albums, but she was uninterested in parcelling herself up as a 'nice package'. Although she lost her way with supper-club pop hits ('It was never really me'), like a homing pigeon, she found it again with the self-written, bluesy album *Hoodoo* in 1990 and the upfront beat pop of *Essex* three years later.

Another woman who resisted attempts to package her up was Tyka Nelson, Prince's sister, a pop singer/songwriter whose self-titled debut came out on Chrysalis in 1988 – it was ironic that in contrast to her brother's lithe and svelte fantasy women, Nelson was overweight and painfully shy. Interviewed that year, she said,

'I get bothered by people saying I should slim. Weight may be a way to hide, and putting a brownie in my mouth may be a way of pushing down the pain, but at least let me have my viewpoint. Maybe I'm testing everybody to see. If you really like me, you'll accept me the way I am and not just think about my physical appearance. It'd be great to break stereo-types: look at Oprah Winfrey – she looks like nobody else on television, yet she's the top in her field. I don't think she was holding on to her weight; maybe it needed to be said. When I'm ready to lose weight I will.'[46]

Another group of women excluded by the pop world are those who are disabled. A blind Stevie Wonder could get away with it because of the rich tradition of blind bluesmen behind him and the sheer breadth of his talent. Former polio sufferer Ian Dury didn't hide his limp and withered arm as the singer of the best-selling Blockheads, and singer/songwriter Robert Wyatt reached the top of the charts while sitting in a wheelchair, his plaintive anti-Falklands-war song 'Shipbuilding' becoming a hit in 1983.

Women with disability, however, are almost invisible, apart from America's most popular jazz singer Diane Schurr, who is blind, and girly punk singer Toyah Wilcox, who danced with a club foot. In the late 1980s, a bright girl with multi-coloured hair extensions called Kata Kolbert tried to break through. Her debut single 'Live Your Life' on her own Nevermore label had cool song-writing and soft vocals that invited comparisons with Nico and Kate Bush. The only drawback was that, restricted to a wheelchair with severe arthritis, Kolbert was unable to promote it in the acceptable way. Her wheelchair was not sexy. While trucking her demo tape round record companies, she was met with both uncomfortable comments and blank rejection. 'I couldn't be a singer in a wheelchair on my own terms,' she said. 'They wanted me to be a brave struggling cripple in a nice long dress.'[47]

Kolbert's influences span folk, pop and alternative poetry. An active member of the disability arts movement in Britain, Kolbert was frustrated with her polished pop being restricted to the disability circuit. On a practical level, though, until venue access improves, disabled performers will be limited to a cultural ghetto. 'Disabled people generally seem outside of normal life,' says Kolbert, 'not part of it. People only think of us if they're made to.'

## Supermodel Superficial

In the face of pressure to be pretty, many female performers, from Tracy Chapman in her dreads to Scottish singer/songwriter Eddi Reader with her librarian spectacles, have adopted a deliberate anti-image policy. Maria McKee, former 'cowpunk' Lone Justice vocalist, who established a successful pop career in the late 1980s remembers,

'I felt no one would take me seriously unless I looked really ugly. I got fat, I didn't bathe for months at a time. Before I'd go on stage I'd untuck my shirt. That's all I'd do to change. I'd wear the same shirt for months and put on black eyeliner, rubbing it around my eyes so it was just a black mess. I thought, OK, now people will take me seriously. Going solo, I had pressure to keep myself together, only for myself. I don't want to be a slob. I wash now.'[48]

Before they grow in stature or confidence, women often start their career either rebelling against or acquiescing in the sex norm. By the time she has made it, whatever her stance, every successful female performer believes fervently that she is dressing or making up to express herself. As novelist Kathy Acker remarked, 'Make-up isn't frivolous; it's another form of art.' But Riot Grrrl fanzine *Pawholes* has asked the legitimate question:

Make-up can be an interesting form of personal expression, but when millions of women are applying make-up every day to mimic a few models who represent the ideal beauty as determined by the fashion and cosmetics industries, just how personal, how unique is this expression? . . . Mass production of cosmetics has led to mass production of 'beautiful' women.[49]

The biggest competitors to Madonna in the early 1990s came not from the pop industry, but supermodels and superwaifs like Naomi Campbell and Kate Moss, fantasy-thin girls marketing high glamour. The fashion industry has always worked in tandem with the music business, one feeding off the other. Hip 'rock 'n' roll' designer Gianni Versace summed it up simply when he said, 'Young people buy things and go and dance in them, basically.' The model–pop star crossover is a familiar combination: French *chanteuse* Vanessa Paradis, for example, took flight as a bird in the Chanel commercial; at the lower end of the scale, topless Page Three girl Samantha Fox launched her pop career with breathy cover versions of 1960s hits, while top runway star Naomi Campbell signed to Sony in 1992, anxious to make it in the rock sphere.

Two years later her debut album, coyly titled *Babywoman*, came out. Although Campbell had worked with a phalanx of top producers including Bruce Roberts (Cher, Donna Summer), Tim Simenon (Neneh Cherry, Bomb The Bass) and celebrated rappers PM Dawn, and *much* was made of her supposedly ground-breaking vocal skills, the record was a flop. It was as if she was on the runway, modelling songs.

But while the musical influence of high-profile models-turned-pop stars is minimal, their visual impact has been striking. When supermodels became bigger stars than those in Hollywood or pop, many women found the results oppressive. Anjali, vocalist and guitarist of British all-girl band The Voodoo Queens, wrote the song 'Supermodel (Superficial)' in response to the media proliferation of Naomi, Christy, Linda and Kate.

'Everywhere I looked they were staring me in the face. It was offensive that they were seen as an ideal form of womanhood. Being bombarded by such pictures when I was young made me bulimic. Problem pages are full of girls saying, I want to kill myself because I don't look like Kate Moss. After the song came out, there was a pandemic sigh of relief from women. They'd come up to us at gigs to say thanks; and both women and men would write to us saying they were so used to seeing it, but no one was saying anything against it. It was about time.'[50]

After a while image is just about manipulation of style. Even Madonna found limitations in the visual sex role when her 'coffee-table porn' book *Sex*, published in 1992 to coincide with the release of her album *Erotic*, failed to stun the world. The *Sex* pictures, parodies of perversion and female fantasy featuring Big Daddy Kane, Los Angeles lesbians and bubbling faucets, coupled with a clumsy approximation of Anais Nin writings, seemed curiously flat. The album, with its disco work-outs and thinly sung version of the taut Peggy Lee classic 'Fever', reflected the fact that it was recorded nine-to-five to a three-month deadline. This audio-visual package was a job, a Warholian facsimile of the peroxide sex persona the public had come to expect. What came across, though, was less erotica than lack of engagement.

The tone of critics became weary. Under headlines like 'Madonna's Anticlimax', she was dismissed as past it by the 'straight' press, and accused by the gay press of being a 'sexual tourist'. 'She's the pure playing with the perverse,' lesbian photographer Della Grace said scathingly.[51] Madonna said later that she was being punished 'for being a single female, for having power and being rich and . . . having a sex life. For enjoying it and for saying that I enjoy it.'[52] On one level *Erotic* was a powerful statement of women's fantasy, but on another she was oversold, overstretched and over-exposed. As the various wannabes in her wake found out, there is a thin line between provocation and pandering. Although some appreciated the sex-toy joke, the irony was lost on a large portion of her audience. Norman Mailer wrote of how she had become 'secretary to herself',[53] while another writer remarked on her 'steely reason-ableness'.[54]

Madonna's solution to the Image Problem was to go into androgyny – a place where theoretically a woman can escape the tyranny of the Body. Throughout the 1980s and 1990s women began to experiment more with cross-dressing and sexuality, finding through their own view of the male world a new kind of freedom.

# She Wears the Trousers

ARTISTRY, ANDROGYNY AND THE
LESBIAN QUESTION

**8**

**Ambiguity:** Double meaning . . . expression capable of more than one meaning
**Androgynous:** Hermaphrodite . . . combining both sexes or opposite qualities
*Oxford English Dictionary*

'Being in a middle place that's neither overtly male or overtly female makes you threatening, it gives you power.'
ANNIE LENNOX, quoted in *Annie Lennox*, by Lucy O'Brien

## Girls Will Be Boys

It's interesting that as Madonna reached a peak in her fame in the late 1980s, she felt free to let the blond girly mask slide, revealing another, challenging, more alluring mask underneath. With her 'Dita' persona Madonna was stating just how much she controlled her image, and controlled the crowd.

Two of Madonna's biggest influences, Marlene Dietrich and Mae West, were apparent in two classic singles that she released in 1990. With 'Vogue' she picked up on the exaggerated catwalk-model poses of a gay underground craze and turned it into a glorious celebration of image – the power of old-style movie-magazine editorial transferred to video. Then 'Justify My Love', shot in monochrome by Jean-Baptiste Mondino in an anonymous hotel, featured Madonna as sex fantasist, exploring the erotic through leather, transvestism and overtones of 1930s Berlin cabaret. Rapping with whispered intensity to a pared-down backbeat, she voiced the deep, private nature of female desire. Teetering between tension and sensuality, 'Justify My Love' was dance ballad as art form. Recurring throughout the video were images of cross-dressing and camp, themes that reverberate in the work of Dietrich and West. The following year Madonna was photographed by Steven Meisel for *Rolling Stone* dressed in a suit with her blond hair cropped short and slicked back 1920s style, dancing and squeezing the behind of a girl in a flapper dress. The pictures were directly inspired by the photographer Brassaï, who documented the gay clubs, brothels and opium dens of 1920s and 1930s Paris.

Madonna may have then shocked the world with her book *Sex*, but seventy years earlier vaudeville comedienne Mae West had been doing the same with her Broadway show of the same name. An amalgam of her own experiences combined with an interest in Freud, Jung and Havelock Ellis, the show ran for a year before the police closed it down and imprisoned West for a week. The follow-up, a play about homosexuality called *The Drag*, ran for only two weeks in 1927, but it consolidated her outrageous reputation. The target of moral crusaders, West toned down her image after a decade in Hollywood, but returned to it again in the 1950s when she toured with a cabaret act including nine musclemen in loincloths.

Dietrich, too, appealed to heterosexual and gay audiences alike, and her movie roles reflected this duality. A German-born star who emigrated to America just before the rise of Nazism, she brought overtones of the cruelty and decadence of pre-war Berlin to her stage act. Projecting an inscrutably cool sexuality, Dietrich could play vamp and seductress in both evening gown and tuxedo. In fact, it is her cross-dressing heroine in Josef von Sternberg's 1930 film *Morocco* that provides one of the most enduring images on screen. Conveying the full power of sexual ambiguity, Dietrich's androgyny has filtered into pop through Madonna's direct imitation. With 'Justify My Love', Madonna showed how gender roles could be swapped, blurred and played with to create a multitude of different identities.

In her act there were also elements of 1930s movie sex siren Jean Harlow, who sealed her stardom in films such as *Platinum Blonde*, *Bombshell* and *Reckless*. Although Harlow conveyed dizzy sexual glamour, she was also an intelligent, witty woman who was harshly attacked when her first husband, production director Paul Bern, committed suicide amid rumours of his impotence. Parallels between Harlow and Madonna can be seen in the way they have been treated as 'ballbreakers'. Such forthright sexual appeal makes men nervous and women suspicious. In 1994 Madonna bemoaned the lack of support from other women in pop like Courtney Love and the sexually frank Chicago rock heroine Liz Phair. 'They slag me off any time anybody asks what they think of me or compare them to me. It's kind of like what a child does to their parent, they denounce you. They want to kill you off because they want their independence from you.'[1]

Madonna's provocative stance alienated many potential supporters. By the end of 1994, however, she was toning down her style, opting for romance rather than sex with her album *Bedtime Stories*. She was growing up and refashioning the extreme sex-blonde image, a role that was beginning to limit her. In the late 1990s she defied expectations again, with a completely new style (see Chapter 14).

The major mark of stars is their ability to transform themselves, to be attractive to both men and women. The most successful stars, then – from Little Richard and Elvis to Prince and Michael Jackson – have both Jungian qualities of masculine and feminine on display. Their mental wardrobe contains a world of possibilities and permutations; when your star is in the firmament, why restrict yourself to something as prosaic as gender?

For male performers there has been a long tradition of peacock drag-queening or sultry ambiguity, of using make-up and style to reinvent masculinity. Within rock 'n' roll conservatism there is still a paradoxical pop celebration of the bizarre. By the early 1990s Madonna was cross-dressing in Dietrich-style top hat and tails for her Girlie Show, presenting a tinge of lesbian cabaret and burlesque, while a beautiful six-foot-seven black drag queen called RuPaul was sashaying on cable screens and chat shows across America. In 1993, when his/her disco single 'Supermodel' flounced out of the club scene to dominate American airwaves, RuPaul said,

'I wanted to do a piss-take on high, high Hollywood glamour. Since Hollywood didn't do glamour any more, I had to go through supermodels and high fashion – models and pop culture are the perfect marriage of image and music. I know them all, their lifestyle is not that different from a working drag queen's. They try on clothes, prance around and serve lots of attitude. That's the drag creed right there!'[2]

Keen to jettison 'walls, barriers, formalities', the former Atlanta 'beauty queen' continued, 'Do I have to just be attracted to men? Can't I be attracted to women who look like men, too? Cross-dressing has everything: yin, yang; day, night; male, female; black, white. It encompasses both sexes, but it's also beyond sex. Our higher selves relate on that level.'

Back at the turn of the century cross-dressing was a staple of music-hall and show-girl vaudeville, with male impersonators such as Vesta Tilley dressing in top hat and tails singing 'Burlington Bertie'. This transferred itself to Hollywood, where Lil Dagover in male attire and monocle performed decadent German cabaret in *Doctor Mabuse*, and Dietrich in full uniform sang 'The Man's In The Navy'. Greta Garbo, Gloria Swanson, Katherine Hepburn and a host of other female stars opted for the power of disguise. The Japanese Takarazuka dance company, formed in 1914 by wily entrepreneur Ichizo Kobayashi and still going strong in the early 1990s, was a large all-female troupe where half the women dressed as men. Performing an impeccable combination of Japanese theatre and Western light opera, the 'men' were regularly told, 'Be more powerful or you'll just come across like girls.' In an ironic twist for such a codified society as Japan, top 'male' stars soon became the focus of unrestrained, female mass adulation.

In the early pop industry, though, this gender play was strictly a male preserve. Mid-1950s female acts were expected to stay in their glitzy gowns, while Little Richard whacked out 'a-wop-bom-aloo-mop' in lipstick and pompadour, and Elvis Presley wore eyeshadow at Nashville's Grand Ole Opry, a conservative bastion of the music business.

It was rumoured that Presley stuffed a toilet roll down his trousers before a live performance, and this, together with the whip of his infamous Pelvis, sent fans into a frenzy. His male part became fetishized, a love object; but, according to cultural commentator Marjorie Garber, he wasn't so much macho as a female impersonator. Transvestite-dressing always incorporates a detachable part, be it codpiece, wig or false breasts, that hides evidence of the 'real' male or female: 'In the Elvis story the detachable part is explicitly and repeatedly described not only as an artificial phallus but also as a trick, a stage device and a sham. Not for the first time the phallus itself becomes an impersonator – and, moreover, a female impersonator, for only a female would lack the phallus and need a substitute.'[3]

## Terribly Taboo

Women didn't fully investigate the false phallus in pop until the cultural mix-up of the 1980s. Before that, cross-dressing was very much part of the male rock 'n' roll rebel pose. In 1968, for instance, Frank Zappa wore a dress on the *Sergeant Pepper* parody cover of the Mothers of Invention album *We're Only In It For The Money*, while Mick Jagger wore a white feminine smock at The Rolling Stones' Hyde Park free concert, and in Nicolas Roeg's film *Performance* dressed up British dandy style in bodystocking, make-up and frilly blouses. The Dandy was popularized even more by former mod David Bowie in the 1970s.

Sixties mods wore expensive suits and were very dapper. 'Make-up was an important part of it: lipstick, blush, eyeshadow, and out-and-out pancake powder . . . It was very dandified . . . very elitist,' Bowie once said.[4] A famed frequenter of London's gay club scene who toured in Lindsay Kemp's dance company, Bowie 'came out' as bisexual early in his career. He first expressed it publicly in 'traditional' drag, on the original sleeve of his 1970 album *The Man Who Sold The World* (which at the time was banned), but by the early 1970s his image became more outlandish, filtering through to glam rock with his feathercut flame-haired alter ego Ziggy Stardust. Sporting skin-tight metallic costume, high laced hunting boots and exaggerated make-up, Ziggy the 1970s space-age hermaphrodite made androgyny fashionable. Much of the inspiration for his look came from his wife Angie Bowie, who claimed later that they were a key part of 'the modern struggle for sexual liberation . . . We were certainly the most famous couple ever to admit and celebrate our bisexuality so publicly.'[5]

While Angie Bowie may have influenced David, she never successfully brought that experimentation into a solo career. In the 1960s and 1970s only a few women created their own version of this theatrical bravado. British girl singer Polly Perkins became a novelty celebrity in the mid-1960s, famed for speaking parlare (gay argot), dressing in Carnaby Street pinstripe suits and singing songs like 'Superdyke'. 'Looking back, I think I was a bit camp for some of them, dear,' she said later.[6] Not surprisingly, she was a one-off destined for obscurity in an era when sex roles were still rigidly defined and lesbianism was taboo.

Sixties heroine Dusty Springfield responded to the pressure of the conventional heterosexual 'dolly' image by presenting an extreme version of femininity, modelling herself on drag queens with her over-the-top gowns, bouffant hairdos and panda-eyed parody of French *Vogue*. They were a strategy to deflect the constant 'gay' rumours, but, even after a decade of hits, those rumours affected her life so much that in 1970 she had to leave the country. US songwriter Allee Willis, who wrote for her the appropriately named 'What Have I Done To Deserve This?', commented,

'Without question the lesbian issue was the icing on the cake of Dusty's "difficult" reputation. It would have been fabulously scandalous if she'd been having hits, but it came at a time when she was tumbling down. You'd never just hear about the drugs; there were the tough females that came along with it. It made her less of a controllable Kewpie doll. It didn't allow her to fall easily into the category of pop songstress, and she was dependent on producers and arrangers to assemble material for her. Her "reputation" complicated matters. She had a bum rap.'[7]

Bobby Woods, one of the musicians who worked on her classic 1969 *Dusty In Memphis* album, said, 'It was a kinda icky situation. I didn't want to get too close to it. At that time people didn't dare come out of the closet.' Coming from the rural American South, Woods admitted that, 'Where I came from, if someone was homosexual you either got hung or ran out of town. It was that strong. I was a naïve Southern Baptist boy. I'm not judging her, that's between her and the Almighty.'[8]

Springfield was also one of the first stars to speak out and put gay sexuality on pop's agenda. After a London *Evening Standard* interview in 1970, in which she said that her affections were as easily swayed by a woman as by a man, the urge by the press to prove she was a lesbian became obsessive. Dubbed 'the woman rumoured to be gay before Navratilova learned to play', she had up to that point been fairly elaborate in her 'het' disguise. She would fend off reporters with photo opportunities, such as her after-show clinch in 1964 with the singer Eden Kane. 'I've taken him home to meet my parents,' she said coyly. 'But we have no definite plans.' After the plans failed to materialize she said, 'Men are afraid of me because I'm famous.' Claiming at the height of her 1960s fame that she was 'living the life of a nun', Springfield said she had been 'too terrified' to take up Mick Jagger's offer of a date, while singer Tony Orlando asked her to send him a telegram when she lost her virginity.

As she shed her inhibitions, so did the tabloids, competing with each other to run 'exposé' stories. By 1978 she openly supported gay issues, giving a lengthy interview to *Gay News* when the Gay Liberation movement was at its height. 'There is a strong anti-gay feeling in Hollywood. Which is extraordinary in an industry that's 75 per cent gay,' she said. 'Because industry heads are very anti-gay, it's very tough for most gay people and difficult to speak out. There's a growing number of enraged people who are not going to put up with it any more.' Her playful frankness also got her into trouble when she quipped to an audience of gay fans at a Royal Albert Hall charity performance, 'It's nice to see the royalty isn't confined to the box!' HRH Princess Margaret was not amused, later demanding a written apology.

Though adept at fielding questions on her sexuality, by the late 1980s she agreed to allay some rumours by telling the *News of the World*, 'I'm sick of being asked about it, so perhaps by talking I'll shut people up. I've tried sex with both men and women. I found I liked it.' She added that the years of criticism had hurt her deeply. 'I think my life and career might have been easier without these constant gay rumours. My sexuality has never been a problem to me but I think it has for other people.'[9]

Closely allied to cross-dressing in pop is the question of sexuality. Although androgyny doesn't necessarily mean a performer is gay, there has always been a historical overlap. As the women's movement grew in the 1970s, Springfield's camp artifice became a relic of the 1960s and more and more lesbian performers sought success on their own terms. In 1972, while Springfield was living in Los Angeles, her career floundering in the face of the 'difficult rep', Helen Reddy had the huge feminist hit 'I Am Woman'. Although her producer pronounced her song 'too butch', and many people said that it would ruin her career, it was an American No. 1. Winning a Grammy for Best Pop, Rock and Folk Vocal Performance (Female) for it, at her acceptance speech in Nashville the Australian-born *émigrée* said, 'I want to thank God because She makes everything possible.' Despite the religious fundamentalist uproar during which she was called everything from a 'ballbreaker' to a 'blasphemous bitch', Reddy stuck by her song. 'It's a chest-beating song of pride,' she said. When she had realized the song expressing a positive feminist sense of self didn't exist, she had decided that 'I was going to have to write it myself'.[10]

By the International Year of the Woman in 1975, Reddy had started her own production company, Helen Reddy Inc. 'The corporate world won't let you play with the big boys,' she said. 'When you've got your own company, you're playing by your rules.' The burgeoning strength of the women's movement was reflected in the establishment of a small independent women's record company in Washington DC known as Olivia Records. Its rules were simple. According to one of the founders and later president, Judy Dlugacz, it was a 'loud, clear statement' about empowerment for women in the business. 'The term "women's music" was an organically developing term, which enabled people to identify that this music spoke about women and to women,' she said.'[11]

Expecting to sell five thousand over a few years, Olivia surpassed that with its first single release, Cris Williamson's 'If It Weren't For The Music', selling more than seventy thousand copies. The melodic singer/songwriter's album *The Changer And The Changed* then sold over a quarter of a million. With the launch of other women-centred record labels in the 1970s, like Redwood, set up by California feminist rock heroine Holly Near, it became obvious that there was a healthy, self-contained and self-sufficient market for 'women's music'. Run along non-hierarchical principles and distributed through alternative channels such as political bookshops or the Women's Revolutions Per Minute organization in Britain, they provided an area where women could write openly about lesbian love without contorting themselves to fit into an admissible mainstream. Dubbed by detractors as little more than 'propaganda in the key of C', female bands, from The New Harmony Sisterhood and Miss Saffman's Ladies Sewing Circle in the US to Britain's Ova and Sisterhood of Spit, nevertheless acted as a flashpoint. Songs like 'Angry Alpha', 'Bury Me In My Overalls', 'Amazing Gays' and 'The Woman In Your Life Is You' may have sounded hilarious and dated in later years, but then they were expressing sentiments in rock music that had never been heard before. Such labels, though, had limited crossover appeal, especially when the term 'women's music' became synonymous with lesbian separatism. The challenge then was in marketing a lesbian presence more central to chart rock and pop.

### Walk on the Wild Side

In the late 1970s punk offered one alleyway to women, though the images were less overtly lesbian than androgynous or broadly feminist, from Poly Styrene's day-glo asexuality to The Slits' defiant parody of femininity. Their precursors were male American No-Wave underground acts like The New York Dolls, transvestite rocker Jayne County and The Velvet Underground's

Lou Reed, who combined trash-guitar rock and flamboyant cross-dressing. They were the perfect messengers for Andy Warhol's factory of the pop avant-garde, a scene that Reed toasted on *Transformer* with the songs 'Make Up' and 'Walk On The Wild Side' with its reference to Holly (Woodlawn) who shaved his legs and transformed himself from a man into a woman. The New York Dolls combined Rolling Stones raunch with heavy borrowings from the girl-group era (The Shangri-Las, etc.), to produce a kind of zonked-out camp. When asked if he was bisexual, singer David Johansen said, 'No man, I'm trisexual. I'll try anything.' Such were the waves that the Dolls created in straight America that Clive Davis, then president of CBS Records, reputedly said that if you wanted to work in the music business, you didn't admit that you went to see The New York Dolls. It was tantamount to admitting you were homosexual.[12]

It was the fusion of glam punk and disco that produced the first female star of androgynous pop. Born in 1952 in Spanish-town, Jamaica, the daughter of a Pentecostal minister, Grace Jones hit the world in 1980 with *Warm Leatherette*, an album of low-slung, sinuous reggae funk played by the cream of Jamaican talent (including Sly Dunbar and Robbie Shakespeare). Wading through established songs such as Chrissie Hynde's 'Private Life' and Roxy Music's 'Love Is The Drug' with a brooding, rasping purr, Jones's sound was wildly different from the traditionally sweet female voice. What set it off, though, was her image – a brutal GI Blues pillbox haircut, angular cheekbones and a tall, taut body in savagely well-tailored suits. She defined her look as 'macho'. 'I don't want to look frilly and, to me, macho means the opposite of frilly. Simple, stern lines, more masculine,' she said.[13]

Having shared a Manhattan apartment with her twin brother, a DJ, when she first came to New York in 1974, Jones channelled her awareness of club culture into three unremarkable disco albums, *Portfolio* (1977), *Fame* (1978) and *Muse* (1979) before hitting gold with her fourth on Chris Blackwell's Island Records. Many couldn't believe that Jones had masterminded such a

**Grace Jones**
on US tour, 1982:
severe andro-
gynous clubland
chic.
(Leon Morris/
Redferns)

striking package herself. In the same way that Dietrich was supposedly the product of Josef von Sternberg, so Jones had to be
the puppet of her partner, French designer and artist Jean-Paul
Goude. 'My career was designed way before I met Jean-Paul.
When I met him I'd already made three records and the androgynous look was already established. He was inspired by me and
used me as a vehicle to make his career grow, and mine grew
along with his,' she said. The effect reached a peak with the
astonishing Goude-directed feature-length video *One Man
Show*, in which Jones appeared with several hundred masculine
cloned versions of herself.

As RuPaul did ten years later, Jones transgressed boundaries of sex and race. 'People feel comfortable with me because I communicate with my soul rather than my colour . . . I had an idea for a film where I would play a white girl. I would be made up as a white girl – it would be similar to De Niro gaining weight for Raging Bull. People have asked me why . . . I like the political implications of it,' she once remarked.[14]

Her success was brief and cataclysmic. The 1981 album *Nightclubbing*, with its stand-out track 'Pull Up To The Bumper', consolidated Jones's reign as the urban disco androgyne, but by 1982's *Living My Life*, the momentum had slowed down. Jones's gift lay more with image than music. Grainy and muscular, her voice was resolutely off-key, and her sound, low on melody, high on robotic rhythm, would never translate easily to pop. By the mid-1980s she had diversified into film, appearing in the James Bond movie *A View to a Kill*. After her pop career slackened off, Jones made several attempts to revive it: in 1989 she released a routine dance track 'Love On Top Of Love (Killer Kiss)', and 1993 saw the subtly titled 'Sexdrive'. Arrested several times in the late 1980s for possessing cocaine, Jones never regained ground in her career, and live performances were tinged with a narcissistic desperation. What Jones did achieve, however, was to imprint a pop moment on mass consciousness, the first woman to redefine images of race and gender on such a wide scale.

Jones's weapon of subversion was video, a medium that postmodern pop diva Annie Lennox exploited with agility throughout the 1980s. 'I wanted to see if I could get rid of the woman completely, and killed Annie of the Tourists stone dead. I knew it would cause a few raised eyebrows; there's something subversive about it that I enjoy,' she said of the provocative image change that occurred when she and Dave Stewart launched Eurythmics.[15] For the video of their 1983 No. 1 US hit 'Sweet Dreams', the duo appeared dressed in suits. Lennox cross-dressed for practical, tactical reasons, for the freedom she discovered once she donned the cloak of neutrality. Wearing a man's suit gave her access, psychologically as well as physically, to the record company boardroom.

'I chose suits not because they were outlandish but because they were neutral. We wanted the strongest symbol of normality we could find,' she said. Suits also represented Eurythmics plc, a business sense that arose out of the feeling that they had no control in their former band, The Tourists. Their album-sleeve designer Laurence Stevens recalled how he invented Dave and Annie's 'D&A' company logo:

'I came up with the Palace script logo D&A; it was like a product stamp. The band Ultravox had the UV stamp that Peter Saville had given to them. It was an important cosmetic image, signalling music with irony. There was new technology with drum machines and synthesizers, it was no longer five guys like The Clash – this was a proper production business, hence the suits.'[16]

The Suit is a powerful uniform in corporate language. Pop stars have historically rebelled against what it stands for, but in the designer-led 1980s Eurythmics were at the forefront of a scene saturated with manipulation and irony. Twenty years earlier a young Bob Dylan played it straight in the search for a deal, donning a suit to meet record company executives. His gesture was one of naïvety and conformity, almost comic considering the protest stance he later delivered, in contrast to Eurythmics adopting the codes of control for themselves. Lennox's role in this was crucial. Her suit, coupled with her cropped carrot-red hair, went further than the titillating theatricality of Marlene Dietrich or Grace Jones; in an unsentimental post-punk package, she made clear points about product, business and female artistic control.

This wasn't an overnight transformation, however. 'I'm not sure she had a good eye for clothes at first. She wasn't confident about her image, and that came out in the way she dressed,' said Carol Semaine, a designer who in the late 1970s made clothes for punk bands like Billy Idol's Generation X and The Vibrators, as well as Lennox. 'When I met her she was in The Tourists and really broke, with the band trying to get out of their contract. You can't have a sleek image if you're living hand to mouth. Annie would get old curtains and I'd cut them up to make into trousers and skirts.'[17]

With her fluffy peroxided hair, wide eyes, jumbled gaudy look and cover version of Dusty Springfield's 1960s hit 'I Only Want To Be With You', Lennox felt she was being stereotyped into the 'British Debbie Harry'. Insecure with the dolly-bird role, she ditched it as soon as she could. 'I don't think she realized at first how stunning she looked,' said Semaine. 'Either that or she knew and couldn't handle it. She never wanted to flaunt her body. You'd never see her in a low-cut dress. If she was whistled at in the street, it'd make her hackles rise.'

After The Tourists broke up in 1980, Lennox continued working with Dave Stewart, but it was the end of their romantic relationship. In the ensuing period of transformation Lennox developed the androgynous look that was to become her trademark. 'I recognize that I am a woman, both as a performer and representative of my generation of women. But there is this double-edged thing about sexuality. Like most women today I am taking control of my own life and you can see my clothes as an expression of that.'[18]

The suit symbolized a control 'behind the scenes' as well as on stage. Once an influential radio producer made a pass at Lennox during a music industry luncheon. She responded by slapping him off his chair and walking out. Jack Stevens, her former A&R champion, recalled,

'Most women in the industry struggle because: a) it's a chauvinistic business, and b) women tend to be regarded as second rate. Annie would never compromise, she was determined to get on in terms of her own intellectualism rather than being a floozy or a stupid girl. As a result she had greater creative insight and was prepared to take the heartache. Very few women are. Working with Annie showed me that a determined woman serious about her career is a better proposition than anything else. Everyone talks crap about female wobblers, but you actually get more with men than you do with women. There was none of those stupid games – with Annie, it was just straight down to business.'[19]

In 1984, fashion columns heralded 'The New Androgyny', a style that arose from the asexual gender play of punk. Groups like Duran Duran, ABC, Culture Club and Eurythmics led an image revolution on video, filling chunks of MTV airtime. *Newsweek* featured Lennox and Boy George on their cover with the headline: 'BRITAIN ROCKS AMERICA – AGAIN'. Androgyny then, though, made US sponsors nervous. Before her appearance at the 1984 Grammy Awards, MTV demanded a birth certificate as proof that Lennox was a woman and not an impersonator. In response she appeared at the Awards show disguised as Elvis, with fake sideburns, a pocked chin and greased-back hair. Despite guffaws from the stage manager, the celebrity crowd greeted her with a stony silence, her masculine edge interpreted as hostile chic.

As Lennox's statement became her entrapment, she began to play with more diverse feminine images, from the angel to the housewife and the whore, culminating in her 'raddled tranny' for

**Annie Lennox** at Wembley Arena, 1989: the suit is a powerful asexual symbol in the world of the corporate music industry. (Tim Hall/Redferns)

the Eurythmics 1987 album *Savage*. A bleak, blond-haired, black-eyed bimbo, she directed her song 'I Need A Man' as much at a gay audience as at her mainstream fans. 'Annie liked the incredible feeling of voyeurism,' said Sophie Muller, the female director of the video, whose offbeat camera angles gave much of her work with Lennox that spinning, fractious quality. Lennox stated,

'I want to set new limits on what women in the music industry are allowed to do. Sometimes I think I'd like to make exquisitely beautiful, sublime music that's almost rhythmless. At other times the most frenzied angry club music you've ever heard – what I think heavy metal could be but never is . . . Heavy metal is very clichéd and sexist, with a chauvinistic swagger. Well, I would like to have a chauvinistic swagger, too. I think I could do it better than any of 'em!'[20]

In the late 1980s that swagger had been honed and toned for a solo career. By then she was a thirtysomething married mother, her image reflecting a more settled sense of self as she moved from casual suit to designer dresses to feather boas and glitter for her 1992 album *Diva*.

At the same time as Lennox opted for male disguise, Culture Club vocalist Boy George invented a look that was less about drag than true sexual ambiguity, his China-doll persona making him the most celebrated 'gender bender' of the 1980s. Interviewed in 1994, he said,

'The stage is a fantasy realm, you can be who you want. Everything's OK if you're a pop star. When I was a little boy I wanted to be like Shirley Bassey, mimicking her gesticulations, the dramas. I idolize women and love colour and artifice – like the old lady with a bright mauve rinse and a spaceship hairdo. I like to see people having their own identity.'[21]

George's 'disguise' arose out of a genuine British gay subculture that reached a peak in the mid-1980s, with male artists such as Frankie Goes To Hollywood, The Communards, Dead Or Alive and Marc Almond scoring major hits in the pop charts. Many lesbians, however, felt that coming out in an industry predicated on heterosexual desire would be too risky. Rocking the institution of the family and the notion of female sexuality that pop clings to so tenaciously, a lesbian is an affront, someone to be labelled 'strange' or 'downright unsellable'. She is a threat to other women as well as men – while shooting the video for 'Sisters Are Doin' It For Themselves' with Lennox, Aretha Franklin, reputedly assuming that Lennox was a lesbian, ignored her throughout the entire session. Despite the boldness of her androgynous image, Lennox fought shy of the 'gay' tag. 'I've had gay girls come on to me,' she said. 'But just for the record, I'm not gay.'

## Constant Craving

Until k.d. lang came out to the pop mainstream nearly ten years later, lesbians felt they had to keep their sexuality hidden. One prominent gay female singer remarked to me in 1988,

'[To come out] would be commercial suicide. Women like Annie Lennox annoy me, making a career out of ambiguity. It's very glamorous to play with lesbian imagery if you're heterosexual, it's considered daring – but if you're not, it's airing your dirty laundry in public. A lot of us have discussed this over and over again, that it shows the massive imbalance of the sexes. If I was a classically beautiful bird in the man's sense of the word, I'd be more inclined to come out . . . but as it is, I'd be labelled fat ugly dyke. I don't want to get lumbered with that. The *News of the World* tried to expose it. In one of the first interviews I did, a female journalist said to me, "You're a lesbian, aren't you?" I was unprepared for it. The best thing was I managed to stop the article because I found out she was as well. I did some heavy research, combating evil with evil!'

Another said,

'It becomes an issue of self-protection. A social ghetto is created with that sort of girly speculation – who is? who isn't? – it's not a happy state of affairs when you have to behave like twelve-year-old schoolgirls. It's funny that all gay boys, as soon as they're pop stars, are off with anyone. It's quite the reverse with women. From being an old slag prior to success, I've become a withdrawn shell of a person. I sublimate it all with cats.'

Many top female entertainers are gay, but fear of discrimination has kept them closeted, or, if they have been open, firmly on the sidelines. Speculation has become a tabloid sport, however. Even after marriage and motherhood in the early 1990s Whitney Houston, for example, was still the target of conjecture and 'outing' campaigns. Capitol Records didn't know how to promote their British singer Horse, who, as well as having a huge, powerful voice, had a butch image and masculine suits. They first publicized her with the line, 'Is It A Man Or A Beast?', an unflattering, misjudged joke. 'They didn't ask me. They thought, "Let's try sensationalism." And it didn't work. They should have concentrated on music as opposed to image,' she told me in 1999.[22]

Several determined individuals nevertheless began to break into the pop market in the late 1980s. Phranc, the self-billed 'Jewish lesbian folksinger', put lesbianism on the map in the major-label industry when she was signed to Island. Though still seen as a marginal novelty when she came on to the scene in the mid-1980s, Phranc was one of the first 'out' lesbians to market her music away from the margins. After touring with Morrissey in 1991, she said,

'Margie Adam and Cris Williamson were my heroes. I really respect Olivia for making a place for women musicians, although most of their artists remain relatively obscure. For me it's really important to be out in the middle of pop music to reach young lesbians and gays who are coming out. I was starved of that. It's strange that it's accepted for Bowie to go through his camp phase, but as soon as women play with gender roles they say, "Oh she's a dyke, she hates men." It's pathetic.'[23]

Apart from other major-label acts Ferron, the Indigo Girls and Two Nice Girls, women artists tend to avoid the sexuality issue by keeping it ambiguous, or relying on 'non-specific gender references' (NGRs) in love songs – the famous 'you', rather than 'she'. When asked how long it would take before lesbians were accepted by the industry, Tracy Chapman, veteran of many women's festivals, said carefully, 'It's going to be a long time.' Though she fought shy of gay categories, Chapman, like

Lennox, found freedom in refusing to dress to please the 'sex sells' cheesecake lobby. When her 1988 self-titled debut went to the top of the album charts she sent a strong signal within the industry that dressing down, or dressing 'asexual', does not mean commercial death.

Late-1980s folk/roots star Michelle Shocked likewise didn't let go of her dishevelled 'urchin' look until her third album *Captain Swing*, feeling that she had a duty to create 'a more realistic image of women'. Her semi-androgynous image arose out of a survivalist tactic when as a hitch-hiker she felt the need to dress as a boy to protect herself. Working in the music industry later required a similar kind of nerve. 'I went to some extremes, starting as a nihilistic punk with a mohawk and a ring in my nose. In the course of life I'll find a middle ground, but I wouldn't want to feel like a sell-out.[24] By 1989 she felt established enough to explore her feminine side, wearing a short skirt and red lipstick for her Robert Palmer spoof 'On The Greener Side'. The move wasn't made without a 'lipstick' crisis, however. 'I carry around a sense of responsibility, an opportunity to defeat existing stereotypes in the media. And if I soften the edges – whether I need to personally or whether it's being imposed on me – I feel I'd be letting down the revolution!' She also felt an onus on her to be an honorary lesbian, even though her sexual identity was never clear-cut, and she eventually announced plans to marry her road manager. 'I felt like I was put in a position where I was damned if I did "come out" and damned if I didn't . . . So for my part, I just leave the question open.'

This strategic ducking of categories was disrupted in the early 1990s when, riding on the crest of Lipstick Lesbian chic – a period when lesbians suddenly became media favourites – singer k.d. lang finally achieved the unachievable: recognition as an openly gay artist and a million-seller at the heart of pop's mainstream, with major-label backing. No mean feat.

She chose to enter it via one of the most difficult routes in the industry: country music. An area where top women like Dolly Parton, Tammy Wynette and Loretta Lynn had to fight their way out of gruelling schedules and oppressive conditions, country expected its women to be sweet, versatile and, above all, non-complaining. In 1977, for instance, when Loretta Lynn was knocked over by marauding fans at Nashville's annual Fan Fair, she maintained a brave silence. One of the unofficial rules for girl country singers was that, no matter how famous you were, you should never offend the fans.

Maybe country music was k.d.'s test case. If she could make it in one of the most conservative genres in the business, she could theoretically make it anywhere. lang didn't subscribe to Nashville's 'the higher the hair, the closer to God' philosophy. She started out as an alternative cabaret artist, discovering a love of country while portraying Patsy Cline in a college musical. Despite her claim that she was the reincarnation of that rootin', tootin' mid-1950s cowgirl, Nashville refused to take k.d. seriously, suspecting that the Canadian cross-dresser was sending them up. If at a 1970s award ceremony star Charlie Rich could tear up the card announcing John Denver as Country Artist of the Year – because the bespectacled one was 'too pop' – where indeed would an androgynous girl in a suit fit?

The answer lies in her background. Born Kathy Dawn Lang in 1961, she was raised in Consort, Alberta, a typical Canadian prairie town with one main street and a skyline broken by tall grain elevators. lang was a tomboy who lay on the floor of her pharmacist father's dispensary, shooting targets hung at the back with revolvers and shotguns. He bought a guitar for her when she was six, and after he left the family when she was twelve she would speed out to the prairie on her motorbike, away from the unexpressed pain at home. 'I love the feel of them. I love the aloneness. I love moving and seeing things. I like the romance of being on a motorcycle,' she said.[25]

Her upbringing was liberal, her mother a supportive woman who admired lang's 'handsomeness'. Hence lang has grown up with a robust self-confidence and a clear will: she is a modern pioneer, ploughing across the prairies to her mythical West. Although not a great beauty – she has an angular, outdoors, butch gait, in some lights she's even plain – she exudes a healthy self-assurance that appeals across gender and music genres. lang is the man every woman would love to be protected by, and the guy every man would have as his best friend. Her prairie-girl persona reflects the world of *Patience and Sarah*, Isabel Miller's famous lesbian love-story set in pioneer America.

Causing a kind of 'lesbian Beatlemania', lang succeeded through romanticism, her lush love lyrics and a sparkling, wayward charm. No wonder Madonna once remarked about her, 'Elvis is alive. And she's beautiful.' Established Nashville star Minnie Pearl also assessed her impact within country. 'We admire k.d. for her voice and because there is nothing phoney about her,' she said. 'I think k.d. represents the freedom we all wish we had.'

From the wild rockabilly of her major label Warners debut *Angel With A Lariat* (1987), to the pure country of *Shadowlands* (produced by Nashville mandarin Owen Bradley) to 1989's *Absolute Torch And Twang*, lang plugged into every feeling and fibre of country, but, according to her, Nashville wasn't listening. In spite of the fact she was selling millions and winning Grammys, country radio gave her no crucial airtime. The only way to deal with a lesbian who wore 1940s suits and teased her hair into an Elvis quiff was to ignore her. That was until 1990, when lang appeared in a People for the Ethical Treatment of Animals (PETA) advert, saying, 'If you knew how meat was made, you'd lose your lunch. I know. I'm from cattle country and that's why I became a vegetarian.'

Although controversy meant that the advert was never broadcast, word was strong enough to ensure that radio stations in the beef areas of Alberta and Nebraska pulled lang from their playlists, the 'Home of k.d. lang' sign in Consort was scrawled with the elegant phrase 'EAT BEEF DYKE' and lang was vilified throughout Canada and the US as a 'cow hugger'. It was this hostility that led to her describing Nashville as a bunch of 'rednecks and Christians'. However, within Nashville there were plenty of influential people rooting for her and some felt that lang didn't understand Southern working-class music, with its female singers too easily written off as 'white-trash wives'. They felt she had *made* herself an outsider. 'For her to say that

Nashville wasn't fair to her when she had the king [Owen Bradley], the man who gave birth to Music Row, produce one of her records?' said one insider. 'Well, she can kiss my hillbilly ass.'[26]

Rejection, self-engineered or not, made lang more resolved. In 1992 she recorded the cross-over album *Ingénue*, attracting a whole new mainstream audience. Three months after its release she declared herself a lesbian in a cover story for *The Advocate*. Madonna's flirtation with butch chic may have conveyed a glamorous hint of lesbianism, but lang was the first to consolidate the work of artists such as Cris Williamson, Holly Near and Phranc by making lesbianism a visible, unequivocal reality. This reached a peak when she appeared on the cover of *Vanity Fair* 'butched up', being shaved by supermodel Cindy Crawford. 'k.d. wasn't too sure about it at first,' said her photographer Herb Ritts. 'But then she relaxed and really got into it.'[27]

'There was a part of me that really didn't think it was important to make an announcement,' said lang. 'But to the gay community, saying "I'm a lesbian" is dispelling any doubt.'

At the level where sexuality and commerce meet, the stakes are high. Behind what appeared to be a simple decision were complex machinations – from the nervous staff at Warners, the politicking on *The Advocate* magazine itself, to the reverberations in the pop industry. Along with the decision came an almost collective sigh of relief. 'I mean, you can't be with the woman and not know she's gay,' said US TV producer June Cross. 'It's like trying not to look at the white elephant.'[28]

Torie Osborn, executive director of the National Gay and Lesbian Task Force, felt that lang's openness was of key importance.

'She's been the first major woman pop star who's out and proud and fine about it. It signals a whole new era of possibility for celebrities,' she said in 1993. lang being the first out lesbian to be nominated for a Grammy gave other lesbians in pop, such as Melissa Etheridge and Janis Ian, courage to come out as well.

lang used the power of androgyny to protect a personal vulnerability: 'Androgyny is important in my life because I can deal

**k.d. lang**
at WEA Records
UK, 1993: the first
'out' lesbian in
mainstream pop.
(Pennie Smith)

with people on a human, not a sexual, level; it's important on stage because both men and women are attracted to me.' Not at ease with her full, womanly body, she covered it up from the start of her career. Only she would dictate when, where and how she would expose herself. She initialized herself k.d. because k.d. is 'a name, not a sexuality'. She said a woman's body was so overused in the entertainment industry that maybe her androgyny was 'deep rebellion': 'I don't understand my own feminine power yet, in terms of my body. I don't know how to use my femininity as a powerful tool. I use my sexuality but I eliminate the gender from it. I think the male thing is just a way of surviving – outside. Inside I'm completely a woman.'[29]

Kansas-born Melissa Etheridge grafted for seven years before her 1993 album *Yes I Am* propelled her through to rock's major league, reaching sales of over 6 million and spawning Top Ten US hits. Ironically her huge success coincided with her coming out. An artist with economic arrangements and a powerful delivery, she has been compared to Bruce Springsteen, and hailed as the first woman artist really capable, as *LA Times* critic Steve Hochman said, of becoming 'a US heartland rock figure'. Her honesty compelled her to be open about her sexuality.

'k.d. lang was the first big star to come out. I was talking to her during that whole time, telling her, "Yeah, go do it!" Then I thought, what am I saying? I need to follow my own advice,' Etheridge told me in 1995.[30]   At the 1992 Gay & Lesbian Inaugural Ball for President Clinton, Etheridge grabbed the mike, made her announcement ('I'm proud to be a lesbian') and phoned her publicist. 'When I signed to Island in 1986, Chris Blackwell said, "We're not into flag-waving." Then when I came out I called the publicist and said, "Hey, here we go." She said, "Well, all right. I guess we'll line up the gay press." Everyone was fine.'

It was interesting how Etheridge's announcement didn't affect her sales in mid-America – despite public support for women's issues and gay rights, she still managed to bring teenage Beavis & Butthead fans to her shows in droves. 'I'm just normal, painfully everyday and of the Midwest. They can see

**Melissa Etheridge** live: 'I have twisted the American Dream . . . I am showing it's available to anyone.' (Mick Hutson/ Redferns)

that and relate to that,' she says. 'Their attitude is kinda, "She may be a lesbian, but she doesn't have green hair and sings in a way I understand. Let's live and let rock".' Etheridge was jubilant that she and lang could combat prejudice:

'I have twisted the American dream. I've come from lower middle class nothing to the big city and built it up. I've got the house, the car and the fame, but I'm not a man, or straight – what the Dream was originally built on. Now I'm showing it's available to anyone.' [31]

## Zami Girls

While lang's image was more an expression of herself than a parody of masculinity, when drag queens became popular again in the wake of supermodels, there was an element of ridicule and hostility in their imitation of women. Careful to protect a non-threatening, gently humorous image, RuPaul said,

'Lots of queens throughout history are fiery 'cos drag puts you in a position of power. When people without power get it, honey, there's no stopping 'em . . . miaow, miaow! Some boys abuse their power as good fairies. It's amazing what comes out of a person in drag – like when someone takes acid for the first time, or after drinking, we ask, is someone a nice drunk or an evil drunk?'

The impulse to 'do drag' has never been restricted to gay men, with male heavy metal artists doing a kind of low-budget approximation of the style. Outfits like Kiss took 1970s glam into the 1980s with full make-up and outrageously teased hair, while Guns 'N' Roses adopted the garb as a statement of male bravado. For Guns 'N' Roses, cross-dressing was less about empowerment than about theatrical rock cliché – a factor at first subverted by early-1990s grunge rock bands such as Nirvana and Smashing Pumpkins, who wore floral granny dresses and smudged lipstick as an anti-macho rock-hero device and a gesture of solidarity with the Riot Grrrl movement. When acts such as Stone Temple Pilots, The Lemonheads' Evan Dando and The Manic Street Preachers started to follow suit, their pose appeared to be more about empty self-promotion than straight subversion.

As if in reaction to this, hardcore rock bands bred within their ranks a movement known as Queercore. Arising from gay urban centres like London and San Francisco, a series of predominantly lesbian bands promoted their version of 1990s dyke culture. Fired by punk and Riot Grrrl, groups such as Tribe 8, Random Violet, The Mudwimmin and Malibu Barbie in the US, along with Britain's Sister George and The Children's Hour, made loud, angry riff-driven rock music on everything from sex, oppression and SIM to homophobia. 'The queer scene and the punk scene have always been linked for me,' said Random Violet's singer Allison Hennessey. 'Both are about being as loud about it as you can, so that everyone will see and hear it.' Their addiction to hardcore thrash flew in the face of the more melodic output of 1970s labels like Olivia, music that had become a drippy, hated orthodoxy to a younger generation. As well as reacting against straight homophobic society, they included among their targets the 'gayristocracy' of white gay men that had formed its own establishment within the music scene – as Sister George's manager said so piquantly on Channel 4, 'those poncy cappuccino-drinking gits in Old Compton Street'.

After the initial flurry of media interest in Queercore, however, by 1994 bands were wishing to establish themselves on the basis of their music as much as their sexual identity. The challenge was in finding a way to be open without being boxed in by media labels. 'I don't want the whole world to buy our records just because I'm a dyke,' said Eliot, lead singer of Sister George. 'I want them to buy our records 'cos we're brilliant!'

Adele Bertei, former keyboardist with avant-garde funker James 2 Chance and singer with late-1970s all-female New York punk band The Bloods, felt she had come full circle by the early 1990s, arriving at a point that was far more positive for lesbians in pop. 'When I started out I met up with these weird androgynes who were just making a row. From there I got my own female band together, The Bloods. We were very outspoken as lesbians, but were unfortunately all going through our heroin period at the time. We were very dysfunctional and kinda crazy.'[32] The band split up in the early 1980s, but Bertei's song-writing was noticed and she was signed to Geffen. In spite of her collaboration on hits with such artists as Jellybean and Thomas Dolby, there was uncertainty about how to market her. Her 1988 Chrysalis record *Little Lives* got good reviews but was not a big seller, partly because Bertei had to be circumspect about her sexuality. 'At Chrysalis I was compromising myself by not always telling the truth. I wrote a song about a Persian boy, but it wasn't about a boy, it was about a Persian woman. But I didn't feel the strength or the courage at that point to come out.'

By 1994 Bertei was writing again, having a hit on Imago with the openly gay rap-club track 'Zami Girl'. (Zami is a term for lesbian love from Andre Lorde's book *Zami: A New Spelling of My Name*.) 'I don't want any skeletons in my closet any more. This is who I am,' she said. Though aware that lesbianism had become 'hip', Bertei wanted the message relayed with integrity:

'It's not just about being flavour of the month, ambiguity in the lyrics or a series of fashion statements. Popular music has always maintained a silence on gay love, and the truth of the oppression we live with has to be spoken, too . . . that we're human beings who have a right to be respected for who we are. I don't think it should be a problem for the record industry. In my mind if someone is upfront about their sexuality and humanism and lives a life of dignity – then people are going to be attracted to them whether they're straight or gay.'

Bisexual singer/songwriter Sophie B. Hawkins echoed this sentiment when she said in *Diva* magazine: 'You have all these artists who come out and never make a stand in their lyrics about themselves or their sexuality. That's why I distrust some of these artists. It's not being true to yourself and I've always tried to be true to myself.'[33] In 1992 she burst onto the scene with the hit 'Damn I Wish Was Your Lover', a seductive, soulful tune about lesbian attraction. Although her first two albums, *Toes And Tails* (1992) and *The Whaler* (1995) were big sellers, Hawkins' record company Columbia seemed to keep her at arm's length. It was rumoured that they were unhappy about her doing interviews with the gay press for fear of her being typecast as 'that lesbo who sang "Damn I Wish I Was Your Lover"'. When her third album, *Timbre*, came out in 2000, they did minimal promotion. She split with Columbia the following year, and re-released the record on her own label. 'It was hard. But I feel like I'm a sail boat that's been through adversity . . . and I've actually come through the other side,' she said.

Some artists brazened it out, and were lucky to have sympathetic record labels. Skin, for instance, the bald, beautiful black frontwoman of rock band Skunk Anansie who was open about her bisexuality became a pin-up for men and women alike. She coined the term 'clit rock' as an alternative to 'cock rock', playfully describing it as: 'slippery, wet, swollen and full on'. Compared to every black female singer from Aretha Franklin to Grace Jones, Skin told me that, in terms of delivery, she had more in common with Robert Plant. She was perplexed that because she sang loudly and made faces, people found her threatening.

'I may seem scary on stage but I don't walk around being scary 24 hours a day. I'm not that one-dimensional. I know I'm aggresive and in people's faces, but what's scary is you have someone like me doing that. If it was just a white guy no one would worry. It's the old black lesbian thing – she's got a bald head, she's hard. It's almost taking away my femininity.'[34]

As her band got bigger, Skin was aware of the pressure to be a more typical 'girly' singer. 'We'll go to a certain point in breaking America, but I won't make announcements that I'm heterosexual,' she said. 'Otherwise you're not happy with yourself, not happy about why you're in this industry. You've lost your integrity.'[35]

Embarking on a solo career with Virgin Records in 2001, Skin was still open about her sexuality, but by then it seemed that the impetus for major stars to come out had stopped at k.d. lang and Melissa Etheridge. The fate of TV comedy star Ellen DeGeneres and movie actress Anne Heche (whose careers suffered immeasurably once they came out as a couple) sent a chill wind

**Skin:**
defying genres, she
coined the term
'clit rock'.
(Sainted PR)

through the world of entertainment in the late 1990s. 'Sorry to say it, but coming out as a lesbian still means a loss of sales,' one gay pop star told me.

Etheridge, however, was still fighting. In 2001 she came out with *Skin*, the best album of her career. A journey through her break-up with long-term girlfriend Julie Cypher, it was a powerful, moving solo set. In promoting the record, Etheridge didn't shirk from telling the truth, explaining the custody arrangements for their two children and what it was like being a lesbian parent. When I asked her if the Ellen DeGeneres/Anne Heche affair had forced people back into the closet, Etheridge shrugged, saying: 'No one will do it that way again. My current girlfriend Tammy says, "Don't throw me on the cover of a magazine just because I'm gay." The path will be different. There's no point in going backwards, you can only go forwards.'

Black women have historically encountered what Maya Angelou termed 'double jeopardy' – the double bind of sexism and racism. Despite being the mainstay and foundation of much of modern pop, they have also been the most stereotyped and misunderstood. By the early 1990s they were ready to let fly.

# 9 I Wanna Dance with Somebody

DECONSTRUCTING THE DISCO DIVA

'I WAS VERY UPSET. Then when I saw her in the videos I said, No, no, no, this can't be happening. There was a rumour going round that she wasn't even a woman. Oh God, I thought, they put a man dressed as a woman! I think it's wrong. A lot of people believed it was her vocals – except for people who knew me and my voice. For a while it was downright awful.'[1]

It took twenty-stone (280-pound) Martha Wash a long time before she could listen to the biggest house record of 1989 'Ride On Time' without 'committing a crime'. Although it was her powerhouse vocals which guaranteed the success of this and several other hits from Italian house act Black Box's hugely successful *Dreamland* LP, she wasn't given a credit on the album sleeve. Then when Wash saw a leggy model with endless hair and a wasp waist fronting the band in videos and on tour, lipsynching vocals originally laid down by Wash herself, she exploded. 'I had to talk about it in print,' she told me after months of lengthy litigation and a court settlement with BMG/RCA Records. 'If someone is trying to take the credit for something you know you've done, you have to speak out.'

When disco returned in the form of house music in the late 1980s, so did the crushing weight of production-line anonymity for – usually – black women vocalists. Many a top house record not only used hooklines from session singers employed for that specific track, but frequently sampled from 1970s soul and hi-energy singers such as Loleatta Holloway, Vicki Anderson or Wash herself. Wash refused to grin and bear it, like so many sessioneers are forced to in the business. Instead she sued; and sued and settled again when producers Clivilles & Cole tried the same trick with C&C Music Factory's breakthrough hit

'Gonna Make You Sweat'. Her story became a kind of industry test case for other singers.

'I was determined not to let people get away with it. Eventually everything was settled and credit was given. Musicians come up to me and say, "We know what you're doing and we're glad."' Wash took a risk that paid off. By 1992 she had her own major album deal on RCA, and later that year was invited to sing at President Clinton's Inauguration bash. Perhaps it was the years singing with disco star Sylvester and as one half of the camp *cause célèbre* The Weather Girls, belting out 'It's Raining Men', that gave Wash the sense of self-worth that fuelled her legal battles.

She also took a stand against the blatant stigmatizing of age and weight on the quick-sell club scene, where the 'sexy black chick' image is often used to market a record. 'We have a hard problem dealing with someone who doesn't look wonderful in front of the camera. If she doesn't look how she should, it's not commercially viable.' The tyranny Wash referred to has affected black women from the beginning of the pop industry, but it was disco that cemented their role as the Voice of synthesized dance music.

## It's Raining Men

'Sisters who sing are the great romantic icons of gay culture, the heart of the music business, and the inspiration for generation after generation of sisters who sing to keep on singing. Sisters who sing are beautiful and soulful. If you're not careful, they'll break your heart just like a real deep blues.'

NELSON GEORGE, *Buppies, B-Boys, Baps & Bohos*

In 1975 the strange surreal sensual sound of a woman's orgasm locked for seventeen minutes into a hypnotic synthesized beat dominated the radio waves. Donna Summer's 'Love To Love You Baby' set a completely new tone for female pop. The apogee of Euro disco, Summer was a Boston singer who went to Germany in 1967 with a production of *Hair*, and stayed. She linked warm gospel vocals with the Teutonic exactness of producer Giorgio

Moroder's epic disco, becoming one of the few divas of the era to achieve longevity as an album artist. In the same way that Billie Holiday rose with the success of the new juke-box in the 1940s, so Summer capitalized on the advent of the 12-inch single in 1976. There are two schools of thought as to what constituted the major musical event of the late 1970s – white rock fans claim it was punk, while dance adherents swear by the invention of the 12-inch. DJ pressure to keep butts dancing and hustling meant that by the early 1970s plain old 45s weren't long enough, with artists like James Brown beginning to release singles in Parts I and II, which DJs segued together on the disco floor. Responding to the need for a new format, American companies manufactured 12-inches first as a promotional tool, then by 1976 as commercial releases. Summer's extended mixes were among the first of the new breed, with hits such as 'I Feel Love', 'Heaven Knows', 'MacArthur Park' and 1979's 'Bad Girls' becoming disco classics. Of the pioneering work she did with Moroder, Summer said, 'In its time it was very different, and I'm thankful that I was the person it was designed for.'

Originating in the New York gay male underground at clubs such as The Garage, by the early 1980s disco had transmuted into hi energy, with the speeding up of bpms (beats per minute). Apart from Evelyn Thomas's huge 1984 hit 'High Energy' and Frankie Goes To Hollywood's 'Relax', hi energy never crossed into the mainstream like disco. Though centred on a few small labels such as Nightmare, Passion and Ian Levine's Record Shack in Britain, and 'O' Records in the US, its influence on house, techno and chart pop was still considerable. As well as basic beats and production, hi energy pioneered a distinctive singing style, with divas of the genre such as Evelyn Thomas, Miquel Brown, Barbara Pennington and Earlene Bentley diving through peaks, crescendos and never-ending high-pitched soprano notes. Thomas in particular rolled a robust gospel voice through hits like 'Masquerade' and 'Reflections' with both a rawness and cathartic expertise that would never have sat easily in the pop charts. Though strong, innovative vocalists, these women were regarded as a kind of substratum within dance music, the unfair equivalent of aspiring actresses who get stuck doing porn movies.

To the gay community, however, they were heroines. 'Their vocals were meaningful,' one gay friend told me. 'They related to gay people's experiences and dreams. Just look at the titles "Coming Out Of Hiding", "Stranger In Disguise", "Cold Shoulder" – they said so much.' These, together with the tongue-in-cheek irony of tracks like 'So Many Men, So Little Time', 'He's A Saint, He's A Sinner' and 'All American Boy' summed up gay men's experience more accurately than the 'straight' romance of the regular charts. That special connection between gay man and dance diva continued well into the 1990s. When singer Jody Watley, for instance, released the single 'When A Man Loves A Woman' from her 1994 *Intimacy* album, the radio-play A side was jettisoned by DJs soon after release in favour of the 6-minute B side 'When A Man Loves A Man'. Ground-breaking in its sensual sympathy, as well as focusing on gay love as a 'beautiful thing', it featured the stark reminder that two men together know the reality of AIDS.

Donna Summer became successful in the 1970s through the support of this key market, but when AIDS began to take hold in the early 1980s, she denounced her following with Born Again fervour. Commercially, though, Summer probably felt the risk of alienating such a core constituency was worth taking – by 1987 she was playing Lake Tahoe and singing about 'Dinner With Gershwin', a supposed step 'up' in showbiz stakes. An unusually enduring personality for the genre, Summer was an atypical dance diva. Most fell victim to the ruthlessness of the disco underground: black women needed more than God, good luck and a decent hairdresser to push through the inequities of club culture, where singers had continually to fight to be more than just a face for a DJ producer's grand plan.

### Heat You up (Melt You Down)

The image of black women in soul music as little more than pliant girl groupies has been a hangover from the 1960s girl-group era. The unprecedented respect for Aretha Franklin's gutbucket soul created a new area of possibilities for women in the late 1960s, but it wasn't until the early 1970s that an all-female space-age group of glam funk rockers styled and managed by a woman really broke the mould.

Former *Ready Steady Go!* producer Vicki Wickham took three black girls, disregarded the dictates of acceptable feminine 'poise' and 'class', and changed a supper-club soul act into the space-age LaBelle. She recalled,

'When Patti first asked me to manage them I was reluctant. The name Patti LaBelle and The Bluebelles sounded so old. I said, "If we're going to do this, it's a new day. You've been together sixteen years, you can't get arrested. You can't wear those nice little frilly frocks and wigs, we've got to rethink it. You've got to make a statement, you're women, there's a lot to be said."

'At that stage they were being managed by a real gangster-type from Brooklyn who threatened to put me at the bottom of a river – real bad news. With me it really was a new day. They had a lot of fun with the silver and feathers – they grew up, and for the first time they were participating in their careers and their lives.'[2]

'She didn't want us to be like Diana Ross and The Supremes,' Nona Hendryx recalled. 'We were LaBelle, an equal amount of energy and personality. We were nurtured to grow to our possibilities.'[3] Their voodoo Creole pastiche on strutting street prostitution, 'Lady Marmalade', was an international No. 1 hit in 1975, flagging their top-selling album *Nightbirds*, a defiant mixture of pop, rock and soul categories. Twelve years later and after the success of her 1986 power-ballad duet with Michael MacDonald 'On My Own', Patti LaBelle said,

'I thought people would boo us because we'd gone too far. I was afraid of change . . . but when we went out and did it, I said, Good! Three outrageous black women who wore and said anything on stage. Although with "Lady Marmalade" I swear I had no idea for a while what it meant, until I asked Bob Crewe who recorded it, "What's *voulez-vous coucher avec moi?*" He told me. "Oh gosh," I said, "what will my mother think?"'[4]

LaBelle enjoyed massive cult success, but despite respectable sales on follow-up albums, there was confusion about how to market the trio, and they split in the late 1970s. The subsequent story of LaBelle encapsulates the divergent streams within post-1960s black music, with Hendryx veering off into more exacting funk rock and state-of-the-art production, Patti LaBelle performing a gospel-influenced pop crossover and Sarah Dash opting for more subtle, jazz-tinged soul. LaBelle imploded, partly due to the differences of three such separate personalities, but also because radio in particular couldn't find a place for strong black women working against the categories. Sisters who sing may swing, but they also have to know their place.

Within the more regular confines of soul and disco, black women created a crucial role for themselves. By the late 1970s the Voice became the pivot around which the new synthesized dance music swung; in the craze for percussive drive and often ruthlessly formulaic bpms the female voice acted as purveyor of emotion, sensitivity and human warmth. Its roots lay in the combination of two influences – the sweeping, orchestrated soul of Philadelphia International stars such as The Three Degrees and Barry White's trio Love Unlimited and the more downbeat 'realism' and street funk groove of acts like First Choice and Betty Davis. A trio signed to Philly Groove, First Choice had a pop hit in 1973 with 'Armed And Extremely Dangerous', but singing about pimps, prostitutes and gangsters, they sold more to a black audience tuned into the new blaxploitation movies. Betty Davis, meanwhile, wife of jazz player Miles, was a self-styled funky chick who growled to rigorously hip street grooves in liberated 1970s style with songs like 'If I'm In Luck I Might Get Picked Up' or 'Anti Love Song'. Both reflected a move away from the idealism and desire for upward mobility that figured in the black community before the 1968 assassination of Martin Luther King. That street funk strand has remained, with the success in the early 1980s of outfits such as The Jones Girls and Bernadette Cooper's Klymaxx, who made cult feminist classics like 'The Meeting In The Ladies Room' and 'Never Underestimate The Power Of A Woman', before Cooper went on to create the similarly liberated trio Madame X.

Set against this trend in 'realism' The Three Degrees were unfairly dismissed by critics as 'black Barbie dolls', though former key member Sheila Ferguson told me in 1994 that there was some truth in the term. 'I'd agree with that. We were as soulful as white people could handle at the time. That was the way the white world perceived blackness – glitzy, slick, feminine and smooth.'[5] Throughout the 1970s Ferguson, Fayette Pinkney and Valerie Holiday had a series of hits that spoke directly to their constituency of women from the bold tones of 'Dirty Ol' Man' to the lush longing of 'Year Of Decision' in 1973 and 'When Will I See You Again?' in 1974, which was No. 1 across the globe. More knowing than The Supremes, they sang of morning-after heartache in a decade of fashionable non-

**The Three Degrees:** Philly International's 'black Barbie dolls': 'We were as soulful as white people could handle at the time.' (Mick Patrick's private collection)

monogamy. The glitz and the gowns were the perfect accessory for their label Philadelphia International, who boasted the Gamble & Huff production team, and the house orchestra MFSB (Mother Father Sister Brother – or, more uncharitably, MotherFuckin'SonovaBitch) who augmented many 1970s soul hits. 'Kenny [Gamble] was wonderful in that he gave me the confidence to sing. He knew I was insecure, and he brought out Sheila. But then we'd take the bows and the record company would take the money,' said Ferguson.

At first the women enjoyed emotional closeness and camaraderie; their worst arguments centred on buying shoes. They left the Gamble & Huff stable in 1975 to work with Giorgio Moroder who, fresh from producing Donna Summer, gave The Three Degrees a few Top Ten hits such as 'Woman In Love' and 'The Runner'. Once the run of hits dried up, though, the strain soon began to show. Fed up with a manager who insisted they 'sit around looking pretty', and who deflated their egos by saying, 'People applaud you because they're sorry for you', The Three Degrees tried to take a new direction in 1983. Ferguson said,

'I wanted to go punk. But the others wanted to stay steady, sequinned and secure. I said, "We're looking like Bassey here, we've got to keep changing." I felt I had to suppress my talent to be equal with the other two. To stay sane I had to get out. It was stifling, strangling, like the full spectrum of a marriage. Once I left, we lost touch. Now I should get a T-shirt saying, "I Don't Know Where The Other Two Are".'

Ferguson went on to write a best-selling book about soul food,[6] and moved permanently to Britain where in the early 1990s she launched her own TV production company and the 1991 sitcom *Land of Hope and Gloria*. Back in the early 1970s her options were more limited. She was performing on a scene where the division between tough funk and swoony ballads was strict, if soft soul was your role you had to stick to it. These definitions began to break down with the arrival of female groups like The Pointer Sisters. Originally a California family group of close-harmony scat singers, by the mid-1970s the Pointers had ditched their 1940s nostalgia material in favour of hard-hitting pre-disco tracks such as 'How Long (Betcha Got A Chick On The Side)'. Their penchant for rock spice didn't fully emerge until the early 1980s with hits like 'Automatic' and 'I'm So Excited', but they projected a new versatility for black women in music.

It wasn't until the end of the decade that another group of sisters cropped up with that crucial commercial hybrid of funk and soul, via the bass-driven Philadelphia disco of producers Bernard Edwards and Nile Rodgers. His band Chic had already broken new ground with hot, tight dance-floor smashes like 'Everybody Dance', 'Le Freak' and 'Good Times' when he picked up on Sister Sledge, an all-girl family outfit previously floundering on Atlantic who had the resonant tones and teen spirit required for a younger disco sound. Originally groomed for Jackson-type stardom, when Joni, Kathy, Debbie and Kim linked their sassy sparkle to Nile Rodgers's bass drive in 1979, they created a dynamic new pop.

Long-legged, with toothy grins, Sister Sledge were welcome personalities amid the faceless glut of disco product, radiating an odd combination of designer style and quirky exuberance. What is interesting about Sledge is that they sang not of traditional female topics like boyfriend trouble, but of being 'down' in club-land, 'Lost In Music', there not to attract a man, but simply to be consumed by the music. Even when they did fancy someone, he had to be the 'Greatest Dancer' wearing Gucci and Fiorucci. Though being a good sheltered Christian girl, Kathy Sledge admits that at first, 'I didn't know who Fiorucci was!'[7] Their pride in being strong, united women was reflected in the smash hit 'We Are Family', a song celebrating church and family values that ironically became a huge lesbian anthem. This song conveyed a strong emotional truth. 'That didn't come from me and Bernard. That came from those girls walkin' into the studio, listening to the track and responding. They did it in one take,' recalls Nile Rodgers.[8]

As disco receded into the gay male underground in the early 1980s, Sledge more directly addressed their young female fan following with pop songs like 'All-American Girls' and 'Frankie'. 'We knew that we were role models for young girls,' Debbie Sledge said. 'That was why we made "All-American Girls" . . . it was about being proud of your womanhood and standing up for your rights.'[9]

Unable to sustain their success, the Sisters disappeared and came back in 1993, but it was only for the re-release of their old disco hits. Barely in their thirties, the girls were being treated like nostalgic has-beens. 'That kind of throws us off, people think we're going to be in wheelchairs when they see us,' Kathy said.[10] Debbie pinpointed the problem when she said, 'After the success of "We Are Family", we felt we had proved ourselves and now it was our turn to get some support. But we didn't get it. And the reason was that we were black and we were women. We didn't have the money, power or influence.'

### Didn't We Almost Have It All?

One night in the summer of 1987 I walked into Sigma Sound studios in New York. I was with a friend interviewing Pat Kane, the singer with Scottish post-modern pop band Hue and Cry, who happened to be recording a track with Sinatra's string section. As we trooped through, I noticed a smart black woman sitting in reception surrounded by beefy guys in leather jackets and chains. Staring at my flat-top haircut as I walked past, she said admiringly, 'Gee, look at the haircut.' I smiled, but didn't answer. When we got into the studio, Pat turned round to me and hissed, 'That was Whitney Houston!' I charged back out, but by then she had gone.

Houston then was a veritable Untouchable at the height of her early fame, thundering out straight power ballads. The fact she could still appreciate a subcultural haircut despite the saccharine nature of her public world pointed to the eternal dichotomy at the centre of the Houston phenomenon. 'She sings great, but she loves funky hardcore. She was not the girl next door when I worked with her,' said deadpan female producer and New York club DJ Toni C. 'She makes beautiful pop, but really likes to kick butt.'[11]

Houston broke the mould for black women soul singers in the mid-1980s by amassing the sort of money, power and influence that had historically eluded them. She achieved mainstream international success, but not without an element of compromise. Accepted by white family audiences, she lacked credibility among 'true' soul fans, her presence a source of knotty debate. 'I knew the critics were waiting for me,' she said, for instance, when the film *The Bodyguard*, in which she co-starred with Kevin Costner, came out. Whatever her apparent capitulation, soul in essence is a privilege, an emotional secret guarded by women. Houston's success, after her mother slogged through the 1960s as the archetypal underrated session singer, was sweet revenge.

'I was lucky because I got the star,' Houston once said. 'My mother, who was also my friend and my greatest teacher.' Emily 'Cissy' Drinkard Houston, who grew up in Newark, New Jersey, with her nieces Dionne and Dee Dee Warwick to become one of the top soul session singers, backing everyone from Aretha Franklin on 'Respect' to Warwick, Linda Ronstadt, Bette Midler and Luther Vandross, was a tough cookie. After her mother died when she was nine, the young Cissy found solace in God, a belief she transferred intact to her daughter Whitney. She also passed on talent, grooming and, together with Warwick, a training that is the envy of any soul sister who sings. Houston's father John said,

'When Whitney was a kid she used to go down to the basement of the house wearing her mother's stage outfits and start singing, and her mother would be doing the dishes in the kitchen, shouting down to Whitney, "You're not hitting the notes, come on, a little higher. That's it, that's the one, baby."'[12]

At seven Houston was in the recording studio, nose pressed up against the glass, watching her mother cut a record with Aretha. As an angular, shy fourteen-year-old she was singing backing vocals in Cissy's nightclub act. This was part of a solid training in which mom, 'aunt' Aretha and cousin Dionne would coach style, poise and delivery to such an extent that when she was signed to Arista in March 1983 Houston was well-primed for the Clive Davis masterplan: to create a star in the 1960s tradition of black female vocalists, but with a 1980s feel. It took years for *Whitney Houston*, the album, to be constructed.

After careful hiring of mainstream soul producers like Michael Masser, Narada Michael Walden and Kashif, plus months of expensive promotion and pitching the product right in the centre of the middle American MTV market, Houston fronted an album that couldn't fail. Both Cissy and John were fiercely protective of their daughter, guiding her through the business with professional commitment. When I saw them backstage after Houston's 1988 Birmingham NEC concert, I was struck by Cissy's determined composure, and by John, exuding street-cool dude in his immaculate camel-hair coat.

Houston had been a phenomenon waiting to happen. With the inroads black female stars had made into pop in the 1960s and 1970s, it was only a matter of time before a woman with the requisite talent would emerge from this competitive hotbed and cross over to pop on such an epic scale. A song fanatic who listened to new material twelve hours a day in his office, Davis harnessed the gospel force in Houston's voice as the perfect vehicle for the pop ballads he loved. Her self-titled debut album, released when she was just twenty-two years old, sold eighteen million copies worldwide. By 1988, with the follow-up *Whitney*, she had made $45 million and surpassed The Beatles' American record of seven consecutive No. 1s.

The resonant purity of her voice gave the corniest material an epic intensity: while much of it tipped into schmaltz, some of her key hits – 'Greatest Love Of All', 'Saving All My Love For You' and the later 'I Will Always Love You' – pulsated with pride and self-determination. While the first two albums went into the charts at No. 1, her third, *I'm Your Baby Tonight*, sold less well. Partly produced by LA & Babyface, it attempted to pick up a younger, hipper audience, but didn't quite straddle the divide. Booed at the Soul Train black music show awards ceremony, Houston's attempt to return to R&B roots was seen as plain cynical. Once asked whether she felt responsibility to the black

community as a black performer, Houston said, 'I don't like that question. It's so heavy! I'm an example to all people.'[13]

Taking criticism face-on, she said, 'When you reach a certain height you will stand out and you will always be criticized. My mother told me this would happen. "You think you're a success? You have seven No. 1 songs. They're gonna mess you up." She wasn't lying.'[14] In 1993, with the massive success of *The Bodyguard* and of the soundtrack album, which gave her eleven *Billboard* awards, the spotlight was almost unbearable. That same year she married rap artist Bobby Brown and retreated to her New Jersey mansion to have a child, a girl named Bobbi Kristina. Unsurprisingly, the world's biggest black female star felt the need to preserve her sanity and take stock.

Houston's success set a relentless standard; like Steffi Graf on the tennis circuit, she looked unbeatable. Maybe if she had been singing in the 1970s her main opponent would have been Minnie Riperton, the Chicago-born singer with the five-octave range whose 'Loving You' was a universal hit in 1974. Riperton's death from cancer in 1979 tragically foreshortened her career, but she would have had the versatility and range to beat

Houston to that top slot. It wasn't until the early 1990s that she had a serious rival in Mariah Carey (see Chapter 14), the young wife of Sony Records boss Tommy Mottola, whose capacity for murdering cover versions with vocal gymnastics on her *Music Box* album was even more flamboyant than Houston's.

In 1996 she was back with a starring role in *The Preacher's Wife*, and a well-received gospel album with choral backing. She followed this up with *My Love Is Your Love*, an album of soulful urban R&B that seemed to chime more accurately with her true taste. There were fewer of the histrionic ballads and more focus on content, as if motherhood had given her music a new grit and maturity. By 2001 she was facing the challenge of younger, fresher rap/R&B acts like Destiny's Child, Missy Elliott and Lil' Kim. Problems were surfacing, with rumours of serious drug abuse. That year she negotiated a $60 million five-album deal with her label Arista, and should have been at the top of her game. When she performed at the Michael Jackson tribute concert at New York's Madison Square Garden in the September, though, people were shocked at her appearance. She looked painfully thin and strained, and talked to no one else that night but her husband Bobby. After years of careful grooming, the squeaky clean image was finally falling apart.

Back in the 1980s, though, Houston had only two serious contenders for her crown. The first was Sade, whose first two albums *Diamond Life* and *Promise* had sold twelve million worldwide when in 1986, just two years after her debut, she appeared on the cover of *Time* magazine as the Queen of Cool. A hauntingly beautiful Anglo-Nigerian from Clacton-on-Sea, Sade turned her background as a St Martin's fashion student to advantage, exercising total control over her image as well as her music – a mix of cocktail jazz, soul and chart-friendly pop. 'You can get to a certain point by your courage. But after that you have to develop some sort of expertise to sustain your success,' she once said with typical professionalism.[15] The only British soul vocalist really to break America in the 1980s, Sade had an interpretation of soul that was European – less about glitz and gospel than understated classicism.

Despite the smooth international pop production of later
albums like *Stronger Than Pride* (1988) and *Love Deluxe* (1992),
Sade lays herself bare in her songwriting, in a way that even US
gangsta rappers appreciated. 'Hardcore rappers, whatever you
might think of them, tend to write from the heart,' she
suggested, 'And I think that they know what we do also comes
from the heart.'[16] In 1996 the birth of her daughter, Ila, led to a
return to a more rootsy sound. For *Lover's Rock* (2000) her
image was more 'natural', less diva-like, and its lilting reggae feel
made her seem positively downhome.

In the 1980s, Sade was slotted under the US trend of
'retronuevo', the recycling of vintage black styles such as
doowop and 1950s jazz R&B in updated formulas. Heading this
new market was Anita Baker, who stunned audiences worldwide
with her 1986 *Rapture* album. Unlike Houston she was not
cosseted to stardom, having to establish financial and artistic

independence through hard, lonely graft. Brought up in Detroit by her Aunt Lois, an imaginative entrepreneur who ran her own beauty parlour, Baker said, 'Lois taught me that a woman must be self-sufficient, and not depend on a man for money or attention. She was married to a guy who didn't meet her needs. She aspired to be her own person.'[17]

Starting out in the late 1970s as lead singer for R&B band Chapter Eight, in 1983 Baker was signed to maverick Otis Smith's LA label Beverly Glen. His manifesto at the end of the disco boom was simple: a return to honest-to-goodness classic soul. The label issued some of the 1980s finest soul albums, including Bobby Womack's 'The Poet' and 'Poet II', and Baker's legendary *The Songstress*. Its controlled mid-tempo tones worked against the fashionable dance music of the time, yet the quality of Baker's tracks coincided with the growing popularity of 'Quiet Storm' radio – a marketing term for slow subtle classic soul performed by such artists as Luther Vandross – and the rise in CD 'adult-oriented' soul. Baker found herself on a stylistic vanguard, but although *The Songstress* stayed in the US charts for over a year, she claims she 'never received a dime for that record', living on $200 a week. Legal hassles with Beverly Glen meant that although she got a deal with Elektra, release of her album *Rapture* was prevented until 1986, when the Houston invasion was well under way.

Baker, however, had a credibility that Houston lacked. Intellectually controlled yet highly emotive, songs like 'Sweet Love' and 'Caught Up In The Rapture' became international hits. With executive production and co-songwriting credits, Baker negotiated a position of power few singers, let alone black female singers, could readily expect on a major label debut. Her follow-up, *Giving You The Best That I Got*, sold less well, and by the early 1990s she had yet to come back with the verve of her first two albums. In 1986, though, Baker and Houston set the pace for wholesale record company investment in the next black female crossover star.

Some key names emerged in the scramble, many of them – Angela Winbush, Brenda Russell, Vaneese Thomas, LaLa

– already established in the business as songwriters or producers. The codes were strict: sophisticated soul complete with sleek delivery and smart dress. Although in one way it gave black women a new dignity and identity, another stereotype was created, that of the Buppie Princess. All were aware of a fight to find individuality in this new medium. Regina Belle, for instance, a determined young woman with a stunning 1987 debut of bluetones and piercing soul entitled *All By Myself*, studied the spiritual canon of Holiday, Vaughan and Washington, saying, 'You have to know your history. Originality seemed unattainable until I started listening to them.' Aware of the way black women were marketed either as Black Chic, animal raunch or gutsy blues, Belle tried to dodge labels with a self-conscious reserve. 'With racism from every standpoint, it's something you can't ignore, it has to be dealt with, or that will hold you back.'[18]

Vaneese Thomas, daughter of Rufus 'Funky Chicken' Thomas and sister of Carla, was a professional songwriter who found a niche for an eponymous solo album in 1987. She described her sound, subtle and web-weaving, as the result of 'an intellect that's hard to be reckoned with. I write about the complexities of relationships, how they work, or why they break down.' Her agenda, as distinct as Houston's or Baker's, led her to say optimistically, 'Black singers have always been there, but now we're thrust to prominence. I don't see it as competitive, there's a niche for everybody. It's time we controlled our own destinies.'[19]

Peggi Blu, a Broadway actress and top session singer for Vandross, Ashford & Simpson and Stevie Wonder who received accolades for her 1987 debut *Blu Blowin'*, was less charitable about the Whitney Effect. 'She's done no more than anyone else. She's pushed forward a certain style which is very calculated, nothing spontaneous.' Angry at the way black women were being lumped in one smooth soul category, Blu instilled poetry in her defiance. 'Some of us paint pictures when we sing. Some of us tell the story when we sing. Some of us sing, not yell.'[20]

Coolly wrinkling up her nose, Natalie Cole's comment just

before the release of her 1987 'comeback' album *Everlasting* was, 'I rate some of the competition, but a lot of them out there are basically doing the same thing.' Like Houston she had confidence born of pedigree, but whereas Whitney did not have to compete with her mother's reputation, merely augmenting it, Cole had to establish herself independently of the legendary Nat King Cole.

'I was comfortable with having a famous father until I started singing. Then it became a problem. Dealing with the force my father was created a stigma I couldn't overlook.' At first she reaped the family benefits, entering the music business almost effortlessly after college. Her 1975 debut album *Inseparable* yielded the classic hit of effervescent vocalizing 'This Will Be', but despite Grammy awards and platinum releases, Cole felt diminished by the inevitable comparisons to her father, disguising her insecurity with a runaway coke habit. 'I was wild and I didn't want anyone telling me what to do. I was successful, I had money: it was all very fast and impressive. Then coke became 90 per cent of my life. I was skinny, sick a lot and in bad shape. The jobs I was used to getting I wasn't getting.'[21]

Cole nearly died along with her career, but after a tough Minnesota rehab programme in the early 1980s, she re-emerged with a valued sense of identity. Cynics say that talking about her drug abuse ensured media coverage for the 'comeback', but despite the sensationalism, Cole went on to prove the longevity of her talent, spanning everything from the Springsteen rocker 'Pink Cadillac' to her thoughtful early 1990s tribute album *Unforgettable*. It was as if she had finally come to terms with her father's bequest.

By the late 1980s a complicated picture was emerging, with black women attempting to break out of more and more categories. In one corner Tracy Chapman sang protest folk, in another reigned Baker-style retronuevo, while Janet Jackson was defying the family and beginning to rival brother Michael as the voice of modern pop. Like Whitney Houston, Jackson was part of second-generation soul, a girl who had grown up in the rarefied atmosphere of a showbusiness family, one of the black aristocracy who dominated 1970s pop.

Growing up surrounded by brothers at the top of the Motown family tree, Jackson watched, learned and waited. A deliberate, careful performer, by the time she recorded her 1986 break-through album *Control*, she knew the industry inside-out, teaming up with the hottest production team of the mid-1980s, former Prince sidekicks Jimmy Jam and Terry Lewis.

Despite her illustrious lineage, Jackson had to struggle hard to create her own sound and image. A stage veteran from childhood, she appeared in the family Vegas show at the age of seven, doing a cutesy impression of Mae West. In a strange way the lewd, provocative and comic 1930s star stayed with her as a kind of alter ego, an inverted shadow self who spoke plainly and lived her sexual life in public. For the shy, guarded Jackson, West, the woman who said 'Too much of a good thing can be wonderful', presented an inspiring model of sexual outrageous-ness. It is a neat irony that West, who has been accused of stealing her act from the vaudeville blueswomen, should in turn influence a black pop star fifty years later.

Jackson played the part of the obedient daughter, acquiescing to her domineering father and manager Joe until in 1984, at the age of eighteen, she eloped with James DeBarge, the son in another major American showbusiness family, the DeBarges. Having made the break, she retreated, moving back into the Jacksons' Encino home with new husband in tow, sister LaToya listening to them make love through the walls. Lasting less than sixty days, the marriage was annulled amid family pressure and rumours of DeBarge's drug abuse.

After the DeBarge fiasco it was as if Jackson had decided to take charge of her life. Father Joe had secured her an A&M deal in the early 1980s, but her first two LPs were unremarkable flops. Her period in the studio with Jam & Lewis resulted in *Control*, an enduring, endearing collection of grit funk, pop soul and street sass tracks, seven of which she co-wrote and produced herself. Unlike Houston, Jackson went straight for the black market first, consolidated herself there and moved with firm foundation into the pop mainstream.

*Control* sold eight million and yielded five Top Five singles, including 'What Have You Done For Me Lately?' and 'Nasty', the latter a classic of modern feminist pop. Jackson's success came through a combination of passion and obliquely cool observation. She laid down 'Nasty', for instance, immediately after a trip to the studio, when loafing men abused her in the street. She said,

'They started shouting seriously sexual stuff, real dirty stuff . . . So many men call women Baby. It takes away your dignity. I've got a name and if you don't know it then don't shout to me in the street. I took a stand, I backed them down. Control meant not only taking care of myself but living in a much less protected world. And doing that meant growing a tough skin. Getting attitude.'[22]

By the time her next album *Rhythm Nation 1814* came out in 1989, she had sacked her father as manager, declaring, 'Business . . . that's what I'm all about.'[23] *Rhythm Nation*, with its 'socially conscious' themes of racism, drugs and homelessness, was her personal manifesto, a kind of female *What's Goin' On?* for the late 1980s. Contrary to record company nervousness about the songs being uncommercial, she began to rival brother Michael for megastardom when the album went multi-platinum with seven million sales, a record-breaking seven Top Five singles, and a sell-out 1990 Rhythm Nation world tour. The following year she moved from A&M to Virgin Records with an approximate $27 million deal that ranked her among the top-earning female artists.

Like Madonna, Jackson exploited the video market with choreography and pyrotechnics: the longform thirty-minute video of 'Rhythm Nation', for instance, won a Grammy. A strong video profile, however, meant a stringent image overhaul. Although on one level she tried hard to be 'down' with the black rap brotherhood, socializing with Public Enemy, and taking the lead role in John Singleton's 1993 'black consciousness' movie *Poetic Justice*, Jackson also opted for the kind of cosmetic surgery and photographic lighting that 'whitened' her image. Although she didn't remodel her face in the same drastic manner as Michael, Jackson expressed anxiety about her features. 'Want to

**Janet Jackson** on tour in Holland, 1992: as one of the top-earning female artists in the 1990s, she rivalled brother Michael's success. (Michel Linssen/ Redferns)

know what I see when I look in the mirror?' she once asked writer Debi Fee. 'Well I'll tell you. I see too much face.'[24]

Up to her early twenties Jackson was plump, but the more successful she became, the more weight she shed. For the first stage of her mega-career she didn't reveal her legs, and was seen only in trousers. But by the time of her fifth album release, 1993's enigmatically titled *janet.*, she made a move that Mae West would have been proud of. Her topless *Rolling Stone* cover shot, with a man's hands cupping her breasts, was meant to be a statement on her new 'happy phase of sexuality', a joyful expression of taut bod and adult self. To others it seemed a cynical marketing exercise, tasteful cheesecake to outdo older sister LaToya's tacky 1989 *Playboy* centrefold. *janet.*, a whimsical slice of more traditional 'sophisticated' soul, outdistanced the first-week sales of Michael's 1991 *Dangerous* album at 350,000, so her new 'sexy' image could have been judged a success. She continued to develop this svelte image, through the risqué tones of 1997's *Velvet Rope* to the more upbeat *All For You* in 2001. Hers became a familiar route. Despite the elegant monochrome of that *Rolling Stone* session, Jackson fell in with an industry that requires black women in particular to be sylphlike and sexualized.

## Wailing Slags

By the late 1980s dance-music producers had become the stars and directors of a scenario in which a girl was muse and vocal clothes-horse. Toni Braxton, for instance, had her 1993 album *Breathe Again* reviewed more as the creation of her producers LA & Babyface, with UK magazine *Blues & Soul* making no bones about Braxton being 'Babyface's lady'.

Braxton was lucky in that at least a face could be put to her name. 'It's just tinkly pianos and wailing slags', was how a member of British techno act 808 State charmingly summed up the contribution of female vocalists to house music. If it hadn't been for 'wailing slags' like Liz Torres, Ultra Nate, Inner City's Paris Grey, or even Debbie Malone, whose 'Rescue Me' must be one of the most sampled tracks in hardcore techno history, most backroom production boys would not have had the hits they did. Unlike the indie rock scene, where at least women performers have notoriety, if not acceptance, the dance underground can be cruel and cheap in its lack of credit. Not surprisingly most female vocalists are keen to move out to where the real money lies, in pop/soul ballads. Some, though, stay to carve a place on the cutting edge of dance.

Ultra Nate was one such diva, her first two albums *Blue Notes In The Basement* (1991) and *Joy* (1993) being more equal collaboration with garage producers The Basement Boys. Small, tough and imaginative, she was one of the few vocalists on the club scene to become an 'album artist', weaving her intelligence into tight lyrics and an intense, pared-down production. Though coming from a soul background she showed how it was possible to turn clichés from the defiant 1990 house hit 'It's Over Now' to the breathy regret of 'I Specialize In Loneliness' and the disco pleasure-queen role of the title track 'One Woman's Insanity', where she wears red boots up to her neck and cold-laughs the night away.

In the early 1990s Nate was a soul rebel fighting against the mainstream tide in the US. The rise of black female vocal group En Vogue had created a new trend in high glamour. Hair extensions and six-inch nails were *de rigueur*, along with a fine line in funky pop with a kick. 'Our costs in gowns, videos and stage sets are enormous,' said Cindy Herron, the most vocal of the super-quintet.[25] Male artists such as Jodeci and Guy had been dominating the US market with the rap/R&B hybrid New Jack Swing, so companies were looking for the alluring female equivalent. In the wake of En Vogue's massive success with two platinum-plus albums, *Born To Sing* and *Funky Divas*, there was widespread investment in New Jill Swingers including Expose, Jade and SWV (Sisters With Voices).

The latter broke through in 1993 with a gold debut album *It's About Time*, an aggressive update on the girl-group era with sweetly sung yet knowing 'ghetto soul' tracks like 'I'm So Into You' and 'Weak ' storming the US Top Ten. I interviewed the New York trio at the peak of their initial success. Affecting boredom, Leanne (Lelee), Cheryl (Coko) and Tamara (Taj) were sulky and unforthcoming, trotting out 1990s commercial mantras like 'We're speaking up for the ladies'. When asked about their saucy ballad 'Downtown', a tribute to oral sex, Coko stifled a yawn, saying almost by rote, 'Usually it's the guys sayin', "Let me lick you." This is the first time a girl group has come out and told a male where to go. It's time for the ladies to take a stand.'[26]

Despite protestation that it is *them* singing the songs, SWV had the air of being manufactured, manicured tomboys, the marketing dream of the man who signed them – Kenny Ortiz, vice-president of black music A&R at RCA. Further chat revealed that they were stressed at being pushed around, forced to do promotion when they were plain exhausted. 'People put so much pressure on you,' said Lelee. 'Nobody cares. You're supposed to be happy-go-lucky all the time, and people don't understand when you have a bad day.'

They brightened considerably when talking about their business arrangements. 'As well as sing, we want to produce, manage and maybe one day have our own record label,' Coko said animatedly. Proud of their all-female management office, it was evident that one of the main lessons soul sisters learned from the girl-group era was how to take care of business. Like En Vogue, who had their own lawyer and corporation, SWV surrounded themselves with a female power-base, creating a girl mafia almost as a defence against financial exploitation. 'People don't manage En Vogue,' said Sylvia Rhone, chairperson of En Vogue's label East West, herself a highly successful black woman. 'En Vogue manage people.'

While that was admirable, in terms of image and material these female acts still adhered strictly to commercial trends. By 1993 US pop had become a serious business, with black radio wielding greater influence over pop as more black music crossed over to the Top Ten. 'Pop radio has even started looking for urban product earlier than black stations do,' said Roland Edison, vice-president of promotion at RCA. SWV and En Vogue, then, were primely positioned.

### Melting Pot

Black women have followed several strategies to avoid being typecast – one of them being the decision to switch countries. With the stratification of American music into separate charts resulting in rigorous stereotyping, from the Whitney Factor to New Jill Swing, many found that Britain, traditionally black American music's A&R and home of eclectic pop, was the place to breathe in. Carleen Anderson was part of a new breed of female soul rebels reinventing the genre for the 1990s by experimenting with a range of sounds and subcultures. A solo artist and former Young Disciples front-woman who wrote their huge hit 'Apparently Nothin'', Anderson found that her startling voice and illustrious parentage counted for nothing in her home country:

'In America they don't care about Bobby Byrd or Vicki Anderson. It's not news. It's like, they haven't had a hit for twenty years. Didn't they die? Take my uncle James [Brown]. A lot of cabaret has pushed into his shows and recordings of late; he probably feels there's no other way to do it now. America teaches you to become so uncomfortable with who you are.'[27]

Her mother Vicki toured with James Brown's revue from 1965 to 1971. 'He said I was his greatest singer, but I never had an album. All the others had an album,' she said from her home in Atlanta, Georgia, soon after the release of Carleen's 1994 solo debut *True Spirit*. Caught between the duties of being wife to JB member Bobby Byrd, 'fit' mother to her children, and a full-time performer, Vicki had to put her solo ambition on hold for over twenty-five years. 'I don't know how Bobby would have felt if I had a deal first. I didn't want to chance it, put myself through jealousies and insecurities. With my health and looks I knew there'd still be time for me. Singing became a way for me to provide a living for my children,' she said.[28]

James Brown was a tough taskmaster, and Vicki often had to choose between the stage and her children:

'James was 25 per cent entertainer, 75 per cent businessman. He took care of his business. He'd have a lawyer, then hire a lawyer to watch that lawyer. I learned a lot, but on tour there were many times I cried. One day we were playing the Copacabana and Carleen was being awarded Honorary Student at a high-school ceremony. I was going to go anyway, but I was afraid James would fire me.'

Vicki kept her job that time, but more often than not her priority had to be Brown's punishing schedule, and it was her parents who looked after Carleen while the JBs were on tour. 'The things that didn't work for me may work out for her. She's seen what Bobby and I have gone through so she's wise. I was supporting them both for years, that's my character. Now I feel it's my turn. Hopefully Carleen can take some time out from her busy schedule to help her mom.'

Finally recording a solo album in her early fifties with three young German producers, Vicki sounded sanguine. Her daughter, though, harboured less cool memories.

'I resented them being on the road the whole time, that's probably why I keep my son round me. Most children of '60s entertainers didn't grow up with them – they were either away in boarding schools or with relatives. People are only now beginning to realize how damaging it is to break up homes; the industry has grown a bit more. Artists didn't have that option before.'

The experience went deep, fuelling much of the existential angst in her material. At the end of her London showcase gig in 1994, Bobby Byrd and Vicki came on stage to hug her and share the applause. Angrily Carleen ducked from under their arms and fled the stage. Her personal conflict, like Natalie Cole's or Janet Jackson's, showed that Whitney Houston's experience of supposedly smooth mother nurture was atypical. It was as if Carleen had to move to Britain to establish a career independently not only of the US industry, but also of her famous family. 'I only started getting to know them when I moved over here,' she said.

Adelaide Hall, one-time singer with Duke Ellington, moved over in the late 1930s, while Madeline Bell, who came over with a gospel musical Black Nativity in 1962 and never returned, liked to think that she was the first of the 1960s vanguard. 'After me came Marsha Hunt, Doris Troy, P.P. Arnold. Then, to my knowledge, there were very few black singers in this country.' She became the 1960s studio singer, backing everyone from Dusty Springfield to The Beatles and Elton John before joining 1970s soul groovers Blue Mink as lead vocalist and having a major hit with 'Melting Pot', a funky plea for racial harmony. In 1993 she said,

'People would tell me what a great singer I was, but I'd say, You can find ten singers like me on every street corner where I come from. Every church has a choir, every choir at least ten girl singers who could sing me off stage. Now it's different – there's a lot of competition from British girls. If someone's coming here to strike it rich, they've got their work cut out for them.'[29]

Her compatriot Marsha Hunt left America because she felt
limited by the R&B/Motown girl-group ghetto, and almost by
accident became a star in the 1960s rock musical *Hair* ('It was
the day before the show opened and they desperately wanted a
black singer'). From there she went on to have several hits,
notably the Tony Visconti-produced 'Walk On Gilded Splinters'.
'Apart from Jimi Hendrix I was the only black rock singer,' she
said. 'The American music scene was still severely segregated.
They wanted me to be a soul singer, but I wasn't into bubble
haircuts and short dresses, I wore leather and a large Afro. I said,
I wanna sing rock. They said, Black women don't sing rock. So I
had to come to London to do it.'[30]

Competition is fierce in any area of music, but for black
vocalists the odds are stacked against them because of the
factory production-line effect. Like the proverbial Hollywood
waiter, every session singer is working on her own project,
desperate to escape the bit part of the anonymous Voice. UK
soul artists like Mica Paris, Dee C. Lee and M People's Heather
Small avoided the trap of session singing by taking the initiative
in their career, but some women need those sessions to get
started.

All-male (often white) bands hiring a strong black female
vocalist for that stamp of soul credibility are taking a risk.
Someone with a mind and voice of her own is an asset, but there
is tension in the arrangement – the likelihood that three hits and
an album or so in, she will fly the nest. 'There's all these bands
who're really pissed off that once they get some success the
female singer leaves to go solo,' one (male) artist told me. The
band feel betrayed – after all, they showcased the Voice – while
the singer feels that it was her sound that made the band.

Within this conundrum is the assumption that the girl singer
has risen above her station. The irony is that many a vocalist
would have stayed, had she been listened to and treated as a fully
fledged member of the band. Becoming a featured vocalist may
be a way out of the session-singing trap, but the boys in the band
can still treat you strictly as Voice and Hairdo, a vehicle for their
songs and their arrangements. 'It ain't easy, let me be the first to

tell you,' said N'Deah Davenport, vocalist with acid jazz outfit
The Brand New Heavies. 'I don't think people understood that
although I was starting anew with The Brand New Heavies I had
a background of my own before.'[31] Having already worked with
George Clinton, Fishbone, Dave Stewart, and even turned down
Madonna's Blond Ambition tour to work on her own album, she
was dismayed at the band's apparent indifference when she first
came over:

'I saw myself as an artist in my own right working with them,
while in their eyes it was, We were this band and now there's this
girl here. My attitude was a bit of a shock to them, I was pretty
feisty, and the adjustments with that took some time.' After com-
pleting a second album with the Heavies, N'Deah felt that finally
it was a 'four-way creative split', in contrast to singer Shara
Nelson who continually felt frustrated as front-woman for the
indie-soul band Massive Attack. 'If you want to do more than be
a guest vocalist you should be given an equal chance. I couldn't
grow with Massive, I felt stifled,' she said. Having worked with
the Sugarhill Gang at fourteen, and been a songwriter for 'as
long as I can remember', Shara decided to go solo with her own
material. The risk paid off, with *Down That Road* one of the
biggest crossover albums of 1993:

'I was an honorary member of Massive Attack, another cardboard cut-out
in the front. It was done very well, but still . . . If you're black and a soul
singer you're perceived as having nothing to do with what makes the
whole thing. Once you branch out and say, Well, actually I do write and I
do have a bit of a brain, they question it. You're a stroppy singer. I left
Massive at the height of their success, and people would say, "We love
what you did and we're so afraid for you." I say, why?'[32]

Nelson was lucky in having a record company (Cooltempo, part
of Chrysalis) interested in serious promotion. Soul II Soul's
Caron Wheeler, however, found it a lot harder in the late 1980s
to get consistent record company support once she was a solo
artist experimenting with everything from country and western
to funk, and by 1994 she was back with the band. Pop history is
littered with lead women who have tried the solo route and

failed, much of that down to industry reluctance to market a dance vocalist as a long-term artist.

Reassured by the success of black women in other spheres (Tracy Chapman, Des'ree), by the early 1990s record labels were more prepared to get behind a vocalist writing her own material and veering away from soul if it was right for her.

## Brown Skin

By the mid-1990s, however, there was an interesting development with what's loosely termed 'Organic Soul' or 'Neo Soul'. The profound influence of hip hop, with its irreverent, multi-genre mixing, had transformed black music. Black women artists like Lauryn Hill, Erykah Badu and Mary J. Blige were no longer soul cyphers, but creating music of strong emotional depth. They were hailed by *New York Times* critic Ann Powers as 'the new conscience of pop music'.[33]

Christened 'the Mother of Hip Hop Invention',[34] Lauryn Hill was born into a middle-class family in South Orange, New Jersey. She had a liberal upbringing, absorbing everything from old school soul to Charlie's Angels and Flashdance. A budding star, she was a teenage actor in TV soap *As The World Turns*, and scored a minor part in the film *Sister Act II: Back In The Habit*. But it was music that proved her most powerful medium – at 13 she was rapping and singing with Wyclef Jean and Prakazrel (Pras) Michel, local Haitian guys who called their outfit The Fugees (short for 'refugees' after the band's African and Haitian roots). Their first album, *Blunted On Reality* (1994), made little impact, but two years later their follow-up, *The Score*, went multiplatinum. Mixing guerilla rock and rap with cover versions of famous songs, it was a strong crossover album. Their version of Roberta Flack's 'Killing Me Softly With His Song', featuring Hill's rich, crystal clear vocals, became a worldwide hit and gave her massive exposure.

Soon the ambitious Hill was writing, arranging and producing her debut solo album. 1998's *The Miseducation of Lauryn Hill* integrated everything from rap to reggae and soul,

**Lauryn Hill**: 'keepin' it real' with Organic Soul. (Paul Bergen/ Redferns)

with songs like 'Doo Wop (That Thing)' and 'Every Ghetto, Every City' showing different facets of her personal world. With her dreadlocks and Levi jeans, her songs about anti-racism, motherhood and 'keepin it real', Hill symbolized a new era. At 22 years old she had a child (against all advice) at a key point in her career. The father of her son Zion is Rohan Marley, son of reggae legend Bob Marley. Hill is careful to keep the illustrious lineage intact. Her album became a byword for integrity, picking up five Grammy awards in 1999, and leading her to high-profile production work with artists like Aretha Franklin and Whitney Houston. Although she was competing in an increasingly sexualized R&B scene, Hill made certain that her music, rather than her cleavage, was upfront. Referring to the steamy sex sirens of

1990s R&B, Hill told writer Gerri Hirshey, 'After they make a certain image popular, they're victim to their own insecurity.'[35]

Though it was downplayed, the fact that Hill had cover-girl looks and was perfectly at home in photo-shoots helped to sell her records. *Miseducation* . . . showed her to be a consummate professional, and was a solid debut, but the critical hype surrounding it was a tad overblown. Rather than being the Second Coming, Hill is one in a long line of powerful female artists. The Fugees gave her a platform that she used with grit and a single-minded focus, but in 1998 she was only just beginning to take her place in a rich soul tradition.

Also emerging in the late 1990s was Erykah Badu, a languid, silver-tongued soul poetess with a fine line in colourful turbans. Born Erica Wright in Dallas, Texas, she changed her name while a teenage performing arts student to Erykah ('kah' meaning the 'inner self' and 'ba-du' after the scat singing of great jazz vocalists). Fusing jazz with R&B and hip hop, her 1997 debut *Baduizm* sold over three million and won numerous awards including two Grammys and four Soul Train awards. Her off-the-wall funky narratives had cross-cultural appeal – as well as doing her own Smokin' Grooves Tour, she played the Lilith Fair (an event that in its first year attracted predominantly white audiences). Badu followed up the success of her debut with the acclaimed *Live!* album, and *Mama's Gun* (2000), an insouciant collection that has her drawling with quirky humour about her pot belly and her ability to rhyme. 'My music is not for everybody. People think the Afro-centric image is a gimmick, a ploy to sell records,' she said, 'That's just who I am and I'm not gonna stop being who I am because I got a record deal.'[36]

2000 was the year that Organic Soul reached critical mass. Record companies talked slow-burning sales strategies like 'stealth marketing' and 'organic penetration', but when artists like Badu, Hill, then Macy Gray and Angie Stone went overground, they knew contemporary soul was much more popular than previously supposed; it had been redefined for a wider audience. No longer about glam, glitz and gospel-inspired vocals, black women were jumping the categories with aplomb.

Macy Gray, for instance, has been hailed as a female Jimi Hendrix – dressing in flamboyant clothes and creating her own brand of psychedelic R&B. All of her messy life was there on her bestselling debut *On How Life Is*; with songs about being an out-of-work LA scriptwriter, a divorcee with three children, and on looking for new love and being disappointed. 'There's no showbiz artifice. She's pure, unedited passion,' said her producer Andrew Slater.[37] For Gray, the appeal of her record was simple: 'Put something hot out there and people will be down with it.' She was also aware that record buyers were sick of the 'whole skinny girl with the sunk-in eyes thing'[38] – women in particular wanted someone they could relate to, someone with a 'regular body' and a point of view.

Angie Stone also rode the crest of the new realism. 'I am not a Whitney, a Monica or a Deborah Cox. I am none of those American dream girls. I am a healthy sister with a natural hairdo and the complexion of charcoal,' she said.[39] Former member of 1970s rap group The Sequence, she created *Black Diamond*, a melodic soul album free of fussy production gimmicks that topped the charts at the beginning of 2000. Spanning edgy grooves and ethereal space funk, it was Stone's life story told with mellow beats, infused with the sense of a life lived. By summer 2000, Philadelphia performance poet and soul singer Jill Scott had enriched the scene further with her debut *Who Is Jill Scott? Words & Sounds Vol. 1*, a multi-faceted record with a jazz sensibility and astute lyrics.

Harlem-born Kelis then stormed the pop arena with multi-coloured afro hair and 'Caught Out There', a screamer of a song that lambasted unfaithful men. Her live shows were a mix of raucous rock and percussive funk, a gritty assertion of self. Atlanta-based India Irie released her own richly-textured *Acoustic Soul* album, and celebrated her heritage with the rootsy hit 'Brown Skin'. A Lilith Fair performer who cited Bonnie Raitt as an influence, Irie felt free to explore different genres, rejecting the notion of black women artists being little more than a writhing body in a formulaic video. There was also piano prodigy Alicia Keys, who combined tough Brooklyn sass with a classical background, and the graceful Aaliyah, a subtly experimental soul chanteuse who scored a worldwide hit with 'Try Again' and was tragically killed in a plane crash in 2001, just as she was about to fulfil her potential.

The market was opening up to new representations of black women, even with its glamorous showgirls. Here, female artists were adding a punchy urban R&B to modern pop, and singing lyrics that steered away from the vacuous to a more defined sense of real life drama.

## No Scrubs

Queen of the new urban R&B gals was undoubtedly Mary J. Blige. With deep, sweet tones nurtured by years of singing in Pentecostal choirs in the South, she has the history of soul music in her voice. With a touch of gospel devotion allied to a street-wise toughness, and an emotionally direct delivery, she takes a song by the scruff of its neck and moulds it with passionate precision. Discovered by Andre Harrell and his then-label Uptown Records, in 1992 she recorded her debut *What's The 411?* at the age of 20. Then she was like a young Aretha, a little rough around the edges, but her sound instantly caught on, with . . . *411* selling over three million worldwide. At first she was rumoured to be the puppet of Sean 'Puffy' Combs, producer of her first two albums and notorious creator of 'nu soul' divas. But by 1997's *Share My World*, she had broken out, working with a number of top names including Jam & Lewis, Babyface and R. Kelly. With each album, she has grown more poised and sophisticated, steadily steering her own direction.

When asked what advice Blige would give to female musicians starting out, she said ruefully: 'I wish I'd taken advice to finish school and read all my contracts before I signed them. If you haven't finished high school, finish. Just beware.'[40] Despite greater awareness of the small print, women artists were still not getting their fair share of the profits. Being a coiffured soul singer, in particular, is a high-risk, high-maintenance business. It can be an agonizingly long time from the first hit to the first

**Mary J. Blige**:
urban R&B diva,
'with the history of
soul music in her
voice'.
(Mick Hutson/
Redferns)

proper pay cheque (average waiting time 18 months), and even then Top Ten success doesn't make the artist a millionaire. Record companies ensure they recoup costs, and by the time they have subtracted their share for the recording, the video, the marketing, the touring, the stylist, the chauffeur and the hairdresser, an artist can end up out of pocket.

Soul diva Toni Braxton found this to her cost. The woman who once turned down a £25 million record deal because it wasn't enough, went bankrupt in 1997. It was reported that she was planning to sue her record label Arista for allegedly trying to 'cheat' her out of royalties.[41] Despite selling more than ten million copies of her 1993 self-titled debut and having a massive worldwide hit with 'Unbreak My Heart' on the follow-up album *Secrets*, the Grammy Award singer discovered huge debts when she fired her managers Arnold Stiefel and Randy Phillips and took control of her business affairs.

Braxton was one of the new divas, singing songs with a sassy edge, such as 'You're Making Me High', a frank exploration of female sexual fantasy. US female rap/vocal trio TLC, too, were part of this audacious 1990s breed, bursting onto the scene in 1992 with 'Ain't 2 Proud 2 Beg'. Sporting baggy hip hop fatigues and condoms, the teenage Tionne 'T Boz' Watkins, Lisa 'Left Eye' Lopes and Rozanda 'Chilli' Thomas sang about sexual openness and responsibility. They grew up quickly in the limelight, swapping the loud colours for a more sophisticated image, but still keeping the message sexually frank. T-Boz in particular took things a step further in 1996 with 'Touch Myself', a solo song about the delights of female masturbation that was banned in the UK by Radio 1. In the video she danced with her male self, playing both glam soul girl and Drag King, complete with moustache and cut-off T-shirt.

Despite their incorrigible confidence, TLC lost a fortune. They filed for bankruptcy in 1995, even though their album *CrazySexyCool* had sold an estimated four million copies and their hit 'Waterfalls' sat on top of the US charts for six weeks. It didn't help that Lisa Lopes faced a $1.3 million insurance claim from her ex-boyfriend, whose home she allegedly burnt down after a domestic argument. But looking at the hyper-production that surrounded their 1998 album *Fan Mail*, complete with expensive producers like Jam & Lewis and Jermaine Dupri, plus lush state-of-the art packaging, it was easy to see where the money was going. Glamorous soul divas are aware that substantial money is to be made in song publishing, but traditionally songwriting has been the preserve of the production team that surrounds them. TLC's song 'I'm Good At Being Bad', for instance, had 16 writing credits – once everyone has been paid their share, there was not a great deal left for the band. The fact that the album's stand-out track 'No Scrubs' became an international hit, propelling healthy sales for *Fan Mail* overall, must have come as a relief.

Keeping it all in the family, though, were Destiny's Child – the next R&B girl group to achieve superstardom. Managed by their father Matthew and styled by their mother Tina, Dallas-born Beyonce Knowles and Kelly Rowland (who had lived with the family since childhood) were well protected from the beginning of their career. In 1991, Knowles was nine years old and already a veteran of talent shows and beauty pageants. She formed a group with schoolmate Rowland and friends LeToya Luckett and LeTavia Robertson, and they jetted round the country playing showcases, in an effort to get a record deal. They would dedicate every summer vacation to the group, rehearsing five hours a day. They would watch archive tapes of The Supremes, analysing the Motown stars' every move. A vocal coach moved into their back apartment and, instead of paying rent, gave the group voice lessons. 'We were young and sacrificed a lot,' Knowles, a beautiful and unusually focused young woman, told me in 2000.[42]

In 1995 they signed to Columbia and spent the next two years recording their self-titled debut. The key track on the album, 'No, No, No' was cut with Fugees impresario Wyclef Jean. Through him, Destiny's Child arrived at their trademark staccato, rhythmic style. 'We were in the studio one night with Wyclef, all really tired; I sang a melody to the fast music track, for a joke, and Wyclef said, "That's hot! Do it like that",' recalls Knowles. At first she refused, saying she sounded like a chipmunk. Eventually she agreed to try. The girls recorded the song in 57 minutes and came up with a No. 1 R&B hit. 'That's how the whole fast-singing, rhythmic thing started,' says Knowles. Riding high, they went straight into recording the follow-up album *The Writing's On The Wall*, which by September 2000 had yielded four hit singles and was shifting 70,000 units a week.

This hardworking act can be guaranteed a fair share of the sales because Knowles takes a major role in songwriting and production. On *The Writing's On The Wall*, for instance, she wrote and co-produced 17 tracks with beat architects Shek'spere and Timbaland, helping to create the Destiny's Child trademark sound of bass rhythms, baroque samples and daring vocal harmonies, a cross between TLC and Kraftwerk. With 2001's *Survivor*, Knowles had graduated to sole producer on most tracks. Despite disruptive line-up changes, the group remained consistently at the top of the charts. Much of this was due to Knowles' leadership and innate sense of what was appropriate for them. 'People have tried to get us into bathing suits,' she says, 'but there's a line we draw. We wear nothin' with our butt cheeks out, our boobs out. We like sexy clothes, but still classy. Not so people can say, "How can they wear that and be a Christian?"' One of the group's most endearing qualities was their un-diva-like humility. As soon as you stop working hard, as soon as you think it's all about you, God takes it away,' she said. "And I don't want this taken away.'[43]

While R&B rebels risked rewriting the rules on soul, black women had been infiltrating other areas of music, building a presence in bastions of male power like rap and reggae. Unlike the soul sisters who had the diva tradition to support them, though, 1980s fly girls and ragga queens were entering true pioneer territory.

# In Search of Our Mothers' Gardens

## THE TRUE STORY OF WOMEN IN RAP AND REGGAE

# 10

SHE WAS TWO HOURS LATE, arriving in a limo with a new leather jacket, '£2,000 worth of bullshit' and curling fingernails painted red and black, set with fake diamonds. World-weary at nineteen, rapper Roxanne Shante had a two-year-old son, a house, a dog and an Attitude. 'I was just thirteen when I came into the business. For me to be a veteran at my age and newcomers to be older than me I think, God, am I old!'[1]

It was 1989 and Shante was promoting her new album *Bad Sister*. Our interview at the offices of her UK record company was frank and playful, but with an edge. She told me about a track she'd written called 'Fatal Attraction' in which a young married man working on Wall Street cheats on a young black woman. 'He's nice-looking, well-groomed, drives a Jag, lives in the country. He cheats one time too many with the wrong girl. She gets tired of it and cuts his dick off.' Barely concealing a yawn, Shante added, 'That's the whole record, to tell you the truth.'

Being one of the first women to grow up early in the hip hop world had taken its toll.

## It's My Beat

The story of women in rap is interesting as an example of the most naked form of self-definition in the business. In view of the overt misogyny they've had to contend with, female MCs could be forgiven for just shooting from the metaphorical hip – yet their material also encompasses intense subtlety, a depth of expression, and, by the early 1990s, a lyrical maturity.

Though a genre that came from the margins, within ten years

of the first hip hop hit, 'Rapper's Delight' by the Sugarhill Gang, rap was to become a lynchpin of the music industry. With its reliance on the marketable stereotypes of black cowboy, pimp hustler, gang leader or black nationalist hero, the growth of rap did not leave much room for women beyond the roles of cheer-leading or decoration. Never perceived as big sellers, women were forced to prove and publicize themselves in spite of b-boy scepticism, evolving their own cast of characters, from fly girl to earth mother to mackstress to black sista. Women's impact in rap, traditionally perceived as little more than 'the girls are doin' it for themselves', is more refined and far-reaching, sometimes echoing in its complexity the best of black American feminist lit-erature.

The history of women's rap begins with a simple one-sided conversation on record. A woman goes through her man's pockets to find another woman's name and number; she then rings her to settle the score. One of the most famous early female raps, Shirley Brown's 'Woman To Woman', clearly set out the rules of love, possession and rivalry. Released in 1974 by the Memphis R&B label Stax, Brown's song was rooted in Southern soul lament, the voice of a lone, defended woman standing up for her meagre love rights. While her approach was understated, 1990s comedienne and Soul Queen Millie Jackson operated at the other extreme, matching lewd male bravado with her own tales of sexual exploits and ridicule. Rap/R&B singer Laura Lee, too, addressed her female audience with directness, giving them frank advice in 1970's 'Wedlock Is A Padlock', and the follow-up 'Women's Love Rights'.

It wasn't until the late 1970s that women figured more specif-ically on the rap scene, with a handful of acts such as Lady B and The Sequence countering male bragging with stories of their own womanly prowess. Blondie (not Deborah Harry!), Cheryl the Pearl and Angie B (aka The Sequence) harnessed their bouncy eccentricity to Sugarhill, recording hit tracks such as 'Funk You Up', recalling the sauce of vaudeville blueswomen in the way they urged men to ring their bell and rock their body. Like all women acts to be first on a male-dominated scene, though, they were treated as a novelty disco alternative, the 'fun' factor at fiercely competitive New York City block parties, where DJs and MCs created an intense virtuoso world of intricate record-scratching and improvised rhymes.

As funk rhythms were pared down to a severe bass beat and rapping took on a harder edge in the early 1980s, male raps weren't just about partying, their tone had become disparaging of women. Though some girls rose to the challenge – such as the Two Sisters in 1983 proclaiming on 'B-Boys Beware' that it was the girls' turn, and simultaneously the Almighty Pebblee Poo at 'five foot two' lambasting macho opportunism on 'A Fly Guy' – it wasn't until 1984 that a female rapper emerged seriously to confront the exclusive b-boy scene. Hailing from Queens, New York, Lolita Shante Gooden was just fourteen when she recorded 'Roxanne's Revenge', an answer to the sexist rap of UTFO's 'Roxanne Roxanne'. Sparking off a host of 'Roxanne' answer records, from 'Roxanne's Doctor' to 'Roxanne's A Man', she found herself at the centre of a debate within hip hop that took years to die down.

Responding from gut instinct as a street-aware teenager, Shante said when the record came out, 'Guys should stop talking about girls because it's not working any more. It's played out!' One scorching summer day in New York City three years later, I met her at the Broadway base of rap label Cold Chillin'. Then her record 'Have A Nice Day', a smart, satirical rap with a crunching backbeat that contained the immortal line on which she claimed to be 'The Boss', was crossing over from street to chart status. Fully involved with the current hip hop debates, she was happy to compete on vinyl in the verbal and gang New York district rivalry known as the Bridge Wars. Though not shy of controversy, she was ambivalent about the effect of the answer-record saga. After all the Roxanne records, UTFO had stumped up their own rival, the coiffured and cute Real Roxanne, who despite her doe eyes could execute a sharp rap and a nifty rhythm, scoring a hit in 1986 with the cartoon cut-up of 'Bang Zoom Let's Go Go'.

Pitching the Roxannes against each other in a grand media

Battle of the Bitches deflected attention from Shante's original message against male put-downs. In 1987 she commented,

'Answer records may be a quick way to pick up fame. But it's a bad way to pick up friends. When I first started out, male rappers reckoned I wasn't gonna be successful, but when I was they resented it. At first they said, "Oh look she's so cute, she's my little sister." Then after a while it was, "I don't want her on tour with me" or, "She good, but she ain't that good." I found it hard to mix and mingle.'

Answer records to her had become a distraction from a girl's inherent talent. 'You should make your own idea, your own spotlight.'[2]

Shante's ruthless rap constantly got her into trouble. One year she was disqualified from the NY New Music Seminar MC contest for ripping a gibbering male MC to shreds. Behind the tougher-than-leather stance, though, beat an intelligent, isolated heart. The day of the interview she went outside to have her photograph taken. 'I have to get ready,' she said. Hair? Make-up? Nails? No, a quick change from a black T-shirt into a blue one. She wandered over to a news-stand and, laughing, picked out a copy of *Penthouse*, looking at the camera with expressions of mock outrage. The energy emanating from her made for a vibrant, colourful picture. 'I'm just a regular hip hop girl who's indispensable and superb with her vocals,' she said.

By the late 1980s Shante had become blasé, using insult as a way to get attention. Less popular among the new female MCs, she had still pioneered a place for female rap that was consolidated later by acts such as Sweet Tee and Salt 'N' Pepa, who paced themselves and handled the aggression of the scene in a more tactical way. 'We're all friends here in New York – at least us newer girls. It's so dumb, the fight, so stupid,' Sweet Tee told me soon after 'It's My Beat', her record with DJ Jazzy Joyce, became a huge hip hop hit in 1987. She refused to comment on Shante who, feeling insecure, had begun to spat with the female competition.

Sweet Tee and Jazzy Joyce were the first successful combination of female MC and DJ. 'There wasn't a girl mixer who had a name for it, that's why I chose one to work with me. It would make the group more powerful to have a girl MC and a girl DJ,' said Tee. 'I was convinced it was a good concept and there was no way anyone would talk me out of it.' It is still difficult for a woman to establish a reputation as a strong DJ, but back then on the edge of old school/new school, the period when rap first crossed to the commercial mainstream, it was even harder. A sassy college graduate, Joyce became interested in DJ-ing through her cousin Chovy Chove, who taught her the basics. She had already triumphed against rival DJ Wanda D at the New Music Seminar when Tee, looking for a DJ, got in touch. Joyce's beats were hard, crunchy and abstract: 'I don't use cartoons or comic characters – they're like games. This is no game. Some people have gimmicks like scratching records with a chair leg, but that shows no skill. Mixing is moving on now – old school had a lot of straight beats, routines and corny lines like "Dip, dip dive, so-so-socialize!" It was fresh then, but not any more.'[3]

As a new rap vanguard moved towards the pop charts, women were briefly at the forefront. Girls have always been an integral part of pop's language, and an ambitious young producer named Hurby 'Luv Bug' Azor saw their potential early on. 'Roxanne diss you and does it good,' he said. 'So I figure two girls dissin' two major rap guys like Doug E Fresh and Slick Rick – people you wouldn't dare diss – would create mayhem in the music industry.' As well as working with Tee and Joyce, he picked up two girls with loud laughs, called them Salt 'N' Pepa and moulded them, like Phil Spector in the 1960s, to become the Ronettes of rap, one of the biggest-selling female acts of the 1990s. 'Girl rappers are a gold mine,' he told me when Salt 'N' Pepa's debut album *Hot Cool & Vicious* went gold in 1987.

Two years earlier he had hauled Cheryl Jones (Salt) and Sandy Denton (Pepa) from their jobs in a Sears & Roebuck chainstore and persuaded them to cut a rap with him called 'Showstopper'. A retort to the Doug E Fresh hit 'The Show', the record drew immediate airplay and chart attention. From that moment, Hurby says, he knew he was away. The girls' irrepressible philosophy spilled out in each clearly enunciated groove of

*Hot Cool & Vicious*, from the opening declaration of 'My Mike
Sounds Nice' to their now infamous reading of the Carla
Thomas 1960s soul original 'Tramp', where the homegirls
attack male street hustlers with the line: 'All men are tramps!'
Where Shante's approach was a teenage female blitzkrieg, Salt
'n' Pepa used mockery and homegirl solidarity.

In 1987 they were staying in a poky North London hotel
room: Pepa was an ex-disco punk fresh out of safety pins
engaged to Fat Boy Markie, Salt a bright yet serious young
business-head in love with Hurby 'Luv Bug'. 'Our first show was
scary,' said Pepa. 'We performed at a club called Inferno in
Manhattan, and we had on high heels. We skipped over verses,
our voices were shaking, and I kept thinking, "What am I doing
here? Why am I on this stage?"'[4] Within two years they would
become serious pop contenders.

### It's My Butt You're Kissin'

After rap went pop with Run-DMC and Aerosmith's massive
MTV hit 'Walk This Way' in 1986 there was an extreme reaction

among the rap fraternity and women were the first to feel the chill. A significant section of the market spearheaded by 'gangster' rap outfits like NWA and Naughty By Nature went defiantly back to its 'street' roots, becoming immersed in the tough localism of hardcore. While their raps both documented and sensationalized racism and gang warfare, a misogynist trend also reasserted itself. Women were a common target within rap, the holdall for young male insecurity about sexuality and power. In the mid-1980s underground rapper Schoolly D spoke of 'breakin' bitches' arms', while Kool Moe Dee blamed women for spreading VD in 'Go See The Doctor', and the Beastie Boys' stage act included a plastic hydraulic penis and girls stripping in cages. This trend took an ominous turn when, in the rap world's version of the whore/madonna dichotomy, women were described as either 'good' or 'hoe's' (whores). The Geto Boys reached a new nihilistic nadir with a kind of video nasty, when they rapped about slitting a woman's stomach and listening to her squeals. Female MCs who had been flourishing in the wake of Salt 'N' Pepa faced a stark choice: go hardcore, where the money and respect seemed to be, or stay with a more 'feminine' style and go under. In 1993 so-called gangsta girl rappers topped the female sellers, with MC Lyte's and Yo Yo's albums shifting approximately 400,000, while Boss's sold 300,000.

'Sorry to say it but harder sells more,' Yo Yo said that year.[5] Her third album *You Better Ask Somebody* dealt with themes of prison and drug-dealing, and the closing track was a duet with Ice Cube called 'The Bonnie And Clyde Theme'. Aching with anger and defiance, it showed little of the sweetness that characterized 1992's *Black Pearl*. 'This is my hardest album. I've always been known as the female Ice Cube. I softened up for the ladies on *Black Pearl*, and had no problem with it, but everyone now feels you have to be tough. Hopefully that'll change.'

Yo Yo began her rap career in a brother/sista face-off with Ice Cube on his track 'It's A Man's World'. A proponent of dark, aggressive 'tell-it-like-it-is' rap, the former NWA member was pulled up short by a black LA homegirl with a cascade of sexy blond braids. 'He wrote his verses and I wrote mine, and it turned into a battle of the sexes.' Stressing that Yo Yo, the gangsta mackstress, was like a horror-movie cartoon character, she was keen to talk more about her 'real life' initiative, the Intelligent Black Women's Coalition. An organization aiming to set up education campaigns for young women in every US city, the IBWC reflected another side to Yo Yo's hardcore culture. 'There's not enough sisterhood in rap,' she said. 'And there's not enough sisterhood generally.' Working with her mother, an assistant in a home for battered children, and a network of women from LA to New York, Dallas and Washington, the organization would raise money for battered women's shelters, for instance, or educational campaigns about teenage pregnancy. The IBWC may have been at odds with Yo Yo's 'on-screen' mackstress persona, but, she said, 'I have to make the public understand that entertainers play different roles.'

MC Lyte, whose 'I Cram 2 Understand U' became a late-1980s hip hop classic, had also gone back to basics. Her 1993 album *Ain't No Other* dealt in straight hardcore, packed with 'reality rhyme' and messages to her Brooklyn homies. At a London gig, for instance, she won over the reserved crowd with a series of good-natured and well-placed expletives. A spiritual tomboy with a warm, quiet confidence, she said that one of the songs she was most proud of was 'Ruffneck', a tribute to men on the less acceptable side of rap's divide. 'It's for guys into hip hop who have to deal with a lot of criticism from other folks regarding how they dress. People can't understand why they want their pants sagging, why they want boots so big and they're not climbing any mountains. Just to give a shout to them – what's up? Hey! you're appreciated.'[6]

In some ways Lyte was the ultimate roots girl rapper joshing with the guys, but her material, strong and tautly written, kept her in that hallowed place as one of rap's most respected artists. So much so that in 1994 she was guesting on Janet Jackson's single 'You Want This', at the heart of the mainstream. Of her work, which combined both humble poetry and the force of ego rap, Lyte said simply, 'I feel there's never going to be another me. Like there's never going to be another KRS-1 or LL. Some things cannot be replaced.' Lyte's confidence about her status extended to a cheerful curse-out of Roxanne Shante on the track 'Steady F—king'. 'She dissed me, so I had to do a song dissing her.' When asked if that was a bit, well, unsisterly, Lyte replied, 'It's just a vinyl war. People have to remember how rap started – this is what people were doing in the South Bronx. I think it's much better to rap on vinyl than actually fight.'

To some extent women deal with sexism much more directly in rap than in other musical genres. The posturing male attitudes they face are so upfront and overt that arguably this allows them to be serious about their music and how they present them-selves. In an area like street rap they cannot afford to be covert, and the sexuality they project is not coy and discreet.

The Brooklyn-born 'Black Widow' of rap, LeShaun was just such a fighter, keen to resurrect the vinyl gender war by goading men into an answer record debate – 'I have to dog 'em first, the way they dog the shit outta us. Me and a few other female MCs out there, if we stick to our guns we could get them mad enough to start writing back,' she said in 1993.[7] Her debut *Ain't No Shame In My Game* dealt with issues affecting her homegirl audience, from date rape ('Neaux, No, Know') to teenage pregnancy ('Young Girlz'). 'The main problem facing young black women today,' she said frankly, 'is young black men.' Many female rappers had reservations about men's use of the term 'bitch', which had become a political football, a barometer of the gender debate – meaning everything from a term of warmth and irony to the more obvious insult. NWA's Dr Dre, whose work with Snoop Doggy Dogg in 1994 made him one of rap's wealthi-est producers, said grudgingly, 'If a woman takes offence to us saying "bitch" that means she must be one.'

On Dogg's three-million-seller debut *Doggystyle*, he made sixty-three references to bitches, in more than one unflattering instance ordering a girl to get down and give him a blow job. Despite such hard-ass lyrics, he had a large contingent of female fans attracted to his sleek, feminine features and laconic drawl, either conveniently not 'hearing' his words or choosing to take them as a joke. Made paranoid by his success and clearly disturbed by the fans hounding him in hotels, during one interview Dogg pointed out a girl to journalist Dele Fadele and said, 'That's a bitch or a hoe. She's trying to get a scam, she's trying to get pregnant, or even get a lawsuit. That's what I'm thinking: "What you wanna fuck me for? You don't even know me." '[8]

While men used 'bitch-hoe' lyrics to insult women they saw as strong, mistrustful or in control, many women reclaimed the term in the way 'nigga' or 'queer' became used respectively within the black and gay communities. Calling herself a 'bad-ass bitch from Brooklyn', Lyte interpreted the term as 'someone who knows what she wants and stops at nothing to get it. A woman that's completely headstrong. If that's a bitch, that's what I am.'

Distinct from Salt 'N' Pepa and their chart-friendly rap, Yo Yo, Lyte and LeShaun were key players in a period when hardcore was at its height and competition centred on who could be the hardest. A Detroit native who moved to LA in search of a record contract, rapper Boss came out with the strongest identification with gang culture, 'packing a piece' for a style magazine photo shoot and talking about guns. 'Your dick'll get shot the fuck off if you keep talking that shit,' was her riposte to sexist rappers. Boss's gun-culture glamorization, though, was not so different from Ice T taking a British TV crew on a tour of his apartment, showing off his 'state-of-the-art' submachine-gun collection. In a world where rap is compared to wrestling, 'males dialoguing with males', Boss believed that bragging about her gangsta qualifications would act as a liberating force. Ironically the same year that her debut album *Push* came out, America's largest gun lobby, the NRA, launched its 'Refuse To Be A Victim' campaign, which hijacked the language of feminism in directly targeting women. Accused of using scare tactics to boost falling membership, their glossy ads played on women's fear of attack. 'When you learn to shoot, your fear falls away from you,' said celebrity 'Women's Empowerment' trainer Paxton Quigley, who appeared in an advert for *Working Woman* magazine dressed in black, her blond hair sleek in *film noir* style, clutching a handgun.

'I didn't get to where I am today by reading *Good Housekeeping*'
ran the caption. The slick pictures did nothing to alleviate gun-
related crime. In 1990 handguns were used to murder ten
people in Australia, twenty-two in Britain and 10,567 in the US.
And of the 330,000 people who died by guns in the US throughout the 1980s, one of the most high-risk groups identified was
African-American girls aged ten to fourteen. The percentage of
those dying of gunshot wounds doubled between 1987 and
1988.[9] In the face of the figures, Boss's stance didn't seem so
cool.

Hardcore females like Boss have also been called anti-
feminist and accused of condoning gang codes or slack male
attitude. Writer Carol Cooper counters, however,

'Rap never evolved from a feminist point of view. Feminism began as a
white middle-class movement and contemporary feminism still has that
taint. With economic inequities, racism will always be greater than gender.
Where do you get off saying a black female rapper like MC Lyte should be
talking about feminist issues? Why should they adopt your political views
when they don't come from your socio-economic background? Gangsta
rap reflects the movies – and Schwarzenegger's body count in his movies is
much more than in a record by the Boss.[10]

As a white woman, Monica Lynch, head of premier rap label
Tommy Boy, was circumspect about the hardcore trend.

'There's this tyranny of hardness that dominates. And though the rap
audience may be racially mixed, in terms of gender teenage males are still
not checking for a female MC. Some women experimented with R&B productions and found that there was a strong backlash from their audience –
they were perceived as soft and a sell-out. The other way round can work
tremendously to your benefit. Rap tends to be a lightning rod for criticism,
because it's primarily a black male art form, and has historically been a
threat to the white majority As a genre rap has always been "in yer face"
lyrically, and given to extremity – whether it's your dick being this big or
your gun this long or your skills on the mic this incredible. The OTT
bragging invites challengers. If you don't like what they're saying, dammit,
get on the mic and refute that point of view!'[11]

In the early 1990s it was still difficult for women to be heard and taken seriously by record companies, so it was unsurprising that so many of them plumped for the commercial hardcore trend. 'Too often women rappers' records are categorized as "We're waiting to see what's going to happen with this artist." They are not considered, "This is the breakout one." So oftentimes they don't get promoted as well, and the initial assessment becomes a self-fulfilling prophecy,' said Carmen Ashhurst-Watson, president of Rush Communications, parent company of one of rap's biggest labels, Def Jam.[12]

The potential 'Diana Ross of Rap' that the industry had been looking for was more likely to come under the spiritual umbrella of the 'Back to Africa' movement. Many saw this direction as more positive than hardcore, with the majority of male and female MCs looking up to one woman in particular, New Jersey-born Dana Owens, or Queen Latifah, as a key inspiration for the rap sisterhood. 'She took this rap thing to another level,' said LeShaun. 'She's building, just keeps on goin'. I got my deal the same time as Latifah, but I got pregnant. She didn't. She started a management company.'

## Nature of a Sista

Strengthening her position as Earth Mother businesswoman, Latifah was the first female rapper to cross over to Hollywood, playing a cameo role in Spike Lee's hit *Jungle Fever* and starring in one of America's top sitcoms, *Living Single*. Like Will Smith, who became a household name via *Fresh Prince of Bel Air*, she diligently expanded her horizons beyond the rap world, forming Flavor Unit, a successful record label and a management company. Managed by her mother, she worked within a solid female power base.

Latifah was signed to Tommy Boy in 1989 and her debut *All Hail The Queen* sold a million worldwide, marking a turning point for girl-rap in its representation of funky female dignity. Dropping each syllable with surefire shot and humour, from the sweet, quirky De La Soul collaboration 'Mama Gave Birth To

**Queen Latifah** in Los Angeles, 1993: Earth Mother as businesswoman – rap crosses over to Hollywood. (Martina Raddatz/ Redferns)

The Soul Children' to her duet 'Ladies First' with Monie Love and the smash dance hit 'Come Into My House', the album rode on optimism and an uplifting message. After the follow-up, *Nature Of A Sista*, it was obvious that Tommy Boy couldn't contain her.

'I'm not just a rapper, a businesswoman, an actress . . . I needed someone to share my vision,' she said. 'Jheryl Busby [Motown president] was that kind of guy.' Though she was only twenty-one, her reputation secured her a favourable deal at Motown in 1993, and her third album *Black Reign* reflected this sense of confidence. Latifah's dignity arose in part from her Afrocentricity, a strand of the 'Back to Africa' movement that had a major impact on hip hop, distinct from hardcore nihilism in its sense of spiritual freedom. The name Latifah is Arabic for 'sensitive', while Queen is a tribute to her African ancestors. She classed herself as rap's 'feminine teacher', showing appreciation for her culture. Regularly called upon to speak on radio, at black feminist groups and for AIDS and ecology charities, Latifah was seen as the poet of a generation. Though she came closest in spirit to the womanist literature of black American writers like Maya Angelou and Alice Walker, she denied that she was a feminist. 'I don't even adhere to that shit. All that shit is bullshit!' she said in 1994. 'I know that at the end of the day I'm a black woman in this world and I gotta get mine. I want to see the rise of the black male in personal strength and power. I wanna see the creation of a new black community for ourselves and respect from others.'[13]

The links between rap and literature, though, are strong. 'Toni Morrison, Zora Neale Hurston, us, it's all poetry, a language in itself – just a different generation,' said LA-based black nationalist rapper Nefertiti. 'We live by a constitution here in America. That's what makes words so strong. We've always followed words through the power of this system.'[14] Like Sethe, the heroine of Morrison's book *Beloved*, who discovers the empowering purpose of 're-memory', rap involves a reclaiming of black history. All the female rappers interviewed spoke with urgency about the need to teach and remember the 'dis-remembered', to recall the tragic impact of slavery and to find past role models of women who survived or rose above their lot, like the charismatic nineteenth-century Unionist Harriet Tubman.

Infusing female rap are metaphors of Queens, Princesses and Ladies. Just as Morrison acknowledged the power of naming, some young MCs took on an authority through the inventiveness of their names – Arabic Queen Latifah, Nefertiti, the fourteenth-century BC Egyptian queen who educated Tutankhamen, Queen Mother Rage – all these harked back to ancestral heroines. Such naming countered anonymity, the legacy of women silenced through slavery. In her book *In Search of Our Mothers' Gardens*, Alice Walker wrote of the troubled, unconscious spirituality of black women in the post-Reconstruction South:

These crazy Saints stared out at the world, wildly, like lunatics – or quietly, like suicides; and the 'God' that was in their gaze was as mute as a great stone.

Who were these Saints? These crazy, loony, pitiful women?

Some of them, without a doubt, were our mothers and grand-mothers.'[15]

The flowering of black women's writing, from Lorraine Hansberry's hit Broadway play *A Raisin in the Sun* in 1959 to Ntozake Shange's ironic scream from the heart, *for colored girls who have considered suicide when the rainbow is enuf*, in the 1970s and the early-1980s jazz rhythms of Morrison and Toni Cade Bambara, showed a reinvention of language through jivetalk, folklore and literary metaphor. Female rappers continue in this tradition, articulating their generation's experience through the bald originality of their own language. Although some feel disconnected from feminist authors associated with the white college establishment, finding expression through their rhymes is the rage of rural foremothers. Predominantly urban, though, like the narrator of Morrison's *Jazz*, this new generation is fully versed in the mores of the street: 'Nobody says it's pretty here; nobody says it's easy either. What it is is decisive, and if you pay attention to the street plans, all laid out, the City can't hurt you.'[16]

The links between music and literature are evident through constant referencing and re-referencing – in the early 1990s, for instance, Alice Walker wrote sleevenotes for the black female a cappella act Sweet Honey In The Rock, as did Ntozake Shange for Nina Simone, and Maya Angelou received a warm dedication in a Pointer Sisters' song. In the rap world, an artist like Nefertiti was trying to solidify the connection, saying, 'My album is trying to let people know what's going on. A lot of people who don't read don't realize how uplifting books can be. It's all about awareness.'

'Awareness' became a buzz word as the ideas of Malcolm X resurfaced in the late 1980s, and black nationalism infused certain sections of hip hop. His doctrine of black pride and self-reliance permeated 'Daisy Age' surreal or psychedelic rap outfits such as A Tribe Called Quest and De La Soul, along with mixed-gender rap acts like the Atlanta-based (rural-South-and-proud-of-it) Arrested Development and the quirky, jazz-influenced Digable Planets. In acknowledging the feminine, these groups made rap's characteristic bass-led, stripped-down delivery more buoyant with surreal raps, psychedelic riffs and samples from 1970s funk. Me'Shell NdegéOcello, an early signing to Madonna's Maverick label, developed this stance within the dance sphere; her 1993 debut *Plantation Lullabies* was a mix of rap, soul and poetry. Using the image of the plantation as a metaphor for modern-day ghetto life, she said, 'My lullabies are the calm before the revolution of the people of color.'[17] The irony of that statement, coming from the stable of a massively successful white woman's operation, did not go unnoticed.

Other women followed a more rigorous agenda. Nefertiti, for instance, who was the strongest, most poetic advocate of the 'Five percenters' (followers of the radical black Five percent Nation of Islam faith) and whose 1994 debut album *L.I.F.E.* (*Living In Fear Of Extinction*) dealt with every issue from ecological survival and genocide to love and childbirth.

Though explicitly political, nationalist rappers Nefertiti and Queen Mother Rage were careful not to criticize their 'brothers', making race rather than sex the priority issue. Rage was the X-Clan 'crown wearer' or messenger of the New York-based Blackwatch movement, one of numerous black rap coalitions that sprang up in the late 1980s. Not strictly Muslim by faith, the group she represented still took rap seriously as a vehicle to heighten black consciousness. 'I'm keen to stress there's more to being conscious than wearing a pendant. We're telling people to look into what they're wearing and why it is that they're wearing it.'

This radicalism reached boiling point when Sister Souljah, part-time female recruit to rap's most influential group, Public Enemy, announced in 1991, 'Hip hop represents the African war drum . . . the call to arms . . . the survival of the memory and the legacy of our ancestors.'[18] A diligent, widely travelled activist from the Bronx projects who was educated at Cornell and Rutgers University, she became involved with rap after realizing its potential as the black community's 'strongest communication network anywhere, worldwide'.

While many applauded her uncompromising stance, her album *360 Degrees Of Power* was a flop, with critics writing her off as a 'humourless second-rate rapper'. It was evident her skills lay more in activism than in musicianship. Undeterred, she said, 'Sister Souljah is not trying to dazzle you with her rhymes. Sister Souljah is trying to give you the information that you need to liberate your mind, soul and spirit from white supremacy and racism.' Pointing out that she worked with multi-million-dollar-selling artists like Public Enemy and Ice Cube, she added, 'So what is really threatening to America is what I'm saying, and not how I'm saying it.'

## Let Yourself Get Down

Perceived mainly as a black medium, rap still has meaning for other cultures, particularly the US Hispanic community, and women there have played an active part in its promotion. Throughout the 1980s Latin hip hop developed as a separate strand, its underlying funky syncopation on hits such as Shannon's 'Let The Music Play' and tracks by The Cover Girls or Sapphire reflecting the feverish groove of Manhattan clubs like Funhouse. The biggest female star to emerge from this scene was Lisa Lisa who, with Cult Jam, had a series of pop/hip hop hits like 'I Wonder If I Take You Home' and 'All Cried Out'. Proud of her heritage, she told me in 1994, 'There's a lot of talent in the Latin community, but like a lot of minorities we don't get looked out for. We've got to get together like the Afro-Americans and show what we can do.[19]

A Puerto Rican native of Hell's Kitchen, the Manhattan ghetto west of Times Square, Lisa Valez met with rap producers Full Force (the svengalis behind UTFO and The Real Roxanne) at the Funhouse when she was twenty. After fronting their band Cult Jam for five years she quit the group in 1991 and had an identity crisis. 'Someone said it was all over for me. I cried. But then you wipe your eyes, walk out there and figure how to kick those people in the ass. I had been a little girl with two guys at the side and six producers up her ass. It was time for Lisa to come out on her own and grow up.' Her debut solo album *LL-77*, a ground-breaking mix of tough club beats, wise witty girl-talk and funky vocals, was partly produced by rock/funk queen Nona Hendryx. Conveying Lisa's salty verve, it combined elements of Latino rap history with a personal narrative drive.

Lisa knew how to integrate rap within her own dance-music culture. Other women have not been so successful. White rap, for instance, has always had a chequered history – with very few white male, let alone white female, artists breaking through with what is overwhelmingly a black cultural force. The Beastie Boys cornered the market in rap for college frat brats, but the female equivalent, if it surfaced, seemed strained and uncertain. Blonde female LA rapper Tairrie B, for example, worked with former NWA member Easy E, released an album in 1990 and disappeared. Trying to be down', she talked about 'packing pieces' on the club scene, breakdancing and tagging her high school. Dubbed 'the Madonna of Rap', Italian American Tairrie committed the ultimate sin of trying too hard. She re-emerged in the late 1990s as a nu-metal rock siren, a role she was far more comfortable with.

Four white girls from New York, Luscious Jackson avoided the credibility trap by focusing on an entirely different audience. 'We're outside the rap community; it'd be false for us to try and be hardcore MCs. We've never played to a straight rap audience, so I don't know how that would go over,' said singer/guitarist Jill Cunniff.[20] Coming from liberal bohemian backgrounds in Greenwich Village, Jill, Gabby, Vivienne and Kate had been friends since they were twelve years old and were veterans of the New York club scene. Their music, like their audience, was mixed. Signed in the US to the Beastie Boys label Grand Royal, their 1993 EP *In Search Of Manny* fused old-school rap, power-funk grooves, 'real' drums and an indie rock sensibility. The stand-out track 'Let Yourself Get Down', with its affectionate girl-rap, was a tribute to female old-school crew The Sequence.

Press attention for this debut EP was enormous, much greater than for, say, MC Lyte, who had released her third album. Cunniff said,

'Most journalists are white, I'm sure that's partly why they like us. We're safe. We look like them, smell like them. Same old shit. We love black women rappers, they've been a huge inspiration to us, and they don't get enough recognition. Also, people are like, "White girl rappers – we're gonna make a lotta money". The temptation is every record company wants you to be the first white girl-rap group. That's just gross.'

Part of the attention came from their association with the Beastie Boys, but Cunniff stressed the girls' independence from the group: 'We'd been friends with them for a long time, as little kids. They went off, got really famous, lost touch with everyone, and got very sexist in their lyrics. We fell out with them but now we've all come back. We're still friends, but we're different from them as artists.' By 1994 Luscious Jackson were moving into more brooding, bluesy garage fusion on their debut album *Natural Ingredients*, with honeyed rap just one element in their groove.

In Britain black women rappers took a lot of cues from their US counterparts. Late-1980s London girl crews such as the Cookie Crew, She Rockers and Wee Papa Girl Rappers received widepread UK press and critical acclaim – they even had a few chart hits – but when it came to the US market they were literally lost in translation. The respect bordering on awe the Cookie Crew duo had for early Salt 'N' Pepa also contained frustration at somehow being in the wrong country. 'If we met them I think we'd break down in tears. We'd like to work with them. We love them,' said one Cookie, Suzy Q. The solution then was either to mix rap with the eclectic dance rhythms so beloved by the British market or relocate.

When I interviewed the Cookie Crew in their South London bedroom in 1987, slouched on the bed was a diminutive teenage girl in denim jacket and jeans. 'I'm going to be the female LL Cool J,' she said. Her name was Monie Love. Within two years she had moved to New York, been adopted by Queen Latifah and the Native Tongues rap collective, worked with the Jungle Brothers, and secured a major deal. Her first two albums, *Down To Earth* (1990) and *In A Word Or 2* (1993), married tickly pop with hard-driven hip hop and sold like crazy. 'Something was shining over me,' she said later. 'I was lucky, being everywhere at the right time.'

Conversely, UK-based rap/singer Neneh Cherry found that her New York background worked better for her in England. The step-daughter of jazz musician Don Cherry, she emerged through the punk club scene of the early 1980s, fronting an outré ensemble called Rip, Rig and Panic. After going solo, with one eye studiously on the dance floor, she plus partner Cameron McVey and a production team that included Soul II Soul's Nellee Hooper came up with one of the biggest rap/pop singles of the decade – 'Buffalo Stance'. With her trademark Lycra, trainers, chains and flyaway hair, Cherry – pregnant and proud of it for the record's promotion – cut a distinctive figure. 'I'm not into male-ego rap,' she said. 'Female rappers manage to be funnier. They're less scared of looking a bit of an asshole and laughing at the whole thing.'[21]

Though always perceived as outside rap's circle – her debut LP *Raw Like Sushi* (1989) was gritty pop, while the follow-up *Homebrew* (1992) ploughed a more obvious dance groove – 'Buffalo Stance' still remains a quirky rap classic. 'It's about surviving,' she said. 'Standing strong. A song for anyone who goes through life determined to be their own person.'

## Ill Na Na

In 1994 it took a legion of hair and make-up artists to coiffure the women in the video for the Salt 'N' Pepa/En Vogue collaboration 'Whatta Man'. Sleek, sensual and sexy were not adjectives usually associated with women in rap. For so long they had had to be tough in sweats, hard on the beats and beating men at their own game – but as female rappers got older and matured, so they felt able to display a more typically feminine side.

Salt, Pepa and DJ Spinderella had always had one eye on the upmarket. When their 1986 debut *Hot Cool & Vicious* was released, they were regular, awestruck homegirls, yet within two years they became pop divas, the first female rappers to go gold. Interviewing them in a Manhattan hotel in 1988, I was struck by the ostentation – swathes of leather, fur and gold. Over-excited, speaking with clarity one minute and collapsing into impenetrable giggles the next, they were charged up by their success. Even then they were talking about wealth and real estate – the desire for a second home in California with glistening cars and a well-stocked fridge. Despite the radical nature of their music, they shone with aspirational chic.

Taking on the mock personae of three sophisticated, middle-aged women, they discussed divorce, carpet-cleaners and costly vacations, sounding like embryonic Millie Jacksons. 'It's our own soap opera,' Pepa told me. 'A pretend for when we're on tour. A game where we act real old – maybe part of our future selves.' Seven years on they had partly fulfilled the fantasy, transforming themselves through four hit albums into tomboy glamour queens. They had played at President Clinton's Inauguration. Producer Hurby 'Luv Bug' was very much on the back-burner. They were all single mothers and their prevailing motto was 'independence'. 'We cater to women. We build up women's self-esteem,' said Salt. 'That's something we've always taken pride in.' Having reached their late twenties, Salt, Pepa and Spinderella were coming of age. They were relaxed in their curves, and their sexual expression was as assured as it was feisty.

As 'Whatta Man' shot into the charts, rivals 7669 emerged, firing: 'Salt 'N' Pepa just follow what's hot and change to it. 7669 is us. It's sensuality,' said El Boog E, one of four New York-based video-stylists who decided to form a frontline female R&B/rap act to out-raunch SWV, En Vogue and Salt 'N' Pepa put together. The sleeve for their debut album on Motown, *East From A Bad Block*, had them topless astride Harley Davidsons, backs to the camera and butts in the air.

The Harley Davidson picture echoed a troubled theme in pop representation of black female sexuality. In 1990 Florida outfit 2 Live Crew were the target of pro-censorship groups, but after a court case lyrics on their album *As Nasty As They Wanna Be* were deemed by a Miami judge to be ribald and tasteless rather than obscene. Nevertheless, the album cover, featuring four black women in thong bikinis standing with their backs to the camera, male members of the group looking up between their legs, was crude in its message.

'In the sexual iconography of the traditional black porno-graphic imagination, the protruding butt is seen as an indication of a heightened sexuality,' wrote commentator bell hooks in her essay 'Selling Hot Pussy'. 'Since black female sexuality has been represented in racist and sexist iconography as more free and liberated, many black women singers, irrespective of the quality of their voices, have cultivated an image which suggests they are sexually available and licentious.'[22]

'Men pick, women choose and pussy rules,' said Jazz, one of the rap trio Hoez With Attitude. Described by writer Rob Marriott as 'three church girls with a gimmick', HWA skirted both the strip-joint market and the lower reaches of showbiz rap, posing for the black US porn magazine *Black Beauties*, as well as undoing the zips on their short shorts for a *Source* photo shoot. 'We're redefining "hoe",' they claimed. 'We're using "hoe" as a positive word. If one little girl can walk down the street and somebody calls her a hoe and she can say thank you and keep going with pride, then we've helped.'[23] Brave words, but in a culture that traditionally viewed the black female body as expendable and available for prostitution, they had an uphill struggle. Unless, of course, their claims were just a cynical attempt to reap the benefits of 'playing slut' – 'Yes, we hoes, and we playing it for all we can.'

By the mid-1990s, two female stars emerged who inevitably plugged into the appetite for semi-pornographic rap: arch rivals Lil' Kim and Foxy Brown. Brooklyn-born Kim dealt in hard-edged, explicitly sexual rhymes and dressed in skimpy bikinis and furs. Her parents separated when she was nine, and Kim lived with her father, a strict Air Force man, until she was a teenager. 'When I was thirteen and wanted to have a boyfriend, all hell broke loose. He called me a "bitch", and that was *it*. Your father calling you a bitch?' she told flamboyant broadcaster Ruby Wax. 'I was so respectful until that time. It was like, whoah, whatever . . . I'm gonna show you bitch.'[24] And with that the persona of Lil' Kim, promiscuous, glamorous and street-tough, was born.

Kim first honed her rhyming skills with the help of rapper

**Lil' Kim:** sexploitation scene queen. (Salifu Idriss/ Redferns)

Biggie Smalls (or Notorious BIG), guesting on an album he was producing with the Junior M.A.F.I.A. gang. A record pulsating with rhyme scenarios of guns, money and sex, *Conspiracy* went gold in 1995 and gave Lil' Kim maximum exposure. Her romantic affair with Smalls was solidified in the public imagination when the latter was gunned down in LA in 1995, just six months after his West Coast rival Tupac Shakur was shot and killed. She became the high-profile grief-stricken gangsta widow, openly mourning her lost love, and teaming up with Smalls' friend and business partner Sean 'Puffy' Combs to work on her solo debut. This, allied with a provocative marketing campaign, meant that her appropriately titled debut album *Hard Core* went to No. 11 in the pop charts the week of its release in 1996. She again cemented the connection with Smalls on her follow-up, *Notorious KIM* (2000).

Kim's detractors criticized the way she sold sex, but her skills as a rap artist were undeniable. 'I don't choose to call it porno-rap,' she said. 'I don't project porno – I see myself as projecting sexiness and sensuality. Sometimes I do get a little bit rough-edged.' She was riding a delicate faultline between tease and sleaze. Admitting that 'sometimes it's a power thing', she was careful to differentiate herself from the 'get-money girls'. 'I'm not a hooker. Where I come from in Brooklyn there's the "get-money girls". I'm not that. We just bad-ass bitches who know how to work our shit with men.'[25]

Kim occupied that place in rap between blaxploitation and entertainment, and in 1996 her only main rival in that area was Foxy Brown. Also Brooklyn-bred, the slender, overtly sexy Brown was a fierce freestyler and fan of hardcore rap. She first came to prominence rapping on LL Cool J's *Mr Smith* album, and worked with Total, Jay-Z and on a remix of Toni Braxton's 'You're Making Me High'. After a major bidding war Brown signed to Def Jam and her 1996 inflamatory gangsta-mack'stress-style debut Ill Na Na shot to No. 7 in its first week. Not surprisingly Kim and Brown have engaged in very public feuding ever since. On Capone-N-Noreaga's song 'Bang Bang', for instance, Brown attacks Kim for being a professional widow using the memory of Notorious BIG to sell records. On the same day that Kim and Capone-N-Noreaga (CNN) appeared at New York radio station for promotional work, there was a six-man, 22-shot gun battle which left one man wounded. Kim and CNN denied any involvement.[26]

Just when it seemed that female rappers had blocked them-selves into a corner, outvying each other with increasingly hardcore, sexual imagery, along came an artist who opened up a whole new avenue for women. The arrival of Missy 'Misdemeanor' Elliott was like a breath of fresh air. In 1997, her debut album *Supa Dupa Fly* revolutionized hip hop with its bouncy staccato beats and surreal lyricism. Here was a large woman who defied the 'bikini-in-a-limo' convention of the day by exaggerating her size and dancing in an inflated rubber jumpsuit on the video for her breakthrough hit 'The Rain (Supa Dupa Fly)'. She was about primary colours and optimistic beats, asserting a vision of womanhood that was creative, comic and sharply 'on the money'. A gifted producer as well as a rapper, she launched her own Gold Mind Inc. label as part of her Elektra deal. Since 1997 she has worked with artists as varied as Eminem, Destiny's Child, Busta Rhymes, Mariah Carey and Janet Jackson, giving their sound added bite and focus. She became a top-name producer on a par with Timbaland, Shek'spere and all the new architects of millennial R&B.

Born Melissa Arnette Elliott in Portsmouth, Virginia, in 1972, her earliest childhood memory was of 'my father stamping my mother in the face with combat boots. I was three or four.'[27] The domestic abuse continued until she was fourteen, and she and her mother Patricia escaped to a safe house. 'That was the scariest time of my life, thinking he was gonna come after us and kill us,' she recalled. Elliott was a troubled teenager who suffered breakdowns and underachieved at school, despite her obvious intelligence. 'I wasn't mentally focused because of living so long in fear,' she said. Hip hop gave a boost to her self-esteem. She

**Missy Elliott:** establishing a new power base for women in hip hop. (Ebet Roberts/ Redferns)

formed a group Sista, which was signed to Elektra in 1991. Although their record was never released, by then she had built up a reputation as a sparky writer/producer, and teamed up with old friend and rising star Timbaland. By 1996 they were working with artists like Aaliyah, SWV and Ginuwine. Then when she was picked up by Sean 'Puffy' Combs and re-signed to Elektra she became 'hot'. 'Everything started changing. You go from people saying, "You're not made out to be an artist", to having every major label there tugging at you.'

After *Supa Dupa Fly*, Elliott's work took a more serious turn with the powerbroking demand for respect that was *Da Real World* (1999). Come 2001, though, she was playing to her strengths again, opting for the psychedelic and surreal on her album *Miss E . . . So Addictive*. Saying, 'you don't have to do drugs because my music is what gets you high', Elliott had created an audacious mix of Indian tablas, Hawaiian guitar and futurist electronic beats. Her songs were about the joy of dancing, about music's entrancing power, and about sex. 'One Minute Man', for instance, was a lighthearted skit on a boyfriend's lack of stamina during love-making.

But though on one level Elliott's message was one of escapism, she was also making strong points about the image of women in pop (that artists didn't have to be sylphlike to be successful), and female assertiveness. Like Queen Latifah before her, Elliott was establishing a powerbase behind the scenes. She dealt with the legacy of her traumatic childhood by supporting Break The Cycle, a campaign group against domestic violence. The organization received profits from her Misdemeanor brand lipstick: 'I gave a million dollars, 100 per cent – I didn't take a penny off the lipstick,' she said proudly.[28] Through hip hop she had found a voice, replacing childhood fear and powerlessness with a message of hope.

## Rude Girls

Whether the word 'hoe' – like the word 'bitch' – can ever be reconstructed is debatable. The argument seemed to have greater urgency on the Jamaican dancehall scene where 'punani watching' had almost become a high-risk sport. 'I've seen a lot of them in Jamaica pin dollar bills to their clothes. They're proud to look and be outrageous. They dance with their hands right in front of their vaginas; they're proud to be women,' said British broadcaster and ragga exponent David Rodigan.[29] Proud of their 'punanis' (Jamaican for 'pussy'), 1990s ragga girls dressed to express, wearing gaudy stretch lamé and Lycra, shorts so tight they were called 'punani prints' or hot pants, known as 'batty riders'. The aim was to reveal as much as possible without being arrested.

The look was meant to suggest sexual control, the desire to attract a man who works to satisfy his woman. 'A worker man is a humble person who knows how to get down with the programme. Once he can love you right, hey, he's a worker man. If you can't love us females right, you're not a worker man, you're a joker man,' said DJ Patra, the first woman to emerge from the dancehall scene as an international artist, explaining to me the philosophy behind her 1994 single 'Worker Man'.[30] At twenty-one she was 'whining' herself towards the young male market with a stage act that left little to the imagination. On British TV she performed the song with two backing dancers who wore impossibly short shorts, grinding and gyrating into the floor. 'I'm sexy but not too sexy,' she claimed. 'Forget the slackness. I give only so much and the guys go crazy.'

Ironically, compared to other women on the dancehall scene, Patra showed a degree of restraint. In the upwardly mobile strive for success, there's a fine line between gaining an audience through controversy and alienating them. Her debut album *Queen Of The Pack*, a combination of rugged ragga and killingly slick mixes, reached No. 1 in the US reggae chart and within a year sold almost a million worldwide, with 'Worker Man' becoming a ragga/rap anthem. Although primarily a dancehall heroine, once she began to cross to the mainstream Patra learned good table manners and made astute international connections. She went into the studio with Cyndi Lauper to record a guest spot on the latter's *Twelve Deadly Cyns . . .* collection, and for her album collaborated with 1970s soul star Lynn Collins and LA rapper Yo Yo. 'Yo Yo's like me: ragamuffin, down to earth. We didn't mix the star shit or anything, we just got down to business. It was great.'

Patra was signed to New York Epic Records by Vivian Scott, vice-president of the Black Music department, who, having brought Shabba Ranks to the label in 1990, was looking for a Queen Consort for her Dancehall King. Scott had already been negotiating with one female DJ when, on a business trip to Kingston in 1992, she saw a young feisty woman pass through the lobby:

'She was stunning, she had this aura about her that she was somebody special. I didn't know who she was, whether she sang, or what. When I asked Shabba's manager, he said, "Aha, that's Patra." So I discontinued my negotiations with the other female DJ, switched on to Patra and got her to sign with us.

'I felt bad about the other DJ, but I knew if I hadn't signed Patra she would always have been in the back of my mind. I saw Patra not only as someone who could sing or DJ, but could have a movie career. Her beauty alone will get her covers. She has a 360-degree star quality about her that I felt the other DJ eventually would have, but it would've taken a lot more time and grooming. Patra just had it.'[31]

Scott came under fire through the Patra project for exploitation of women, but she insisted that Shabba and Patra had to come to Epic warts 'n' all:

'I wouldn't have signed them had I not agreed with how they wanted to get their message across. In Patra videos you see women very scantily dressed and dancing sexually. I go to any street corner in Kingston, and I'm gonna see the same thing. It wasn't a device to sell records. The key point on her "Queen Of The Pack" video is that you never see men interact with her, you never see her shaking and whining up to men in those videos. It's a very independent thing.'

Jamaica is very different from liberal black America. On a scene where women were still very much considered adjuncts of men, Patra herself, pristine and sparkle-eyed, was keen to emphasize her independence. Of her labelmate Shabba, she said, 'He's my big brother. He brought me into the business and gives me a lot of encouragement. He has taught me things, but I take what I want from it. I don't take too much because I'm a very smart woman. I give him all my respect but he doesn't control me.'

With the Epic deal and a move to Manhattan, Patra was able to develop her career more the way she wanted, in contrast to the late 1980s, when, reacting to peer pressure, she had tried to outdo in 'cockybully' notoriety other female DJs such as Carla Marshall, Lady Mackerel and Lady Saw. Songs like 'Teaser' and 'Visa Hole' she would rather not talk about. '"Visa Hole" meant I have a good hole for all the men,' she said. 'It was just gimmicks, stupid stuff.'

Competition is raw on the Jamaican dancehall scene: on a poverty-stricken island where one of the biggest exports is music, it is hardly surprising that women fight with tried-and-tested techniques. Some felt that they could disrupt the sexual stereotypes. 'I like breaking rules men set. I'm a dancehall goddess, to the top. I'll wear a batty rider and my printers, but they're warrior clothes,' said Toronto DJ Carla Marshall.[32] In the sex war she was able to turn male taunts into own goals – like the time at New York's Ritz when Louie 'Typewriter' Rankin, a male DJ who regularly scoffed at women, asked Marshall over the mike if she had ever been fucked by a fourteen-inch cock. 'Louie, I want you to know the only way me done is if you dick more than two inch or your tongue bigger than you wood! Watch it!' she chanted back, to an appreciative roar from the crowd.

'When you act shy, they boo you, so you have to act brave,' said another female DJ, Princess Goldie. At a dancehall jam men were so reluctant to pass the mike to a woman that when she got the chance she had to be larger and more explicit than life to get noticed. While on one level Marshall, Lady Saw, Lady Mackerel *et al.* provided an example of 'buddy terrorism' with songs like 'Mi Man Pon Mi' and 'Everyday Cock', the girls that imitated them in the crowd were maybe less confident and therefore easily exploited. 'In dancehall some of the girls are so young. They're wearing revealing clothes and all these guys are just lined up, watching them, like in a meat market. It felt really threatening,' says one Jamaican female friend who went to early-1990s dancehall nights. To many women, though, it's a night of forgetfulness and celebration, holding a Canei (flavoured white wine) in one hand, while waving the other in the air. To others it's the route to teenage pregnancy and a life of even more limited options. While women (rightfully) take pride in their punanis, all too many men feel free to take advantage of them.

'I don't have kids. I can't because I'm just thinking about music,' said Patra. She thought for a minute, then added, with emphasis, 'I'm a single woman, too.'

### Bed's Too Big without You

Reggae and its later offshoot ragga have never been an easy scene for women to break into, but they have always been an important presence, from the women at the turn of the century who sat down with their family to recount folk tales, to the New York and London MCs many decades later presenting their own version of the oral tradition.

When US rap impacted on 1970s roots reggae to create a raw-edged ragga hybrid, the music began to reflect the violent gangster Yardie culture of the ghetto. Artists had come a long way from Sir Lord Comic's coy toasting about Adam and Eve's sexual high jinks. By the early 1990s teenage ragga star Buju Banton was at the centre of moral controversy with his song 'Boom Bye-Bye', which encouraged the shooting of 'batty-boys', or homosexuals.

Many of the generation who began singing in the 1960s and 1970s were bewildered by the effects of dancehall, which seemed nothing more than an X-rated porn movie. Though a large number of dancehall fans were female, women were among its most vocal critics. 'It's having a severe effect on children out there. There has to be some censorship as to what's played on the air. Like magazines - we don't want to see our child pick up *Playboy*. You have to set standards and values. Besides, a positive message can be just as exciting,' said Carlene Davis, a Jamaican star who has been performing her moving mix of R&B, soul and dub since the 1970s.[33]

While the 1990s saw women making strides through dancehall, the unsung heroines of more traditional reggae were the lovers' rock singers of the previous two decades. In the same way that blueswomen made blues commercial via vaudeville, so women fused reggae with pop to create their colony of lovers' rock. Reggae emerged in the late 1940s with basic sound systems and the recording of mento, Jamaica's raggedy calypso style. With the influence of American R&B in the 1950s, it transmuted into the chopped guitar sound of ska, with key producers on the scene such as Leslie Kong and Clement 'Sir Coxone' Dodd opening their own studios, the latter's Studio One being the most important. By the mid-1960s ska had slowed down into 'rude boy' music and rock-steady, with hits like Prince Buster's 'Judge Dread' and Desmond Dekker's '007 (Shanty Town)' pointing out social injustice.

Described by writer Elena Oumano as 'a ramshackle boys' club controlled by "uptown top rankings"', reggae was very male-dominated, but it was a woman who gave it its first international hit. Signed to London's Island Records, the label established in the 1960s by white Jamaican entrepreneur Chris Blackwell, Millie Small had a worldwide hit in 1964 with the cheeky charmer 'My Boy Lollipop'. Despite her success, women didn't have much impact on the scene until over a decade later, when Althia and Donna took their light-hearted skank 'Up Town Top Rankin'' to the top of the British charts.

With the rise of Rastafarianism and the use of ganja (marijuana) as a meditative aid, 1970s reggae slowed down even further to its characteristic hypnotic, pulsating bassline. The phenomenal success of Bob Marley and other rasta acts such as Burning Spear, Third World and Steel Pulse meant that from the mid-1970s onwards women were relegated to the shadows. 'Reggae was very rootsy, radical and male,' said British lovers' rock singer/songwriter Carroll Thompson. Of the few who broke through, Judy Mowatt and Marcia Griffiths already had international exposure as part of Marley's backing trio the I-Threes.

A clear-voiced stylist and Jamaica's finest female vocalist, Griffiths kept her message religious rather than feminist: 'Because our music is truth and it is positive, so it definitely has a spiritual force. We are all players and singers for Almighty God,' she once said.[34]

Thompson, whose career took off in 1980 with the Leonard Chin-produced hit 'I'm So Sorry', had a less idealistic view. 'Roots reggae was synonymous with rastas, and rasta then was about suppressing women. Also it was difficult for record companies to perceive women singing love songs on reggae, even though the sound was successful on the street,' she said.[35] When she started, Thompson noticed a dearth of female role models. 'Marcia Griffiths and Judy Mowatt were the only females who had albums. Millie was a one-off, and not my generation. Then a British woman, Janet Kay, had a major hit in 1979 with "Silly Games" and I realized it was possible to do reggae music and get noticed.'

Although lovers' rock singles in the wake of 'Silly Games' began to flood the market in Britain and Jamaica, the genre was dismissed by purists as too weak and watered down. But since Lorna Bennett's 1972 hit 'Breakfast In Bed', women had been busily and brilliantly welding the clarity of pop melody to a compulsive reggae beat. Throughout the late 1970s and 1980s a series of mournful classics were recorded, from Sheila Hylton's 'Bed's Too Big Without You' to Deborahe Glasgow's 'Knight In Shining Armour', Barbara Jones's 'Please Mr Please' and 'Can't Be With You Tonight' by Judy Boucher. They cornered the market in cover versions, reinterpreting and paring down rock songs to a bell-like pop base. Foxy Brown, for instance, turned Tracy Chapman's 'Fast Car' into a cheeky yet heart-rending reggae anthem.

In a tough, insecure industry where men are singled out for the longevity of album deals, women have found it hard to build on their singles' success. Deborahe Glasgow was one of the younger generation poised to make a breakthrough, her vocal versatility spanning both the ragga and lovers' rock world, but tragically she died of cancer in 1994. 'There are a lot of estab-

**Marcia Griffiths** at Reggae Sunsplash, 1992: former member of Bob Marley's I-Threes and Jamaica's finest female reggae artist. (John Kirk/ Redferns)

lished females in the reggae business,' said Thompson. 'But none have broken through. There should be a female Maxi Priest – quite a few of us could have done it. And Marcia Griffiths still doesn't have the recognition she deserves.'

Like the high-energy heroines of the disco boom, many lovers' rock artists suffered through quick-turnover independent deals. 'I felt stifled. I was forever haggling for money. I never knew how much I'd sold. The business wasn't run efficiently or effectively,' said Thompson who was signed first to the small London label Ital and then to Virgin, where they tried to make her drop reggae in favour of pop/soul. When she left Virgin to form her own reggae label Carousel and had hits with artists such as Sugar Minott, Winston Reedy and girl group Saffrice, Thompson thought she had found a solution. 'The trouble was I'd included my boyfriend. Love is blind. I had to fold the company. I found it very difficult to create a stronghold in the business – all my ideas had to be sorted through my boyfriend, he was the mouthpiece. It was demeaning to me as a woman.'

Another woman who found it difficult to consolidate her first overnight success was Sophia George, a personable, bubbly woman who at the age of twenty-one had an international hit in

1985 with 'Girlie Girlie'. Lambasting a man for having too many affairs, the jaunty song proved popular with women the world over, from Jamaica to Britain and the US. 'My brother wasn't amused. He had a lot of girls and said, "I can't believe you're my sister. How can you say that about me!" Also, a policeman told me that song had made his girlfriend leave. "You're too 'Girlie Girlie'," she'd said. Women? They all said, "Thank you very much for mashing some of those men for me,"' George said in 1994 from her home in Kingston.[36]

Though she was twice voted Female Reggae Artist of the Year, after 'Girlie Girlie' George had only intermittent hits, mainly in Jamaica. Signed first to Winner Records, then the New York-based Pow Wow, she grew to adopt a sanguine, almost passive attitude. 'It's a male-dominated world and we have to work extra hard to be good, but I don't get frustrated. I listen to music, do my voice exercises, and just try and write as if nothing is happening. Then if anything does I'll be prepared.'

Marjorie Whylie, musicologist, pianist, percussion player and veritable *grande dame* on Jamaica's music scene, offered me her interpretation of reggae's treatment of women: 'Reggae started life as music of protest, social commentary. It represented a cosmology, and values came out of experiences at the base of society where women are strong in a supportive sense – which meant that those carrying the message to the forefront would be male.'[37] As yet she still had to see a woman 'go the full journey' and 'interpret people to themselves' the way Bob Marley did.

Starting out on the eclectic Jamaican scene of the 1980s, Whylie played in many different bands, leading her own combos in a mix of jazz, blues, Latin and reggae. 'When I was growing up it wasn't respectable for a woman to be a musician, she had to be a piano teacher. But I wanted to develop my own music. What I play is a kind of hybrid, a European bias with African retentions, a whole acculturation process. We are a Creole society, and what I do is represent the many-faceted nature of our culture.'

One answer for women in reggae was to broaden their base. After the struggle of her early years Carroll Thompson went on tour as backing singer to top stars such as Boy George, Billy

Ocean and Natalie Cole, in an effort to learn about the music business outside reggae. She then used that business experience in the early 1990s to set up via a Japanese company the independent label Cairn, releasing the reggae she had always wanted to sing.

Carlene Davis, too, found that time away from Jamaica – first as a teenager in Berkshire, then as a successful star in Toronto performing pop and rock as well as reggae – gave her confidence to pursue her own style once she returned. 'Having soaked up everything in Canada, I felt it was time to get across-the-board acceptance from my own community,' she told me. 'In 1980 I did Reggae Sunsplash, and it was a big turnaround for me. Once I focused into reggae music, I felt totally at home.' Signed to Island subsidiary Gee Street in the late 1980s, her sound had fresh energy. 'As female artists we may not make international success, but we're consistently there in the ethnic market, putting out records, getting airplay. Trust me, we are there.'

By the late 1980s women in rap and reggae had begun to move in from the margins, remoulding by their presence the hip hop and digital dancehall that underlay mainstream pop. Their visibility challenged pop's Eurocentric white profile, its reliance on rock-guitar supremacy and the four boys in the band. Coinciding with their rise was the long overdue crossover of a new genre, decades old but freshly marketed – world music. A catch-all term for anything 'ethnic', it provided an opportunity, however haphazard, for female artists previously on the borders of pop to be heard, consumed and adored. It was a chance for them to become the new Stars.

# 11 Oye Mi Canto

HEAR MY VOICE: WOMEN IN WORLD MUSIC

'A dream came to me that the whole world was dying, with famine, floods and people drowning in quicksand. The earth was very disappointed, feeling no mercy or kindness towards us. I could see all that as if it was happening, it was terrifying. Then there came thousands of women's voices, singing together. It was the only thing which was heard by the earth. The planet then became kind and all the bad things stopped. But it was only the voices of the women which could be heard.'

STELLA CHIWESHE, Zimbabwean mbira player, author interview, Surrey, 1994

'Everything's changed now. My generation is another generation. Seventy per cent who marry don't want problems with polygamy.'

OUMOU SANGARÉ, Malian female star, author interview, London, 1994

'I'm a heroine in Miami, because Cuban stars before me had to disguise their names to become popular and not sing Spanish. I'm proud of being the first generation not having to hide where I'm from.'

GLORIA ESTEFAN, Latin superstar, author interview, London, 1988

WHILE WESTERN WOMEN PERFORMERS tend to lose themselves in love songs, groove songs and the selling of sexual commodity, their 'Third World' sisters are coming through with unashamed, clear-eyed and poetic focus about what it means fundamentally to be a woman in society – from Bamako to Birmingham, the underlying humanism of their message pulsates across territorial and cultural boundaries. Artists such as Sangaré and Chiweshe address issues with a simplicity that would make sophisticated Western stars squeamish. But while they may not be shown on MTV, they are huge stars on their own continent and unofficial ambassadors of music local to their country or community. Their music offers a stark truth less easily seen and more easily lost in a Western industry swinging on the pivot of unit-shifting and aggressive marketing. Undoubtedly the more African artists in particular cross over to the West, the more they will be affected by its values, but a new spiritual dynamism has been created in the process.

World-music influences are a disparate hotchpotch, but overall they have become a major influence on the rhythms of mainstream pop. In the early 1990s there was a period of transition when female artists began to emerge as international stars while simultaneously remaining close to their roots.

In 1987, in a small upper room in a North London pub, disciples of international ethnic music gathered around a table to discuss a marketing strategy for all those non-Western pop artists who ended up in stock rooms, bargain bins and 'Misc.' racks all over the country because shop managers didn't have a clue how to display them. Hence the all-encompassing term 'world music' was born, keenly promoted by stars such as Peter Gabriel, who championed Senegal's Youssou N'Dour, as well as establishing WOMAD and the Realworld label. Paul Simon meanwhile had recorded with South African musicians for his 1986 *Graceland* album, David Byrne explored Brazilian and African forms on his post-Talking Heads solo releases, and Londoner Jah Wobble began fashioning his peculiar vision of 'global beat' with indie rock. In the late-1980s barrage of publicity that followed the invention of this term, world music (or worldbeat) became the single biggest growth area in record stores and a number of male artists emerged as big sellers in the West, such as N'Dour, Salif Keita and Mory Kanté.

## Mother Africa

By the early 1990s women had yet to break through on the same scale, but there were female stars threatening to take Keita's crown as Europe's biggest world-music seller. Mali, for instance, a poor but proud landlocked country in West Africa with vibrant pre-colonial traditions, had a burgeoning sorority of female recording artists, probably the highest number of any African country. Emerging mainly from the Wassoulou region of southern Mali, singers such as Oumou Sangaré, Sali Sidibé and Nahawa Doumbia were assiduously carving out a major form of female expression. Evolved from traditional hunting dances performed by men and sung by women, the sound is active, exciting, incorporating shades of delta blues rhythm and traditional instruments such as the djembe drum and kamalengoni gut-strung guitar with modern bass and keyboards. Unlike the *jalis*, hereditary musicians who sing for money in praise of battles, historical patrons, noble lineage and local businessmen, the Wassoulou artists sing of social issues and everyday problems.

Spearheading this new breed was Oumou Sangaré, whose debut album *Moussolou* was 1991's best-selling cassette in West Africa and whose second, *Ko Sira*, spent three months at No. 1 in the European world music charts, outselling even Salif Keita's ground-breaking 1987 *Soro* album. As writer John McLaverty said, 'From Mali to Benin, her voice blasts from cassette-players and her face beams from T-shirts and bar murals.'[1] Sangaré was successful because she addressed her audience with a direct clarity. Other young rivals took a more oblique approach, whether it was Nahawa Doumbia's high-tech poetry and metaphor, or Sali Sidibé's deep-textured rough Muslim songs of respect. 'Every week I receive letters from young women in the Ivory Coast, Senegal, Nigeria, Togo, as well as Mali itself – women who find themselves encouraged by the music I'm making. It's the first time a woman has sung about their problems she said.[2] Among the most explicitly feminist of Mali's singers, Sangaré, a tall, good-looking artist whose dynamic vocals animate a rich weave of kamalengoni and percussion, tackled the issues of arranged marriage and women's oppression with candid outrage. Her song 'Dugu Kamelenba' (The Womanizer), for instance, lambasts polygamists who 'seduce and deceive', controlling several wives through a personal policy of divide and rule. 'Sigi Kuruni' (Advice To New Bride) tells the female listener deadpan to expect bullying and disrespect, not only from her husband, but also his entire family, while 'Bi Furu' (Modern Marriage) says that in the bartering of vested interest, a woman's dignity is treated with contempt.

A high point of Sangaré's set was when her two teenage backing singers picked up half-calabashes strung with cowrie shells to throw and catch them on the beat in a celebration of female verve. Though she wore dazzling damask and the traditional long tie-around skirt on stage, the day I interviewed Sangaré in a cramped East London house, she looked as if she had come straight off *The Cosby Show*, with her designer leggings and high-top trainers. A restless feminist ambassador keen to convey abroad the experience of African women from a country where many women talk only through their husbands or male 'intermediaries', she spoke directly for herself: 'It's time for women to be heard. Women have an equal spirit.' An admirer of Madonna, she said, 'She's fighting for women. I love the message and the music even if I don't like the way she's dressing!' Like La Ciccone, in Sangaré's music women take control – like the desired and desiring heroine of 'Mani Djindala' (Mother Stands In Front Of Her House) who feels free to choose her own husband.

Sangaré assumed a certain amount of freedom in her songwriting partly because she was not a *jali*. Ami Koïta, a *jali* and Malian star from a slightly older generation, was as much a paid praise singer as an entertainer recording commercial cassettes. While her father was a farmer by trade, he was also a renowned orator with a detailed knowledge of noble family genealogy. *Jalis* were historically in service to their patrons, but as the finances of the noble families crumbled, the role of the *jali* broadened. As well as praise singing at weddings or at the invitation of the wealthy, Koïta made it known that she would sing for whom she wanted, rich or poor.

An assured and authoritative singer, she was one of the first Malian women to perform abroad, astonishing Western audiences when African fans threw cash on stage which she deftly tucked into her full sleeves. An elegant diva whose mother and grandmother both sang, Koïta was used to receiving cars and jewellery as presents for her singing. But she was careful to develop her role further than just social functionary, drawing emotional female issues into her music. The song 'Simba' (a person's name), for instance, is dedicated to her mother's village Kirina, a place of pilgrimage for childless women who wish to conceive, while 'Diarabi' (Passionate Love) is about a woman obsessively in love.

While Sangaré and Koïta stayed in their home country, other female artists moved west to launch an international career. The most prolific base for African artists, particularly those from francophone West Africa, is Paris, where top producer Ibrahima Sylla – architect and promoter of big-name sounds such as Salif Keita and Mory Kanté – holds sway. Sangaré spoke disparagingly of the Senegalese producer, who pays musicians flat fees rather than royalties, but his Paris/Abidjan-based Syllart operation guarantees a wider audience for young, ambitious performers.

Guinea's Oumou Dioubaté, for instance, is a griot singer/songwriter who relocated to Paris in 1987. By 1993 her joyful, fluttering sound was harnessed to sophisticated studio production on her international debut *Lancey*. Deyess, too, the 'Little Goddess' from Zaire, recorded her powerhouse debut with Sylla in Paris. But even more successful is the diminutive Benin-born Angélique Kidjo, who left West Africa for Paris in the early 1980s. By the time her second album *Aye* (Life) was released in 1994, she had worked with Branford Marsalis, Manu Dibango and Ray Lema, recording her own brand of elastic, exuberant 'voodoo funk' in Paris, London and Paisley Park, Minneapolis. When I saw her perform to a packed, ecstatic crowd at the London Forum in 1994, with everyone from schoolgirls to middle-aged drunks singing to her music, it was obvious she was becoming a major international star.

'I'd love to stay in my country and do what I'm doing now,' Kidjo told me from Paris in 1993. 'But in Benin there is no infrastructure to help you become an international star. Youssou N'Dour stays in Senegal, but it's OK if you have the support of the government. Benin is just fighting to survive and eat, music is not their priority.'[3] On an entire continent where, it is estimated, there are fewer recording and manufacturing facilities than in a single European capital city,[4] the odds are against

African musicians being heard outside their locality. Although global sales of the international music industry exceeded $20 billion in 1990, little of this share went to Africa. The majors have no substantial interest in Africa beyond local sales (for instance, Sony-CBS concentrate on Nigeria and Kenya, EMI on South Africa), so it is rare for an artist, particularly a female performer, to get a major deal in Europe. By the early 1990s, however, Kidjo had been signed up to Island Records (a former independent bought by Polygram), and a large budget meant more immediate exposure and promotion for her than for her sisters at home. Far from being a novelty star, however, Kidjo had a drive and a canny ability to feel out grooves that would work in the West alongside her West African cross-rhythms and dance beats, and could place herself squarely and with little compromise in the Western pop market. In crossing over, though, she carried a sense of guilt and struggle.

'Journalists ask me if my music is still African – what do they know about it?' she burst out angrily. 'You go to the market in Africa, it's not only traditional music, we listen to everybody. When I was ten years old I was listening to the Stones, the Beatles, Hendrix. People didn't say you should only listen to African music. It makes me so mad!'

Brought up in a large liberal family who never stopped her going on stage, Kidjo was outspoken about the role of female artists within Africa – where social pressure dictates that unless a woman is constantly accompanied by a husband who grants her respectability and protection, she is judged to be a prostitute.

'If you're a woman in Africa and you don't have your family behind you, forget it. The fight will take up more time than the music. When I started singing people would look at my parents like they were from planet Mars, saying, "You're putting her into prostitution." My parents didn't keep me from what I wanted to do, they wanted me to be in harmony with myself. Now I'm successful their critics are congratulating them. I hope my example will help people see it's not that bad.'

In Europe, too, she had to fight against the pressure to market her as African exotica. 'I'm black and African – so what? I've been told, "Why don't you move your ass like an African?" I don't want to have to show off my breasts and my ass. Sometimes I get mad and say, Fuck you!' A 1990s Josephine Baker in cropped hair and Adidas trainers, Kidjo had an exceptional energy, a gift for uniting audiences with lyrics that embraced everything from race and homelessness to the environment. She hoped fervently that future African artists would be able to work in their home country, yet still attain international success. 'I see so many young African women coming up as performers. I'm amazed at how much knowledge they have about capturing the public and their space on stage. They have TV and videos, they watch how people move, and combine it with their own traditional moves.'

Caught between Africa and the West, Kidjo expressed the keenness of her separation in songs like 'Logozo' (Tortoise), a hymn to the tortoise who lives alone in a folded shell. She sang of the pains of living alone in exile, away from family and friends.

Whether the result of war, brutal dictatorship or simple grinding poverty, exile is a constant theme among female artists making a living in the West. Cécile Kayirebwa's story was particularly poignant She has been based in Belgium since 1974 to escape the war, and it has been a source of sadness to her that she could not return to her home in Rwanda. Split by a civil war that escalated in the early 1990s, with the traditional ruling Tutsi minority fighting the Hutu majority and an estimated 500,000 hacked to death by Hutu extremists, Rwanda was in 1994 a country torn by massacre, its tragedy compounded when thousands of Hutu refugees fleeing to the borders died in a horrific cholera epidemic.

With its stark beauty and haunting fluidity, Kayirebwa's album *Rwanda*, released during that year, is music composed in exile. Shaded with an ethereal sadness, it combines the Catholic Gregorian chants of her youth with pastoral Rwandan song to create a living tribute to her country's culture. 'I have been in

Belgium twenty years, and I suffer enormously. The rare occasions I'm able to go to Rwanda are a source of energy and inspiration,' she told me.[5] Soon after her arrival in Belgium, Kayirebwa formed the theatrical ensemble Inyange as a form of cultural exchange for exiled Rwandans. A thoughtful woman, Kayirebwa saw herself as 'the link between traditional culture and today's generation', safeguarding tradition as a cohesive force. It was important to her that her music convey 'a universal language that everyone, including those in the West, could feel and understand'. 'I would like to show another side to Rwanda apart from the war!' she said. 'The beauty, the poems, the melodies, the graceful dances and the richness of Rwandan culture which, I believe, helps to alleviate the pressures of the war.' As she is a Tutsi herself, it wasn't surprising that the Tutsi-led RPF (Rwandan Popular Front) had picked up on her songs, suggestive of hope for the future, but it meant that her music, though intended for everyone, was deemed politically sensitive.

Unlike stars working in big-budget Western pop smoothed by commodity gloss, African artists often have to deal with pressing social issues that directly affect their music. In South Africa, for instance, black female performers were silenced, exiled or ignored for decades by the apartheid regime. 'Queen of Africa' Miriam Makeba, the major inspiration for countless African female artists, said,

'In our struggles, songs are not simply entertainment for us, they are the way we communicate. It hurt to have my records banned, but even though the regime did that, they could never get me out of the minds of the people. Many of the songs I did while in exile were never heard, of course, but even though they don't know them, they know who Miriam Makeba is. Even the young people – I walk down the street and they say, "Hey, Mama Africa!"'[6]

I interviewed Miriam Makeba in an East London recording studio one hot summer afternoon in 1994. At sixty-two she had a lined and tired face registering the legacy of decades of apartheid. Her conversational style, though, was drenched in irony, her eyes playful. Exuding a mature dignity, she had the

relaxation of someone who had struggled enough and no more. 'I always knew if I lived long enough I would see the day,' she said of the historic 1994 election when Mandela was voted President of South Africa. 'It had to come, it just couldn't go on.' When Makeba appeared with her old friend Hugh Masekela at London's celebratory Viva South Africa concert that summer, the young noisy crowd at the front of the stage stopped respectfully to listen. On a bill that included the younger generation of female stars – firebrand Brenda Fassie and the queenly Yvonne Chaka Chaka – Makeba represented the trail-blazer, the first African woman to become an international star. Like those of 1950s star Dorothy Masuka, princess of jazz variety and the itchy marabi beat, Makeba's earthy revivals of traditional song on albums such as 1988's *Sangoma* may have been dated to the ears of an impatient new audience, but as a role model she was still revered.

She began her career in 1955 as female lead in the South African jazz opera *King Kong*, and after an appearance in the documentary *Come Back Africa* was invited to the Venice Film Festival and London, where US star Harry Belafonte took her under his wing, acting as a mentor. By the late 1950s Makeba was performing sell-out concerts across America, a symbol of the black South African struggle against apartheid. Received by world leaders from a political spectrum that included President Kennedy and Fidel Castro, she became a threat to the Pretoria regime, and in 1960 her passport was revoked. Three years later her records were banned.

An eloquent campaigner against apartheid, Makeba became a United Nations delegate when she relocated to Guinea in the early 1970s. Although in 1986 she won the Dag Hammarskjöld Peace Prize, her fame and success had not come cheap. Personal family tragedy and a lifetime of upheaval gave her words depth and a residual sadness. 'But it's not made me tough,' she said. 'If anything I'm probably softer. When you go through such problems you learn to be humble.'

In marked contrast was Brenda Fassie, the tenacious young star whose bubblegum pop contained a raw gospel ringed with defiance. Criticized by some as disregarding the traditions of her own people, Fassie was provocative in the face of sexist and racist convention, talking as openly about sex as Madonna – 'When I sing I make love' – and publicly kissing the girl gang that accompanied her wherever she went. Born the youngest of ten children in 1964, Fassie was once described as 'sounding like the townships', one of a hardy young generation fully versed in pop and rap.

Just as popular but more easily marketable was her contemporary Yvonne Chaka Chaka, the honey-brown-eyed Soweto-born star who exuded a cheeky elegance and sang a combination of pop with the South African umbaqanga beat. Her debut No. 1 single 'I'm In Love With The DJ' had become a South African dance-pop anthem – an indicator of how easily the country assimilated Western pop, yielding a high number of crossover acts.

'We never thought we'd see people like Hugh and Miriam, we thought they'd die in exile. But here we are together,' said Chaka

Chaka after appearing on stage with Makeba.[7] With five platinum albums and a major deal with Polydor UK, she rather than Madonna had been chosen by Pepsi to represent the corporation in Africa. While Makeba was keen to keep alive traditional roots in her music, bemoaning the fact that South African radio had become dominated by American pop, Chaka Chaka was at the forefront of a new generation of South African singers prepared to leave the country voluntarily to make it. 'If the best part of my career is in New York, for instance, I'll move there,' she said. 'I'll hold on to my roots but I'm willing to experiment with Western sounds. I have to compromise some things.'

Chaka Chaka would sing uplifting songs for freedom, but while the regime was in place during the 1980s, she had to be circumspect. After one of her 1986 stadium concerts ended in a riot, with youngsters throwing stones at the police and newspaper headlines declaring 'CHAKA CHAKA CAUSES CHAOS', she decided to stick to love songs to be safe. 'One had to be careful to stay away from politics. I imagined myself on Robben Island.' Her message still filtered through, however, with Nelson Mandela telling her personally that her hit 'Umgombothi', a cry for unity and freedom, kept him going while he was in jail. In making resistance less explicit Chaka Chaka was able to stay and perform in her country. Protected by her platinum status and the political developments of the 1990s, Chaka Chaka was luckier than many of her older, less high-profile sisters who had to struggle alone or in exile.

Busi Mhlongo, for instance, a dramatic Zulu soul vocalist who sang with 1970s African high-life superstars Osibisa before touring with her own band Twasa, had to leave her daughter behind and come to Europe to make any headway in her career. Apart from Margaret Singana, the top female singer of the late 1970s who had a hit with 'I Never Loved A Man' and for a while was christened 'Lady Africa', black South African women in the 1970s were rarely given decent record deals, let alone a platform to express their views. Mhlongo said,

'In the old South Africa I was a very angry woman. But in leaving I learned to love myself. Before, you would imitate white stars from other countries, but you learn to admire your own country. The success of people like Miriam Makeba was important – she was the first person who sang about what was going on in South Africa. It kept us alive.'[8]

Like Kidjo's and Kayirebwa's, Mhlongo's recording career took off when she went to Europe – but international success also brings the problem of cultural translation, particularly if the artist signs a major deal. Aster Aweke, for instance, the shimmering, silver-tongued star of Ethiopia whose cassettes saturate the market at home, found herself lost in the CBS machine six years after she moved to America:

'CBS got excited and signed me, but didn't know how to distribute my product. I was their only African artist. You couldn't find my records anywhere, they didn't put them into all the outlets, the record shops. But I'm OK – CBS was the best thing to happen to me whether I liked it or not. I've had good press coverage. Publications like *Time* and the *LA Times* are interested in me, they're on my side.'[9]

It is strange that, despite the strong cultural force of Afro-Americanism, the market for African music in the US is relatively small, with patchy understanding and support of African artists. Consequently many expatriates stay within the limits of their own transplanted communities. When she moved to Washington DC in 1983 to further her education, Aweke began singing in nightclubs to expatriate Ethiopians. On hearing one of her cassettes via a contact in Ethiopia, Iain Scott, the enterprising boss of the UK's Triple Earth Records, tracked her down and, after much persuasion, drew her out of that world into the recording studio. Matching her fierce Amharic scales and piercingly ornate vocals to the demands of Western pop was a challenge, but her 1989 debut album *Aster* was an immediate critical success. The follow-up, *Kabu*, was even more accessible, combining elements of jazz and soul that worked with, rather than battled against, her vocals. There were also traces of her great American heroine and role model, Aretha Franklin, in the delivery. In one sense she has become fully integrated into US culture — she smokes, drinks and is a sophisticated shopper — but in another way she remains wary of the white audience. 'Singing in my language for a non-Ethiopian audience I thought was undreamable, unacceptable. It's very challenging,' she said. 'I know a white audience don't understand me, so I try and attract them by expressing my feelings.'

By concentrating so hard on communication, she has improved her performance, raising it to an international standard without diluting her graceful emotional strength and the frantic, full-tilt delivery of those obsessive love songs. When Aweke recorded her 1993 album *Ebo*, a graceful return to roots initially aimed at the Ethiopian community, she was confident enough to ask Iain Scott, 'D'you think we could sell this to white people?' Part of her creative impetus comes from this straddling of cultures, and the freedom of being away from the family that initially disapproved of her singing career, preferring that she went into medicine or law. 'I couldn't face them,' she said. 'But after I got here I was more free. I started creating and sending songs back home.'

Aweke's decision to sing was difficult enough, but working harder against women is the resistance to them playing instruments. While Africa has produced many fine female vocalists, the number of public women instrumentalists is minuscule. Notable exceptions are the Amazones de Guinée, a fifteen-strong all-woman band from Guinea who frequently tour abroad. Formed in 1961 as a police band, some of its members are from Manding griot families, among whom women are not permitted to play instruments, so their place in a modern pop orchestra is most unusual. While the Amazones can perform openly, all-woman outfits tend to be relegated more to the background. Zambia's Masiye Dancing Queens, for instance, a female group who sing of social issues, can only get bookings as front-line dancers for male bands.

Individual instrumentalists, too, have to persist in the face of hostility or indifference. Zimbabwe's Stella Chiweshe was seventeen when she first heard the mbira, a thumb piano with iron keys that has a deep, plangent sound. 'It was so powerful, it didn't leave my head.'[10] Though aching to play the instrument, she was actively discouraged by her family. When I interviewed her in the early 1990s, more and more young women were beginning to play mbira, but in 1963 Chiweshe was the only one. Because of its power to plug the listener into their spiritual source, the mbira was outlawed by the powerful Zimbabwean Christian missionary church. 'After death it was believed your soul would go to Satan if you played the music,' recalled Chiweshe. Mbira is usually played on social occasions for long stretches, sometimes twenty-four hours. There is a trance-like intensity about the music, and for Chiweshe it is a channel for her mediumship, a source of meditation and renewal.

'I've discovered this music is healing,' she said. 'It heals if you have stress or disappointments or confusion inside, like medicine. The music takes over, and it is music not just for the people of Zimbabwe, but for everybody.' If mbira enables people to find the source of their strength, it's not surprising that there is male opposition to women plugging into their own power. The reasons used to discourage them are many: when she began playing, her grandfather cautioned Chiweshe against neglecting her home and children for a life on the road. Women were not supposed to play mbira while menstruating, husbands wouldn't like to see their wives playing amid men, and, most importantly, women's tender hands would get blistered. 'You get pain and cramps, but if you want to play you ignore the pain. Maybe they thought we couldn't stand it, but that's not as painful as bringing a child into the world.'

Chiweshe had her two children in her late teens, almost unconsciously getting her 'duty' out of the way before she could concentrate on her musical career. In a society where women are stifled by having constantly to seek male permission, she was relieved when her first husband left for Portugal on a football contract. 'It was my luck that he left. He didn't like me playing mbira.' Now Chiweshe holds workshops all over Britain and America, casting a spell with her whooping, scarred vocals and plangent mbira backed by Western instrumentation. A tall, relaxed woman with wise eyes, she sees a message in her method. To her, mbira is connected to the earth: 'It's the earth's music played by us human beings. Before it was separated by water the earth was one, meaning we're one people together. We work with borders, the oceans between, when actually everything is coming from the earth.'

Referring to the dream she had where the earth turned its back on people, sending pestilence and floods, she said, 'And women singing were the only voices that could be heard. They were so powerful because we are the people who feel the pain of bringing a baby into the world. This pain the men will never experience. They cannot imagine how it feels.' She set about realizing the dream in 1993, organizing an international women's music conference in Zimbabwe called Mother Earth. Drawing on all her contacts throughout the US and the UK, Chiweshe envisaged a forum for 1995 where hundreds of women could gather together to match a fraction of the thousands of voices she heard in her dream. 'Then the earth may listen,' she said with a smile.

## Im Nin' Alu

Another facet of world music that operates within the heart of pop culture is 'global dance', the mixing of different ethnic sounds within Western beats. In the remixing frenzy of the late 1980s, for instance, British producer team Coldcut added the spiralling Yemenite vocals of Ofra Haza to Eric B and Rakim's hit 'Paid In Full'. On first hearing the rappers weren't convinced – 'What is this wailing shit?' being their rumoured response – but once that version shot into the British charts, they readjusted their view. For Haza, a singer from Israel who came second in the 1983 Eurovision Song Contest, crowning by UK club culture was praise indeed. Her 1988 album, *Yemenite Songs*, a reworking of traditional numbers to a dance beat, was a big hit and a deliberate attempt to woo young people less tuned into the traditional music of her Yemenite roots. 'Through the discos we felt they would be interested. People need something new, a little bit strange,' said Haza.[11] The words of the title track 'Im Nin'

Alu', for instance, come from a devotional love poem by the sixteenth-century Yemenite Jewish poet Shalom Shabazzi.

After scoring seventeen gold albums in her home country, Haza seemed poised for international stardom when she was snapped up by East West Records UK, but after two moderately successful albums, *Desert Wind* (1990) and *Kirya* (1992), she was dropped. It was not so much her Yemenite roots showing through as her love of MOR pop. Her culture was tinselly Euro-vision as well as pure Yemenite vocals, and 'the kids', eventually, weren't interested. Cross-cultural collisions need a fine balance in order to work.

Britain's Natacha Atlas, for instance, has worked on the vanguard of indie club culture. Unlike Haza, who didn't fully understand the disco beat beefing up her vocals, Atlas is immersed in the club scene. Raised in the Moroccan district of Belgium, with an English mother and a Sephardic Jewish father from Jerusalem, she is proud of her mixed Middle Eastern origins, expressing that through compelling Arabic vocals. 'Arabic music seems to connect me 100 per cent with my ancestry, my roots,' she said.[12]

After working as a belly dancer in Brussels' Arabic clubs, she moved to England in the mid-1980s with an idea for fusion music. Although her ideas coincided with the rise of Peter Gabriel's WOMAD, Atlas was interested in something more streetwise. After collaborating with fusion guru Jah Wobble and Asian ragga artist Apache Indian, she joined world-dance experimenters Trans-Global Underground. By 1994 she was working on her own album, mixing Middle Eastern rhythms with Hindi film music and songs in Arabic and French.

Despite the trendiness of 1990s 'ethno techno', Atlas initially found it was a battle to be accepted. She railed against 'white-boy rock' orthodoxy as being racist, because it blocked out any other sounds: 'You get up on stage in your T-shirt and jeans strumming full-throttle guitar. It's like they want to express themselves so hard, but can't. An attitude of Bored White Youth comes across with this white noise. It seems very linear, nothing from other cultures. I don't relate to it.' When interviewed in

1994, Atlas was also sceptical of the vogue for techno acts adding an Asian vocal to their mix, in much the same way as white pop boys in the 1980s gained credibility by drafting in black female backing singers. 'It's like the icing on the cake. In the beginning I was seen as an exotic bird wailing half-naked in the corner.' But as world beat seeped into the dance charts and then pop consciousness, the attitude changed. 'In London particularly, there are so many people from mixed backgrounds and people exposed to other cultures through friends or travel, it instantly became hip.'

An important part of her image is the belly dance, something she wants to wrestle away from the corny wriggling temptress of James Bond films. 'It's a very powerful dance, a woman's dance. It's not really erotic; it's so hard to make those movements the last thing you're thinking about is shagging. It's strenuous, but the lines the body makes are very spiritual and artistic.' By 2001 she had become a major alternative star, welding her soaring voice to Egyptian orchestration and electronic beats.

Much of her inspiration comes from the great Egyptian female singers such as Asmahan, Warda and Om Kalsoum. A proud, private woman whose rich Oriental song dominated the Arab world for four decades, Kalsoum rose to fame in the 1920s. By the 1960s, her records were broadcast so much on Egyptian radio she requested they be played less in order to preserve a degree of public anticipation She influenced governments – it was her song 'Love Of The Nation' that persuaded President Nasser not to resign after the 1957 Six-Day War with Israel – and when she died in 1973 there was international mourning. An unprepossessing figure with a heavy face, severe hairstyle and static stage style, she showed how a woman could gain increasing respect throughout her career rather than be discarded, as so often happens in the West, when she is judged to be past her prime.

## From Bollywood to Lollipop

While Atlas experimented with an Arabic fusion, growing in Britain from the mid-1980s was a rich mix of Asian and English pop – reflecting the strong Indian community in the UK. Taking its cues from Bollywood, the Indian film industry that has produced world-class singers such as Lata Mangeshkar and Asha Bosle, Asian pop in the UK can be very self-contained, a kind of outlet for the Mother Country. As reggae acts record pop cover versions aimed at West Indian fans, so Asian artists do the same for their own UK community. Amar, for instance, daughter of famous film singer Mangal Singh, recorded as a fourteen-year-old schoolgirl a Hindi version of Whitney Houston's 'I Will Always Love You' in 1994. Selling more than 30,000 units, it would have been a chart hit but for the fact that Asian retail outlets weren't included in the official UK chart database.

Amar then proved herself able to cross over with the English-language hit 'Make It Easy On Yourself'. In her late teens she was experimenting with drum 'n' bass and leftfield dance music, one of many young UK Asian women – like Susheela Raman, fusing blues with Asian and African music, and DJ Ritu with her dynamic Sister India project – who'd become adept at mixing genres.

By the early 1990s a fresh term had been coined – New Asian Kool – the result of rap Bhangra (Punjabi pop) and Asian ragga outfits emerging through clubs such as London's Bombay Jungle. Vocalist with 'trance dance' group The KK Kings, Radical Sista was one of the scene's first female Bhangra DJs, while the best-selling Bindu began as a backing singer for Bhangra bands before releasing her solo debut in 1992. On a predominantly male scene, the few female Bhangra singers often find themselves frustrated. 'You're taken less seriously; on stage you do your numbers and that's it. In the beginning I did a lot of Bhangra tracks with their beat folk melody, and the Punjabi language sang in a harsh, powerful voice,' said Bindu. 'But then I started using classical melodies in my songs, and that brought out my unique style.'[13] One of her key releases was 'We've Got Feelings Too', a collaboration with black artist Sheena Staple that reflected 1990s multiculture in its ragga/Bhangra mix. Despite her sophisticated 1990s appeal, Bindu reserved greatest respect for the majestic playback singer Mangeshkar, who by the mid-1980s had cut a record-breaking 25,000 songs. 'When I started I tried to copy her. Her voice is very clear, her command of language brilliant. I try and watch her breathing – you can never tell when she's taking a breath.'

While women like Bindu and Sasha worked within commercial pop or club music, other Asian vocalists explored more 'leftfield' mixes. Sheila Chandra, for instance, began in 1982 with the band Monsoon, singing the swirling pop hit 'Ever So Lonely'. After going solo less than a year later, her career was marked by increasing experimentation, the instrumental backing being pared down to let her warm voice pulsate centre stage. Her seventh album, *The Zen Kiss* (1994), wove Islamic and soul vocal with shimmering Gregorian chant, while the six-minute stand-out track 'Speaking In Tongues IV' had pioneering vocal percussion – a hypnotic, shamanic babble she had created with tongue twisters and Indian syllables. 'It was to give a voice to the chatter that goes on in the mind. To remind people that being a creator means facing all the dark, dangerous bits. When it comes from the depths you have a responsibility to express it, otherwise it could destroy you,' Chandra explained. Reluctant to be seen specifically as an Asian singer, she went on, 'What's liberating is to go into that world of imagination and drop the fact I'm female or Asian. The only thing I take with me is that (in the new millennium) I have access to an incredible array of musics.'[14]

Part of her resistance may come from being catapulted into the limelight with Monsoon when she was only seventeen. 'It was difficult being asked to be a cultural ambassador. There was virtually no one else Asian in the mainstream media at the time, so it was easy to lose individuality and become a cultural phenomenon, a great angle on someone's show.'

In terms of image stereotypes, Najma Akhtar, a vocalist who has successfully combined the Indian classical music of ghazals with jazz, has found that there was constant pressure to be marketed as Indian exotica. 'I remember when I wanted to cut my hair my record company told me not to. They liked the Indian image of long hair and sari. I used to wear a lot of Indian clothes when I travelled around, but that's not me. I wear jeans, track suits, miniskirts – whatever I want.'[15] Although she sang Asian poetry that was centuries old, she did not want to present a fossilized tradition – hence the jazz influences. Likewise, her dress accurately reflected the attitude of an Asian woman born and raised in Britain. World music can be a liberating force and a source of solidarity across cultures. Performing in Japan once, Akhtar was astonished when she looked down at the crowd. 'I saw Japanese women in the audience singing Urdu with me – they knew the meaning of my lyrics. It was unbelievable!'

With its avid consumption of Western styles, Japan, too, has thrown up some female hybrids. 1980s pop cabaret duo The Frank Chickens were two Japanese women who moved to

London to escape the restraints of their home country. Their act, exploring everything from geisha girl to Manga cartoon, developed into a pastiche of Western ideas of the Japanese. More straightforward were the all-female rock group Shonen Knife, whose buzzsaw guitar, girlish harmonies and late-1980s record deal with independent British company Creation led to them being picked up by the alternative rock elite. Whether this was through rock prowess or sheer novelty value is debatable. Though Shonen Knife's sound toughened up the more they were exposed to the Anglo music industry, when they first emerged from Japan (where they have been stars in their own right since the mid-1980s) Naoko Yamano (guitar), her sister Atsuko (drums) and Michie Nakatani (bass) veered towards kitsch guitar bubblegum.

In person the trio's polite charm masks a private determination to succeed. When I spoke to them in 1992 they were the only rock band apart from Yellow Magic Orchestra, male or female, to cross over from Japan, a country dominated by teeny 'Lollipop' groups or Western imitations. Referring to their US tour that year with Nirvana, Nakatani said, 'It gave us the opportunity to see real rock musicians on tour. Normally Japanese bands can't have such experiences.' As women they had to be very clear about their goals. 'In Japan neighbours are very important,' said Naoko. 'If I wear dirty clothes and have a guitar my neighbours make rumour that I'm crazy. It is bad for my mother.' Despite disapproval, they picked up rock guitars and pursued what is normally a male white Western dream. Their sly humour emerged when I asked if they wanted to live the rock 'n' roll lifestyle: 'Smash TV,' said Naoko. 'Throw TV out of hotel window,' added Nakatani. 'Guns 'N' Roses wild.'[16]

While African and Asian women have made substantial inroads into the pop mainstream, Oriental, particularly Chinese, women are restrained even more by family mores and a tradition highly suspicious of the West. A tough Beijing daughter of former high-ranking Communist Party officials, writer/musician Liu Sola moved to London in the late 1980s after her work, a mixture of Western blues and Chinese music, was denounced by the Chinese government as treacherous. Stultified at home, she found her career took off in the UK when she wrote a rock opera, *Blue Sky Green Sea*, and collaborated with 'ambient' groups such as Durutti Column. Representing the post-Tiananmen Square drift of a younger generation hungry for new ideas, she used pop as a vehicle for ideas. 'Young people in China don't know enough about world popular music, they need good music to make them more sensitive and enrich their understanding,' she said.[17]

## Rhythm Is Gonna Get You

Apart from African music the world beat that has been most influential on pop, particularly North American pop, is Latin. In the rich, varied but macho music culture of Latin America, certain key female performers have emerged supreme. Hailed as 'the Latin Ella Fitzgerald', Celia Cruz was a major star of salsa improvisation scat and popular song in her own community decades before she gained the international stature she deserved by the 1980s. 'Many Latin women are fine singers, but we're very badly paid in comparison to American stars,' she said. 'Because so many Latin Americans are on the poverty line, we can't expect to be like Donna Summer in Las Vegas with a full house each night.'[18]

Born in 1921 in Cuba into a family of fourteen children, Cruz studied at Havana Conservatory, singing Afro-Cuban religious songs before expanding into showbusiness in the late 1940s, fronting the top popular band La Sonora Matancera for fifteen years. Her operatic range and disciplined training meant that she could extract nuance and projection with every syllable, an ability that has left audiences breathless. Cruz brought out the healing joy of salsa music, as well as its angry, syncopated self-definition. Since she defected from Fidel Castro's Cuba in 1960, New York has been her base and she has won a katin NY female vocalist award every year between 1975 and 1982. A flamboyant, hard-working heroine with a penchant for wigs, impossibly high heels and lurid pink dresses, by the late 1980s she had

recorded over fifty albums, a good proportion with Fania Records, the main salsa label in New York City.

Cruz has long been an ambassador for Cuban music and the salsa sound which evolved in the 1970s, surviving trends by keeping her material relevant and continually developing her vocal edge. She is one of the few Latin stars to have gained a crossover audience in America, performing in the 1992 hit movie *The Mambo Kings* with her touring partner Tito Puente, and duetting with David Byrne. Cruz is versatile in technique – musician and producer Johnny Pacheco said that watching her improvise lines for 'Caramelo', a song about fruit, was amazing: 'It was like watching a computer: she listed every tropical fruit you can imagine at a speed I couldn't believe.'[19] She also avoids banality, addressing pertinent subject matter in her lyrics. In 1985, for instance, she sang 'Las Divorciadas', a song about divorced women which would have been taboo twenty years earlier. As a young woman Cruz had to be constantly chaperoned, negotiating her way round a minefield of respectable mores – until she married Pedro Knight in 1961, the first trumpeter in her big band.

Such restrictions may have eased by the 1980s when Gloria Estefan came to the fore as a pop/salsa superstar, but although she didn't have an official chaperone, from the start of her career Estefan had the public protection and support of her husband, Miami Sound musician Emilio. She spoke of his jealous 'Latin temperament' and was careful to say that despite the attention of her many fans, she only had eyes for him.

Coming from the younger generation of Cuban *émigrés* to Miami (she still has the $26 airline ticket with which she fled the Cuban revolution at two years old), Estefan climbed to international stardom with caution. Her father, a former political prisoner in Cuba, contracted a disease akin to multiple sclerosis, and she nursed him throughout her teenage years until he died in 1974. While an introverted student at Miami University, she began singing as a hobby for Emilio Estefan's Miami Sound Machine. With his encouragement, music became a full-time occupation and she took centre stage as lead singer. The band's first seven records were in Spanish, until their ebullient, part-English high-octane 1984 hit 'Dr Beat' enabled them to cross over to the mainstream pop market. By the time I interviewed her in 1988, the band were filling stadiums worldwide with their lush Latin disco pop. Estefan had been so successful that even Madonna picked up on the possibilities of the Latino market, recording 'La Isla Bonita' the year before.

'It's only Anglos who see her as having popularized Spanish,' Estefan said, smiling widely. Dressed in a fitted jacket with brass buttons and military-style epaulettes, she exuded a neat and wholesome air undercut by a sparky humour. 'Madonna's a bit confused about her Spanish. She mentions a tropical island in the sun – that's Puerto Rico, then samba – that's Brazil, and then flamenco guitar – that's Spain. There's a mishmash of everything in the song. But hey, every little bit helps.' Seeing herself as a link between the conservatism of her parents' generation, patriotic for pre-Castro Cuba, and the Americanized young, she said,

'My parents' generation all came at the time of the coup. Because they felt homesick in America they re-created the lifestyle they'd had at home,

keeping hold of it within their communities. The next generation born
here rejected everything about Cuba and embraced America as their
home. And now there's an even younger generation accepting and celebrating their Latin culture.'[20]

While Latin musics like salsa and samba have their own socialist
language for the displaced and dispossessed, Estefan is pro-
Republican and, because of her family's experience, anti-Castro.
Despite her commercial, slimmed-down, sexy MTV image, she
is a good role model for Cuba's daughters. 'I don't do anything
to offend,' she said. 'But,' she added defensively, 'that's me. I
wouldn't pretend to be anyone else. And I don't hold back from
saying something if I want to say it.' As she fully immersed
herself in US pop, some referred pejoratively to Estefan as
'selling out' to the white market. English-language success,
however, has given her the space to pull out the occasional
Hispanic percussive cracker – such as the glorious salsa-driven
track 'Oye Mi Canto' (Hear My Voice) in 1988 and *Mi Tierra*,
the album of 1940s mambo-based originals she released in 1994
after the film *The Mambo Kings* created a new Latino craze.

By the late 1990s she had sold over 70 million records, and
she and Emilio had set up a virtual business empire in Miami

with their own label, TV company and a collection of restau-
rants. She became so identified with Miami that fan mail
addressed to 'Gloria Estefan, USA' would reach her. A former
US delegate to the United Nations, she also became a key figure
in 'exile politics', the link between old and new Cuba. Referring
to her 'Spanglish' lyrics, Estefan said: 'Had we been raised
somewhere else, our music would not be what it is. Culturally, I
am that mix. I grew up listening to old Cuban records that my
mother had. Then I listened to pop music. I really have both
influences in my life very strong.'[21]

Though she was established enough to move with ease
between genres, it helped Estefan's career to live in the centre of
the US music industry. There the market tolerates a cultural mix
reflective of the US 'melting pot' tradition: singer Linda
Ronstadt, for instance, has delved into as much ranchera as she
has rock – ranchera songs she has recorded were simply derived
from what her father, a Mexican immigrant, used to sing in their
home in Tucson, Arizona. In Latin America itself women do not
have such a wide range of options, especially if they want to
produce outspoken material. In the 1980s Brazilian singer Leci
Brandão worked on the bitter, cutting edge of samba. The
vibrant music of the Rio Carnival, samba was popularized by
'Brazilian bombshell' Carmen Miranda, the 1940s star whose
comic accent, six-inch heels, fruit headgear and quirky hit
records are a far cry from the later gritty street sound that char-
acterizes Brandão's work. The latter's frank songs on Brazil's
social inequalities and prejudice against her as a woman may
have led to her expulsion from samba competitions, but she felt
strongly that samba music had a place conveying everyday experience under the tourist gloss.

While Brandão found herself sidelined as a result of her fierce
focus on roots, there are problems, too, in diluting material for a
Western market. Singer Margareth Menezes was a star on the
Salvador club scene singing electric Bahian rhythms, but after
she was 'discovered' by David Byrne, supporting him on a US
tour in the early 1990s, her records were confused by a dated
thrash rock that just sounded clumsy in the US. Because of its

wide popularity, Latin music also has in places become debased currency. Tom (Antonio Carlos) Jobim once spoke with horror of the number of 'airport lounge' cover versions of his bossa nova song 'A Garota De Ipanema' (The Girl From Ipanema) after Astrud Gilberto made it a Top Five US hit in 1964. The lambada, likewise, a vigorous dance music from Amazonian Brazil, was exported in the late 1980s in a much lighter, more synthesized Bahian version, losing the distinctiveness of the original sound.

Even if they court the international scene, therefore, female Latin artists are assured greater success and credibility if they keep the essence of their native music. Along with the Brazilian stars, certain performers have become popular national matri-archs – like Toto La Momposina, whose hair, flair, tensile voice and raw, driving rhythms have acted as a galvanizing force for Colombian music, and Mercedes Sosa, the Argentinian folk diva whose repertoire ranging from Andean music to Argentinian tango made her by the 1980s the 'voice of the Americas'. Part of the 1962 Argentinian Circulo de Periodistas (a Latin American cultural coalition formed in the face of US imperialism), she was among the first singers to unveil *nuevo cancionero*, a revolution-ary manifesto that recognized the power of political expression in music, with the guitar as gun and the song as bullet.

Meanwhile Bolivian Emma Junaro used her mix of pure-voiced Andean folk, husky jazz tones and subtly subversive songs to maintain a vital communication link between people in a country dominated by repression after Garcia Meza's 1980 coup.

## Mouth Music

It is not just the music of non-Western countries that has kept alive a sense of roots culture and resistance. In Spain Carmen Linares sings flamenco from her Andalusian community, redefining it in her own rigorous style for an international stage. 'I interpret flamenco music my own way. With my experience, the countries I've been to, I see that people respect flamenco – it is quality music, it has roots and authenticity,' she told me shortly after a British concert in 1993. 'I want to do it well to show the depth of the music and the professionalism that exists within flamenco.'[22]

Britain and America, too, have their own 'world music', spanning Louisiana cajun and Celtic folk. Women have always been at the forefront of folk traditions, and in the early 1990s one of the most exciting experimenters with ancient rhythms and modern pop was Talitha MacKenzie, an artist who welded intricate Gaelic vocals to a techno house beat on her album *Sòlas*. Originally from the US, MacKenzie consolidated a long fascination with Gaelic music and her Scottish roots by moving to Edinburgh in 1984. There she explored *puirt-a-beul* or mouth music – literally, 'instrumental tunes from the mouth' – along with Gaelic folksong:

'I love Gaelic because it's a really expressive language – of grief as well as joy. I take songs in their purest form and enhance what is special about them. Some provoke different textures, so I'll play with parallels in anything from Bulgarian music to funk. The Highland community had strong feelings about me as an American "tampering" with their material, but I do my homework. I try to tackle different musical areas with as much integrity as possible.'[23]

When I spoke to her in 1994, MacKenzie was planning to release a 'white label' dance track into the clubs – an example of Scottish culture far removed from 'mass band pipes or five bonny lasses singing in a glen!' More in the mainstream were Maire Ni Bhraonain and her sister Enya who with the family-based group Clannad brought Irish folk into pop's epicentre – veering between vague synthesized soundtrack wash and strong atmospheric feeling. Enya's 1988 No. 1 solo hit 'Orinoco Flow', for example, was a jaunty, magical wade through feminine fantasy.

Cross-breeding will always antagonize those who wish to preserve music in its pure, almost fossilized, form, and a woman who came under more fire than most for doing this was Samiland's (better known as Lapland, in northern Norway)

Mari Boine, a singer who brought a soulful jazz slant to *joik*, or Sami chanting. A leading figure in the Sami cultural independence movement of the 1980s and 1990s that rejected Norwegian dominance, she was still criticized by traditionalists who claimed she was corrupting Sami culture by opening it up to pop. 'She is commercializing the music and ignoring the savage side of the songs,' said purist singer Ante Somby, overlooking the dramatic defiance of arresting Boine songs like 'Vilges Suola'.[24]

## International Times

In the grab bag of musical styles that emerged through the 1980s to shake previously set definitions of pop, it was mainly Western male stars such as Peter Gabriel and David Byrne who got attention for their 'patronage' of world music. Female artists like Ashley Maher and Toni Childs working in a similar way were given less devoted column space. Already sidelined as women, serious experimenting with African and Asian sounds put them even further outside the category of 'sexy' female rock act.

A singer/songwriter since the early 1970s who didn't get her first major solo deal until 1985, Childs learned to shrug off the hurt of that marginalization. 'For so much of my life I've been trying to fit in with the boys; I felt I'd missed the boat – the women's boat. But now I know I've been on it all along,' she said in 1994 when her third album, the richly layered *Woman's Boat*, was released.[25]

Though their role has been played down, women have always been active promoters of world music. London-based broadcaster, producer and musicologist Lucy Duran, who went to Gambia in 1976 to study kora, recalled how difficult it was in the late 1970s to get a European tour and record deal for her teacher Jobarteh. 'Media interest in "world music" was non-existent. It was regarded as a quaint curiosity. I was always on the defensive. "It may look like a strange instrument but it's wonderful music!" It's great now to feel part of a wider community.' Proud of the fact that she has contributed towards making African and Latin American music better known, Duran still said, 'It's hard to find women producing this music. There's not enough women behind the steering wheel.'[26]

Lois Darlington, writer and editor of *Tradewinds*, the influential newsletter produced by London's main African music outlet and record label Sterns, found that despite a depth of knowledge gathered since the mid-1980s her opinion was not always valued. 'If I recommended a band I'd seen as really good, people would ignore me. But if men had seen the same band, then they'd take notice.'[27] Though her experience mirrors that of women generally in the industry, with its tight budgets and logistical difficulties world music is an even harder area in which to make an impact. If you are operating outside the festival circuit, strict immigration controls, high air fares and the hotel costs needed by the typically large line-up of world-music bands often make promotion prohibitive. 'Men pass business on to each other first,' said Debbie Golt, who in 1990 set up with her partner Alexa Dalby the first UK female world-music promotions agency, Half The Sky. A former activist with Rock Against Racism, and manager of UK-based pan-African band Taxi Pata Pata in the 1980s, Golt arrived at the idea for Half The Sky 'by combining fierce feminism with music. I wanted to promote women because I felt they were hidden.' For Dalby, a writer who had also worked for Thames TV selling programmes worldwide, there was a gap in the market for world-music women. 'Men get that prominence because promoters think they're the bigger stars.'[28]

With patience, perseverance and much negotiation through husbands and intermediaries (before even speaking to Malian singer Sidibé, they had to speak to five men in her house), in their first two years alone, Half The Sky organized UK tours for Ami Koïta, Oumou Sangaré and Stella Chiweshe along with key Women In Music festival dates. Confidently promoting their artists in the mainstream, Golt and Dalby noted a big step forward when women like Koïta and Chiweshe became 'critics' choice in media bastions of white male middle classdom'. After her work with Half The Sky, Golt went on to become an international DJ at www.gaialive.co.uk and to manage the male Moroccan band MoMo.

By the 1990s, female world-music artists were beginning to pack out venues alongside men: from Sangaré's Malian feminism to Cuban ambassador Celia Cruz to the liquid melancholy of Cape Verde's 'barefoot diva' Cesaria Evora. The latter, in particular, became a millennial star later in life, with two best-selling albums, *Cafe Atlantico* and *Sao Vicente di Longe*. Her soulful, salty 'morna' ballads mixed African, Brazilian and Caribbean influences, winning such celebrity fans as Ricky Martin and David Byrne. Madonna wanted Evora to sing at her wedding to Guy Ritchie, but the diva gracefully refused. Evora sang barefoot as a mark of solidarity with those she left behind, the poverty-stricken children of the Cape Verde island interiors. Unfazed by stardom, she said: 'I wasn't astonished by Europe and I was never impressed by the speed and grandeur of modern America. I only regret my success has taken so long to achieve.'[29]

As more women like Evora moved into mainstream pop, the phrase 'world music' sounded like an anachronism. To a veteran like Miriam Makeba progress lay in the eventual abandonment of the term:

'I hate when they put artists in categories. What is world music? I think they're being polite. What they want to say is Third World music. I resent that. Where did jazz come from? Africa. And people have stolen from jazz. Africa has contributed to every sphere of music, yet we're sold as something separate. It's a way of keeping us in our place. If it's Third World music they don't have to pay these artists much or give them the same treatment they would a Western artist.'

To the younger club culture vocalist Natacha Atlas, who played in Eilat in 1994 to a thoroughly mixed crowd of Israelis and Palestinians, the answer was an even simpler one of unity:

'Where the fuck else can music go? Everything else – rock 'n' roll, pop – has been done. I know other people who are Anglo-Indian, Anglo-Czech, French-Arabic, French Tunisian . . . there are a lot of young kids growing up with dual nationality and awareness of other cultures. Integration is the only way; globally it's the future of mankind. And musically, that has to be the future.'

Come 2001, a host of new female artists was emerging: there was Susana Baca, delving into her Afro-Peruvian heritage to create a minimalist mix of bossa nova and pop; the enigmatic Virginia Rodrigues singing spare songs of Christian devotion to Brazilian and Yoruba rhythms; and South Africa's Sibongile Kumalo, melting audiences worldwide with her jazz-tinged repertoire. Also being re-discovered were older divas, such as Cuba's feisty Omara Portuondo, and Cheikha Remitti, from western Algeria. Like an Arabic Piaf, the latter began singing on the seaports and streets of Oranie in Algeria, and flouted Muslim convention by singing about the pleasures of sex and alcohol. In 2000 she played her first British date, at the age of 76. A tall woman with waist-length black hair and flashing eyes, Remitti is known as the 'grandmother of rai', or 'el ghedra' (the root). Accompanied by a spritely band of young musicians, she slowly paced the stage of the Barbican Centre, singing mesmerizing drones in a deep, cavernous voice. A female dancer appeared and wiggled decoratively, but couldn't compete with Remitti. With just one suggestive shake of her ample hips, the older woman conjured up the vision of a musty, exotic, ancient world.

Amid the explosion of cross-cultural music in the late 1980s there was a similar revitalization of protest pop. Just as women in world music demanded to be heard, so female artists in rock and pop developed a more open political voice. This was a stance, however, that did not come risk-free, and, in testing the boundaries of politicized rock, many encountered marginalization, suicide and madness – a precarious place to be free.

# 12 Talkin' Tough

## THE ENEMY WITHIN: WOMEN AND PROTEST POP

**Protest:** Polarity . . . antagonism . . . non-co-operation . . . challenge . . . cussedness . . . resist . . . recalcitrant . . . repulse . . . unsubmissive . . . disobedient . . . mutinous . . . struggle against . . . kick . . . not take it lying down
*Roget's Thesaurus*

'I said in concert once, "In my humble opinion", and burst out laughing. I've never had a humble opinion in my life. If you're going to have one, why bother to be humble about it?'
JOAN BAEZ, quoted in *International Herald Tribune* by James Gavin, 1992

POLITICAL DISSENT has always been a rich strand within pop music. From the angry blues singers of the 1940s to Communist folkies in the 1950s and the various vast stadium Aid spectacles of the 1980s, performers have used the medium of rock as a mass vehicle for protest. Stars can publicly endorse or criticize political parties, hence the knowledge for politicians that music is a force to use, manipulate or fear. Protest makes automatic heroes – whether or not they had feet of clay, artists such as Woody Guthrie, Pete Seeger, John Lennon, Hugh Masekela, Stevie Wonder and Bob Marley had all at one time been victimized for taking a public stand on particular issues. In the arena of political pop, it is the male voice that attracts the most attention. Seventy-five per cent of Robin Denselow's *When the Music's Over: The Story of Political Pop*[1] is taken up with men's stories, with women given fleeting coverage – usually (as in the case of Joan Baez and Peggy Seeger) as wives or partners of the dissenters.

Traditionally viewed as less authoritative, the female protest voice has long been powerful. Women protest singers did not clamber out of the 1960s folk scene but were in evidence during the 1920s and 1930s. Miner's daughter Aunt Mollie Jackson (Mary Magdelene Garland), for instance, born in 1880, was jailed at ten years old for union activities, later becoming a union organizer. Her mother had died of starvation in 1886 and her brother, husband and son all died in mining accidents, another brother being blinded by further mining misadventure. Jackson sang at meetings and on picket lines, eventually arriving in New York in 1936 after being blacklisted throughout her home state of Kentucky because of her beliefs. In New York, together with her half-sister Sarah Ogan Gunning, she recorded mainly for the Library of Congress, and made one commercial single for Columbia called 'Kentucky Miner's Wife'. After her death in 1960 some of her Library of Congress records gained an album release through Rounder.

Another protest balladeer, Ella May Wiggins, was shot dead near Gastonia, following her activities in the Kentucky coal-fields, while a link between protest generations was made when Joan Baez and Bob Dylan covered songs such as 'What Have They Done To The Rain?' and 'Little Boxes', written by veteran campaigner Malvina Reynolds.

Although a female assertion of identity within a male-dominated sphere is arguably an act of protest in itself (from Madonna's populist attack on Catholicism to Tina Turner strutting her survivalist ethic in stadiums throughout the world), this chapter focuses on key women who have made their per-formance explicitly political, who have taken themselves perilously close to a personal edge in pursuit of a moral ideal. One definition of protest is: 'a formal statement or action of dissent. To affirm solemnly one's innocence, especially in reply to accusation.'[2] In a rock medium that regularly trivializes female opinion, a woman risks isolation when she makes an open statement. And she is not even guaranteed the cachet of heroic status.

## From Where I Stand

When rock 'n' roll was in its infancy in the 1950s, Communist folk musician Pete Seeger racked up hit after hit with his harmonic pop outfit The Weavers. Once McCarthyism began to bite, his group was effectively blacklisted, despite the fact there was nothing overtly political in the innocuous nature of their pop material. From then on he returned to his role as a tireless political campaigner, adapting and popularizing radical folk music, bringing songs such as 'Where Have All The Flowers Gone?' and 'We Shall Overcome' to mass audiences. Along with brother Mike Seeger and the radical British folk artist Ewan MacColl, he did much to establish a history and heritage of political struggle within pop culture. Like Shakespeare, though, he had a sister.

At fifty-three the author of over 140 songs, Peggy Seeger is a sensitive woman with a sparky, intelligent smile. Perched on the edge of a sofa for our interview in 1994, she spoke of how her brothers Mike and Pete, and Ewan MacColl, her husband for thirty years, acted as mentors in her life, before she grew into a

**Peggy Seeger** with husband/collaborator Ewan MacColl – creating folk song as protest and documentary. (Courtesy of Peggy Seeger)

sense of her own purpose. 'I was running around with a long-neck banjo and jeans. I wasn't pushy, more a push-over.'[3] Born in New York in 1935, Seeger grew up in Maryland in a large, sprawling musical family. Her father was an ethnomusicologist, her mother Ruth Crawford Seeger, an inspiring modernist composer who taught young Peggy the piano. As well as learning songs from half-brother Pete, she taught herself to play the banjo with Mike – so by the time she arrived in England as a penniless student traveller in 1956, she was an accomplished musician and songwriter.

It was when she joined folk revivalist group The Ramblers in the late 1950s that she fell in love with one of its charismatic members, MacColl, and married him. They forged a prolific partnership, writing and recording for TV and film, while she herself released more than thirty solo albums. While he expounded a radical Marxist philosophy through his touring Theatre Workshop or organizations like the London Critics Group, she wrote songs to document the activities of women's groups and peace organizations, from the CND Aldermaston marches to Greenham Common. During the high-profile 1976–8 Grunwick strike, for instance, when up to eighty-five strikers, the majority of whom were Asian women, diligently picketed their anti-union film-processing plant in North London, Seeger interviewed their prime mover, Jayaben Desai. Rather than write a rallying call, she decided instead to compose a song about the strike through Desai's own words.

'Desai had been a well-off Kenyan Asian when she was expelled from East Africa. Brought up with a silver spoon in her mouth, she then became one of England's persecuted minority and was thrown to the top of an incredible strike. She was a survivor, a woman without "High English" speaking on platforms about the strike. "I do not speak your language High," she'd say to me. "I speak High in my language." Her language was one of continual translation – she'd come out with evocative phrases like "Now husbands proud to see saris on the picket line" or "Born rich in the womb." After a twelve-hour interview I cast the song in an Appalachian style with an Indian mode. She was fascinated, saying, "It sounds Indian, I can hear myself talking."'

It was this painstaking research technique that gave Seeger's songs their immediacy and colour. Interested in the personal effect of politics, she was too sceptical to be ruled by dogma:

'I've been on every demo possible – like businessmen have everything packed up, so I had my walking boots, sandwich box, flask and emergency numbers. I got beaten up by police in an anti-Vietnam demonstration, and I've written songs for each major issue, but I'm no good at rallying songs. I'm stronger for women. I'd like women to be writing about more than just love. Everything in the world needs to be reshaped in our own imagery.'

By the time she wrote the women's peace camp anthem 'Carry Greenham Home' in the early 1980s, she had become more and more interested in feminism and her relationship with MacColl began to shift. Instead of seeing him just as a father figure and mentor, she realized how her solidity gave him a nest from which to operate. 'I brought musical knowledge and instruments, and took care of him domestically. He got me a sweet thing, but as I used to say, Ewan, you were all right 'till feminism got you. He tried to adapt but couldn't.' After his death from arteriosclerosis in 1989, Seeger continued to write and perform, publishing 139 of her songs five years later in a book, *Peggy Seeger, 40 Years of Songwriting*. A legacy of late maturity, Seeger was finally getting due recognition outside her circle of heroic men.

## No Lipstick, Flat Shoes, a Guitar

'You take this little pickle at age seventeen and a half who's given a mantle and an identity at a time when I still thought of myself as a dumb Mexican from southern California. Then here I was, the Virgin Mary,' said Joan Baez, of her sudden elevation from obscurity to sainthood after her emergence at the Newport Folk Festival in 1959.[4] The half-Mexican, half-Scots Baez has referred frequently to the division between her canonization as political activist Saint Joan and the fun-loving, hedonist and unreliable feminist icon Queen Joan. Like Seeger she found herself overshadowed by her male partner when in 1963 she introduced Bob Dylan, a new young singer she had taken under her wing, to her audience at the Newport Folk Festival. They had become lovers, the 'King and Queen of Folk Protest', but as his fame rocketed she was dogged by insecurity. The young bard would refuse to let her on stage time after time, he was unfaithful and insensitive, but for many years she clung on to the affair: 'Don't you think that if somebody is just out of reach, you keep grabbing for it?' she said later, with philosophical hindsight.[5]

Despite the undermining effect of her relationship with Dylan, Baez still managed to become a key voice for the 1960s generation. Though self-deprecating about her efforts, Baez was a major female star who kept political conviction firmly on her pop agenda. A strong supporter of civil rights, she marched with Dr Martin Luther King Jr, and appeared on a platform with him at the historic 1963 March on Washington singing 'We Shall Overcome'. She refused to appear on the TV folk programme *Hootenanny* because of ABC's blacklisting of Pete Seeger; she told the IRS that she would not pay the percentage of her taxes earmarked for defence spending; and she was twice thrown in jail for protesting against the draft. Not many stars have actually been imprisoned for their beliefs.

In the early 1990s while watching a TV show about Mick Jagger, free love and the levitation of the Pentagon, she wondered, 'Where was I during all this? I was in jail', and commented, 'Except for the intensity . . . I don't have nostalgia for the details of what went on in those years, and for my general grimness.'[6] The first performer in twenty-five years to be denied use of the Daughters of the American Revolution's Constitution Hall in Washington because of her opinions, Baez became an important voice in the anti-Vietnam movement, releasing 1973's *Where Are You Now, My Son?* as a document of her visit to fiercely bombed Hanoi the year before. She told me later: 'I would have liked to have learned by that early age to have fun and be present in the moment in the way that I was preaching. I did so much for others – I just wish I'd been there!'[7]

With her pure, precise voice, Baez was the million-selling singer of other people's stories. Never considered an 'authentic' folk artist – once described as an 'outsider singing to outsiders'[8]

– she still conveyed the integrity of rural song, from the Appalachian mountains to Arizona badlands. Apart from only a few singles hits, including 1971's 'The Night They Drove Old Dixie Down' and 'Diamonds And Rust' in 1975, she was an album-chart regular, six of her records registering gold. By the mid-1970s, though, she fell victim to the problem of musical sleep-walking, a scourge that can grip even the best protest performers who concentrate on politics at the expense of their music. 'I stayed with what felt safe for me,' she said. 'I would be reading the editorials in the *New York Times* during breaks in recording, rather than concentrating wholeheartedly on the album I was making. Then music shifted, the whole socio-political atmosphere shifted . . . I found myself left behind.'[9]

Derided as droopy Dylan pastiches, her later albums were unsuccessful – until the early 1990s when she returned to the studio in the wake of an industry friendly to folk again, enlivened by the success of Tracy Chapman and Suzanne Vega. *Play Me Backwards*, her 1993 album, showed concentration, verve and a fresh fighting spirit. At a live concert that year in London, she played to a rapturous crowd, showing her Saint and Queen Joan image, combined in an enthusiastic anecdote about dancing on a table top with inhabitants of war-torn Sarajevo. 'Even though bombs were going off around us, our hosts could still sing and drink me under the table till four in the morning.'

Chiming with anti-Vietnam and civil rights protest, Baez's views in the 1960s had an enthusiastic audience, but by the late 1970s punk dismissed 'hippydom' as a failed experiment, and the knowing ironists of the post-modern MTV 1980s derided notions of acoustic 'authenticity', leaving the traditional protest voice submerged. But as if in reaction to the right-wing cynicism that pervaded the 1980s through Reaganomics and Thatcher-ism, there was a mounting (and lucrative) folk-roots revival. Suzanne Vega was the first million seller of this new female acoustic breed. Apart from 'Luka', her Top Ten hit about child abuse, Vega's affiliations were veiled and subtle. Michelle Shocked, however, was a Texan-born hardcore hobo who took up just where Baez had left off.

A veteran of the San Francisco punk squat scene, Shocked had led a nomadic existence, guitar in tow, hitching round women's peace camps in Europe and actively campaigning with the squatters movement in Amsterdam and New York, when her life was transformed by a British indie record executive. The impromptu Walkman recording of her raw songs of love and protest late one night at the Kerriville Folk Festival, complete with passing trucks, was released by Pete Lawrence's Cooking Vinyl in 1987. Reaching No. 1 in the indie charts within a few weeks, *The Texas Campfire Tapes* went on to sell over 40,000, securing a follow-on deal with major label Polygram. By 1988 Shocked was stunned, working firmly within the system she thought she had rejected. 'My reason for dropping out was that I didn't agree with the competition in the market-place, but now I'm in the most competitive industry possible. I feel as though I'm playing with fire,' she said.[10]

Caught between commercial pop and political credibility is an uncomfortable situation to be in, but Shocked negotiated it in a way that was true to herself. Her second album *Short Sharp Shocked* featured a picture of her being arrested and man-handled by police on a 1984 'Stop the City' demonstration in San Francisco's financial district. In one way it could be seen as packaging rebellion, but in another it was Shocked levelling a broadside at the capitalist system that had 'co-opted' her. Had 1960s pop machinery been more sophisticated, and its con-sumption more self-aware, Baez would have faced the same dilemma.

By the time of her third album *Captain Swing* in 1989, Shocked was focusing on the single issue of homelessness. Disgusted with Reaganomics, she had exiled herself in England for several years, but with a planned march on Washington by the homeless movement, she felt ready to return to the US. 'My solution would be, once you're there, squat on the White House lawn. During the '30s Depression they had Hooverville, where people built these cardboard shanties. The mobilization among the homeless is an encouraging sign for me, it's one area I feel I can speak with authority,' she said. Although we were sitting in Polygram's plush office, I could see her struggling with the paradoxes of her position. Then she was still living on a houseboat ('called Courgette, because it's long and green') in North London's Tottenham Hale. 'You can see music as a means to an end,' she sighed. 'But it's so easy to be corrupted working inside the system.'

Another female artist also weaving political issues into her work was Natalie Merchant, alternative star and lead singer of the band 10,000 Maniacs. In 1988 when their album *In My Tribe*, a collection of heartfelt, melodic rock songs, made her the darling of the college circuit, Merchant spoke with earnest clarity on issues ranging from the Contras and US policy in Central America to domestic violence and the environment. '*In My Tribe* – the album title basically sums up America – First Person, possessive, active. It's the frontier mentality. There it is, it's free, I'm gonna get it, it's mine. I'll kill you if you want it,' she said.[11]

Five years and three best-selling albums later the Maniacs had split up, and with a solo deal, Merchant's politics had become more circumspect. 'By supporting so many different causes I've been called a political firebrand,' she said. 'I've done lots of benefits, but I'm not sure where I am on the political spectrum.'[12] Less about general injustice in the world, her focus had shifted to her particular place as a woman on the scene. 'At the MTV Music Awards I was appalled at the male-to-female ratio. I was the only female singer asked to give an award. Janet Jackson and Madonna were there, but they're corporate artists, more like Las Vegas showgirls, while quality female acts like Lucinda Williams weren't getting the recognition they deserved.' In turning her attention to the industry that she worked in, Merchant struck a note resonant with a personal sense of insecurity and anger. In directing energy to the 'external' enemy, protest artists can lose a sense of self, and for women this can seem oddly detached. An artist whom Merchant championed from the beginning of her career found herself in an uncomfortable position as talisman of the Left, and detached herself for her own creative survival.

Until Tracy Chapman was beamed worldwide by satellite to sixty-three countries at Nelson Mandela's birthday concert in 1988, she was a shy young black girl with a guitar, a sackful of songs and a low-profile deal with Elektra. Overnight her life was transformed into a nightmare of media attention and fan adulation. She became the key request for everyone's benefit concert, the voice of the new 'twentysomething' generation 'Talking 'Bout A Revolution'.

Before she battened down the hatches for a few years in the face of painful media glare Chapman talked politely to me about

a tough childhood in Cleveland, Ohio, a scholarship to a liberal
boarding school via Kennedy's ABC programme for the disadvantaged, her discovery of folk music through the white pupils
around her, and her graduation from Tufts University. It was
while busking in coffee-house Cambridge, Massachusetts, that
she met Brian Coppelman, son of Charles, president of the
powerful SBK Songs. Coppelman Sr became her manager and
secured the deal with Elektra. Not long after came Merchant's
invitation for Chapman to support the Maniacs on their next
tour.

When I asked what inspired her, her reply was circumspect:
'I'm intrigued by the way people relate to one another . . . I've
seen a lot of horrible things.' Bad experiences? 'I feel I'm with a
therapist!' she said, and then blurted out, 'A lot of it has to do
with growing up poor, black, working class and female in
America. There're a lot of obstacles in simply trying to live your
life, let alone trying to do anything outrageous or grand. Just to
simply get by. Discrimination, humiliation – you just don't

forget those things. I deal with a lot of those feelings in the songs.'[13]

Unfairly criticized as dealing in 'professional disillusion',[14] Chapman's ground-breaking self-titled LP was considered too anodyne for a black audience. Half the songs on her debut, however, were covered by reggae artists, with the track 'Fast Car', a poignant picture of urban poverty and escape, becoming a hit for reggae star Foxy Brown. Chapman's initial core audience may have been white festival-goers used to folk ('and why not? I get a lot of my support from grassroots political movements'), but with her second album *Crossroads*, her message began to filter through to the black community. Celebrity photographer Herb Ritts may have shot her in air-brushed monochrome, the country twang on her follow-up may have been a calculated bid for the Nashville radio that had previously ignored her – but her collaboration with Spike Lee on her 1989 'Born To Fight' video became part of a text on black history for US high-school students, and as she said, not without irony, just before playing a Brixton ANC benefit, 'People try to tell me that black people aren't into my music and don't know who I am, yet I am consistently recognized more by black people than by white people. It's not just my face, but my music.'[15]

In 1988 *Village Voice* writer Nelson George hailed Chapman as 'Today's Black Woman', leader of a consumer group 'shamefully under-represented in record bins . . . college-educated, upwardly mobile, politicized black women – neither buppies nor b-girls, but with street sense and tempered careerism.'[16] She continued to plug into this politicization on her third album, *Matters Of The Heart* (1992), directly addressing themes of racism and poverty. Her biggest crime, it seems, was in crossing over so easily into the pop mainstream. She may have been a reluctant icon, but Chapman represented in the 1980s a rich tradition of black women's civil rights protest.

## Mama Didn't Raise Me to Be Foolish Like That

Chapman was not the first black woman to voice protest in a supposedly white folk tradition. In 1953 Odetta Felious, a singer who played off-beat guitar and looked like a young Bessie Smith with a crew cut, was performing her own brand of power folk/ blues at the Tin Angel on San Francisco's waterfront. Her set included Guthrie songs, gospel traditionals and the song 'I've Been 'Buked And I've Been Scorned', which she sang with a peculiar blood-curdling spirituality.

Born in Birmingham, Alabama, in 1930, she grew up in LA, studying music at the City College before her itinerant spirit took her via San Francisco to a New York residency at the Blue Angel in the late 1950s. There, the artful integrity of her style, moving from silky voice to rasp in one phrase, attracted the support of luminaries such as Harry Belafonte and Pete Seeger. Early recordings like *Odetta Sings Ballads And Blues* on the Tradition label may have been uncomplicated and folksy, but later her classical training and theatrical virtuosity led to symphony concerts, appearances at Carnegie Hall and even a movie career, with roles in such films as *Cinerama Holiday* and *Sanctuary*.

Despite the later *Odetta With Strings*, she is just as well known as a folk heroine, performing at the historic Student Non-violent Co-ordinating Committee (SNCC) March on Washington in August 1963, where Dr Martin Luther King gave his 'I have a dream' speech and top black artists from Mahalia Jackson to Josephine Baker registered their support for civil rights. An active protest singer, Odetta also campaigned against US involvement in Vietnam, appearing alongside Joan Baez, Phil Ochs, Pete Seeger and newcomer Paul Simon at the free 'War Is Over' concert in New York's Central Park, after the last Americans were airlifted from Saigon in April 1975.

Back at the same SNCC rally in Washington in 1963, Odetta shared the bill with a young Bernice Reagon, a key SNCC Freedom Singer who would eventually form one of the most powerful female gospel protest a cappella outfits, Sweet Honey

In The Rock. Active in the civil rights movement since she was thrown out of school after being arrested on one of the first marches in Albany, Georgia, Reagon joined the SNCC Freedom Singers in 1962. Headed by her future husband Cordell Reagon, the Singers harnessed the 'close to life-threatening'[17] force of Southern gospel and toured the country as a truly political pop band, campaigning for voter registration and telling audiences news of the struggle that had been suppressed. The 1960s protest for civil rights was fuelled by the urgent survivalist anger of black America. In the same way that gospel has been dubbed 'the music of necessity', it was vital that voices like the Freedom Singers be heard, as resistance in the face of an institutionalized racism that threatened to suffocate the Afro-American spirit for good.

Bernice Reagon linked this force with the burgeoning women's movement in the 1970s, the decade when politics became unfashionable. 'People say it was the decade when everyone went to sleep, but in terms of women there was a real unleashing of energy. A lot of causes were centred around women – so of course they say that nothing happened!' she said.[18] After singing with all-black female line-up the Harambree Singers, she formed Sweet Honey in 1973, a five-strong female vocal group whose self-titled debut on Flying Fish in 1976 serves as a dynamic blueprint of their work against racism and sexism, and on the environment. Much of their focus was on big campaigns, playing rallies in support of the jailed radical West Coast academic Angela Davis, for instance, or the Wilmington Ten, black students jailed after protesting against harassment in the wake of desegregation, and Joan Little, a woman charged with murder for killing the warder who tried to rape her in jail.

Sweet Honey express the most potent female connection between voice and protest, using every sound from doowop chest bed bass to declarative 'shout songs', spirituals and airy flying ballads. Twenty years after their formation, on the sleevenotes for the eleventh album *Still On The Journey*, Reagon wrote about her ensemble as if it were an independent being, an abstract female warrior. 'Sweet Honey is formed out of today's requests – out of my dreams – her songs and singing give focus to my efforts to stand steady against the howling winds of societal insanities . . . we plow the path forward with sound . . . a path . . . lit by the chatter of the ancestors.'[19]

Reagon forged Sweet Honey out of her activism, unconcerned about whether they would become 'stars' in the US showbiz mainstream. Those women who try to do both inevitably pay dear. 'Brown-skinned' female artists from Paula Abdul to Sade now find they can move more easily between the categories of modern pop, but for cabaret star Eartha Kitt back in the 1950s and 1960s, the more successful she became, the more threatening her 'difference' appeared to the Establishment. When the anti-Vietnam movement was blazing, for example, Kitt spoke frankly to President Lyndon Johnson, only to find herself blacklisted. 'He asked me, "Why is there so much juvenile delinquency on the streets of America?" I said, "Our boys are running away from joining the army, not because they don't like America; they just don't want us involved in an unwinnable, unfair war." Within two hours I was out of work in America.'[20] Mixed-blood Cree Indian Buffy Sainte-Marie, a singer/songwriter who had a huge hit in 1971 with the soundtrack for Mike Nicholls's film *Soldier Blue*, also found her political work suppressed when she started campaigning for Native American civil rights. 'When Johnson came to power the lid came down . . . and a letter campaign from the White House "advised" radio networks against work by people like me, Eartha Kitt and others, stating that they "deserved to be suppressed". On the *Tonight* show I was told not to sing anything to do with Indian people,' she said.[21]

Nina Simone, too, was cold-shouldered by the Establishment when she began playing SNCC benefits and her song 'Young, Gifted And Black' became the anthem of young black America. 'It was no accident that most active black musicians couldn't get major label deals in the late 1960s and 1970s,' she said. Years of straddling the opposing worlds of evening-gown jazz with political street soul took its toll, and in 1968, after King's assassination, with a legion of friends exiled, dead or under FBI surveillance, she played the Montreux Jazz Festival crying her eyes out at the keyboard.

In 1992 Simone referred to the LA riots that happened earlier that year in the wake of the Rodney King case.

'I was disgusted. Nothing's changed in the United States, so I'll go on singing my protest songs. The songs I sing are just as applicable in 1992 as they were in 1963. It amazed me when I saw all the burning and looting on TV. I saw it and said my people should burn down the United States, they should tear it up and burn it *down* – they'd let the world know they're not gonna tolerate what's been done all these years.'[22]

While the civil rights movement raged in early 1960s America, its parallel political flashpoint was South Africa. Throughout the 1960s and 1970s there was growing consensus among musicians that playing Sun City in the Bophuthatswana 'homeland', the Las Vegas of South Africa, was fuelling propaganda for the apartheid regime. But despite intensified repression following the formation of the ANC's armed wing Umkhonto we Sizwe in 1961 and detention without trial, the idea of a Western cultural boycott was in its infancy. So when a white convent-educated British Home Counties girl with blond hair resisted the apartheid laws by refusing to play to segregated audiences, she became an isolated case and an unwitting political football. Her concerts at New York's Brooklyn Fox with members of the Motown soul contingent coupled with a growing awareness of the civil rights debate meant that Dusty Springfield became the first British artist to include a 'No Apartheid' clause in her contract. After just four non-segregated shows in South Africa in 1964 she was deported, returning home to an ugly controversy and questions in the House of Commons. Springfield's action was condemned by top entertainers such as Max Bygraves and Derek Nimmo, who accused her of publicity-seeking, and condoned in more liberal quarters such as the Musicians Union who applauded her for advancing 'the cause'. Caught between the two, a bewildered Springfield protested, 'I'm strictly a non-political girl. I know nothing whatsoever about politics.' Then later, 'Whatever your personal political feelings are, if you become involved in them publicly you're bound to come out the loser.'[23]

Springfield's action may have made her feel temporarily victimized, but she still continued to have a successful pop career. Had she been black, the outcome would probably have been very different. Miriam Makeba, the first African female artist to become an international star, used her status to speak out against apartheid, only to find herself exiled by the regime in 1960 and her music banned three years later. The fact that she was highly influential meant she was a threat not only to Pretoria, but also to the government of her second home. When she married Black Panther leader Stokely Carmichael, her link with the US civil rights movement was cemented, and she was effectively blacklisted. 'I thought, I'm not going to fight this. If my own country could ban me, someone else's country [blacklisting me] was not half as bad. I just left, and in good time came back,' she said decades later.[24] As a friend once pointed out, 'She would never have been so shoddily treated if she had been a man.'

In 1987 she was at the centre of another political controversy, but this time in a way that could have compromised her credibility. When in 1980 the UN passed Resolution 35/206 supporting an official cultural boycott the position for entertainers was made clear. Among pop stars the consensus was against performing in South Africa, so when Paul Simon decided (without consultation with the ANC) to record his 1986 *Graceland* album there with South African musicians, there was uproar in anti-apartheid circles, many artists accusing him of breaking the cultural boycott. When Simon tried to add legitimacy to his blunder by touring the album with veteran campaigners Makeba and Hugh Masekela, the debate exploded, particularly in Britain where he and his entourage faced a hostile press conference and his Royal Albert Hall date was picketed. Makeba recalled,

'Boy, did I suffer. Masekela and I were the ones who had to answer all the questions. It was only when we were on tour I found out that there was this controversy. Because I found myself in the hot seat I went to the ANC and asked, "What is the rule?" They said no one should perform in South Africa. So I asked Paul, "Did you perform in South Africa?" "No, I was just in the studio making a record." He didn't perform in South Africa. When we came to Britain there were people demonstrating outside the Albert Hall saying, "Sell out! Sell out!" So I said, "Let them in. And by the time we were through they were dancing. That show was very political, we sang what we needed to sing and finally it was OK. A lot of people stirring things up were jealous, saying he'd used us. Who doesn't use anybody? We're always using someone.'

Makeba refused to take the accusations seriously, but for a while there was disappointment that her tour with Simon may have weakened the cultural boycott. Being so public a figure meant that she would always be seen more as a symbol than a simple entertainer. It was not an easy position. Most artists in the late-1980s rush of satellite stadium charity shows from Live Aid to Nelson Mandela's 70th Birthday Tribute opted for safety in numbers, while growing media consciousness meant that pop stars could unite with a sense of solidarity. By 1994, after Nelson Mandela's election victory, the path was wide open for artists to play South Africa. That year Whitney Houston did the largest-scale production tour for an international artist in South Africa, ensuring that tickets were sold in townships and factories as well as in the usual outlets. Her children's charity concerts flagged her high-profile investment in New Age Beverages, the large black-owned and managed Pepsi Cola bottling venture in South Africa. Protest had become allied to big business.

Back in the 1960s, however, isolated individuals found that political protest marginalized them and made them an industry target. A friend of Makeba, jazz singer Abbey Lincoln committed commercial suicide several times by speaking out. 'Some people say I was political. I never was political. I just went looking for myself. In a world where you can't be yourself you may as well slit your throat,' she has said.[25] During the 1960s she and bandleader husband Max Roach played benefits for Malcolm X, the NAACP or the Black Muslims when radical black nationalism was perceived as the devil within. With the rise of rap in the 1980s, there was a resurgence of black nationalism, and the Nation of Islam was sold on MTV. Lincoln noted this trend with disgust: the politics that gave her a 'difficult' reputation and damaged her career in the 1960s seemed to have been packaged and sold as safe nostalgia twenty years later. 'Everything is not for sale, and when it is, you can kiss the baby goodbye,' she said, adding (particularly on the subject of selling sex), 'My mama didn't raise me to be foolish like that.'[26]

Her statement, however, underestimated the integrity of the next generation. Not just marketing outrage, radical black acts like Nefertiti, Queen Mother Rage and X Clan trod a fine line between record company policy and promotion of their own passionate politics. Nefertiti, for instance, was careful to 'use uplifting metaphors instead of hate/devil words' in her lyrics.[27] Her message may have been radical Nation of Islam, but its delivery was sophisticated and poetic. Less easy to stomach for the white mainstream was artist activist Sister Souljah, whose rap was purely a political vehicle. An articulate part-time member of Public Enemy, she took an extreme almost adversarial role and was singled out for public censure, an effective tactic for undermining power.

When in 1992 Souljah told the *Washington Post* that she could understand anti-white feeling during the LA riots she was targeted by Clinton during his presidential campaign for what was perceived as anti-white racism. Claiming that she was being scapegoated for the Democratic debate on racism Souljah fought back, saying that if Clinton could not respect her for the 'strong, independent, educated black woman' she was, what hope was there for young black people who had already 'opted out' of the system?

Souljah's comments became a matter for national debate partly because of the speed of the media and the extent of its proliferation through TV, magazines, cable etc. The self-aware media-conscious 1980s and 1990s meant that protest pop could never be as simple as it was in Joan Baez's day. Its last great agit-prop blast was in the late 1970s, when campaigns such as Rock Against Racism (RAR) and its more muted sister Rock Against Sexism dominated the British punk scene. Organized by the militant Socialist Workers Party, RAR was an initiative packed with male heroes and supportive women. 'We want rebel music, street music . . . Crisis music. Now music', read the message on Tom Robinson's 1978 debut album *Power In The Darkness*, a typical rallying call to young punks 'kicking against the pricks'. The slogans may have applied to everyone, but apart from a few all-girl bands such as The Raincoats and The Slits performing benefits, female artists did not have a high profile in RAR. Again, when the Labour Party cultural youth coalition Red Wedge toured the UK in the late 1980s spearheaded by acts like Paul Weller and Billy Bragg, it wasn't until leader Annajoy David organized a Red Wedge Women's Tour that female acts were foregrounded in the campaign. This was not just a male music-business conspiracy to keep women dumb when it came to voicing protest: women themselves fear isolation and condemnation if they speak out. Less automatic heroes, they are more likely to be branded 'mad'. What would have happened had John Lennon, working-class hero and Bed Peace activist, been a woman?

In the mid-1990s a new voice emerged from the protest folk scene to cross over spectacularly into the mainstream rock market. Ani DiFranco had multicoloured locks, funky songs and robust, rhythmically inventive guitar. Born in 1970, DiFranco came from Buffalo, New York, a blue collar town in the heart of what is known as 'the rust belt'. Buffalo's steel plant closed down in the 1970s, leaving empty buildings and a vast swathe of unemployment. DiFranco told me that her sound, unembellished and direct, was influenced by her plain surroundings. 'There's no pomp or circumstance.'[28]

In 1990 she released a self-titled debut on her own Righteous Babe label, and steadily built a fanatical following. Despite her lack of glitz, DiFranco's 1995 album *Not A Pretty Girl* went overground, shifting 112,000 copies in the US alone. By the time she released 1997's bestselling *Dilate*, she was being feted by the *Wall Street Journal* and *Time* magazine as the indie success story of the decade. Although approached by major labels, DiFranco remained resolutely independent, controlling everything from

**Ani DiFranco**
live in London,
1998: 'The music
industry is a fuckin'
zoo . . . I've never
felt like watering
my experience
down to make it
radio-friendly.'
(Carey Brandon/
Redferns)

music to image to artwork, and earning more royalties per record than the average superstar. According to DiFranco:

'The music industry is a fuckin' zoo. I find it hard to accept rebel music in a corporate setting. Because you know all those people have to play that game. They all have to show up to the photo shoot with the stylist and make-up artist and pose like good little rock stars. Fuck that. Fuck all of that.'[29]

DiFranco asserts that as a folk singer she can be a true alternative. She has sung about everything from her bisexuality to abortion rights to trashing racism. 'People talk about the *issue* of abortion or the *issue* of queer sexuality. But to me they are not issues. This is my life,' she says, 'I've never felt like watering my experience down to make it radio-friendly.'

Hailed as 'Rock's Most Unlikely Superstar', the prolific DiFranco has carried on producing an album a year, beholden to no one's schedule but her own. She became a role model for legions of young women, and an authentic example of millennial Girlpower. 'When a whole bunch of women say, wow, thanks for saying that, me too, that in turn makes me feel I exist,' she asserts.

## Not Mad, Female

'I've always been called crazy. So for the video I said, "No crazy stuff, I'm not gonna look crazy." Warner Brothers saw the video and talked to Billy [her husband/manager]. Billy said, "So how was Kristin – she look OK?" The guy said, "Well . . . I don't want you to take this the wrong way . . . but she looks like a lunatic." "A lunatic?" "Yeh. But we think we can sell that."'[30]

It was 1994, and Kristin Hersh, guitarist in The Throwing Muses, one of the most influential bands on the US 'alternative' scene, was disussing the video for her single 'Your Ghost', a duet with REM's Michael Stipe of sweet madness and haunting obsession. A surprise hit from her acoustic solo album *Hips And Makers*, 'Your Ghost' made insanity marketable.

The skittish, explosive tensions or surreal meanderings that make up the most striking output from female performers are jokingly called Pre-Menstrual Rock. Women such as Joan Baez, Michelle Shocked and Sister Souljah are atypical in the way they directed their message outward. Political protest is seen as an external fundamental dissatisfaction with one's place in society in relation to the world outside. Male acts tend to express that disturbance outwardly in musical slogans, by destroying their guitars, the speaker stack or each other – hence Pete Townshend's claim that smashing his guitar on stage was in the style of Gustav Metzger's 'auto-destructive' art. Women more often take the route of turning suffering on themselves with introspection, or, in the extreme case of Katie Jane Garside from rock band Daisy Chainsaw, self-mutilation. This inner protest, this statement of dis-ease with one's place in the world, is one of the riskiest routes for women to take. Erratic and destabilizing, it does not obey rules of political engagement, yet still conveys the message of untamable, and therefore radical, female power.

Madness doesn't sell. At least, that used to be the prevailing view within the music industry: Beware the Kooky Woman, beware she with the Difficult Reputation. But amid the critical mass of 1990s female rock acts, certain off-kilter voices emerged with raw strength.

Diagnosed as having a bipolar disorder or schizophrenia, Hersh had long struggled with what it meant to be a 'crazy' woman in rock. 'It upset me a lot to be a songwriter. I didn't know what was happening to me. I had seizures and a constant fever for ten years. I could feel my hair stand on end like electricity, I'd throw up, have a seizure and a song would happen. It's like I had to get the song out of my body,' she said.

Averse to the notion that music is just therapy she stressed that there was art in her catharsis, a disciplined objectivity that enabled 'the music to talk as well as myself'. In conversation Hersh is alert and active, with wide eyes trying to take in everything at once. It may not be relaxing, and in terms of writing music, her disorder could be painful, but she was reluctant to dampen it down. 'It's hard not to believe people when they tell you that you have to take drugs to numb what you're seeing, and that what you're seeing isn't real. If you're serious about anything, they think you're sad. If you're strong, they think you're angry. They project all these bad emotions on to you.' Hersh learned to ease the songwriting process with her own resources, and having children helped put it in perspective – 'That's way more important than writing a fuckin' song!'

Coming on like a 1990s West Country Clytemnestra, PJ Harvey, too, allowed angst to billow out on record. Her 1993 album *Rid Of Me*, a catalogue of blood, blues and revenge, emerged out of a 'couple of breakdowns . . . I just couldn't do anything for weeks on end – really little things like having a bath and brushing your teeth. I just didn't know how to do it. It was horrible and I never want to go back there again.'[31] PJ was criticized for letting it all hang out at the expense of her art, but one person's emotional honesty is another's madness. Rose Carlotti of former indie band The Heart Throbs pinpointed the dilemma by saying, 'Male angst is celebrated in rock music. Female angst, passion and lust is an area that's very dodgy. Sometimes going into a record company or going out on stage I'd be scared of being aggressive and being abandoned. I used to feel trapped by that. I have doubts and vulnerabilities – should I express those?'[32]

Carleen Anderson, ex-vocalist with acid-jazz band The Young Disciples, had no qualms about expressing herself as a solo artist, in fact it was a necessity. 'I'm fortunate with my record company because I've been able to explore my feelings through my music. They still say they can market it. The nightmare is when you express yourself and they say, "We don't know what we can do with it." Then it's, "Where's the nearest window!"'[33]

Her 1994 hit 'Nervous Breakdown', a tempestuous dance song about a lone mother's emotional collapse, covered very unsexy ground, but its bitter, soulful edge struck a chord with record buyers. Rather than trying to hide her experiences of depression, Anderson used them as fuel for powerful songwriting:

'Therapeutically it's excellent, it's kept me from going over to the deep end loads of times. The process can be hazardous. It can carry you to the deep end as well. When I recorded "Mama Said", for instance (a song about leaving a relationship), I was in a painful place. That period in my life has passed, but it's my job to perform this, and for people to believe it I can never lose all the pain. Sometimes you have to pull yourself up, then be up high and pull yourself right down, in order to deliver.'

Despite her courage, musical exorcism exacts a price. It's one that Carleen's forerunner Chaka Khan paid in full. A vocalist who has been inspiration to countless female performers since the late 1960s, Khan had a massive hit in 1984 with the Prince song 'I Feel For You', but she never consolidated that with the expected smooth ride to superstardom. In a business that likes its soul singers malleable and chic, Khan consistently exposed her anarchic self, leading to the frustration of a chequered career. Her open support of black supremacist (and reputed anti-Semite) leader Louis Farrakhan also did her no favours. 'There's a thin line between genius and insanity,' she once said. 'People who say I'm a genius have probably mistaken that for madness. I don't think I have a special gift but I do feel I have a special ability to convey things.'[34] Khan would talk publicly about the unacceptable, whether it was racism, sex addiction or menstruation, her openness clearing a space for subsequent female artists.

Sinéad O'Connor, too, blazed through in the late 1980s and 1990s with a free-thinking chaos that put pop taboo topics such as child abuse, religion and errant nationalism firmly on the rock agenda. 'Whether you like her or not as an artist she's been attacked because she has *raged*,' said Carlotti. When I met O'Connor in 1990, shortly before the release of her second ground-breaking album, *I Do Not Want What I Haven't Got*, a mixture of Celtic melodies and dark, angry dance beats, she was doe-eyed and slightly defensive. Quietly spoken, and already bitten by her free-flowing words being quoted out of context, she recorded our interview on her own Walkman. Refuting the fact that people considered her mouthy, she said, 'I don't think I ever was big-mouthed. People judge books by their covers and build up an image of me based on their own narrow-mindedness. If they think a certain way about a woman with a shaved head, bomber jacket and boots, that's their problem, not mine.'[35]

As if gouging out her feelings, from her muddled yet caustic debut *The Lion And The Cobra* to the ambitious visionary angst of *Universal Mother*, O'Connor has regularly taken herself to the edge, not just musically, but in headline-grabbing protest.

Seeing herself as a 'communicator' rather than an 'entertainer', she once gave vocal support to the IRA (and then retracted it), refused in protest to the 1991 Gulf War to allow 'The Star-Spangled Banner' to be played before a concert of hers in New Jersey (Frank Sinatra said she deserved a 'kick in the ass'), and tore up a picture of the Pope on prime time TV. 'If the Virgin Mary were here today, she'd be ripping up pictures of the Pope. The Catholic Church has done such a lot against her as a symbol for all women,' she told me later.[36] O'Connor continued to grow up in public through the early 1990s, giving painful accounts of the childhood abuse she suffered from her mother. Drawing comparisons with the troubled Guns 'N' Roses singer Axl Rose, O'Connor said, 'We're famous because we want help. We want our stories told. We don't understand what's happened to us, and we're in a lot of pain . . . The only reason I ever wrote songs was because I was so fucked up in my head that I had to figure things out . . . [Songwriting] became a kind of journey inside myself, to rescue myself.'[37] Part of that journey included seeing her country's political history as a metaphor for her own life. 'I see Ireland like a child that's been battered,' she said. 'We lost our history, we lost our language to the British.'[38]

Wearing her 'Recovering Catholic', PWA (Paddies With Attitude) and 'Irish Princess' T-shirts, the 'torch singer of resistance'[39] had a sometimes incoherent, arbitrary logic that found its most intense focus on organized Catholicism. Referring to the 'church triumphant' and the 'church militant', she said, 'Church triumphant is basically God and the saints and everybody else; the church militant is the church on earth which I have no respect for.'[40] Opposed to their draconian attitudes on sex, abortion and birth control, she claimed the Vatican-ruled church had created a culture where 'people are controlled through fear'. Political pop stars rarely focus on the injustices of religion apart from easy-target fundamentalist Christianity, probably because women are the constituency most severely affected by it. Unlike Madonna, who sugared her anti-orthodox Catholic pill with humour and MTV gloss, O'Connor unrepentantly rasped against it. It is not surprising that her roots lay in the Dublin post-punk scene; as The Raincoats' Ana da Silva – a woman who moved from conservative Catholic Portugal to Britain in the late 1970s – commented, 'Catholicism is so much part of you. It gives you a strong sense about right, wrong, guilt and repression. And trying to come out of that in the strongest possible way you use punk.'[41] With her punk-inspired yells, O'Connor is hardly the Singing Nun, yet ironically a strong strand of mysticism runs through her music. Like an inverted saint, she has followed the edicts of her own faith to come up with a pure spirituality both piercingly original and tender. It seems appropriate that one of her heroines is the 'good soldier', Joan of Arc, and it seemed logical that in 1999 she became ordained as a Latin Tridentine priest in Lourdes by rebel divorcee Bishop Michael Cox. Not surprisingly, her ordination wasn't recognized by the Church.

O'Connor's public and contradictory stance earned her condemnation, particularly within the music industry. She was booed off stage at the 1992 Madison Square Garden Bob Dylan tribute concert, for instance, and when she refused to accept her BRIT Award for Best International Female Artist, in a sardonic industry move, her slot at the ceremony was filled with a clip of Whitney Houston singing 'Star-Spangled Banner'. Publicly alienated, O'Connor took body-writing to an unexpected level when she appeared on prime-time British TV in a long dress and wig, the word FORGIVENESS written neatly round her neck like a strange necklace.

Amid the controversy a few women began speaking up in support of O'Connor – particularly Annie Lennox. Using her clout as an oft-nominated favourite within the business, in 1992 Lennox penned a public letter to the *Independent* praising O'Connor's talent and criticizing BRITS producer Jonathan King for a gesture that was 'puerile and embarrassing'. In reply King ticked off both women in an astonishing display of 'keeping them in their place'. O'Connor he accused of being 'hypnotized by celebrity . . . I'd love her to take herself less seriously as a social commentator and concentrate on making [non-political] gems like "Mandinka"' – while he verbally slapped Lennox down for 'egging [Sinéad] along the path to self-destruction'.[42] An older woman who should know better was irresponsibly encouraging a younger sista's rebellion – within that was the implicit warning that no matter how favoured she appears to be, if she puts one foot wrong in the industry the older woman is 'out'.

Columnist Suzanne Moore also voiced support of O'Connor's explosive anger. 'Angry women don't always make a pretty sight . . . yet the outrage she generates is a precious thing.' Underlying the chaos of O'Connor's views is a refusal to be assimilated that speaks volumes. 'Name me another woman who can generate this kind of publicity without taking her clothes off,' said Moore.[43] 'Sinéad O'Connor: she's more rock 'n' roll than all of us,' Chrissie Hynde said admiringly.

By 1993 O'Connor had driven herself to desperation, pulling out of the major Dublin Peace Together concert and printing a full-page poem in the *Irish Times* in explanation, saying that she had to retreat to attend to her 'inner child', a part of her 'tortured and abandoned and spat at and abused'.[44] Two months later she attempted suicide with an overdose of sleeping tablets. After waking up alive she sought recovery through therapy, and started writing songs again, this time with new depth.

When I met her again in 1997, O'Connor was a calmer, mellower thirty-year-old. 'I'm on the other side of recovery,' she said, 'I'm finally on top of the hill, and I can see the other side, whereas before I was right down the bottom.' She could look back to 1993 and see that 'I wasn't a well girl. In a way, I'd lost my voice. I was so sad, I couldn't sing above a whisper, I had no energy to sing joyously or even angrily. Your voice is your spirit and your sexuality.'[45]

Another artist who has explored outrage is Tori Amos, whose song 'Me And A Gun', a searing account of her experience of rape at gunpoint, struck a chord with many women. In response to all the female fans who came up to her after shows talking about their experience of rape or abuse, Tori set up RAIN in the mid-1990s, a US national helpline and counselling service for victims. 'I'd like to think that RAIN is a sort of emergency room, like ER,' she told me. 'Sometimes you're looking for lawyers because you've got an underage gal who if she leaves will be arrested, yet her stepfather's raping her. You walk into the realms of law in certain states. The men and women who're involved in RAIN are a gentle, nurturing force. There are so many artists who've been touched by it who're nothing to do with me. It's taken on a life of its own.' She says it's difficult to keep a non-government-funded organization going, but there is no shortage of sparky fundraising ideas. 'Somebody came up with a birthday concept, for instance. On my birthday there were drag queen shows in New York, and Latin nights across the country – people bought tickets and raised funds for RAIN. It's a big round table of people and ideas now, it's really grown.'[46]

Like O'Connor, Amos has managed to mobilize a great deal of support, but her anger has also been ridiculed. After she sang about the grief of miscarriage on her 1998 album *From The Choirgirl Hotel*, for instance, one newspaper headline read: TORI AND HER LATEST TRAUMA. Amos finds this exasperating.

'People were saying, "We've lost Tori now to depression and drugs". Where did drugs come into it? People misread the shamanic journeys I did, sometimes with a little Ecstasy. Well, of course, I was grieving. But why does it have to be that, as you walk on the edge of sorrow? RAIN aren't afraid to traverse the trenches, they'll go with you in the valleys. Why can't the dark night of the soul be a powerful journey we respect. This is not about smiley faces, guys. There is a walk to be walked.'

Male performers such as Lou Reed, Leonard Cohen and Bob Dylan are taken seriously when they explore dark emotions, but for women artists, this is less acceptable. For all its sharpness, its voice on the verge of a nervous breakdown, O'Connor's music speaks with purity about a woman's struggle for identity. Amos, meanwhile, has written with poetic honesty about rape and mis-carriage – subjects traditionally sidelined as 'women's issues'. Like all rock's 'mad' girls, Amos and O'Connor have driven out further than many dared to go. In that act, all definitions about good/bad girls and the crushing socialization of the need for approval dissolve. That way – inwardly personal or outwardly political – lies inspiration. By the 1990s this voice was growing stronger, with female artists making headway in all genres. Less progress was being made within the industry itself, however. Women were striving to establish their presence in the crucial bargaining positions of money and power, the place where an artist's career can be made or broken.

# 13 Talkin' Business

NUTS 'N' BOLTS AND ALL THE NECESSARIES

'Women are allowed to excel in publishing, human resources and the International department – all jobs that men don't want, and that don't lead to running major corporations.'
> DIANA GRAHAM, MD of Arista Records UK (1991–5), author interview, London, 1994

'I should have given heads of department a good sacking once in a while to be seen as a strong manager, even if they're good at their jobs. I handled things practically rather than politically.'
> LISA ANDERSON, MD of RCA UK (1989–91), author interview, London, 1994

'If you can't be a snake in the grass you gotta hire one.'
> TONI C, New York DJ and dance producer, author interview, New York, 1994

FEMALE PERFORMERS have been the most visible example of women's progress in the history of rock and pop. But what about those working behind the scenes within the business itself? Traditionally excluded from the 'serious money talk, women have always fought to achieve decision-making power and substantial budgets. Pop is a young business and women have found there a degree of mobility that's comparatively higher than in other, more established industries, especially in the US, where they are becoming vice-presidents (VPs) and combining childbearing with senior management in increasing numbers. Although in 1993 only 25 per cent of VPs and department-head positions in the corporate sphere were held by women, in the music business women were six to eight times more likely to get to this level. The snag was that they made roughly 74 per cent of what men in similar jobs earned – only marginally more than the Bureau of Labor national average, according to which women earn 71 cents to the man's dollar.[1] But while their organizational skills are exploited in management, women are still hugely under-represented in creative areas of the business such as A&R or production. In all parts of the industry women's progress has been slow, though they have stealthily made certain jobs their own.

## Management Matriarchs

Any aspiring artist needs a manager, there to negotiate a deal, supervise finances and act as buffer between artist and record company. The 1960s was the era of celebrity managers, with Brian Epstein, Kit Lambert, Andrew Loog Oldham and Allen Klein almost as famous as the stars they managed. Management involves tough talk and an ability to negotiate the best for your artist. Women are not seen as heavyweights in this area. Journalist Caroline Coon, for example, temporarily managed The Clash at the height of their success, after their split with Bernie Rhodes. Although the band were polite, she could tell '[they] would have been much happier if I had been male',[2] and that they were relieved when they eventually found a man for the job.

Apart from the matriarch Eve Taylor, who worked with Adam Faith and Sandie Shaw, up to the late 1970s female managers were the exception in pop. Vicki Wickham, who has managed LaBelle, Cameo, Nona Hendryx as a solo artist and Dusty Springfield, was one of the first to break through in the early 1970s. Like many women in the industry, she claims she got there 'by default'. After her experience as a producer of the cult British TV pop show *Ready Steady Go!*, she went on to work for The Who's manager Kit Lambert, who gave her a sense of what could be achieved when she got an unknown R&B act, Patti LaBelle and The Bluebelles, signed to his label Track:

'I hadn't the slightest idea what I was doing – I just knew that Pat had a great voice, that I liked black and rock music, and I knew what a good song was. I learned so much from Kit. He taught me to try things – if you make a mistake, fine, do so and move on. It didn't matter. He had that marvellous dangerous edge. I met him once in New York: he had a huge suitcase with literally just one pair of socks in it. I asked him why he was carrying it. "Oh, I might have something I want to put in it."

'We'd have dinner with the best brandies and wines; what I didn't realize was that he was selling his mother's silver and father's cufflinks to pay for it. We lived every moment for the moment. If it was four in the morning and he suddenly thought, "Let's go to the Revolution", we'd go in a limousine whether he could afford it or not, have the best champagne and see if we could pull the prettiest people there, because it was fun. I learned not to be so inhibited, so serious. We were in showbiz, there was a lot of show in it.'[3]

This flair paid off when she transformed the Bluebelles into a spaceage vision of glam androgyny called Labelle that had a massive worldwide hit in 1975 with the salty 'Lady Marmalade'. 'With me it really was a new day. They had a lot of fun with the silver and the feathers – they grew up, and for the first time they were participating in their careers and their lives.' Coming from an empowering female perspective, Wickham enabled Patti LaBelle, Nona Hendryx and Sarah Dash to open up and experiment with their potential.

Wickham worked with men, too, succeeding through strength of personality. Macho US superfunkers Cameo, for instance, accepted her as an equable oddity:

'Was I a hippy chick; did I dance? No! I was a complete sore thumb. I only once took acid and thought I was gonna die. That's what worked, because I was so different to everybody else. It was like, here's this odd English girl, can't understand half of what she says, but she seems to be able to contact people we can't get on the phone, chatting them up and calling them love – she must be all right. Oddity has got me through the door. Having said that, it's still very much a boys' club.'

Men often come from a different perspective, so it is not surprising that many female acts now have a woman manager – from glam ghetto-soul trio SWV ('She understands women's things, y'know') to British dance artist Dee C. Lee, whose manager Gill Stein remarked: 'We are a team, and when men think they can take the piss out of two women, Dee and I back each other up.

"If you don't like it, fuck you, we'll do it on our own."[4] Too often a male manager pushes a female artist into a bracket of 'sex quotient', even sexual favours. Amanda Freeman, head of press for Island Records in the early 1990s, once told me of a distasteful episode: 'We had an artist who was there one minute, gone the next. Her manager actually said to me, "Any male journalists, you know, if you need her to help out in anyway – go out for dinner, have a good time, she's a friendly girl." We were absolutely gobsmacked.'[5]

Some male artists, too, prefer working with women, trusting them to get on with the job without posturing. Ragga star Shabba Ranks, for instance, is managed by Babsy Grange with C. 'Specialist' Dillon, while Jane Rose handles Keith Richards, and Sharon Osbourne negotiates for several heavy-metal acts, including her husband Ozzy. All have found their own survival strategies within the industry. Gail Parry, manager of the outspoken alternative star Henry Rollins, deals with 'the boys' club' by disregarding it:

'You'd have to do a lot to sexually harass me. I'd just laugh. I have no female/male thing. The majority of top people are men, but rather than dwelling on what I'm up against, I just work to get something done. It helps being independent. I know there's a big disparity with what women and men get paid in record companies, but I don't experience that because I work for myself.'[6]

Before becoming a manager, unlike most women who arrive at it via record company A&R or press, Parry took the unusual route of sound engineering and stage-managing acts such as the Dead Kennedys, Dennis Brown and Bow Wow Wow on the 1980s punk/roots circuit. This tough, technical work gave her 'a basis for understanding music from the ground up,' she explained. 'It makes my job easier that when I go to record artists I can pull apart an amp rack and fix it.' Admitting that 'there aren't that many women on the road', she said that being a roadie and sound engineer was a definite entrée into tour management, though 'you have to have the personality to get out there and do it. It's hard to come in cold and be a girl with all-guy bands.' She decided to work for Rollins after taking a break from the business, going to law school and practising in the late 1980s in LA with civil litigation and music business projects. Armed with knowledge of legal contracts as well as knowing where to put a jack plug gave Parry a breadth of experience that enabled her quickly to move Rollins from cult minority-interest status to a star on the early-1990s college rock circuit and key tours like Lollapalooza. 'I wasn't looking to left or right, I learned by trial and error, an inspirational thing.'

### Does She Have Ears?

There have yet to be top-level female managers on a par with Allen Klein, Albert Goldman or Simon Napier-Bell, doing stadium acts, but with their organizational and nannying skills it's an area in which women should theoretically excel. Much harder to crack is the jealously guarded bastion of A&R. At the nexus of power and creativity, the A&R person is responsible for signing bands to the label, then developing them. It is one of the most sought after and potentially heroic positions in the music business. Women are slowly making an impact in this frontline department, but it can be a lonely haul.

When Fredric Dannen's book *Hit Men* came out in 1990, A&R producer Ethel Gabriel wrote a letter to *Billboard* taking issue with his statement that while there is the industry term 'great record man', there is no such thing as a 'record woman'. 'To earn this tribute,' he wrote, 'you must have ears, which is not quite the same as good taste.' Gabriel countered that with, 'Unfortunately, Dannen has joined the "boys' club" by ignoring the accomplishments of women in the record industry.'[7] Producer of more than 2,500 records, head of million-dollar lines and A&R for everything from big-band swing to country and pop at RCA for over thirty-five years, she was described as 'the architect of beautiful music' at a time when 90 per cent of FM-radio time featured her recordings. 'Without "ears", I could not have accomplished this,' she stated.

When I spoke to her in New York three years later she said,

'I never had a reply from Dannen. Typically, women's issues are ignored. When I was hot as an A&R my husband would say, "Honey, they're still treating you like a secretary." If a man had accomplished what I did at RCA, they would be at least a vice-president. The most I got was acting VP until they brought someone else in – a man. They're still making money on my product, I see it all over the place.'[8]

When Gabriel began her career in the mid-1940s women were rarely granted titles or due recognition. Born in 1921, Gabriel was a dance-band leader in her teens, and studied trombone in Philadelphia before she brazened her way to New York in 1948, landing a job as secretary to the international-sales manager at RCA. 'I thought I was the cat's miaow. I used to come to work with a trombone slung under my arm.' Her musical expertise proved an asset when she became an A&R assistant, editing and breaking new records. By the late 1950s she had officially become the first woman A&R producer in pop, working with such artists as Geraldo, Chet Atkins, Roger Whittaker and Perry Como. Although at the helm of the million-selling Camden and Pure Gold lines, she was frequently taken for granted.

'At first I didn't realize I was doing everything the guys didn't want to do. That was the kind of commitment I had. I caught on to a lot of their tricks, though. I let them use me professionally because in my heart I knew that if they picked my brain, it was a well that would never dry up. I was often given tough artists, especially ones giving A&R trouble. I was used but probably because I could handle it. I was a tough sonovabitch.'

Aware that for too long women were scared to show solidarity in the business ('No one knew what networking meant, they were so busy making coffee for the bosses'), towards the end of her career at RCA in the early 1980s, Gabriel persuaded the company to subsidize a women's group for lectures and seminars. 'At least let me teach women how to be executives,' she told the then RCA boss Jack Craigo. She was granted the group, partly as a salvo for never having been given her due promotion. Although Gabriel was held back, her encouragement to others has reaped results, with younger women such as Nancy Jeffries and Linda Moran heading up record-company depart-

**Ethel Gabriel** and engineer Bob Simpson at RCA Recording Studios, New York: as an A&R producer, Gabriel invaded one of the most hallowed male areas of the music business. (Courtesy of Ethel Gabriel)

ments – 'I felt like mother to some of those girls.' She is a warm, enthusiastic and brave woman, yet there was disappointment in her voice when she said, 'I always thought everybody liked me. Now looking back, a lot of people resisted me or ignored my progress. That was strategic.'

Senior vice-president of A&R at Elektra in 1993, Nancy Jeffries worked hard for the official recognition that was denied her mentor Gabriel. Former singer in a late 1960s jazz/rock band called The Insect Trust, Jeffries entered the business in 1974 at the point when the job of in-house staff production was changing into modern A&R. It was while she handled accounts for the head of A&R at RCA that she heard a young singer from Philadelphia called Evelyn Champagne King and insisted that the company signed her. 'They did,' she said. 'Sure enough, her record "Shame" went on to sell a million copies. After that they said, "Oh thanks. Here's another bill to pay." I said, "OK, I'm leaving." When I went in to resign they said, "Don't leave – what d'you want to do?" "What I just did. I signed an artist who did well. I want to continue doing that."[9]

Jeffries got her A&R position at RCA before moving on to A&M, Virgin US and finally Elektra, in the process signing Suzanne Vega and Dee-Lite, and having a hand in signing Ziggy Marley, Iggy Pop, Keith Richards and Lenny Kravitz. Although Jeffries has had a long run of success, she identifies the continuing problem for women in the industry as that of just being heard. During her interview in her office on the sixteenth floor of the towering New York Time-Warner building she told me,

'There is still this whole thing about being a doll. Older men especially think they should be participating in the advancement of women, taking advantage of their talents, but they don't really know how. I can see them trying. The head of A&M tried so hard to understand me that having a conversation with him would wear me out. We'd have lunch and I'd be exhausted at the end because I could see him trying to make sense of this. He was thinking so hard about how he should be listening, he never heard a word I said. Never.'

When he suggested she go and see Suzanne Vega, Jeffries was at first resistant: 'A female singer/songwriter. I thought it was so predictable – they'll take that from you, but not understand if you come in with a really hard rock band.' When she saw Vega perform, though, Jeffries was stunned. 'She communicated something unique and moving. It's great when a woman has an intelligent perspective but at the same time is still kinda sexy. That's so important. If you let the men choose all the female artists, they'd just be pink and bubbly.'

When Jeffries started her A&R career in the late 1970s, there were only a handful of women working in this area for major labels. One of the rare breed was former *Rolling Stone* writer Karin Berg, head of A&R at Warners East Coast who helped to bring Dire Straits, Television, The Roches, The B-52s, Tom Verlaine and Hüsker Dü to the label, and in co-ordination with her 'LA right hand', Roberta Peterson, signed Laurie Anderson. Berg attributes much of her success to trusting instinct. 'I make my decisions where my heart lies, and that's something women do a lot. This is an industry where you can do well following your instincts – that's something men have to learn and women have to learn not to lose.'[10] When you are a woman surrounded by men, however, it is not easy to stick with decisions that could invite ridicule:

'I was out one night in the late '70s surrounded by A&R guys. They were discussing a tape someone had got from a band called The Cars, and wasn't it dreadful. "Karen, did you hear it?" "Yes, I did. Yeah," I told them. "I wanna sign them." Everyone exchanged glances. She's out of her skull. It was hard to be in that situation and not think, am I crazy?'

The band proved to be one of New Wave's biggest sellers, racking up ten Top Twenty singles and seven hit albums. A quietly intelligent woman dressed in post-punk black, Berg has never been interested in the sometimes forced camaraderie of the A&R scene. 'In the beginning it was lonely. I went to a club by myself, listened by myself, and left. I didn't "hang out" – I went specifically for the music. I still like doing that, though I feel less isolated with more women in the industry now.'

Women also seem less likely to enter ego-boosting 'bidding wars' while A&R men, like hounds on a chase, will run after a hot band. Kate Hyman, one of the new generation of 1990s A&R women, who came up via 1980s street-artist label Z Records through MCA and a VP position at Imago before setting up an independent A&R/management consultancy, says, 'It's "Let me prove I've got bigger balls by winning this band." The band loses in the process because they become a commodity the A&R guy is trying to gain. It's a very macho thing. A lot of A&R guys think that because they signed a successful act, they're a star. They're not. They should be looking after stars.'[11]

While it is hard enough being female, being black involves another set of obstacles. Vivian Scott, VP of Black Music and A&R at Sony, realized that although she signed two of the world's biggest-selling 1990s ragga dancehall acts, Shabba Ranks and DJ Patra, she could get stuck in the black music area, with no room to expand:

'There is a ceiling, and part of my education as an executive is not only to read the Urban Music section of *Billboard*, it's to read International and Retail. I am beginning to learn pop radio, since black music is crossing over to it heavily from the underground. I see integration of the two departments. It's the right time to be here.'[12]

Arriving at A&R via concert promotion and publishing, Scott says she had support from other 'firsts', such as Sylvia Rhone at East West and Prospective's Sharon Heyward, the first black women to head companies:

'I've never felt lonely, just challenged and pioneering. Also the Each One Teach One mentality is very important to me. Because I was once there, I always encourage my assistant, 'cos she is going to have to grow at some point. I want people to say, "Yeah, Regina Robinson, she used to work with Vivian Scott, she's baad!" It makes me feel good that we're nurturing young black women.'

## I Write the Songs

When artists have been signed and their songs are played on TV or radio, collection of their royalties is down to publishing companies – the repositories of hit songs and one of the most lucrative areas of the business. Pop music originated in sheet music, its focus by 1900 on Tin Pan Alley – a concentration of song publishers, writers and pluggers in offices on Manhattan's 28th Street. Sentimental tunes for family sing-songs round the parlour piano soon gave way to the more sophisticated material of Broadway composers such as Irving Berlin and Leonard Bernstein. During the big-band era, out of the few successful female songwriters battling to establish a catalogue, Gladys Shelley reigned supreme. A former ballerina and model with pretty, vivacious eyes, she was a published poet at eight, and with a neat turn of phrase on male/female relationships, she became the Daphne du Maurier of Broadway. Also dubbed the female

Irving Berlin, she has written over 3,000 songs, such as 'A Man Is A Necessary Evil', recorded by Pearl Bailey, 'Just Like Taking Candy From A Baby', performed by Benny Goodman and Fred Astaire, and her big hit 'How Did He Look?', covered by over thirty-five artists including Carmen McCrae, Connie Francis, Mel Tormé and Anne Shelton. Though Shelley's output has been prodigious, including songs for everyone from Nat King Cole to Peggy Lee and Sarah Vaughan, she is rarely afforded space in pop encyclopaedias: like Ethel Gabriel, she emerged with the 1940s generation, where women's achievements were frequently overlooked.

By the 1960s, women were more visible, if only because they constituted 50 per cent of the most lucrative sound of the era – the Brill Building's girl-group phenomenon fuelled by the three main husband-and-wife songwriting teams of Ellie Greenwich and Jeff Barry, Carole King and Gerry Goffin, and Cynthia Weil and Barry Mann. Greenwich, who co-wrote many of Spector's hits such as 'Be My Baby', 'Da Doo Ron Ron' and 'River Deep, Mountain High', recalls that although she had a degree of creative control both in her lyrics and in the studio, it was not the same on a business level. 'In dealing with attorneys I'm not so sure they took us females seriously, they would rather deal with men. When Jeff and I got divorced I was established and taken seriously as a creator, but suddenly I was a free female. Suddenly men couldn't separate Ellie the producer and Ellie the single woman. That took adjustment.'[13]

She also found that without her husband as a 'shield', she had to fight much harder for respect. 'When Jeff and I were no longer together I seemed to be left out of everything.' It was Greenwich who had met an unknown songwriter named Neil Diamond, and she who introduced him to Barry. It was her suggestion that the three of them form a company – Tallyrand Music and Productions – which published all of Diamond's early hits including 'Cherry, Cherry'. But in 1965, when she and Barry separated, Greenwich was left behind:

'I was shoved aside. Neil was the number one male vocalist in the country. Suddenly he wanted to leave the label. Jeff and Neil would be talking and gallivanting, and I'd be like, "Hello? Anybody home?" I was the one who put the company together and they were asking me to sell shares. I remember sitting in the attorney's office, crying, and they'd say, "Typical, a female crying." I felt alone and paranoid that the men were against me. There, I felt the crunch severely.

'None of us were business people, we just did what we loved. People say we were ripped off. But since then women have got smarter, more business-minded. Madonna, for instance, came in professionally, setting up companies before projects got underway. She set the ground rules long before things got moving, we didn't.'

After the legal battle with Diamond, by 1967 the Greenwich/Barry collaboration was over. Taking control of her own life and finances, Greenwich went on to form a jingle production company. In 1973 she released a solo album *Let It Be Written, Let It Be Sung* on MGM/Verve, and went back to writing for other artists from Nona Hendryx to Cyndi Lauper right up to the 1990s. In 1983 her life was immortalized on Broadway with her best-selling musical *Leader Of The Pack*, a tribute consolidated in 1991 when she and Barry were inducted into the Songwriters' Hall Of Fame.

Greenwich's accolade was hard won, however. Historically she started at a time when modern pop was in its infancy and 'you were out there as a kid, barrelling along doing your thing. Then twenty years later it's classic music.' It has taken several decades for women to build up control and confidence in their publishing careers. Franne Golde, whose songs have been recorded by over sixty artists including The Commodores (with the Grammy Award-winning 'Nightshift'), Whitney Houston, Diana Ross and Alexander O'Neal, began writing songs in the mid-1970s to support her performing career. 'One of the few places where there is comfort and security is as a songwriter – there have always been women songwriters, it's somewhere to fit in. It's not like trying to run a record company,' she says. 'Having said that, though, the one place I have felt frustration is the business side, because it's primarily run by men.'[14]

By the early 1990s these business lessons had been learned.

One of the most successful female-owned operations in the music industry was Diane Warren's Realsongs, named *Billboard*'s Top Singles Publisher in 1990 and Top Five Publishing Corporation in 1991, beating industry giants with legions of writers like Warners, Virgin and EMI. Together with her senior director Doreen Dorion, Warren has secured financial as well as artistic control over her prolific output. An ebullient, earthy woman whose life is centred around her Los Angeles home studio, Warren scored twenty-five Top Ten hits in the first ten years of her career and was named the Association of Composers, Authors and Publishers' (ASCAP) Number One Writer three times in the early 1990s (1990, 1991 and 1993). Working with exhaustive dedication, she monitors the markets and carefully follows the process of a song, from demo to final product.

'A song is a lot like real estate,' she said in 1993. 'It doesn't lose its value. As people license it for use in radio and commercials it becomes more lucrative. It's the real estate of the record business – when Berry Gordy sold Motown, he held on to his publishing company.'[15] Born in 1955, Warren describes herself as 'an infamous Valley Girl', an obsessive songwriter and an ardent pop fan. She grew up on Brill Building hits and, after years as a teenager honing her craft, had her first break in 1982 when Laura Branigan began recording her songs. Three years later DeBarge turned 'Rhythm Of The Night' into a No. 3 pop hit, and then Warren was on a smooth run, from Starship's 'Nothing's Gonna Stop Us Now' to 'If I Could Turn Back Time' by Cher and Michael Bolton's 'How Can We Be Lovers'.

'There has to be a great marriage of words and music in my songs, a unique slant, and a melody that gets to you, stays with you,' she says. As well as being a gifted, single-minded writer, Warren knows how to capitalize on her talent. Mentored by her late father David Warren, who bought her a guitar at the age of eight and, when she was in her late teens, steered her round publishers, record companies and clubs, she learned to operate within the business, earning the respect of A&R and label executives as well as that of artists themselves.

**Diane Warren**
in 2001:
'A song is a lot
like real estate.'
(Courtesy of
Realsongs)

The key to this is an ability to negotiate. Women have built up
a strong presence within the publishing business through a
combination of assiduous attention to detail and people management. Vice-president/general manager of Imago Songs in
New York between 1991 and 1993, Ann Munday began her
career in early-1970s' London with Charles Hansen Music Publishing, moving on to Big Pig Music where she worked with
Bernie Taupin and Elton John before joining Chrysalis Music in
1976. Based in LA and New York she expanded its American
catalogue for the next nine years. Gaining a reputation as a

shrewd operator, Munday attributes much of her success to tenacity and patience rather than aggression. 'Men and women doing business don't circle each other,' she says. 'There's a lot of bullshit spoken in this business, and as soon as people find you're not into bullshit, they relax more. Too often men put on a kind of mental feathers and war paint.'[16] Talking about work, Munday referred to the budgeting skills her grandmother taught her when she was a child. 'A housewife manages a small company, dealing with different jobs and personalities. Can you imagine circling round the electricity man? You'd never have the time.'

Despite her formidable track record, Munday encountered the glass ceiling in the mid-1980s when she was told point blank that she wouldn't run Chrysalis Records – because she was a woman. Disillusioned, she left publishing for five years to concentrate on artist management with several acts including Carlene Carter. After returning to head Imago Songs she went independent again in 1993. She spearheaded a successful music campaign for the UK Commission for Racial Equality, raising money and awareness of key issues. She also set up MundayThruSunday Music, marketing music for the US film and TV industry. Munday has always recognized the importance of marketing to women: 'There are so many good women artists out there, plus a strong market. Women, after all, spend most of the money in the household.'

Ann Munday, a ground-breaker in music publishing: 'Too often men put on a kind of mental feathers and war paint.' (Courtesy of Ann Munday)

## Who's Boss?

Munday is a good example of the female 'brain drain' to the independent sector. More and more women, frustrated with a corporate world they find restrictive and baffling, are opting to move sideways within the industry, rather than continually crash their head against the vinyl ceiling. 'Corporations have not served us well, that's why we're independents. Out of all the small businesses, the ones run by women are more successful,' says Lisa Anderson, former managing director of RCA UK between 1989 and 1991.[17] When I interviewed her in 1994, she was still one of the industry's most successful women, working as a top-level freelance consultant on music/TV projects such as the BPI Awards and Virgin Records' Twenty-first Birthday bash, earning more than she ever had as an MD. 'I work side by side with the big guys now, I'm respected, I can say what I want. For all their protestations about encouraging you to be different, in a hierarchical structure the bosses want you to say what they're saying.'

A common story regardless of gender, but Anderson found that as a woman her problems with reading and dealing in power management doubled. When she was first offered the top job in 1989, she was incredulous. Although she had been in the industry over sixteen years, running A&M's promotion department in Paris, then becoming international-marketing manager at Virgin and the label's first female director, before being poached by Polygram UK to head their international-marketing division, her first reaction was still 'Why did they choose me, when will they find me out?'

It was a highly political position at a crucial time for the company. The newly appointed chairman John Preston was keen to name a woman as his successor – she would be the first to head a major label in Britain, a fact that stood to his credit. In the attendant publicity, Anderson found that 'practically all the women in the industry were rooting for me, there was an enormous amount of goodwill.' This positivity, however, didn't help her when she tried to sift through the male protocol at executive level. Firstly, her management style was a problem. Usually heads of department were expected to fall in line with the MD – 'But these were people good at their jobs, earning money. I asked them what they thought. Instead of consensus that, this is nice, we're being consulted, they'd say, "There's no leadership."'

Testing, too, were the week-long management seminars where corporate 'family' bonding was expected, but as the only woman MD amid twenty-five men Anderson inevitably found herself under the microscope:

'I was aware that it was not just about how I presented my ideas, but whether I looked fat in a swimming costume. It was deeply uncomfortable, as if there were a series of unwritten rules. A hideous example was tennis at dawn with the president. God knows who should lose. The irony was that men would come and tell me they hated the whole set-up – they wouldn't tell that to other blokes.'

Although she was a reluctant icon for other women, Anderson put in place concrete changes regarding childcare, doubling time off on full pay from the statutory six weeks to twelve, as well as securing paternity leave and an extra maternity bonus, relaying a message to women in the company that if they had a baby they would not be replaced. It took Anderson a year of hard bargaining to get an annual concession which overall 'would cost them as much as a video that didn't make *The Chart Show*.'

Unfortunately for Anderson, she only had time to put in place one business plan (the first she inherited) before the industry was plunged into recession, two major acts left the label ('and £7 million turnover floated out the door') and the chairman decided to revive the career of a dinosaur 1970s rock band. Anderson made the mistake of telling him that it would be difficult to make the album work.

'I discovered too late that rather than thinking more about running the company I should have "managed upwards". You have to be politically adept, something women haven't learned well yet. You have to be prepared to know what's going on, to ditch people to save your skin. When the album sold only 35,000 and dented the US charts for one week, I should have blamed the head of sales. I should have given heads of department a good sacking once in a while to be seen as a strong manager, even if they're good at their job. I handled things practically rather than politically. '

In the 1991 round of redundancies Anderson lost her job. There was dismay and sympathy within the industry: 'The general consensus was I should have had three years rather than two. Men get away with more, whereas we don't assume we can: we'll never have equality till we can fuck up the same way as men.' At first she felt like 'a forty-year-old bimbo who no one would speak to ever again', but after reinvestigating her self-worth and strengths, Anderson launched a consultancy that met with 'spectacular' success.

Another example of corporate wastage of female talent is Lisa Denton, the first female marketing manager of a UK company. She was forced to leave Phonogram in the late 1970s when the marketing director job went vacant and it was given to a man who had never done marketing before. 'The MD called me and said "This guy will need all your help and support,"' she recalls. Although devastated that a man less qualified was promoted above her, Denton tried to work with him. Within months he felt threatened enough to want her out. 'They couldn't fire me because I hadn't done anything wrong, for two years we'd come in within budget and that had never happened before. For a long time I refused to resign, until it became so impossible I negotiated a settlement and left. I should have got another job but there were few other women at that level.'[18]

Like Anderson, Denton brought new perspectives to her job. In many ways she redefined record company marketing, resisting the urge in the 1970s to employ 'white goods' men in the business, and keeping a sane balance between 'artist' and 'product'. 'There's a lot of classic structured marketing that you can't apply to the business. You can't really do market research, for instance. With normal products you could make demos and get feedback panels. You can't do that with creativity. No one said to Van Gogh, "Do me a dozen visuals and we'll see what works."'

Instrumental in signing top 1970s Phonogram acts such as The Stylistics, 10 C.C. and Steve Miller, after leaving the company Denton ploughed her skills into management, working with off-beat pop artists like B.A. Robertson and Sam Brown. Although by the early 1990s she was involved in dynamic TV and publishing projects, when I interviewed her in 1993,

Denton's disillusionment with a music business that rejected her talent was still tangible.

Compared to their US counterparts, 1990s women are making slow progress in the British music industry. Lisa Anderson attributes this to a small, inward-looking industry where 'old gender values' hold sway. In 1993 Moira Bellas at WEA and Diana Graham at Arista were the only female MDs of major British companies, and in Vox magazine's 1994 list of the industry's 'Twenty Most Powerful People', not one woman was included. By their criteria of innovation and drive, Diana Graham should have at least had an honourable mention. Recruited by Arista in 1991, four years after she had set up BMG music publishing's international office in London, Graham took over what was 'a tokenistic label with not much repertoire apart from the occasional Whitney Houston hit'[19] and expanded. Within two years Arista was the top singles label in the UK, sporting a roster that included Houston, Lisa Stansfield and dance giants Snap. Graham is cool and unsentimental about what women should do to succeed. 'It's a male game, no question. But life is. I'm not stridently feminist – you have to learn to play the game and change the rules within, or you don't stand a chance.' The game maybe proved impenetrable however, because in 1995 news came of her resignation.

Jill Sinclair, MD of ZTT Records and CEO (corporate executive officer) of SARM studios, also prefers to put the gender question on the back burner. 'I've never had a problem being a woman,' she says, but then she notes that people identify her as wife of top pop producer Trevor Horn more often than as an executive and manager in her own right. She also feels she is considered a 'bitch' rather than 'astute or strong'. 'Men prefer to let things slip. Women don't mind grasping the nettle. I'm confrontational, I just want to sort it out. If there's a dog turd there, let's deal with it rather than hide it. I'm perceived that way. Horn says I've got more neck than a giraffe.'[20]

The difficulties facing women are not just of their imagining. Many men in the industry agree that there can be fundamental blocks to women's career progression. Colin Bell, MD of London Records UK, said,

'Strictly speaking there is not a glass ceiling. But there is an in-built chauvinism in those who advance women's careers. In my position you have to go out of your way to find women, so when you do promote a woman, say to head of department, it's almost a political statement.

'There is also the problem with women that you're never sure what the agenda is. Men always have one agenda – a successful career. With women the second agenda is childcare. In a fast-moving business people don't like it if you disappear for a while. It's a twenty-four-hour business and no matter how dedicated you are, if you have a baby you have a responsIbility to it. Everything comes back to the old roles and most of the men I meet are still fairly traditional.'[21]

In the States there appears to be a more enlightened attitude, with less of a split between the fast track and the 'mommy track'. Women seem to have greater mobility, particularly in the music industry, where in 1993 they occupied 25 per cent of upper management positions, as compared to the Fortune 500 companies where men accounted for 499 of the corporate executive offices, and held more than 95 per cent of upper management jobs.[22]

By the early 1990s women such as BMI head Frances Preston, Michele Anthony, executive VP at Sony, Sylvia Rhone, chairwoman of East West America, and Polly Anthony, then general manager of Sony 550, were reaching top corporate positions and keeping their own strong management style. They were all aware of the painful groundwork: 'The roles of women in the corporate structure have changed dramatically,' says Rhone. 'The power behind the throne, the unsung heroes who are women, are now stepping out in positions of power and influence.'[23]

Mimi Jordan was one such 'unsung hero'. The child of Russian Jewish émigrés, Jordan entered the business in the early 1940s after a career in rep theatre during the Depression. She began as music programmer for a small New York station, WMCA, that featured everything from classical to pop and swing. Jordan's work brought her into contact with Tin Pan Alley publishers, so music copyright was a logical next step. From being manager of the copyright department of Decca subsidiary London Records, in the late 1950s she was made head of three departments: foreign distribution, copyright and publishing. 'I was one of the first women to have a CEO position in a huge world company,' she told me in 1994.[24] We sat across a small formica table in the kitchen of her downtown Manhattan apartment. Although she was in her eighties, her memory was sharp and clear:

'I encountered prejudice in many subtle ways. For instance, I was friendly with the composer/conductor Mantovani. I'd negotiated and acquired some of his songs for our publishing company. We were good friends but when he came over and dinners were given, I was never invited. Also the chairman in England would let me rep all over Europe, but invited me only to luncheons with wives of the men who came over. I was excluded from the social network because I might get too big for my boots.'

Happy to exploit her skill and creativity, the company none the less paid her two-thirds the salary of a man in an equivalent position ('I found that out from the accounting department'), and when the company was foundering in the mid-1970s, she was 'let go' after twenty years of service:

'July 1975. The date is etched on my brain. I was let out first because I was a woman. They gave me no advance notice. I was called into the president's office and told I was through. By then I was older, but still productive and healthy – the president himself was seventy-two. They said they had no more use for my services. I was devastated. The shock of being let out so suddenly was terrible: one day I was a senior, the next on Social Security.'

Jordan pulled her life back together and did what she'd always wanted to do, go back to college – graduating from Fordham Lincoln Center with an English Literature BA. Now a private tutor, she still seems troubled by the treatment she received in the industry. One thing she is proud of, though, is the encouragement she gave to other women, employing them wherever she could in a way that was almost subversive.

'I worked well with men, but I employed all women – I wanted assistants, not just secretaries. I always had the feeling that women were never given enough of a chance. I was entrenched in this cause for women, but I did it my own way in my own organization. I had a wonderful opportunity to do it. And the women I trained got wonderful jobs afterwards.'

One woman employed by Jordan was Helene Blue, head of Paul McCartney's publishing company MPL Communications. When she joined London Records in 1968 as a young 'gal Friday', Jordan was her first boss. 'I got a tremendous sense of dignity from her,' recalls Blue. 'She dealt with tons more prejudice than my generation, yet operated with more dignity than anyone else I've met since.'[25] Eager to progress, Blue flowered under Jordan, learning all she could about publishing, from rights acquisitions to international copyright. As general manager of MPL, she dealt with a catalogue that stretched from Jelly Roll Morton to Bessie Smith, Buddy Holly and McCartney himself. 'Life gave me luck and Mimi Jordan, but I had the smarts to deliver,' she says.

Jordan's experience contrasted strongly with Frances Preston. In 1994 Preston was president and CEO of BMI, the industry's most powerful performing rights company with $300 million in annual royalties and 125,000 writers who account for 70 per cent of the country charts. Voted one of America's Fifty Most Powerful Women by *Ladies' Home Journal* in 1990, Preston ran her office like the White House. A Southern belle in her late middle age with a generous blond bouffant and a firm, killer smile, she received me graciously into her Manhattan office, a plush, ornate affair filled with crystal, china and huge lilies, and said,

'Most women in the industry would agree that it's important to avoid cliques. Having so-called female support groups does more damage than it does good. In our business we've gone beyond that. I certainly look to hire women, but by the same token I'm looking for the best person for the job.

'I've been the only woman on so many boards it's unbelievable. I remember my first board meetings: it'd be, "The meeting will come to order, gentlemen. Oh. Now, gentlemen and lady, gentlemen and woman, gentlemen and Frances . . ." They'd go through all these, and I'd say, "Just

**Frances Preston**
in 2001: president
and CEO of BMI
Music Publishing
and corporate star.
(Courtesy of BMI)

say gentlemen, it doesn't matter, whatever makes you feel comfortable." I
always tried to put people at ease because I knew it was a first for them.'[26]

An admirer of Henry Kissinger and Hillary Clinton, Preston is a
consummate politician. She began her executive career in 1958,
albeit at a more modest level than Mimi Jordan, but, unlike the
latter, established herself by tenaciously going after business as a
corporate 'player', building success in a rapidly growing rather
than (as London Records became) an ailing company. After a
stint as a radio station receptionist, she was appointed by the
fledgeling New York BMI to open an office in Nashville. At first
she encountered resistance from men who told her, 'I only deal
with New York.' Rather than panicking, she plugged away: 'I
didn't push it. I gained their respect and friendship. One by one
they'd come around and start calling you. I had a rough time for
six months, then it settled in and was easy.'

Her steady rise through management culminated in the presi-
dency in 1986. A woman on the board of numerous business
associations and charities, she attributes her success to thinking
'as a business person, rather than as a woman'. When I asked her
to name other industry women she admired, there was a long
pause. 'Top-notch executive women in the business are so much

younger than I am,' she said carefully. 'I see them at meetings, but I haven't been that close to them. I admire the good jobs they're doing, and their achievements, but as for looking up to them . . . not really . . . they're so much younger.'

Among the younger generation of executives, Sony's Michele Anthony feels that women are now beginning to be assessed on their skills rather than gender. A confident woman who grew up within the industry, in many ways Anthony had a head-start. As well as being Tony Bennett's manager her father brought to the US English rock bands such as Jethro Tull and Traffic. She worked at her father's management company during school vacations, and toured with Humble Pie in Japan and Europe as a teenager. After qualifying as a lawyer, she practised with a major entertainment firm, helping to make the Seattle 'grunge rock' sound an industry phenomenon. Picked up by Sony in 1990, Anthony moved rapidly from a position as senior VP to executive VP in 1993. The rate of her ascendancy is unusual, but seen positively, it could be read as a future indicator for women's career progression. 'Gender has not really been an issue,' she claimed in 1993, 'and I know that's not typical. I have always found that intelligence, passion and creativity can really break through.'[27]

Also optimistic is Polly Anthony (no relation), former head of CBS radio promotion, appointed general manager of Sony's 550 label when it was launched in 1993 with the million-selling artist Celine Dion, plus a range of strong acts from rock to rap. 'Things are improving, but there's another level to be achieved,' she told me shortly after her promotion. 'It looks good – some have the potential to be major role players in this business. Michele Anthony is phenomenal, she's broken through gender barriers, but you don't dwell on it. You make mental notes and move forward.'[28]

Polly Anthony is used to competing in the fast track. She joined what was then CBS in 1978 as a secretary, working her way up to become head of promotions. Driven by big bucks, hard sell and powerful charts, radio is not an easy medium for women, but Anthony found it invigorating. 'It's not a job for the faint-hearted.

**Polly Anthony,** head of Epic Records US: 'I'm innately curious and ambitious.' (Courtesy of Epic Records)

You don't have time to advance a sale, you have to do it from week to week, and there's a lot of adrenalin rushes. But to get a certain artist exposure, to hear them on the radio while you're driving – I still almost drive off the road!' Anthony's experience at CBS differs from that of Lisa Anderson at RCA UK:

'I was fortunate to work with great people who let me stretch my wings and make mistakes. Promotion is traditionally a boys' club, but I became the mascot. I'm innately curious and ambitious. I have the work ethic, I can insinuate myself into the right scenarios. It's about making relationships, love of music and selling something intangible – you're selling yourself and your team.'

By 2001, Anthony's talents had been rewarded with the top job at Epic Records. Her appointment sent out a message of hope to other women in the industry – that talent and dedication rather than gender might be the main factors considered in promotion.

## Going Single

Many women, put off by the demands of cheerleading a corporate identity, fare better in the independent sphere. In less mainstream areas such as soul, rap, blues and indie rock, there is space to expand, even run or establish your own label. Archivist Rosetta Reitz, for instance, has uncovered scores of successful female blues singers from the 1920s, 1930s and 1940s, releasing them successfully on her Rosetta Records compilations. She plugs into alternative distribution networks such as the UK's WRPM (Women's Revolutions Per Minute), a female company headed by Caroline Hutton that ensures less commercial women's music gets heard.

In the pop sphere Florence Greenberg was one of the first female label owners, founding Scepter Records in 1959. Together with her partner, black producer/songwriter Carl Dixon, she had seventeen R&B hits and fourteen pop hits in two years. Her flagship acts were The Shirelles and Dionne Warwick. 'I was the best "promotion man" in the business,' she said. 'Even when my artists were being bought by big record companies, and I didn't have enough money to compete, I couldn't bring myself to sell . . . I knew I wasn't the kind of person who could work for somebody else.'[29]

Jill Sinclair at ZTT, home of top-selling acts such as Seal and Frankie Goes To Hollywood, finds herself better suited to the independent sphere. 'In my dreams I would love to run a large corporation – but in reality my own business means I'm far more on the cutting edge. I've never had a Madonna record plop on my desk and all I've got to do is sell it. I'm more a go-getter. I'm not good at big corporate politics, I don't give much mental space to what I *should* be saying.'

Despite its misogynist image rap music, too, has a number of significant female entrepreneurs, from Sylvia Robinson, who ran the pioneering Sugarhill label in the 1970s and 1980s, to Rush Communications president Carmen Ashhurst-Watson and artist Queen Latifah's Flavor Unit Productions in the 1990s. 'There've been tremendous opportunities in rap,' says Monica

Lynch, president of Tommy Boy, the stable that launched best-selling acts such as Afrika Bambaata, De La Soul, Naughty By Nature, Queen Latifah and Digital Underground. 'When we first started out rap wasn't an industry at all, and there was a chance for Afro-Americans and women to get in on the ground floor where the stakes were not so high.'[30]

A feisty Midwestern girl, Lynch sang in a punk band and worked as a go-go dancer before joining Tommy Boy in 1981 as assistant to its founder Tom Silverman. In 1982 she became VP of the two-person company and in 1985 was made president. When Warners acquired an interest she was made a VP there too. Typical of younger women, who have a more broadly analytical view of their career progression than older women in the business, Lynch is perhaps the most realistic role model for the new generation: firmly in touch with 'the street', business-minded and culturally aware. 'I don't feel I have to be one of the boys,' she says. 'I try to be myself because people can sense it if you're not.'

In the UK, former publicist Liz Naylor decided to start her own label in 1992 when she became disillusioned with the men she worked for on key independent labels such as Blast First (Sonic Youth) and One Little Indian (The Shamen, Björk). 'You're meant to give all this dedication to indie music and these fuckers are flying off to LA having meetings with the head of Sony. It's not right. The female plugger [radio promoter] was on twice my wages with a car, and all the other women were kind of twittery. I found it hard to fit into that.'[31] A straight-talking Mancunian ex-punk, in the late 1980s Naylor was advised by many to start up her own label. She said,

'Then it was just boys with guitars, really boring. And people would be trying to foist dodgy lesbian folk singers on me. I'd say, No, why aren't there any bands like I wanted to be in? Then by pure chance I heard a Bikini Kill "Riot Grrrl" track, went to see Huggy Bear and suddenly it was, fuck, yeah – it was there. I stepped back into it, like a calling on the road to Damascus. Like, you will form this label.'

Ten years in the business meant that she had an array of solid contacts to call for advice. Within months she had organized a distribution deal for her new label Catcall and signed the UK mixed gender Riot Grrrl band Huggy Bear. 'Everyone was chasing them – I'd turn up at gigs and there'd be loads of record company people there, but I played on the fact that, hey, I'm a girl, this is my first label. They liked the idea, as a kind of split collaboration.'

Her first record with them, 'Her Jazz', sold 6,000 in the first week and went to No. 2 in the UK indie charts – a major achievement for a debut single. Naylor then tracked down Bikini Kill in the States and licensed songs for a compilation ('I wanted to call it Cock Rock, but irony doesn't translate in America'). She admits that she 'pulled favours all the way through. But men do that all the time, only on a grander scale.' By 1994 the brief, glorious burst with Huggy Bear had come to an end, and she moved to the forefront of the Queercore scene, signing defiantly gay bands like Sister George.

Naylor found her niche once she set up her own company. Before that, she had been trying to slot in with established industry practice, albeit 'alternative'. In the mid-1980s, for instance, she set up an all-female promotion company called Pro Motion, yet despite their relative independence, the job still felt like low-level servicing.

'You'd spend your time mothering bands who're too fuckin' witless to get to airports. Everybody else can get to airports – what is it about being musicians that you can't? It's also comparatively low status. I remember trying to explain to my stepfather, this awful Northerner who worked for Walls' sausages for fifty years, what my PR job was. He said, "So, you're in telesales, then?" And I was like, yeah, you ain't far off it. Ringing up some jerk at the *NME*, grovelling . . . oh, here's the record, and would you like double glazing, too? I don't know why so many women go into it, it's a horrible job.'

Regine Moylett, former head of press for Island Records in the late 1980s, turned a 'horrible job' into a creative venture when she established her own independent company in 1990 with an impressive list of clients that included U2, Gavin Friday and the ground-breaking rap/soul group Massive Attack. Moylett enjoys doing press, but didn't like the way she was expected to operate within a company:

'The job is devalued as soon as women do it. When I ran the press office, we'd have five meetings a week, and they were all men. Sometimes they'd guffaw uproariously when looking at press pictures for a female artist, then make me feel like I was whingeing when I said, "Somebody's bottom is nothing to do with her music."

'I just got tired of their company, having to readjust, translate everything in my mind, work with male methods. I was continually being told my methods were ridiculous – you have to have the neck of a rhinoceros not to feel done in by it. For instance, when I was doing a press campaign on U2 I kept all the papers involved, despite people telling me I should lie and play one off against the other. It actually worked fine without telling unnecessary lies, and everybody was happy. Men get a certain pleasure out of being devious, they like to powerbroke, saying things like, "We stitched that paper up, but we're too big for them never to talk to us again." It was very schoolyard.'[32]

When she left, Moylett took U2 with her, determined to operate on her own terms. By 1993 she had an all-woman team consisting of ex-ZTT publicist Sharon Blankson and another ex-head of Island press, Amanda Freeman. 'It works because none of us come from the darling, darling, kissy school of PR, and people like our no-bullshit approach,' said Freeman. With the biggest rock band of the 1980s and 1990s on her list, Moylett admits that they haven't had to trawl for talent to represent. 'People generally come to us.' A former *NME* writer from Dublin with a wry manner, she exudes an intelligent, aesthetic approach that's rare in PR. 'We can't do something unless we believe in it,' she says. U2 appreciate having an all-female team: 'They always say they're lesbians trapped in men's bodies! They've got a good attitude to women, and there's a lot working in their organization. Their manager Paul McGuinness says that women work harder and do a better job.'

The snag is that women do often work harder, but for less money. Being independent, Moylett can command the fee she

deserves, but record-label publicity departments are traditionally viewed as a female ghetto where labour comes cheap. 'When
I started at Virgin in 1981 I was being paid £5,000 a year. After
eighteen months I discovered that a man employed at the same
level as me was being paid double my money. When I threatened
to resign, they insisted it was an oversight and upped it to
£10,000 overnight,' says Sian Davis, head of press at Virgin UK
until she lost her job in the 1992 EMI takeover, when Richard
Branson sold his shares out for £510 million. 'People say that
there's an asking price. It's nothing to do with loyalty or qualifications – it's your market value, like a football player. And
unfortunately men are considered to be worth more.'[33]

Sandy Sawotko, former head of press at Imago in New York,
agrees that the practice of paying men double is widespread.
'Men are so unusual in publicity they're treated really well and
put on a pedestal,' she says. 'Men who call someone important
will more often than not have their call taken. I once had a male
assistant, and found that when he called people for me who we
didn't know, he was able to get through more consistently than I
was. People hear a male voice and think it's authority. It was so
frustrating.'[34]

## Dispatches from the War Zone

Being a female music journalist has its particular obstacles, too.
Starting on *NME* in 1983 as a regional 'stringer' from Leeds, I
gradually wormed my way on to the paper full-time two years
later. It took me that long to build up confidence and realize
that, like a London cabbie, I had to get 'The Knowledge'. As a
woman working in the business, knowledge is your weapon and
the source of your power; it means you can hold your own in any
conversation, and be 'accepted'.

Once I was established, though, like many female journalists, I
found that 'serious' long articles inevitably went to the male
writers, while too often we were kept to writing reviews, short
pieces or doing interviews with women artists. Women are not
considered heavyweight enough to comment on the top male

acts of the day – be it Public Enemy or Iggy Pop. Women rarely get staff positions with power to commission other writers. In 1994, for instance, the senior editorial team of *Rolling Stone* consisted of ten men and two women, while among their contributing editors (including Kurt Loder, Greil Marcus and Robert Palmer) there were three women and twenty-seven men. *Spin* did marginally better with six female and twenty-seven male writers on the masthead, plus one woman among their six top editors. Britain's *NME* had four in an editorial staff of eighteen – two in research, one sub-editing and the fourth working as editorial assistant. The oft-heard cry among male editors is either 'Women just don't cut it' or 'Our readership is mostly boys anyway, so we have to reflect that.' In effect the music press is one of the most gender-conservative areas of the business.

'Pursuing excellence in any field is lonely, but it's like bench-pressing, you feel good about it,' says Carol Cooper, top US freelancer for various titles including *Village Voice* and *Billboard*.[35] The first black female music writer to break into mainstream white publications, Cooper forged a specialism for herself from the late 1970s in emerging musics such as Latin, Worldbeat and rap. 'My motivation was clear and simple throughout – no one was writing stories I wanted to read, so I wrote them myself. I liked to look at the sociological underpinnings.' Getting commissioned, though, was a 'gruelling, competitive process. Because I was an anomaly – not screwing someone, or white or male – I wasn't the first person an editor would think of.' Persistence and originality meant that Cooper gradually built a solid reputation. Her research formidable, her commitment tenacious, Cooper shows music writing at its best. But not until 1995 could she write for *Rolling Stone* on her own terms – 'white writers imitating Lester Bangs: I didn't aspire to be him.'

Male writers jealously guard their space, so the few women who have broken through do so by being definitive. When the pop press was more an adjunct of PR in the 1960s, Penny Valentine at UK's *Disc* magazine elicited more personal revelation than her contemporaries from the key stars such as The

Beatles, Scott Walker and Dusty Springfield, becoming a Swinging London celebrity herself. In the 1970s a new generation battled into the music press, with writers such as Vivien Goldman, Caroline Coon, Julie Burchill and Jane Suck (Solanas) reporting back with wit and verve from the war zones of reggae and punk. In the US, female writers such as Cooper and Gerri Hershey (whose *Nowhere To Run* has become a classic of soul writing) found it even harder to make it as serious commentators on a national level where huge circulations meant a huge vested interest in keeping the 'jobs for the boys'. With the fragmentation and redefinition of the music scene throughout the 1980s, more young women started to emerge through small titles and fanzine culture, while older writers with staying power began to get the grudging respect they deserved.

Val Wilmer, a UK writer and photographer who has travelled widely, covering jazz, blues and African music since the 1950s, began her career as a lone female hustling for interviews backstage. 'The hard part was the people who hung around the musicians – they treated women as an annoyance or on the game. I was young and considered a likely chick.'[36] Then her work was at times literally hazardous, and she became famous in the mid-1960s within the industry for thumping Dizzy Gillespie, a notorious harasser of women.

'Backstage politics could get hairy, I was scared the promoter – a very powerful figure then – would ban me from further interviews backstage, but he was fine. Musicians thought it was very funny. A few years ago I was out with my friend Herb Lovell, and he said, "Yeh, I'm happy to be out with you. Let's face it, you were the chick who gave Dizzy Gillespie the hiding he deserved. I'm proud of my baby!"'

When I spoke to her in 1994, Wilmer was in her fifties and had adopted a sanguine attitude. 'I survived a lot of traumas that would've stopped most women. I was privileged to discover the music and a world most people I grew up with never experienced. All of us white guests in various black societies have a duty to put back from what we've gained. I'd like to leave my work as a legacy for those who come after.'

**Annie Leibovitz,** celebrity photographer, at the opening of her London National Portrait Gallery exhibition, 1994: on tour with The Rolling Stones in the 1970s, she set out to 'de-glamorize life on the road'. (Emily Andersen)

Unlike men caught up in the ego rush of being a 'personality' journalist like Lester Bangs or Nick Kent, women tend to foreground themselves less, seeing the challenge as being a perceptive documentalist of people's stories. This is nowhere more graphically illustrated than through a camera, and it's not surprising that some of the most lasting images in rock and jazz have been taken by women – Val Wilmer, Annie Leibovitz, Pennie Smith, and film-maker Penelope Spheeris – almost advantaged by their position as passionate Outsiders.

'I was not a rock 'n' roll photographer. I'd been taught pure photography. In fact, you didn't even sell your work,' says Annie Leibovitz, *Vanity Fair*'s celebrity photographer, who began her career on *Rolling Stone* shortly after graduating from San Francisco's Art Institute in the early 1970s. 'In the early years of *Rolling Stone* there was a dichotomy. Even though I loved the excitement of working there, I felt I'd "sold out". I was uncomfortable with friends at the Institute who just took a photo when they felt moved. But at the same time I was young, and the lives and rooms I entered were so fascinating to me, it was like being on a journey.'[37]

When in 1975 Mick Jagger requested that Leibovitz go on tour with the Stones, she jumped at the chance. 'They were the band of the '70s, and I ended up doing a very strong set of pictures, I never really put my camera down.' She caught some classic shots: Jagger dark eyed and pale in a lift, looking like a hung-over transvestite; Keith Richards, comatose on a studio floor. A fan of the Cartier-Bresson school of personalized street photography, Leibovitz set out to 'de-glamorize life on the road', and before she got caught up in the Stones' mayhem, it was her very innocence of the rock 'n' roll lifestyle that enabled her to take such dispassionate pictures. 'I had no idea how music was made, how consumed one could get with drugs. I went on tour with my tennis racket, thinking I'd go from city to city and play tennis. They just laughed. It's true. After the first date I was never seen in the daytime again!' Unlike the stylized composition of her later work, Leibovitz's pictures captured the sultry rawness of rock, the ambiguities of its macho stance. When asked what it had been like operating in such a male world, she replied, 'I don't think it's all that male. Jagger has a very feminine side to him!'

Pennie Smith, meanwhile, who shot most of the covers for *NME* throughout the late 1970s and early 1980s, also had a monochrome reportage style. An admirer of war photographer Don McCullen, Smith took pictures, particularly during the punk era, which have the air of dispatches from a battle zone. On tour with The Clash for six years, she captured the famous image of Paul Simonon smashing his guitar on stage at New York Palladium. A fast action shot that somehow encapsulates the myth of chaotic rock hero, it has since been syndicated worldwide. 'I'm there to document what they do, I have no high moral ground,' she says. 'Joe Strummer once said to me, "If I get electrocuted, take the picture, and then pull the plug out." I thought, "Great – I'm there to do that job, not be sympathetic."'[38]

A solitary North London girl who began her career in the

underground press accompanying Nick Kent on interviews, she 'graduated' to *NME* in the mid-1970s, going on tour with top bands of the day such as Led Zeppelin and Roxy Music. Her innovative style signalled the move away from 'formal group shots, residue of '60s staid stuff'. 'I like to live with risk – clutching a case and two cameras, working with available lighting rather than setting it all up neatly in the studio,' she says. Ironically she has found male subjects much easier to photograph than women:

'The problem with women is they always want to be pretty. There's very few who are unconcerned about make-up. It puts me off if they won't let their head go a certain way because hair will fall in their eyes. Two exceptions to this were Debbie Harry – she knew what she was up to and did it – and Patti Smith, who did her job, went on stage, looked like rubbish half the time but had an endearing attractiveness because of it.'

In certain areas the music industry attracts and rewards those who veer towards a fearless individualism. Pennie Smith found that her instinct and critical reserve paid off well within photography, but in a sense the camera de-sexes and protects women – once they are behind it, they are invisible. UCLA graduate Penelope Spheeris found that to her advantage when she recorded the starkly revealing scenes of LA punk life that made her 1980 film *The Decline of Western Civilization* such an 'anarchy carnival' classic. She took this further with *Part 2: The Metal Years*, and even spoofed it in 1992 with the super-hit feature *Wayne's World*.

### Smokin' Spinderellas: the Girl DJ

In front of the camera or the mike a woman's personality is under much greater scrutiny. Having to bear in mind both presentation and journalism, the female radio DJ imparts her musical enthusiasm while fighting the notion that it's men who are the serious custodians of music: taste, trend, B sides, catalogue numbers 'n' all. An early-1990s British Atlantic 252 survey of independent stations found that only 2 per cent of women DJs were presenting daily shows. Reasons for this varied from the claim that women's voices are 'too shrill' and 'not authoritative', to the assumption that women lack the technical skills.

Janice Long, who graduated from a slot on local Merseyside radio to become the first female DJ at BBC Radio One with a daily show, recalls,

'One of the DJs said, "Hang on, what's she doing here, she's a woman, she won't know about music", so you were always proving that you did. They'd say things like, "We've heard another woman and she's really good, so watch out." Why would I have to go for another woman to come in? Also, looks were much more taken into account if you were a woman. Once when I was going to Japan I was told to dress like a star so of course I wore my scruffiest clothes on purpose. What did they expect me to dress like, Shirley Bassey? With blokes they wouldn't say, "Oh his jeans are baggy" or "He's got a pot belly."'[39]

An enthusiastic Northerner who introduced many new indie rock acts through her show between 1983 and 1988, Long tried to provide an alternative to the station's rigid chart playlist base. Her career with Radio One came to an abrupt end when she became pregnant. 'The controller Johnny Beerling called me into his office and said, "Take it from me. I know my wife when she had children. You'll breast-feed, get post-natal depression and have no commitment."' Keen to show that she was still able to do her job, Long planned to take just the basic six-week maternity leave, but before she came back she was 'relieved' of her post and offered a marginal weekly slot on a Sunday. Long refused the meagre offer, issuing a press release in explanation. 'To this day Beerling has held it against me, but I felt I had to stand up to him and his attitude, even if it meant losing my job.'

When I spoke to her in 1993, Long worked as a freelance producer/presenter, and was active in the establishment of the key UK alternative radio station XFM. A year later a new regime at Radio One under Matthew Bannister ironically ushered in a looser, more alternative playlist, and a female presence stronger than the traditional 'bit of fluff' reading the weather report.

The changes took an interminably long time. Angela Bond, a

freelance broadcaster who began her career as a DJ in the USA and Hong Kong, returned to England in the mid-1960s during Beatlemania to become a producer at the BBC. Together with Derek Chinnery and Johnny Beerling she drew up the 1967 document for Radio One, and signed up pirate DJ talent such as Tony Blackburn and Johnnie Walker. While Chinnery and Beerling later rose to become controllers of the station, Bond found her own path infuriatingly slow:

'In 1967 a woman conducting a government survey into women's progress in industry interviewed me. She returned ten years later asking, "Are you where you thought you'd be?" I said, "No, it's taken me three times the period as a woman to get the same grade level as a man." "If it's any consolation," said the woman, "this is the trend throughout the business. In fact you've got the timing exactly right."[40]

When Bond told me this story at the beginning of the interview, she was the bluff realist, saying, 'You can't let it upset you, it's a fact of life.' By the end, when she referred to it again, there were tears in her eyes. 'I was very hurt inside.'

While Bond and Long were fighting marginalization on national radio, from the late 1980s a new generation of female DJs began to grow on the fiercely competitive UK dance scene, with women like Smokin' Joe, Nancy Noise and drum 'n' bass stars Kemistry & Storm establishing themselves as serious musical aficionados. Unfortunately Kemistry was tragically killed in a car accident in 1999, just as she was working to forge links and create a club culture that was more women-friendly. Tasha Mardin, aka Killer Pussies, a tall, slim techno DJ who has been hauling her record boxes round clubs and raves since 1990, spoke of the constant pressure as a woman to argue for your time on the decks, even when you have been officially booked. 'Once I was booked to go on at three, but I kept being put back by the promoter, with all these male DJs put on before me, so I didn't get on till five or six in the morning. Since then I stand my ground to make sure I get on at the right time.' Starting in the time-honoured fashion by mixing records in her bedroom, Mardin began to 'play out' when she got fed up with the obscurantist approach of DJs trying to impress their male peers. 'They were playing new tracks that no one had heard yet – I wanted to hear things relevant to me, for when I was going out. The crowds on the dance floor seem to appreciate that, and female party-goers find it nice seeing a woman DJ, someone they can relate to.'[41]

By 1993 Mardin was beginning to make that crucial jump from the dance floor to the studio. As dance music mushroomed wildly from the late 1980s with a hundred different versions of house and bpm sampling, so former DJs such as Pete Tong and Paul Oakenfold began to move into record production. 'It's an area I have to learn more about, particularly working with computers,' says Mardin.

## Take Back the Board

Whether the chosen route is via DJ-ing, engineering or perform-ing, production is one of the most powerful areas of the music business. While many established female artists such as Janet Jackson and Lisa Lisa are negotiating their own co-production credits, there are very few female producers working on male acts, particularly in the rock sphere, where work goes to a select 'name' coterie of Good Blokes, such as Steve Lillywhite, Glyn Johns and Jimmy Iovine. A Toronto producer who launched her own record label chi'me.ra in London in 1994, Sadia had multi-platinum success throughout the 1980s with David Wilcox, a Canadian guitar rock act that she worked with from the first demo, producing each of their nine best-selling albums. She says,

'Although EMI Music in Canada treated me decently and I've made a lot of money for them, they never once offered me another band. Can you think of an A&R department with a producer whose albums are going gold and platinum not being offered other projects that come along? That does have something to do with the politics of power relations. I know how good my production values are, I sit as the only full-time female member on the directorate of REPRO (the British Record Producers Guild). Part of the problem is that when you're handing over the administration of large sums of money to an individual there's enormous power invested in that.'[42]

The ingrained male attitude is one of not trusting a woman to be assertive enough with a budget, or be confident enough to direct a bunch of errant musicians. 'The studio is a male enclave where women are referred to as tarts only allowed in for a quick shagging. It's not so much budgets you've got to deal with – more the leery guitar player who wants to shag you rather than listen to you,' says Jill Sinclair. 'Women have a civilizing influence, and a lot of rock groups don't wish to be civilized.' Sadia remains unfazed by this. 'I'm interested in developing a sound that's unique to the artist I'm working with, instead of trying to impose preconceptions,' she says. 'I'm capable of drawing good performances from people. When an artist walks into a studio I want them to feel sheltered, secure and completely free.'

Ann Dudley, producer of the Art of Noise and arranger for a plethora of pop acts from ABC to Wham!, Frankie Goes To Hollywood and The Pet Shop Boys, says that she prefers the latter role. 'As a producer you have to take record company political flak – if a record fails it's down to you. Whereas an arranger can stand back and just get involved in the music.'[43] The main block she sees for women is the hours. 'To get into production you need to be an engineer – the craziest job in the world. You work longer hours than a hospital doctor. No woman in her right mind would take that work for those hours and that money, especially if she has children.'

Another bar to women's progress is 'techno-fear', nervousness about negotiating the technology of the mixing desk. 'The language of computers is so alienating, incomprehensible and inhuman; that puts a lot of women off. It's obvious these things are marketed at boys,' says Manda Glenfield, one half of Britain's production team The Beatmasters, ex-commercial jingle samplers who began producing and re-mixing pop hits from the late 1980s with such acts as the Pet Shop Boys, S-Express, The Shamen and Blur. Glenfield, who admits that 'to a certain extent I'm protected because my work partner is male', learned how to use studio gear 'in a friendly environment that doesn't exist for most women. I still feel isolated, though. For instance, if I see a female friend for lunch it's such a contrast being with her, then stepping back into the techno-speak and constant laddish bantering of the studio.'[44]

The technological revolution that arose through dance music signals the future for the industry as a whole. Glenfield feels that this is where women should be directing more energy. 'There's a danger that women will be seriously left behind as technology becomes more and more powerful in our everyday lives. I'm worried that people say things are better for women. I still think that's cosmetic.' White all-girl rap band Luscious Jackson also believe strongly in producer power. 'The Riot Grrrls kept saying, "Take back the pit" [the prime place just below the stage]. We say, "Take back the board." Y'know, learn technology, learn to engineer yourself,' says guitarist Jill Cunniff. 'Too often women are rapping over a man's track. We pick and produce our samples – we're in control of every single thing we do.'[45]

Women such as Bernadette Cooper (with her female outfits Klymaxx and Madame X), Angela Winbush, LaLa, Nona Hendryx and Ann Dudley have been an innovatory force within dance or pop production, but unlike male heroes such as Frankie Knuckles or David Morales, they have yet to receive due recognition. Toni Colandreo (Toni C), top New York songwriter, arranger and producer for a variety of artists including Whitney Houston, Will Downing, Jocelyn Brown and Deborah Harry ('She's supersonic, smart – the first person in the business who gave me my first survival lessons'), emerged through the club culture of the late 1970s and early 1980s. A fast-talking Italian from Washington DC, Colandreo came to New York in 1976 to play bass in a number of punk/jazz bands. Frustrated with group politics, she moved into electrical engineering, doing lighting design for clubs such as the Electric Circus and becoming house DJ for Xenons:

'I met Madonna in the booth. Along with Shep Pettibone and Arthur Baker we were all in that scene together – I was right in the middle of the dance industry. One day in 1979 I was underneath a console fixing a huge lighting show, covered in dust, when a DJ came in the box. "Who are you?" I asked. "I'm Jellybean." "Jellybean," I said. "That's a *name*?"'[46]

Before long she joined Jellybean's 'A team', poring over studio manuals with Steve Bray, and working with a range of top artists. Colandreo never took full production credit for her work, but she admits that she surrendered her own power:

'I was behind the scenes, I wanted to seize the limelight, but I gave up the power. Jellybean's the artist, the producer while it's my songs, my arrangements. I grew up with the idea that a man would take care of me. I expected Jellybean to take care of me, but of course no one would. Women are not so much afraid of technology as afraid in general. Yes, it is scary and people are mean, but you have to find the supports, like any minority. If you can't be a snake in the grass you have to hire one.'

Colandreo is also frank about the role drug abuse played on the dance underground. 'I had substance-abuse problems. There were so many casualties. In 1984 I remember playing the Eurythmics' "Sex Crime" at about 4.30 a.m. looking out on to the dance floor, packed with arms in the air and thinking this can't last, we can't keep it up. Then the whole AIDS and drug thing hit.' After coming through the hangover of the late 1980s, Colandreo picked herself up, went sober and built her own twenty-four-track studio in her East Village front room. A small room cluttered with wires, records and equipment, it is regularly visited by the cream of the dance crop. 'The industry has paid me homage,' she says. 'It's about time.'

## Thank Heaven for B Sides

The long-term habit of linking all women together under the generic term 'women in rock' has left its own legacy of suspicion, in all areas of the business. In a desire to be recognized on their own merits, ahead of gender, many women distance themselves from systems of support that could work for them. Boston female music lawyer Patti Jones, who represents hardcore rock outfits such as Tree and Slughog, emphasized this lack of trust when she told me in 1994, 'Women artists have no balls, they're not supportive of other women, they'll talk to me and then go to a guy. It seems as if they'll be easily manipulated by men rather than go to a lawyer sensitive about female issues.'[47] To perceive men as having that ultimate stamp of authority can only foster divisiveness between women. One way women have learned to beat that isolation (and alienation) within the business has been to establish their own networks. Women In Music, an organization that since 1985 has been holding workshops and seminars throughout the US music industry, is a prime place for women to 'network' and share skills. 'I saw it as a great opportunity to meet other women. Networking is the best thing for me to get moving. There's so much turnover in this business that I've got success through being stable, consistently "out there" and putting 150 per cent in,' says Linda Lorence, East Coast creative director for the performing rights society SESAC.[48] President of WIM between 1992 and 1994 and in her early thirties, she was representative of a younger generation clear about the careers they were entitled to. WIM, though, is more enabling than activist. 'We got a lot of flak from aggressive members ashamed we wouldn't take a stance – but we're just a place women can go regardless of political views.'

Women In Music UK has also been an active body since 1987, when a group of angry female contemporary composers including Nicola Le Fanu, Gail Thompson and Sophie Fuller formed a group promoting the visibility of women in classical music. This grew into a fully-fledged national organization by the mid-1990s, crossing all genres. As well as organizing festivals and conferences, WIM provided a valuable service with its magazine *NOW*. It had arts funding for women musicians, and networking opportunities galore.[49]

There was also the Woman of the Year Awards for the Music Industry and Related Media – the brainchild of leading women in the UK music industry. First staged in London in 1995, the annual event celebrates the achievements of all women working in the industry, but highlights some women in particular and their contribution – all of whom have left a definite mark within their field. In 2001, for instance, PR pioneers Barbara Charone and Moira Bellas won Woman of the Year, while feisty promoter Jenny Marshall collected a Lifetime Achievement award. The event is also a much needed fundraiser for the two main industry charities, Nordoff-Robbins Music Therapy and the BRIT Trust.

Some women impatient for change, though, have organized outside 'the system'. Modelling itself more on AIDS campaigning groups like ACT UP, SWIM was WIM's angry younger sister. 'We're kind of mature Riot Grrrls,' says Juliana Luecking, a spoken-word performer and part of the small core of journalists, artists and DJs who conceived SWIM in 1993, initially as a radical discussion forum with a monthly showcase of women's bands. Before long their frustration with the industry spilled over into activism: at the College Music Journal convention that year they were disappointed to see a twelve-foot naked blow-up doll with bullet nipples towering over the vendors by the Sony Mercury Records stand. 'Ten of us marched down with magic markers and scissors. We wrote on it SEXISM SUCKS and THIS IS NASTY, and punctured it with scissors.' In the ensuing mêlée, security guards had to disperse the crowd. Sony went on to sue CMJ. They didn't press charges, but received $3,000 from CMJ insurance. 'It wasn't a campaign as such,' says Luecking, 'more a spontaneous graffiti act. Very satisfying, too.'[50]

Whether it's through guerrilla tactics or gentle networking, women are becoming a much stronger presence within the industry. Music matters. Music is a powerful force in everyday life, and women want full involvement.

It is outside the industry, however, that there is the weak link – at the level of consumption. In a small but qualitative survey in 1994 of twenty-three men and twenty-three women up to the age of forty, London-based Women's Studies researcher Victoria Rutherford found that 'women don't buy music. They internalize and use music differently to men.'[51] Though boys and girls up to puberty are equally interested in music, boys learn quite soon that they are not supposed to like 'girls'' music, veering towards the loud and noisy while rejecting romantic pop. This divergence widens during adolescence: although pop's biggest market is teenage girls, by the time they reach their twenties, their interest in music significantly declines. Reasons cited include less time (because of childcare demands) and less money, but perhaps more fundamental than that is the sense that women are in direct competition with men for access to music, and in the tussle women either give ground or lose out.

David Terrill, marketing manager of HMV, the huge music megastore chain, says,

'Music is a badge and a means of identification. With males it's the Number One activity, pastime or form of conversation – i.e., who's the best band, the latest band. With girls fashion is the most important, while pop music comes second.

'Also there are two different ways music is used. The group leading the market and establishing trends is 70 per cent male. They're down at the clubs voting with their feet. By the time a group has hit songs they're on to the next one. The other group is pop, and here women are 60 per cent in the majority. They pursue chart activity once it becomes chart activity – they're less concerned than young men about pursuing the credibility factor.'[52]

Part of the reason women are less active consumers is a reflection of the male bias in outlets of information. In an HMV marketing survey, for instance, of a mixed cluster group, 12 per cent of the men bought NME, as opposed to 4 per cent of women, while for the monthly Q, the ratio was 13 per cent men, 4 per cent women. Rutherford comments,

'I think men continue to enjoy music because they want its pleasure uninterrupted. They want to control and colonize it, thereby consciously or unconsciously excluding women. Teenage boys in particular are very competitive about music, they use it as a gauge of sophistication . . . and the most knowledgeable go on to work in the industry, becoming technicians, producers, marketeers.'

A startling finding in her survey was that, when asked to name their top ten favourites, most of the men didn't mention one female act. The exception was a black correspondent who chose Roberta Flack and Ella Fitzgerald – an indicator as much of culture as gender.

The way women artists are ignored is reflected time and again in music press polls: in an *NME* 1994 all-time Top Fifty Albums listing, for instance, only two were by women. But Terrill maintains that it is as much about attitude as gender.

'It's down to certain sounds. There are certain female artists whom men have taken on board, such as Björk. She's not perceived in terms of sex. More, she hits the male on the head for a particular attitude. When Eurythmics were seen as cutting edge, a lot of men were behind Annie Lennox – now her fan base has settled to a more fifty/fifty split.'

One male marketing manager for a record company bemoaned the fact that women were passive consumers, saying that various ploys they had been working on to attract female buyers included Tampax-sponsored music tours, and (in the same way washing powder is included with new washing machines) placing a copy of a current woman artist in all new Renault Clio tape decks. These initiatives ignore the male-orientated bias that underpins and undermines the place that music has in women's lives. This is an irony, when it is women who make an act mass-market, tipping the balance for a band from cult to chart success. 'For years REM were bought by men,' says Terrill. 'But what really broke them was the album *Automatic For The People*. Women loved it, and the proportion of women in the mass market is much higher.' This influence is not acknowledged when it comes to selling.

On a practical level, the sale of hardware (record decks, CD players, speakers, etc.) is generally directed at men, so there is a disincentive for women to buy the 'software' if they are not given easy access to hardware in the first place. As a 1994 catalogue from electronics giant Philips stated, 'Over 50 per cent of women will take a male companion with them when buying a hi-fi.' Emotionally, as well as in collecting both knowledge and records, music is a way for men to channel and express 'unacceptable' feelings, while women tend to use it more functionally, for relaxation, leisure, or as a backdrop to their lives. San Francisco Women's Studies graduate Lynn Peril, who has a vast record collection spanning blues, jazz, punk and 1920s novelty pop, believes that collecting is a way of fighting passivity: 'For me and my friends the acquisition of material goods has turned into a form of self-expression . . . Women are only supposed to know about clothes and make-up; their bodies are their only officially approved area of obsession . . . You need audacity to find things out for yourself.'[53]

While active and knowledgeable consumers of staples like food and clothes, women feel that music is somehow periphery. Many women listen to a boyfriend's or husband's record collection rather than prioritizing their own. This is an extension of the pop wife/groupie tradition, where women vicariously experience the power of music through their men. It is interesting that avid, active female consumers often need to feel a sense of separateness or freedom from men to create their own musical identities. A hidden factor in the 'active/passive consumer' debate is the huge female tape underground that exists.

According to the HMV survey, women are the largest group purchasing cassettes; rather than buy records, many women tape compilations for themselves or friends. It is a common form of cultural referencing and cross-referencing, a network of exchange particularly among lesbians. This kind of consumption, completely outside the realm of chart shops and the expected commercial outlets, has created a separate and powerful arena through music, a new female 'social map'.[54]

A pleasant addendum to this chapter is the fact that by 2001, women were becoming more active music consumers, with record stores reflecting that in promotional campaigns and advertising. HMV, for instance, liberally placed adverts for the *Funky Divas* compilation and their HMV Classics line in the women's consumer press. Women were obviously responding to the greater availability of music from female artists in a range of genres. There had also been changes in the music press – in

2001, for example, there was a concerted effort on the part of that former male bastion, $Q$ magazine, to attract more female readers. The drive to increase sales led to more 'women-friendly' articles, and more women artists featured in the magazine.

Gennaro Castaldo, HMV's Head of Press, said that there was a '60:40 male bias' in the ratio of male/female record store customers, but 40 per cent is a large minority. According to Castaldo, the most interesting development was the amount of girls wanting to work in a music store: 'This is a growing trend. We have a record amount of female employees coming through into store management, approximately 25–30 per cent for managers. That may not sound a great deal, but it was only a few years ago that record retailing was a bit of a male preserve.'[55]

As women have made their demands known as consumers, the music industry has gradually played 'catch-up', with the result that, come the millennium, women as a market were being tapped as never before.

# Girlpower!

## THE NEW GENERATION

**14**

IN 1994, FIVE GIRLS WERE CHOSEN from an advert in UK entertainment magazine *The Stage*. 'R.U. 18–23 with the ability to sing/dance?' it enquired. 'R.U. streetwise, outgoing, ambitious and dedicated?' Out of the 400 who replied, father and son management team Bob and Chris Herbert picked Geri Halliwell (Ginger), Melanie Brown (Scary), Melanie Chisholm (Sporty), Victoria Adams (later Beckham) (Posh), and Michelle Stephenson, a girl who was ambivalent about the group and left to go to college, to be replaced by Emma Bunton (Baby). The girls vaguely knew each other from auditions – 'We were always the crap ones left behind', Mel C once said with startling frankness.[1]

The five girls were ensconced in a three-bedroom house in Maidenhead and given songs to sing. By March the following year they had worked out their choreography and ditched the Herberts in favour of top-flight pop manager Simon Fuller (who later launched mega-teen band S Club 7). 'They had no substance. There are so many wanky managers out there,' Beckham said of the unfortunate Herberts.[2] The girls were teamed up with songwriters Stannard & Rowe, Absolute and Elliot Kennedy, who were signed to Fuller's 19 Management. The alert went out to record companies that there was a feisty girl group available, and by summer 1995, the Spice Girls were in a bidding war. In September that year, Virgin Records signed them for a reputed £2 million advance, beating competition from RCA, Sony and Polygram.

The girls began to make a series of appearances at industry events such as The Brit Awards and the Charisma race day. They launched surprise guerilla attacks on the media: prominent TV

producer Isabel Hutton was won over by an impromptu medley in the ladies' toilets at London Weekend Television. A more bewildered and sceptical staff at pop magazine *Smash Hits* were treated to an a cappella set in the office. By July 1996 the well-orchestrated media campaign reached fever pitch with the release of their debut single 'Wannabe', a catchy piece of pop that celebrated female friendship. 'Wannabe' went to No. 1 in 31 countries, and launched that much-maligned concept, Girlpower.

Within a year of their first hit, the Spice Girls had gone global. US business bible *Forbes* listed them as the 32nd richest entertainers in the world, and their debut album, *Spice*, had already earned £30 million. They made approximately £14.5 million from merchandising and *Spiceworld – The Movie*, and £5.5 million from sponsorship deals. 'They keep blowing up any rules. Everything they do breaks down received industry wisdom,' claimed *Music Week* commentator Paul Gorman.[3] Sponsorship deals included Impulse body spray, Walkers crisps, endorsement of 40 Asda supermarket products, and a 'joint-partnership' with Pepsi (their first live date was in the Turkish capital Istanbul because it was one of the few cities in the world where Pepsi outsells Coca Cola). Over-exposure was clearly not a worry.

'No one has more marketability than the Spice Girls,' music business lawyer John Toone told me for *Q* magazine.[4] Formerly a Virgin lawyer in the original Spice Girls deal, he said: 'Up to ten per cent of their income comes from sponsorship, whereas for most artists that figure ranges from zero to one percent. Spice Girls exposure is massive, and marketeers see them as great vehicles to sell product. No one else has achieved that in modern pop culture.' Until then, pop sponsorship had been limited to touring or one-off promotions like Pepsi with Michael Jackson. By endorsing so many products, the Spice Girls cemented the burgeoning relationship between pop music and corporate culture. 'The Spice Girls are a brand, and a very protected one at that,' declared Rick Blaski, then head of Music & Media enterprises, the agency that put Clearasil spot cream together with UK boy band 911.

The Spice Girls appealed to young girls who were brand-aware enough to become a consumer group in their own right. Dubbed 'tweenagers', this sophisticated, fashion-conscious group of ten- to thirteen-year-olds flocked to the High Street to

**Spice Girls:** getting busy with product endorsement: launching UK's Channel 5 TV in March 1997. (Kieran Doherty/ Redferns)

buy Spice Girl boob tubes and leopardskin jump suits. A report by UK market research company Datamonitor showed that the spending power of the tweenager was rising faster than that of any other group in the youth market.[5] Their ready cash was largely attributed to the high divorce rate; that is, the children were being indulged by both sets of parents. While no one doubts their affection for their young fans, the Spice Girls were perfectly placed to exploit this new pop market.

By the end of 1997, the Spice Girls had won Brit, MTV and *Billboard* awards, met Nelson Mandela and Prince Charles, and become tabloid celebrities. Their manager Simon Fuller talked of 'teamwork' and a record company who let him follow his hunches. 'It just shows what you can do when everyone is prepared to kill,' he trumpeted. But what of the real girls behind the cartoon? And what about the music? And was it really Girlpower, or a well-calculated marketing exercise? Spice Girls made Girlpower their brand, but the concept came from somewhere else.

Ironically the term Girlpower arose from the explosive Riot Grrrl movement, the 1990s daughter of punk rock. The Riot Grrrl fanzine network reflected a new kind of feminism, one where the good, bad and plain unconventional sat side by side, and diverse sounds from the girlpower underground began to surface in the pop mainstream with bands like Hole and Bikini Kill. When the Spice Girls appeared, they were the only all-girl group amid a host of pimply boy bands, and Girlpower, an attractive, hip and very 'nineties' slogan, was adopted as their selling point.

Bidisha Bandyopadhyay, a former Riot Grrrl fanzine writer and now a successful novelist, remembers working on the launch of a short-lived but energetic magazine called *Girlpower* in 1994. A combination of Riot Grrrl attitude and glossy production standards, it was influenced by fanzines such as *Girlpride*, which Bidisha launched in 1993 when she was fourteen. 'There was a lot of interest in a punky, independent, forthright publication, because there was nothing for young, politicized women in the shops. It was all about going to gigs, making music, networking and hedonism. It was about being a visceral female presence at gigs, it wasn't commercial. It was literally walking the walk and talking the talk.[6]

Does she feel that the Spice Girls appropriated this concept? 'The Spice Girls were so manufactured, they wouldn't know about Riot Grrrl if it hit them in the face. When they first came out I hated the sight of these very silly young girls talking about Girlpower without making concrete points to back up what they were saying. It was selling feminism-lite to children.' Five years later, however, she admired the fact that they were: 'amongst the highest-earning women in the arts industries. I don't mind that they were created by men, they earn more than them now anyway. Why should we expect Posh Spice to come out with rhetoric as honed as Naomi Wolf? We're in a capitalist society and she's a pop star.'

What many found objectionable about the Spice Girl phenomenon was the mutual industry backslapping at the massive success of some rather mediocre pop music. The Spice Girls were presented as the 'acceptable' non-threatening girl band, with members who would never get too 'difficult' or political. In a record industry obsessed with the bottom line, the Spice Girls provided a perfect model of how female artists should be, and many more substantial, more *musical* female acts were marginalized. Geri Halliwell's famous Union Jack minidress and cartoon pout, for instance, roused the anger of many a female musician. 'I don't see how wearing a push-up bra and knickers on the front cover of a magazine has *anything* to do with moving forward the cause of female equality,' fumed Shirley Manson, lead vocalist with rock band Garbage.[7] The charismatic, steely-eyed Edinburgh rock singer emerged in 1995, the same year as the Spice Girls, but fronting a band with very different values. Formed by Nirvana producer Butch Vig, Garbage played sophisticated post-grunge rock, with songs like 'Stupid Girl' and 'Only Happy When It Rains' expressing a dark undercurrent of emotion. Manson gave interviews speaking in language a roadie would be proud of: 'I'm naïve. I make mistakes, but I don't give a rat's arse how I'm perceived,' she said frankly. She became an alternative heroine in the vein of her idol Chrissie Hynde, and was understandably scornful of commercialized Girlpower.

Singer Ani DiFranco joined in the debate, saying: 'This is where the life gets sucked out of feminism, and the word becomes a meaningless bumper sticker.[8] Phil Spector, that noted architect of the girl-group sound, called them 'the anti-Christ', while Sinéad O'Connor pointed out that Spice Girlpower was flawed as a model of feminism because, 'it would be wonderful if the world was a safe place and young girls could all wander around half-naked, but it isn't.[9] Chrissie Hynde elaborated on the unease that many felt about not just the Spice Girls, but the whole commercial branding of pop and rock. 'Self-promotion has become so much part of the game now,' she told me in 1999. 'It never used to be like that. Your record company promoted you and you just kinda showed up. When I started, I wanted to play guitar in a rock band. You weren't even thinking about the fame. You were thinking, will I ever get a band together? Are these songs good enough? How am I gonna find a place to rehearse?'[10]

Somewhere along the line, she felt, basic values had been overturned. 'Now people are thinking about the fame aspect first and then, oh fuck, I've got to get some songs together and learn how to sing. I've got to back up my fame with something. People don't talk about music. All you have to do now is pull your pants down and say "Hey, over here!" and you get anyone to write an article on you. It's completely back to front.'

In November 1997 the Spice Girls won an MTV Award for Best Band in the World (beating Oasis, Radiohead, Prodigy and U2). Encouraged by their success, they seemed to believe the monumental hype, that they were indeed the best band in the world, that they had, indeed, invented girlpop. This was a major leap of faith, considering their passing interest in music history. Mel B, for instance, let slip that the first gig she ever went to was a Diana Ross concert in 1996, several years *after* the Spice Girls began.[11] This made a mockery of women's real achievements in music – from the iron-hard vaudeville blues of Bessie Smith, to the glowing soul of 1960s girl groups, to the punk poetry of Patti Smith, and 1990s pop mavericks like Tori Amos, Björk and PJ

Harvey. Amid the Spice Girl circus, new female artists who didn't want to play corporate girlypop were sidelined.

The tide slowly began to turn against the Spice Girls when they turned on the man who had helped orchestrate their meteoric rise. After the 1997 MTV Awards, at the peak of their success, they sacked manager Simon Fuller and announced that they would manage themselves. 'He's a fantastic manager, as business goes,' Mel C said later. 'But he needs to work with robots who have absolutely no emotion. And no brain. And that's where he fucked up.'[12] Within six months the much-touted group friend-ship began to fracture, Geri Halliwell left to go solo, and the Spice Girls continued their first world tour as a foursome.

The band continued to sell, despite the loss of loud, charis-matic Ginger. Their success launched a veritable army of imitation girl groups. First there were All Saints, whose R&B pop was presented as a West London street-cred alternative to the cartoon Spice Girls. Three of the band members, however, had been to stage school, as had many of the female acts record labels churned out during 1999 and 2000. In the year 2000, over 45 girl bands were launched in the UK, and only a handful, including denim-clad Irish girls B*witched, the sultry Atomic Kitten, and the slightly awkward Honeyz, made it past Go! It appeared that the public appetite for formulaic female pop, along with the fortunes of the Spice Girls, had peaked.

The Spice Girls had an elemental energy, but once that began to fade, the true limit of their talent as a group surfaced. Their third album *Forever* was a lacklustre attempt at R&B, made all the more forgettable by thin vocal performances. They chan-nelled their energies into solo careers, with varying degrees of success, and became involved with the celebrity whirl – selling their wedding pictures to magazines like *Hello* and *OK!* It was only Mel C, the one with the discernable singing voice, and Halliwell, the most relentless showgirl of the original fivesome, who made real impact on the album charts. Halliwell, the vociferous supporter of Girlpower, demonstrated what happens when ambition outstrips talent.

At the music industry Brit Awards in 2000, she caused a media stir when she appeared, singing and dancing, from within a giant sculpted vagina and open pair of legs. Though taking cues from Madonna's risqué style of pop vaudeville, Halliwell lacked the incisiveness of her heroine, and the set piece seemed like a desperate bid for attention. 'If this is Girlpower, I don't want anything to do with it,' wrote rocker Suzi Quatro, in a scathing attack on Halliwell's performance. 'A real woman would realize that true power is not about lying on your back with your legs apart . . . Women have struggled to be taken as serious professionals rather than viewed purely as sex objects, particularly in the music industry. Surely Geri realizes the damage she is doing?'[13] Girlpower, it appeared, had reached a nadir. Although many critics saw Spicegirlpower as 'a harmless bit of fun', there was a large constituency of women artists and those in the business who saw it as, at best, a distraction from real talent, and at worst, a distortion of women's achievement. Since when did making large amounts of corporate money qualify someone as role model and heroine? Unless, like Madonna, there is true sense of satire at work. 'Geri, it's up to women like you to carry the banner into the next generation,' concluded Quatro. 'Don't let us down.'

## Lilith's Revenge

Despite the super-dominance in the late 1990s of what was eloquently termed 'crap pop', a new, dissenting sound was emerging, particularly in the US. There was a grassroots swell towards 'authenticity' and music that fully expressed anger, love, bitterness and hope. The success of Canadian artist Alanis Morissette took lyric-driven female rock to the heart of the mainstream. Her hit 'You Oughta Know', a spikey, enraged missive to an unfaithful ex, became a female revenge anthem, and her sassy debut *Jagged Little Pill* went on to sell 28 million worldwide. As her first world tour gathered momentum throughout 1995–6, it was apparent that she had tapped into a twentysomething *zeitgeist*. 'I saw the same thing with Madonna.

The girls caught on first, and it was mainly women at her gigs. Then they brought their boyfriends along, and the thing went mainstream,' her manager Scott Welch told me on the Sydney leg of Morissette's 18-month tour. 'Everyone, male or female, has had a "You Oughta Know" in their life.'[14]

Like Carole King's *Tapestry* in the 1970s, *Jagged Little Pill* articulated a moment, captured the feelings of a generation. Although Morissette says that 'it was written from a desperate, dark, almost pathetically sad place within my subconscious,' her deadpan style resonated with a young audience hip to Oprah Winfrey-speak, struggling with issues of life, love and independence. Morissette symbolizes the move from the surface sheen of sparkly girlpop to a more direct and defiant articulation of feeling. Born in suburban Canada, she was just ten when she launched herself into the music business with money she had earned from acting in a TV soap opera. By her mid-teens she was a national star, with frosted hair and a cheerleader smile. She released two albums and sang the national anthem at football games. She was playing Miss Perfect, and something had to give. 'I felt emotionally like fourteen, but acted like I was 40,' she told me. 'I was in a very adult environment. I had a lot of people around me, but as far as feeling connected, that was pretty rare. I wasn't very connected with myself. The damaging effect of being Miss Perfect is somehow being told, particularly if you're a woman, that being exactly who you are is not enough.[15]

The crisis came when she turned 19 and in the early 1990s turned away from bland pop to strike out on her own. 'When I was young I was about entertaining, making an audience smile, so I got approval from my parents and teachers. As time went on, I remembered the fulfilment I'd gotten from writing poetry: a real, unfettered, stream-of-consciousness. I knew that was possible with music, but not with the kind of environment I was in. I had to get away from that structured, black-and-white pop music.'

She left Ottawa and ended up in Los Angeles, working with rock producer Glen Ballard. He encouraged her to let go emotionally, and *Jagged Little Pill* was born. Madonna immediately saw the strength and spark of Morissette's talent, and the latter signed with Maverick. 'She reminds me of myself when I was young,' Madonna said indulgently. Critics were surprised at the bitter invective that coursed through Morissette's work, and dubbed it 'man-bashing'. But this sense of alienation was allied to memorable melodies and punchy beats, and it went global. Suddenly women's anger became marketable.

It was expected that Morissette would follow up her debut with more pithy, melodic songs about love and hate. Instead she took 18 months off and travelled around India with her friends. Refusing to be moulded into the corporate rock star, she then released an album that was wilfully uncommercial. *Confessions Of A Former Infatuation Junkie* (1998) was ambitious, rambling and introspective, packed with discordant chords and psychedelic riffs. At first it was critically panned but it became a 'slow-grower' inveigling its way with artistic ease into the pop consciousness with hits like 'Thank You' and 'Joining You Pts 1 & 2'. Accused of self-indulgence, Morissette said brazenly, 'It's *amazingly* self-indulgent. I think that's what art is. It's an intense record.' Having established herself so successfully with *Jagged Little Pill*, Morissette was able to continue at her own pace and with her own sound. When it was rumoured in 2001 that she was unhappy with Maverick, feeling pressure to dilute her material, Madonna cut short a world tour to persuade her to stay on the label. By then, female rock was big business.

Women singer/songwriters who had been steadily ploughing a furrow through the early 1990s finally reached critical mass. There was Berklee music graduate Paula Cole, whose dramatic, rhythmic pop broke through with her huge 1997 hit 'Where Have All The Cowboys Gone?' There was Lisa Loeb singing gentle, acoustic songs about love; Seattle-bred firebrand Meredith Brooks toting her guitar and celebrating the 'Bitch' in everywoman, and South Dakota songstress Shawn Colvin mixing country with deadpan pop and sophisticated lyrics on life and relationships. From the UK, Norfolk lass Beth Orton seduced the world with her downhome folkrock debut *Trailer Park*, while former Australian soap star Natalie Imbruglia created moody, melodious pop, and New Zealander Bic Runga went triple-platinum with pared-down Björk-ish ballads.

One of the trailblazers of the 'angry young women' music phenomenon was Chicago-born Liz Phair whose demo cassette 'Girly Songs' led to a deal with Matador Records and her 1993 debut album *Exile In Guyville*. Her salty, humorous songwriting won her a legion of fans, and even more came on board for the 1994 follow-up *Whip Smart*. When asked if she felt competitive with other women artists, Phair said, [Yes], but it's a fun thing. The best thing about having a lot of women in rock is that now I have peers. I don't have to make the guys like me; I have to make Meredith Brooks like me. And at this point in my life, I prefer proving things to other women.[16] There was lively debate on this flowering of women's rock. According to Fiona Apple, the New York überbabe whose intense, burning piano-led debut *Tidal* made her a star in 1996, women artists had been disregarded, and were now like a rash that had started rising. 'It has not healed, but at least it is visible, and at least we're aware of it,' she said graphically. 'The rash has risen. It is better. It is not cured.'[17]

It took one perceptive, practical woman to harness this energy and put it on the road. In 1997, singer/songwriter Sarah McLachlan launched Lilith Fair, a 35-date all-female tour that became the biggest hit of the summer. A clear-eyed, self-deprecating musician from Halifax, Nova Scotia, McLachlan achieved major success with the hymnodic ballads of her albums *Fumbling Towards Ecstasy* and *Surfacing*. Lilith, she explained, was Adam's second wife, the goddess exiled from Paradise because she refused to acquiesce to his demands. 'She was the world's first feminist. Now we're restoring her to her proper position in society,' McLachlan told me in 1998. 'We're celebrating.'[18] When she hatched plans for Lilith, she jokingly called it Girlapalooza, parodying the title of that predominantly male rock fest, Lollapalooza. The idea had formed back in 1996 when McLachlan experienced writer's block for her fourth record, and her manager suggested doing a few shows to loosen her creativity.

'I didn't want sole responsibility so I brought in other female acts, like Patti Smith, Lisa Loeb and Aimee Mann, to make it more fun. At this point there was no political motivation. But then a lot of promoters were hesitant about becoming involved, saying an all-woman show wouldn't work. I respond to a challenge. From then on I wanted to prove them wrong.'[19]

More than 60 women took turns on the first tour, with only McLachlan playing every city. Established arists like Suzanne Vega, Tracy Chapman, the Indigo Girls and Natalie Merchant joined newcomers Fiona Apple and Paula Cole, in a show that triumphed over the 'stupid old-school attitude' that women don't sell. Female consumers flocked to every sold-out date. In droves. There was criticism that the tour was biased towards white acoustic rock, but by the time it expanded the following year to 57 dates, Lilith had become a very successful brand, attracting performers from all genres – such as Erykah Badu, Queen Latifah and Missy Elliott. There was mass PMS,' jokes McLachlan. 'We would all commiserate together. Natalie Merchant walked by me one day with such a look in her eye. "Bad mood?" I said. "I've got PMS," she growled. "Me too," I said – so we ended up laughing, no longer two warriors suffering alone. Forty per cent of the crew were women too, so we hung out and had mass crying sessions. It was all good fun.'[20]

Apart from McLachlan, the tour's biggest stars were two artists who have proved many times over that there is a mass market for intelligent songwriting: Sheryl Crow and Jewel. Born in 1962 in Missouri, Crow studied classical piano and taught music before moving to LA in 1986 and singing back-up for

**Sheryl Crow**: stetson, guitar and 'Raymond Carver-style narratives'. (Paul Bergen/ Redferns)

such artists as Michael Jackson and Don Henley. She began performing with music veterans at a weekly LA jam session known as the Tuesday Night Music Club. This led to her 1993 debut album of the same name, which sold eight million copies and spawned three Grammys. Crow credited her fellow musicians, but had to shake off criticism that she had been 'created by guys'. The follow-up, *Sheryl Crow*, and 1998's *The Globe Sessions*, with its bitter-sweet Raymond Carver-style mini narratives, are most definitely her own. She admitted that she spent most of the 1980s 'being unsignable because I was a woman'. When hawking her demo tape around, people made favourable noises, but weren't prepared to take a risk. 'Women writing lyric-driven music were a curious thing as far as record executives went,' she said later.[21] By the time of Lilith Fair, she was optimistic: 'I think the stigmas are slowly starting to change, because undeniably women are becoming marketable and something to be reckoned with.'

Despite comments that Lilith stars were guarded with each other, on-the-road concert footage of the 1997 Lilith tour tells a different story.[22] There's Sheryl Crow in a backstage jam with the Indigo Girls. Crow might have been the bigger star, but she is gracefully humble in the presence of Amy Ray's talent. The Indigo Girls have been prime movers on the live scene, and a huge influence on many musicians, from REM to Joan Baez to Crow herself. 'The perception of the media is that we're all these backbiting women and there's no sense of community. An interesting outcome from the Lilith tour was a defiance of that. Not only can women get along beautifully, there is real camaraderie there,' claimed Crow.

The camaraderie was tested that year when McLachlan appeared on the cover of *Time* magazine in Canada, but in the US the cover featured a new young folk singer with the line: JEWEL AND THE GANG. 'I was a bit pissed off, but unfortunately, politically it made perfect sense,' McLachlan said later. 'Time Warner owns *Time* magazine [and] Jewel's record label. There you go.[23] Jewel was also the glamorous, saleable face of this new women's movement. Her 1995 debut album *Pieces Of*

*You* bombed on its release, yet through the 'word-of-mouth' effect gradually clocked up 10 million sales worldwide. For an album with no choruses and simple acoustic musings on love, injustice and the incredible lightness of living', its success was phenomenal.

But although Jewel received a lot of the attention, it had taken the 24-year-old Alaskan many years to get there. My record was like the mutt pony that somehow won the Kentucky Derby,' she told me.[24] Brought up on an Alaskan homestead with no running water, she sang in bars from the age of thirteen, and ended up living in a van in San Diego, performing her songs for peanuts. Even after being 'discovered and signing a deal with Atlantic Records, she still had to hire a rental car and drive across America doing an average 500 shows a year for four years, playing everywhere from High Schools to record stores. Like so many of her singer/songwriter peers, Jewel worked from the grassroots up.

By the late 1990s female songwriters had emerged, blinking, from the underground to become a major commercial phenomenon. As well as Lilith, they had their own radio format in the US (Modern Adult Contemporary). There have always been lone female songwriters (see Chapter 6), from Joni Mitchell and Laura Nyro in the 1970s to Suzanne Vega in the 1980s, but their presence was tokenistic. The closing scene in Martin Scorcese's *The Last Waltz*, for instance, a film of The Band's 1976 farewell concert in San Francisco, has all the guys packed onstage for the final number. In the midst of Dylan, Van Morrison, Keith Richards *et al.*, stands a lone woman – Joni Mitchell. We were always out there, but like UFO sightings. It was like *Close Encounters Of The Third Kind*,' says Emmylou Harris, Mitchell's contemporary and a Lilith Fair artist. 'Now women are there in much larger numbers, speaking to a large percentage of the people. Something is in the air.'[25]

In the early 1990s the picture was different. Received wisdom in the music industry was that women singer/songwriters were dullsville. Ron Shapiro, General Manager of Atlantic Records in New York, found it an uphill struggle breaking Jewel as a new artist on a scene dominated by male grunge rock bands like Soundgarden and Nirvana. 'In 1995 when we went with Jewel to radio, programmers looked at us like we were insane. There might be 40 acts on their playlist, and all 40 would be male,' he says.[26]

Then Jewel's uplifting song 'Who Will Save Your Soul?' became a massive 'sleeper' hit, as did Joan Osborne's cool, twanging 'One Of Us'. When either of these songs were put on the radio amid male depressing grunge, they stood out dramatically. There was something that stopped you dead in your tracks,' continues Shapiro. 'Implicit in the sound was heart, hope and warmth, and people responded to it.' By the millennium, the irony was that many US radio playlists were half or three-quarters women. 'At a time when the stock market is crashing, there's genocide, the American president is causing public scandal, people want to know what the meaning of life is. Women tend to address that more often and more viscerally.'

For Jewel, it was a question of taste. 'People were ready for music again, without pretence. Music in America had become so male ego-rock driven. It was all about belonging to a scene,' she asserts. 'That was alienating for the real music fan. Lilith Fair was 30,000 people dead quiet at a concert, listening to the songs. My first record is not very accomplished or slick, but it's sincere, and I think kids respond to that sincerity. That's nice for me because it lets me be who I am.' A significant number of her fans are women, but men also found meaning in her songs. 'You get the college student who saw you on TV and thought you were cute. You get the guy who's gay who feels he can be emotional because you're emotional. And you get the straight white male who says, 'I wanna understand myself better, my life better.'''[27]

Lilith Fair appealed because it seemed to put its money where its mouth was, with eco-friendly sponsors and a dollar a ticket going to local women's charities. Singer Natalie Merchant liked doing the tour because 'it was organized by a woman artist and not a corporate entity.' People feel good about buying into organic pop – it's as 'real' and radical as organic food, a way of resisting the fake emotion of airbrushed pop. But although female songwriters were not marketed as mass confection, they were still marketed. 'Grassroots' 'honesty' and 'authenticity' became buzzwords, while the number of photoshoots of female artists in a naked 'artistic' foetal position (Paula Cole and Alanis Morissette for instance) was alarming.

In Britain, the Lilith Fair didn't tour so well, with one cautious London date in 1998. 'That stripped down, left-of-centre ballad intensity doesn't travel here. The UK market is more pop and dance driven,' suggested Bobby Hain, Director of Music at Virgin Radio. With a 'slight male bias' in its audience (i.e. 57 per cent male: 43 per cent female), only 30 per cent of Virgin's playlist featured female artists. For a new artist like Bic Runga, breaking the UK was a challenge. 'In America, Bic has had a really good response. We find radio programmers more open to female singer/songwriters now, rather than saying, "Crikey what's this?",' remarked her manager Campbell Smith. 'But the UK is a lot harder. It's almost impossible to get her on the radio. The sound is not as fashionable here as it is in the States.'[28]

By 2000 it looked like the British market was catching up when *Songbird*, an album of smokey, sensitive ballads sung by the late Eva Cassidy, shot to the top of the album charts with minimal marketing. And laid-back British singer/songwriter Dido scored a slow-burning hit that year with her debut album *No Angel* – success helped, no doubt, by Eminem's sampling of her song 'Thank You' on his international hit 'Stan'. More low-key female artists were tapping into a cultural undercurrent that had always been there; it just took time to grab public attention. 'I have a real bonding to the underdog,' claims Jewel. 'And you know what? I think everyone feels like an underdog. Even if you're the most popular girl in the school there's always some sense of not being good enough at a deeper place.'

## New School Divas

While artists like Alanis Morissette and Sarah McLachlan got down and got organic, at the other extreme were The Divas, a phalanx of female artists for whom high theatricality, slick choreography, and gallons of hairspray were *de rigeur*. Never mind Girlpower, this was Womanpower *in excelsis* – groomed, airbrushed and overblown to perfection. The word 'diva' originated from Italian, meaning 'divine'. It meant a great female singer, previously an operatic prima donna, but now the term applies to a leading woman artist in any genre, be it jazz or R&B. Mass-market pop divas, from Diana Ross to Whitney Houston, Mariah Carey to Celine Dion, have become modern icons. By the mid-1990s this was reflected in the fact that the word 'diva' had became a marketing concept, shorthand for international sales and global domination. There were top female artists keeping entire corporations afloat. Mariah Carey, for example, boosted the fortunes of Sony by breaking the record for most No. 1 hits by a female artist, while it was reckoned that, in 1998, Epic Records' Celine Dion was selling an album somewhere in the world every 1.2 seconds. The music industry was waking up to the fact that there was a vast untapped audience of women consumers. When cable channel VH1 aired their *Divas Live!* concert series in 1999, over 63 per cent of the audience was female.

Was it that record companies had just become adept at leading global campaigns, planting an attractive woman with a big voice and a big ballad at the helm? Or did divas have more individuality than that? A common thread with all the divas in this book, from the vaudeville blues mamas to the present day, is their single-minded focus and the possession of an extraordinary voice that demands to be heard. It can be a voice of bravura show-womanship, echoing the classical divas in its demonstration of technical prowess. In the 1960s, Barbra Streisand and Shirley Bassey were the key proponents of this style – following the idea that the larger the voice and the bigger the gestures, the greater the impact.

Streisand is the diva supreme. In her 40-year career she has sold over 120 million albums, and her 16 films, including *Funny Girl*, *The Way We Were* and *A Star Is Born*, have grossed $1.5 billion. Among her many awards she has won two Oscars, ten Golden Globes and eight Grammys. Yet in the first flush of her career in the mid-1960s she was described as having 'the face of a bulldozer and the stridency of an ambulance siren.'[29] When asked to account for her success, Streisand once remarked with her characteristically frank humour: 'On stage I'm a cross between a washerwoman and a princess. I'm a bit coarse . . . a bit vulgar . . . But I'm also part princess – sophisticated, elegant and controlled. I can appeal to everybody.' The diva is, to some extent, anti-fashion. In the 1960s when rock culture was burgeoning and the song-and-dance musical was pronounced dead, Streisand's portrayal of the forthright Fanny Brice made *Funny Girl* one of the most successful films of the decade. The diva's purpose is to pull out emotional showstoppers that have mass appeal, and Streisand has always obliged.

Divas are also expected to be temperamental. Film composer Paul Williams once said that working with Streisand was like 'having a picnic at the end of an airport runway,'[30] and it is that precipitous larger-than-life quality that cements their place in the public imagination. A diva makes impossible demands because she can. Shirley Bassey, the UK's answer to Streisand, was christened 'Leather Larynx', and famed for her outrageous feather boas, unstable love life and over-the-top performances. The mixed-race singer from Tiger Bay, Cardiff, began on the late 1950s variety circuit, and achieved international success in the 1960s with her film work. Her rendition of the theme to James Bond film *Goldfinger*, for instance, is a florid, risqué classic; as is 'Big Spender', her hit from *Sweet Charity* and another Bond theme, 'Diamonds Are Forever'.

In the 1990s the old-fashioned showgirl made a comeback with the phenomenal rise of Mariah Carey and Celine Dion. The latter emphasized that connection when she duetted with Streisand on her 1997 album *Let's Talk About Love*. True to the diva tradition of early struggle, Celine Dion was brought up in extreme poverty in the Francophone village of Charlemagne in Quebec, the youngest of fourteen children. She used her powerful singing voice as a way out, and by the age of twelve had released her first album. A French-language star in her teens, she won the Eurovision Song Contest for Switzerland in 1988. At that point her career could have stalled, but through the advice of her manager René Angelil (whom she later married), Dion took a Berlitz course in basic English, and signed up with international record label Sony. A self-confessed 'hick from the sticks', she still had to work at attaining diva-esque stature. 'Even then, there was no question that she had the voice and technique necessary to be one of the world's great popular singers. What we needed to work on was the image,' said a diplomatic Paul Burger, CEO of Sony Entertainment UK, and then president of its Canadian equivalent.[31] We needed to develop the sort of personal style that would allow her to be marketed successfully to English-speaking audiences.' That meant not just having her teeth straightened and a more streamlined wardrobe, but a set of dramatic ballads and impeccably produced pop-dance numbers.

Three years later the slog paid off, and Dion broke through to the huge English-speaking market with her album *Unison*, and the follow-up *The Colour Of My Love* (which included the hits 'The Power Of Love' and 'Think Twice'). By 1996 she was a superstar, with the album *Falling Into You*, and later the theme song to the film *Titanic*. Critics were unimpressed with her high-octane performance (one remarked that it was 'too much ham on the bone'), but her worldwide audience loved the broad brushstrokes of emotion. 'Our Love Will Go On', her theme song to the film *Titanic*, for instance, is one of the most-requested songs for funerals. In 1998 she appeared to be unstoppable. In an interview with *Q* magazine, she compared her job to a game of golf. 'Playing golf is like showbusiness,' she said. 'You put a ball there, you . . . focus, and you need a lot of strength and concentration. Then when you're ready, you make your shot. And when it's done, you transfer your weight and the ball goes on forever . . .'[32]

**Mariah Carey:** poster girl for twenty-first-century pop divas. (Paul Bergen/ Redferns)

The other hyper-diva to emerge in the 1990s was Mariah Carey. The youngest of three children of an Irish opera singer and black/Hispanic Venezuelan father, she too encountered struggle early on with a difficult childhood. Her parents split up when she was three, partly under pressure of Long Island racists burning their cars. Her sister became a drug addict and a prostitute, while her brother had cerebral palsy. Childhood problems only drove Carey's desire to escape from the suburbs and to be heard. She sang backup for Brenda Starr, and came to the attention of Sony executive Tommy Mottola. Overwhelmed by Carey's eight-octave range and pussycat eyes, he signed her up, sent her into the studio for a year, left his family and married her. His old business partner Randy Hoffman became her manager.

Carey now claims that the first few albums she recorded were very much in Mottola's image – wholesome, sweet and full of vocal pyrotechnics. After winning a Grammy for Best New Artist in 1990 she went on to rack up fifteen No. 1 singles (rivalled only by the Beatles and Elvis in that regard), and sold 150 million albums. At the 2000 World Music Awards she was titled 'Best-selling Female Artist of the Millennium'. It was a major feat, but at a cost.

It seemed that Carey was a pop princess with the charmed life. 'It pisses me off when people try to make out it's this princess thing with this girl who walked into fame and never had to struggle. People have no clue about my personal struggles and what I continue to go through,' she said in 1997.[33] That year she left Tommy Mottola, anxious to be more than a trophy wife. Admitting that most of her output until then had been schmaltzy MOR', she changed tack, enlisting the help of hardcore rappers such as Wu Tang Clan's Ol' Dirty Bastard and Bone Thugs-N-Harmony to give her sound a more streetwise feel. Her 'divorce' album *Butterfly* was a long way from the smooth duets recorded with Luther Vandross and Boyz 11 Men. Although it still featured power ballads, her voice was more restrained, the production underscored by an R&B sensibility.

Carey's image also underwent a drastic overhaul, going from cute dresses to raunchy leather and tight tops. Although this signified her move from good girl to woman with 'total control', there was a hint of desperation in her provocative 'soft-porn' look. She finally moved out of Mottola's orbit when she left Sony and signed to Virgin in 2001. Despite her much-trumpeted independence, the pressure proved too much. She split from long-standing boyfriend Luis Miguel over her rumoured affair with rap star Eminem. Then in August 2001, during promotion for her debut Virgin album *Glitter*, she appeared rambling and incoherent. She had a breakdown, and, as the *National Enquirer* so delicately put it, was 'carted off to a mental ward'.

The divas of the 1990s were the apogee of a music industry marketing machine that had grown so sophisticated it could arrange artists' lives with military precision. For women performers, required constantly to look slim, sexy and be in good voice, the pressure is particularly intense. The perfectionist drive that helped to create their success in the first place can later become a physical and psychological trap. No wonder Carey went off the rails. No wonder Whitney Houston was rumoured to have drug problems. No wonder Celine Dion halted her punishing tour schedule in order to conceive a baby. Even in the rock world, top female artists were expected to present themselves with immaculate, diva-like attention to detail. 'I felt like my make-up had to be perfect, my lipstick perfect, that I had to be slim. People are constantly looking at you,' Cranberries singer Dolores O'Riordan told me. 'You can't look like crap, like Helena Bonham Carter. Women like her say, what the hell and go out in their runners and stuff. Coming from the country I felt I had to keep it together.'[34]

O'Riordan and her band came from rural Limerick in the west of Ireland, to take on the world. In 1993 their melodic, anthemic rock hit America with the Top 10 single 'Linger' and sales of their debut *Everybody Else Is Doing It, So Why Can't We?* propelled them into the superleague. At 20 years old, O'Riordan had sold 8 million albums and toured every major venue from the UK to Asia and Australia. By the time of the Cranberries' 1996 album *To The Faithful Departed*, they were playing 250 gigs a year, and the strain was beginning to show. An impossibly thin O'Riordan walked out of interviews and cancelled a worldwide tour. 'When you're young, you're naïve and presented with great opportunities. If you grow up in Hollywood you're used to that scenario. But I grew up in lush, green Ireland. I went from one extreme to the other. I was smiling, saying, I'm in control, but somewhere along the way the cheese slipped off my cracker.'

She stopped 'hiding and running', gave up the band for two years, and started a family. By the late 1990s she was back recording with the Cranberries – calmer and more relaxed. At the time of their fifth album, *Wake Up And Smell The Coffee* (2001), she admitted that women at the 'diva-end' of the business were vulnerable. 'We have biological clocks. We'd like to have a kid, but think, no, it'll ruin the career. You go away and it might all be gone. So we keep going and going, driving ourselves. We can't take maternity leave like any other job.'

In her absence, Irish band The Corrs stepped in, featuring three gorgeous sisters, Andrea, Sharon and Caroline, on lead vocals, violin and drums. Their sultry looks were perfectly groomed for the crossover Celtic pop/rock market, and their silky melodies sold millions. Their way of coping with success was to adopt a gracious but carefully guarded demeanour. Sharon Corr said the pressure of keeping a shiny family image intact meant that 'it was difficult to get that space', but they were willing to make that sacrifice. According to Andrea: 'I was going to study drama, something in the humanities, but sure I've learned more about drama and . . . humanity in the Corrs than I ever could have anywhere else.'[35]

Despite the rigours of diva-dom, after the millennium there were a host of new ones on the scene – from country goddesses like Shania Twain and Faith Hill, to flawlessly perfect live Barbies like Christina Aguilera, Jennifer Lopez and Britney Spears. Entering the pop business at the age of 29, Lopez was a relative old-timer. She had already carved out a lucrative career as a movie actress, though, and in 1998 when she starred opposite George Clooney in *Out Of Sight*, Lopez was the highest-paid Latino actress in history. She was born in the Bronx, of Puerto Rican descent, and dabbled in musical theatre as a child. By her teens she was a regular in TV dramas, and her smokey, photo-genic looks helped her land choice parts. Film exposure plus an ability to sing meant that the transition from movies to pop music with her 1999 album *On The 6* was fairly seamless. Of course it did no harm to her pop celebrity status to have a powerful boyfriend, 'the rap production supremo Puff Daddy. Her Latin-tinged 2001 sophomore album, *J. Lo*, was also a success – but there is a sense in which J. Lo, with her flyaway hair, famous bottom and rather average voice, was acting the part.

By contrast, Christina Aguilera and Britney Spears are in direct competition for real diva-hood. 'I never work out, although I should because I could do with some muscle tone, but I'm a singer, not a model,' Aguilera once said in a pointed dig at opportunist MAWs (Model/Actress/Whatevers).[36] She admitted that as a child she rehearsed her acceptance speeches in front of the mirror, and stressed: 'I'm here for the long haul.' The daughter of an Ecuador immigrant father who served in the military, Aguilera travelled the world before the family settled in Pennsylvania. As a child she sang at 'pool parties, block parties, anywhere people would have me', and at the age of twelve she went from local talent shows to singing on the Disney Channel's *New Mickey Mouse Club*, alongside Britney Spears and NSync's Justin Timberlake. By the time she was fifteen she had landed a record deal with RCA, and her 1999 self-titled debut scored a No. 1 hit with the single 'Genie In A Bottle'. The album sold 10 million its first year. It was the same year she sang in front of President Clinton at the Super Bowl game, and won a Grammy for Best New Artist. With her sonorous, surprisingly mature voice, Aguilera has the talent and the adaptability to be a diva. The follow-up to her debut was *Mi Reflejo*, a set of Spanish-language songs with some firing Latin remixes. She was determined to have longevity, but, ironically, it was her Mickey Mouse rival Britney Spears who most caught the popular imagination.

With her pneumatic grace and twenty-first-century Barbie-doll looks, Spears was the quintessential teen diva. There was something compulsive about her performance. A former gymnast, she had a shapely body and a robust constitution. She attacked dance routines with vim, vigour, and a strange kind of pent-up anger, and songs like 'Oops, I Did It Again' had a similar muscular quality. No shrinking violet or skinny super-model, she appealed directly to her teenage girl audience. The raunchy schoolgirl look she wore for her breakthrough hit video 'Baby One More Time' also proved irresistible to a male audience, as did the shiny red catsuit for 'Oops . . .' Her provocative lyrics, plus the fact that she hired soft-porn director Gregory Dark to shoot her video for 'From The Bottom Of My Broken Heart', implied that she was not so innocent. Coming from a

devout Baptist background, however, Spears protested that she was still a virgin. 'Marriage is a major commitment and I want to enter that commitment untouched,' she said. 'I really believe that true love waits.'[37] That mix of the virginal and the sexually aware made for an explosive combination. No wonder that 'Britney naked' became the most popular request typed into Internet search engines.

Born in 1981, in Kentwood, Louisiana, Spears was groomed for stardom early on. Although her family were poor, her mother Lynne scraped together money for dance lessons, and trawled Britney round the junior beauty pageant circuit. After years spent in local revues and church choirs, she worked as an off-Broadway child actor before joining the Mickey Mouse Club at eleven years old. She began auditioning for pop bands in her teens, and was offered a deal with Jive Records. Groomed by producer Eric Foster (Whitney Houston, Boyzone) and Swedish songwriting maestro Max Martin, Spears topped the US and UK charts at the beginning of 1999 with 'Baby One More Time', while her debut album *Baby One More Time* went on to sell 27 million copies. A determined star ('She's a fully-involved artist,' maintained her A&R man Steve Lunt; 'she comes up with the concepts for her live shows and videos'), Spears grafted with Madonna-like ambition to stay on top. 'I practised so hard I was almost delirious,' she once said of a night rehearsing a video routine.

The parallels with Madonna didn't stop with Spears' ability to work hard. Like her heroine, Spears wasn't shy about combining pop music with an assertive sexuality. Maybe that is why Madonna namechecked the younger diva by having 'Britney Spears' emblazoned in glitter on her T-shirt during promotional shows in 2000. 'I'd love to have a career like Madonna's,' gushed Spears. Out of all the young divas, she is the one that just might.

## Trickster

Madonna has proved to be the most enduring of the modern pop divas – always a self-aware populist, always at the centre of the mainstream, yet distinct from her rivals because of her ability to plug into subcultures and underground trends. In 1996, it looked like her dream of breaking Hollywood had come true, with her starring role in Alan Parker's film *Evita*. This was the new, chaste Madonna in traditional diva guise. Emoting from the presidential balcony in Buenos Aires, arms outstretched, singing to the crowd as Eva Peron, she summoned up the ghosts of 1940s and 1950s movie sirens, and harked back to the surface decorum of another age. When it became known that she was pregnant with her first child, Lourdes, the world was ready to take back a seemingly repentant Madonna after the debacle of her *Sex* book.

Only Madonna wasn't going to apologize. 'I wonder if I could ever have been the kind of sweet, submissive girl that the world

idealizes,' she mused in her *Vanity Fair* diary of the *Evita* shoot.[38] Later, when reflecting on the torrent of criticism following *Sex* (see Chapter 7), Madonna said: 'If in the middle of all that chaos some positive message got out, then I won. But it's not terribly much fun, being a rebel or being a pioneer . . . because you become a target for everyone's fears. You have to be incredibly resilient and there were times when I wished that I hadn't been so outspoken, because it was so exhausting to constantly have to defend myself.'[39] Madonna found liberation in the fact that she didn't have to court approval, but after a while she wished to retreat, to experience motherhood and personal fulfilment away from the celebrity treadmill.

Lourdes Maria Ciccone Leon was born on 14 October 1996, five months after the filming of *Evita* ended. For 38-year-old Madonna, this marked a new phase. The relationship with father Carlos didn't last, but Madonna's true focus was always on her daughter. Motherhood seemed to open up new parts of her character, with friends commenting on a 'kinder, gentler' Madonna. The star said that Lourdes was a healing influence on her life, and named after a memory of her mother. 'Lourdes was a place that my mother had a connection to. People were always sending her holy water from there. She always wanted to go there but never did.' At this time Madonna gave up her relentless schedule at the gym and took up Ashtanga yoga. She also reassessed the function of fame in her life, studying the Kabbalah and exploring a more spiritual path.

Her detractors said that musically she was all washed-up, but, still keeping a weather eye on dancefloor trends, she made one of the strongest records of her career. For *Ray Of Light* she eschewed big name pop producers in favour of William Orbit, then a cult producer on the British dance scene, famed for his electronic soundscapes. In collaborating with him, Madonna delved deeper into her musical persona, creating a set of songs that reflected the optimistic beats and sparkling innovation of rave culture. As she had done with the *Like A Prayer* album ten years earlier, Madonna resurrected memories of her mother, only this time she went to the darker side. 'Mer Girl' is a chilling *pièce de résistance* about confronting the death of her mother from cancer, along with the fear that drove Madonna to the top. When she recorded it, Orbit knew she had crashed through a personal barrier. 'She stepped out of the vocal booth, and everybody was rooted to the spot,' he later recalled. 'It was just one of those moments. Really spooky.'[40]

1998's *Ray Of Light* certainly rehabilitated Madonna's image. Up to that point she had still been written off as an average pop glamour girl who got lucky, but with this record she reached a whole new audience, proving that she was a good songwriter with an intensely productive talent.

Fired up by the critical and commercial success of *Ray of Light*, Madonna was soon back in the studio. Again, she picked a left-field producer to help realize her sound. To her, the electronic bubble funk of French writer/producer Mirwais Ahmadzai was 'the sound of the future'. An experimental artist from an avant-garde punk background, he later admitted that

Madonna 'took a big risk with someone like me. When you arrive at that kind of level of celebrity, you can just work in the mainstream, and just stay there. Everything . . . for her is like a challenge.'[41] Madonna again enlisted the help of William Orbit, and by the end of January 2000 had completed *Music*, her tenth studio album. A mix of electronic pop, sparse, funky grooves, and acoustic balladry, this was more 'uptown' than *Ray Of Light*. The title track, especially, with its nod to 1980s disco, was an anthemic call to arms, celebrating the rush of the dancefloor.

Madonna knew she had a hit on her hands. Soon after recording she sat in an LA restaurant and told friends: 'I have to stay current . . . God help me, but I guess I have to share radio air time with Britney Spears and Christina Aguilera. What choice do I have?' When it was suggested that she retire, she joked: 'But what would the music business be without me'.[42] The year 2000 was shaping up to be important. Her romance with British film director Guy Ritchie became headline news when it was announced that he was the father of her second child. In August she gave birth to a boy, Rocco, and despite the fact he arrived two weeks early because Madonna was haemorrhaging with a condition known as placenta previa, by September she had recovered and was celebrating the release of her album, along with Ritchie's new film *Snatch*.

Madonna was on a roll. In November she performed an 'intimate' gig at London's Brixton Academy to 3500 fans and press, and several million worldwide on the Internet. In December, amid a feverish blast of publicity, she married Ritchie at a closely guarded ceremony at Skibo Castle in the Scottish Highlands. In a bizarre bid to join the ranks of the British upper class (she had always admired Princess Diana), she took up clay-pigeon shooting and bought a country estate famed for its grouse-shooting. This move towards the old-fashioned Establishment seemed an odd direction to take, considering her love of cutting-edge arts and culture – but then Madonna has always thrived on contradiction. Like the ultimate diva, she goes grouse-shooting and makes leftfield pop because, well, she can.

By the summer of 2001, she embarked on the Drowned World tour, a multi-media spectacular that took in avant-garde operatic sets, Country & Western line-dancing, and a nostalgic reprise of 'Holiday' and the early 1980s New York Danceteria scene that spawned her. She concluded with the sparkling neo-disco of 'Music', while projected on a huge screen behind her was image after image: Madonna the Virgin, the Material Girl, the *Vogue* dancer, the tortured Mary Magdalen, the cross-dresser, and the conical-busted Blond Ambition. On one level it could be seen as crowing – move over Kylie, Britney *et al.*, this here's the Queen of Pop. But on another, it was Madonna showing that, despite accusations of bimbo-dom, she was an artist with longevity and an aesthetic sensibility. She was also sending a clear message that marriage and motherhood did *not* mean retirement. She was still a major influence on women in pop. As singer Liz Phair one said: 'Madonna is the speedboat, and the rest of us are just the Go-Go's on waterskis.'[43]

On the post-millennial music scene, it became apparent that a new generation (dubbed the Third Wave) was looking to rock music and popular culture, rather than academic text, for its feminist idols. 'Early feminism was text-driven. There were all kinds of theoretical polemicists people had to read and keep up on,' said US academic Camille Paglia,[44] referring to books like Andrea Dworkin's *Pornography*, Mary Daly's *Gyn/Ecology* and, of course, Germaine Greer's *Female Eunuch*. 'Feminists should be concerned about the personalities in rock 'n' roll because they will be the primary means by which young women get the feminist message,' Paglia went on to say. According to New York cultural critic Cathay Che, female rock icons 'push the frontiers of what it means to be female'.[45]

Though top stars like Madonna and Chrissie Hynde ('she's a tough broad, the ultimate role model,' said Paglia) were inspirational figures, it was also less well-known acts like Le Tigre, Sleater-Kinney and Bratmobile, women rooted in left-field music and subculture, who fired up a younger feminist genera-tion. In 2000 in Olympia, Washington, site of the first Riot Grrrl meetings, Ladyfest was born. A festival of feminist arts and rock, it attracted a crowd of 3000. 'It was the most inspiring and empowering week of my life,' says Lee Beattie, who promptly went back to the UK and organized Ladyfest 2001 in her home town of Glasgow. A committee of seventeen young women worked hard fundraising and making links with other Ladyfest events that year in Chicago, New York and Indiana. Beattie stresses that they were not organizing a new Lilith Fair. 'Lilith draws more on acoustic artists, it's more mainstream and less grassroots. Ladyfest is back to basics. Half of our acts are unsigned.'[46] When I spoke to her in 2001, Riot Grrrl had already become 'hidden history'. Beattie was thirteen when Riot Grrrl was 'at its height', and didn't discover it until she was seventeen years old. In the way that much of women's music history has to be periodically resuscitated, she ironically found out about Riot Grrrl through reading the first edition of *She Bop*. 'I see Ladyfest as a continuation of that movement, a continuation of Third Wave.'

One of the best-attended workshops of the festival was 'Feminism and Identity'. 'Initially girls had just come for the music, then after the workshop discussion, they realized that feminism is not what the media says it is,' asserts Beattie. 'It was perceived as rooted in academia. If you hadn't read Betty Friedan, you weren't a real feminist. Everyone appreciates '70s feminism – without it Riot Grrrl wouldn't have existed – but there were too many regimented rules about what to wear or who to sleep with. Now feminism is about how you lead your life, there's room for everyone, and we have more role models to draw on.'

By 2001, these young bands were acknowledging the potency of musical history – Le Tigre, for instance, whose sharp pop-punk stage show featured slides of past heroines like Audrey Hepburn, the B52s, Delta 5 and the Go-Gos. UK outfit Electrelane, meanwhile, namechecked everyone from Bessie Smith to Dusty Springfield, Gertrude Stein and Virginia Woolf on their debut album *Rock It To The Moon*. 'We have to make a statement about women's achievement,' said their drummer Emma Gaze.

Despite all the gains made by women in previous decades, Electrelane were still coming up against the same problems: 'It's hard to start doing it and for people to take you seriously. Men aren't particularly welcoming. And if that negative attitude is the first thing you encounter, that'll stop you carrying on,' says Gaze.[47]

The band, however, fought their way through to the first level, releasing a debut of mesmerizing, abstract rock in 2001 to critical acclaim. Most of their songs are instrumentals with electronic beats and swathes of krautrock-style cyclical guitar. No vocals means that their music can be androgynous, giving them the freedom from being judged by gender. 'We didn't want to be clichéd women singing sad little love songs,' says keyboardist Verity Susman. For them, liberation came when they stopped worrying about male approval. 'We don't get embarrassed or belittled at soundchecks now. We had to toughen up. A lot of women don't even get to that point,' adds Susman.

For those who push past initial hurdles, there is a rich lineage to draw on. From the late 1980s, artists such as Tori Amos, Sinéad O'Connor and PJ Harvey (who went on to win the coveted Mercury Music Prize award in 2001 for her album *Stories From The City, Stories From The Sea*) opened up pathways. This led to the outpouring of 'angry rock' from acts spanning Babes in Toyland and Hole to Ani DiFranco (see Chapter 12), Alanis Morissette and Fiona Apple. 'It almost gets competitive,' observed Amos. 'Well, what happened to you? The billboard of pain. The media try and make it a catfight, but we turn on ourselves before men even need to lift a finger by saying "So and so's copying me". If you know what you've contributed you can hold that inside yourself. You owe that to your soul.'[48]

Amos is modest about her role. 'The younger artists – they're all very unique women with their own take on it, with their own language and story to tell. Listen, there's room for everyone to claim their own story, there cannot be a hierarchy.' Effectively summing up the importance of a women's history, she says: 'Some have paved ways, and women before me have taken their machete into the jungle, parts of the jungle that are not so traversed, like Kate Bush and Joni Mitchell. Other offshoots, Alanis and Fiona made their own. You honour the women before you and after you. There isn't a copyright on this story.'

# Notes

In the case of author interviews, only the initial quotes have been sourced.

INTRODUCTION

1 Garratt, Sheryl, 'Je ne regrette rien', *Face*, October 1994.

## 1 RIFFIN' THE SCOTCH

1 Feinstein, Elaine, *Bessie Smith: Empress of the Blues* (Penguin, London, 1985), p. 29.
2 From *Brown Sugar: The Beginnings*, Channel 4, 3 September 1988.
3 Author interview, New York, 1993.
4 Feinstein, *Bessie Smith*, p. 95.
5 Garon, Paul and Beth, *Woman with Guitar: Memphis Minnie's Blues* (Da Capo Press, New York, 1992), p. 84.
6 Penman, Ian, 'In My Billie-tude', *Wire*, March 1992.
7 Holiday, Billie, with William Dufty, *Lady Sings the Blues* (Penguin, London, 1984), p. 9.
8 *Ibid.*, p. 86.
9 From *Arena: Billie Holiday – The Long Night of Lady Day*, BBC2, 9 November 1984.
10 Holiday, *Lady Sings the Blues*, p. 24.
11 Author interview, London, 1994.
12 O'Day, Anita, with George Eells, *High Times, Hard Times* (Limelight Editions, New York, 1993), p. 272.
13 Shapiro, Harry, *Waiting for the Man: The Story of Drugs and Popular Music* (Quartet, London, 1988), p. 83.
14 Holiday, *Lady Sings the Blues*, p. 119.
15 White, John, *Billie Holiday: Her Life and Times* (Omnibus Press, London, 1987), p. 64
16 *Ibid.*, p. 76.
17 Author interview, London, 1993.
18 *Ibid.*, 1994.
19 *Ibid.*, New York, 1994.
20 *Ibid.*, London, 1993.
21 Gillett, Charlie, *The Sound of the City* (Souvenir Press, London, 1983), p. 251.
22 Fordham, John, Ivy Benson Obituary, *Guardian*, 7 May 1993.

23 Author interview, Surrey, 1993.
24 Letter from Gracie Cole's private collection, 28 August 1952, Surrey.
25 Author interview, London, 1993.
26 *Ibid.*


**2** STUPID CUPID

1 O'Day, Anita, with George Eells, *High Times, Hard Times* (Limelight Editions, New York, 1993), p. 102.
2 Author interview, London, 1993.
3 *Ibid.*
4 *Ibid.*
5 Lee, Peggy, *Miss Peggy Lee* (Bloomsbury, London, 1990), pp. 54–5.
6 *Ibid.*, p. 126.
7 Caron, Sandra, *Alma Cogan: A Memoir* (Bloomsbury, London, 1991), p. 19.
8 *Ibid.*, p. 57.
9 *Ibid.*, p. 65.
10 Haskins, James, with Kathleen Benson, *Lena: A Biography of Lena Horne* (Scarborough House Publishers, Lanham, Maryland, 1991), p. 152.
11 *Ibid.*, p. 137.
12 Author interview, New York, 1994.
13 *Ibid.*, London, 1994.
14 *Ibid.*, 1989.
15 *Ibid.*, 1992.
16 *Ibid.*
17 *Ibid.*, Sunningdale, 1988.
18 *Ibid.*, London, 1988.
19 *Ibid.*, Los Angeles, 1988.


**3** THE REAL THING

1 *Concise Oxford English Dictionary* (Oxford University Press, Oxford, 1976).
2 Author interview, New York, 1993.
3 Douglas, Susan, *Where the Girls Are: Growing up Female with the Mass Media* (Times Books, New York, 1994), p. 77.
4 Hoerburger, Rob, 'Power of Love', *Guardian Weekend*, 24 July 1993.
5 *Ibid.*
6 Joel, Billy, in the Introduction to Spector, Ronnie, with Vince Waldron, *Be My Baby* (Pan, London, 1991), pp. xiii–xiv.
7 From *Top Ten Girl Groups*, Channel 4, January 2000.
8 Ribowsky, Mark, *He's a Rebel: The Truth about Phil Spector, Rock and Roll's Legendary Madman* (E.P. Dutton, New York, 1989), p. 273.
9 *Ibid.*
10 *Ibid.*
11 Clarke, Donald, ed., *The Penguin Encyclopedia of Popular Music* (Viking, London, 1989), p. 1054.
12 Hirshey, Gerri, *Nowhere to Run: The Story of Soul Music* (Pan, London, 1984), p. 140.

13  Grieg, Charlotte, *Will You Still Love Me Tomorrow?: Girl Groups from the 50s On . . .* (Virago, London, 1989), p. 105.
14  Author interview, London, 1994.
15  *Ibid.*, Los Angeles, 1993.
16  Sullivan, Caroline, 'Miss Ross the Boss', *Guardian*, 1 December 1993.
17  Reitz, Rosetta, sleevenotes to album *Sincerely, Sister Rosetta Tharpe* (Women's Heritage Series, 1988).
18  Williams, Stacey, 'The Queen of Gospel', *New Musical Express (NME)*, 4 March 1972.
19  Jones IV, James T., 'Soul of the Queen', *Vanity Fair*, March 1994.
20  Tobler, John, and Grundy, Stuart, *The Record Producers* (BBC Books, London, 1982), p. 31.
21  From *The Atlantic Story*, Channel 4, 2 September 1993.
22  Author interview, London, 1988.
23  *Ibid.*
24  *Ibid.*
25  *Ibid.*, 1989.
26  Smith, Giles, 'The Only Bird in a Beat Boy's World', *Independent*, 12 October 1993.
27  Author interview, London, 1986.
28  Patrick, Mick, 'The Buddhist, the Aristocrat and the Blonde That Shocked Coventry', *That Will Never Happen Again*, Nos. 5/6, 1988.
29  Unpublished interview with writer Patrick Humphries, Dublin, 1994.
30  Author interview, New York 1993.

## 4  CAN THE CAN

1  Joplin, Laura, *Love, Janis* (Bloomsbury, London, 1992), p. 191.
2  Author interview, Santa Cruz, 1999.
3  *Ibid.*
4  Tyler, Andrew, 'Growing Old Gracefully', *NME*, 14 June 1980.
5  Elliott, Paul, 'Queen of the Stoned Age', *Q*, May 2001.
6  Author interview, London, 1993.
7  Grieg, Charlotte, 'A La Moe', *Guardian*, 1 June 1993.
8  Smith, Patti, 'We Can Be Heroes', *Details*, July 1993.
9  *Ibid.*
10  *Ibid.*
11  O'Brien, Lucy, 'How We Met: John Cale and Patti Smith', *Independent on Sunday*, 25 August 1996.
12  *Ibid.*
13  Pearson, Deanne, 'Women in Rock', *NME*, 29 March 1980.
14  Stambler, Irwin, *The Encyclopedia of Pop, Rock and Soul* (Macmillan, London 1989), p. 622.
15  Author interview, New York, 1993.
16  *Ibid.*, 1996.
17  Tobler, John, and Grundy, Stuart, *The Record Producers* (BBC Books, London 1982), p. 201.
18  Author interview, London, 1993 .

19  Tobler and Grundy, *The Record Producers.*
20  Martin, Gavin, 'Whomping the Suckers with a Superball', *NME*, 10 April 1982.
21  Townsend, Martin, 'Simply the Best', *Daily Mirror*, 17 February 1992.
22  Cleave, Maureen, 'Tina the Brave', *Observer*, 14 September 1986.
23  Toop, David, 'Out of the Blues', *Sunday Times*, 23 February 1992.
24  *Ibid.*
25  Author interview, New York, 1994.
26  *Ibid.*, Boston, 1993.
27  *Ibid.*, London, 1994.
28  Henke, James, 'Bonnie Raitt, the *Rolling Stone* Interview', *Rolling Stone*, 3 May 1990.

**5**   FINAL GIRLS

1  Author interview, London, 1990.
2  O'Brien, Lucy, 'The Woman Punk Made Me', ed. Sabin, Roger, *Punk Rock, So What?* (Routledge, London and New York, 1999), p. 185.
3  Author interview, Seaford, 2001.
4  O'Brien, 1999, p. 193.
5  Author interview, London, 1986.
6  Author interview, London, 2001.
7  Nicholls, Jill, and Toothpaste, Lucy, 'I Play the Vocals', *Spare Rib*, June 1979.
8  *Ibid.*
9  Author interview, London, 1998.
10  Author interview, London, 1990.
11  Gaar, Gillian G., *She's a Rebel: The History of Women in Rock & Roll* (Blandford Press, London, 1993), p. 259.
12  Mareus, Greil, *In the Fascist Bathroom: Writings on Punk 1977–1992* (Viking, London, 1993), p. 107.
13  Burston, Paul, 'Lightning Strikes Twice', *Guardian Weekend*, 23 January 1999.
14  Iley, Chrissy, 'An End to Blonde Ambition', *You Magazine*, 11 July 1993.
15  Burston, 1999.
16  *Ibid.*
17  Wrenn, Mike, *The Pretenders: With Hyndesight* (Omnibus Press, London, 1989), p. 10.
18  Unpublished interview with writer Patrick Humphries, Dublin, 1994.
19  O'Brien, Lucy, 'The Great Pretender', *Guardian*, 27 April 1999.
20  Wrenn, *The Pretenders*, p. 16.
21  *Ibid.*, p. 31.
22  Cavanagh, David, 'Special So Special', *Q*, May 1994.
23  O'Brien, 'The Great Pretender', 1999.
24  Author interview, New York, 1994.
25  Pearson, Deanne, 'Women in Rock', *NME*, 29 March 1980.
26  Author interview, London, 1997.
27  Author interview, London, 1994.
28  *Ibid.*, 1987.

29  *Ibid.*, 1990.
30  O'Brien, Lucy, 'Bad Girls Sing the Blues', *Diva*, April/May 1997.
31  Author interview, London, 1993.
32  Pearson, 'Women in Rock'.
33  Evans, Liz, 'Borrrn in the (Med)USA', *NME*, 13 March 1993.
34  Reynolds, Simon, 'Clarity's Angel', *Wire*, March 1992.
35  Author interview, London, 2001.
36  Author interview, New York, for *The Ballad of John & Yoko*, BBC2, 6 January 1998.
37  Author interview, London, 1990.
38  Juno, Andrea, and Vale, V., eds., *Angry Women* (Re/Search Publications, San Francisco, September 1991), p. 106.
39  Author interview, London, 1984.
40  Juno and Vale, *Angry Women*, p. 21.
41  *Ibid.*, p. 17.
42  Author interview, London, 1997.
43  Evans, 'Borrrn in the (Med)USA'.
44  Blase, Cazz, 'Beginnings', essay from unpublished book on Riot Grrrl, *Screaming in Public*, 1998.
45  Author interview, London, 1994.
46  Corrigan, Susan, 'Who Are the Riot Grrrls?' *i-D*, April 1993.
47  Author interview, London, 1994.
48  Wolf, Naomi, *The Beauty Myth* (Chatto & Windus, 1990/Vintage, London, 1991), pp. 201–2. Reproduced by kind permission of Chatto & Windus.
49  Author interview, London, 1993 .
50  *Ibid.*, 1994.
51  *Ibid.*, 1993.
52  Evans, Liz, 'Rage Against the Man Machine', *NME*, 6 March 1993.
53  Author interview, Los Angeles, 1993.
54  *Ibid.*, Almeria, Spain, 1986.
55  Fax to author, from Seattle, 14 April 1993.
56  Gumbol, Andrew, 'Will She Rock Their World?', *Independent on Sunday*, 4 March 2001.
57  Baillie, Stuart, 'She Puts On Women's Clothing', *NME*, 24 April 1993.
58  *Ibid.*
59  *Ibid.*

**6**  LADIES OF THE CANYON

1  Woolf, Virginia, *A Room of One's Own* (Panther, London, 1980), p. 90.
2  Author interview, London, 1994.
3  Mellers, Wilfrid, *Angels of the Night: Popular Female Singers of Our Time* (Basil Blackwell, Oxford, 1986), p. 141.
4  Echols, Alice, 'Thirty Years with a Portable Lover', *LA Weekly*, 25 November–1 December 1994.
5  From *Top Ten Girl Groups*, Channel 4, January 2000.
6  Mayes, Sean, *Joan Armatrading: A Biography* (Weidenfeld & Nicolson, London, 1990), p. 33.

7   *Ibid.*, p. 38.
8   Author interview, Birmingham, 1992.
9   *Ibid.*, London, 1988.
10  Collins, Jim, *Uncommon Cultures: Popular Culture of Post Modernism* (Routledge, New York/London, 1989).
11  Jonssen, Marianne, 'Rubber Souls', *Vox*, November 1993.
12  Solanas, Jane, 'The Barmy Dreamer', *NME*, 15 October 1983.
13  Vermorel, Fred, *The Secret History of Kate Bush (And the Strange Art of Pop)* (Omnibus Press, London, 1983), p. 87.
14  *Ibid.*, p. 85.
15  *Ibid.*, p. 92.
16  O'Brien, Lucy, 'The Mad Life and Crazy Death of Tammy Wynette', *Q*, August 1999.
17  *Ibid.*
18  *Ibid.*
19  Author interviews, London, 1992 and 1993.
20  *Ibid.*, New York, 1993.
21  *Ibid.*, London, 1993.
22  *Ibid.*, Toronto, 1993.
23  *Ibid.*, London, 1988.
24  Caveney, Graham, 'Nanci Griffith', *City Limits*, 12–19 September 1991.
25  From *Righteous Babes*, Channel 4, 22 December 1998.
26  Author interview, London, 2001
27  O'Brien, Lucy, 'Call of the Wild', *Vox*, October 1995.
28  Author interview, New York, 2000.


7   LIPSTICK TRACES

1   Author interview, London, 1993.
2   Lurie, Alison, *The Language of Clothes* (Bloomsbury, London, 1992), p. 213.
3   Harris, Thomas, 'The Building of Popular Images: Grace Kelly and Marilyn Monroe' in *Stardom, Industry of Desire*, Gledhill, Christine, ed. (Routledge, London/New York, 1991), p. 43.
4   Dellar, Fred, 'Why "Unprofessional" Mamas & Papas Had to Break Up', *NME*, 24 June 1972.
5   Mayes, Sean, *Joan Armatrading: A Biography* (Weidenfeld & Nicolson, London, 1990), p. 51.
6   *Ibid.*
7   Author interview, Birmingham, 1992.
8   Clarke, Steve, 'Kate Bush City Limits', *NME*, 25 March 1978.
9   Kent, Nick, 'Summer Sweethearts', *NME*, 22 September 1973.
10  Tyler, Andrew, 'Hi, I'm Karen. Fly me', *NME*, 16 February 1974.
11  Kinnersley, Simon, 'A Death Too Cruel', *News of the World*, 20 November 1983.
12  Driscoll, Margarette, 'My Sister Karen', *Daily Mirror*, 8 October 1983.
13  Orbach, Susie, *Hunger Strike* (Faber & Faber, London, 1986).
14  Kinnlersley, 'A Death Too Cruel'.
15  Eliot, Marc, *Rockonomics: The Money Behind the Music* (Omnibus Press, London, 1990), p. 188.

16 *Ibid.*, p. 193.
17 Paglia, Camille, 'Madonna II: Venus of the Radio Waves', in *Sex, Art and American Culture* (Penguin, London, 1993), p. 9.
18 Kinnersley, Simon, 'The Real Madonna: "I Just Call Her Daisy"', *Mail on Sunday*, 1989.
19 *Ibid.*
20 *Ibid.*
21 'Madonna Speaks!!!', *Smash Hits*, 28 June–11 July 1989.
22 *Ibid.*
23 Author interview, New York, 1994.
24 *Ibid.*, London, 1994.
25 *Ibid.*, 1988.
26 Hill, Dave, *Prince: A Pop Life* (Faber & Faber, London, 1988), pp. 128–9.
27 Jones, Dylan, 'God's Gift?', *Observer Magazine*, 11 April 1993.
28 Author interview, London, 1990.
29 Page, Betty, 'The Witch Report', *NME*, 9 May 1992.
30 Cosgrove, Stuart, 'Only Women Bleed', *NME*, 16 August 1986.
31 Author interview, London, 1994.
32 *Ibid.*
33 *Ibid.*
34 Marks, Craig, 'Girls On Film', *Spin*, April 1993.
35 Author interview, London, 1994.
36 *Ibid.*
37 Duerdon, Nick, 'Wish You Were Here?', *Q*, September 1999.
38 Agnew, Katie, 'The C Word', *Marie Claire*, October 2000.
39 O'Brien, Lucy, 'The Great Pretender', *Guardian*, 27 April 1999.
40 O'Brien, Lucy, 'Billie No Mates?', *Q*, July 2000.
41 Author interview, London, 1997.
42 Leerhsen, Charles, with Jennifer Foote and Peter McKillop, 'The Many Faces of Cher', *Newsweek*, 30 November 1987.
43 Jackson, Alan, 'Dress Minimal, Stay the Course', *The Times*, 27 April 1992.
44 Iley, Chrissy, 'An End to Blonde Ambition', *You Magazine*, 11 July 1993.
45 Author interview, London, 1993.
46 *Ibid.*, Minneapolis, 1988.
47 *Ibid.*, London, 1988.
48 *Ibid.*
49 Rubin, Julie, 'Making Up With Mom', *Pawholes* (Back to School issue, 1992).
50 Author interview, London, 1994.
51 Grace, Della, panel contribution to 'Unwrapping Sex', ICA discussion on Madonna's *Sex*, 30 March 1993.
52 Garratt, Sheryl, 'Je ne regrette rien', *Face*, October 1994.
53 Mailer, Norman, 'Mailer Meets Madonna', *Esquire*, September 1994.
54 Sandall, Robert, 'Let's Get Metaphysical', *Sunday Times*, 19 May 1991.

**8**   SHE WEARS THE TROUSERS

1  Garratt, Sheryl, 'Je ne regrette rien', *Face*, October 1994.
2  Author interview, London, 1994.
3  Garber, Marjorie, *Vested Interests, Cross-Dressing and Cultural Anxiety* (Penguin, London, 1993), p. 367.
4  Bowie, Angela, with Patrick Carr, *Backstage Passes: Life on the Wild Side with David Bowie* (Orion, London, 1993), p. 23.
5  *Ibid.*, p. 5.
6  Kirk, Kris, 'The Dyke, the Weightlifter and the Chocolate Button', *That Will Never Happen Again*, Nos. 5/6, London, 1988.
7  Author interview, Los Angeles, 1989.
8  *Ibid.*, Nashville.
9  O'Brien, Lucy, *Dusty* (Sidgwick & Jackson, London, 1989), p. 157.
10  Bronson, Fred, ed., *The Billboard Book of No. 1 Hits*, third edition (Guinness Publishing, New York, 1992), p. 324.
11  Gaar, Gillian G., *She's a Rebel: The History of Women in Rock & Roll* (Blandford Press, London, 1993), p. 125.
12  Savage, Jon, *England's Dreaming: Sex Pistols and Punk Rock* (Faber & Faber, London, 1991), p. 61.
13  McKenna, Kristine, 'The Ice Lady', *NME*, 25 June 1983.
14  *Ibid.*
15  O'Brien, Lucy, *Annie Lennox* (Sidgwick & Jackson, London, 1991), p. 77.
16  Author interview, London, 1989.
17  *Ibid.*
18  O'Brien, *Annie Lennox*, p. 77.
19  Author interview, London, 1990.
20  *Ibid.*, Cannes, 1989.
21  *Ibid.*, London, 1994.
22  O'Brien, Lucy, 'A Woman Called Horse', *Diva*, November 1999.
23  Smyth, Cherry, 'Phranc and Still Gutsy', *Capital Gay*, 11 October 1991.
24  Author interview, London, 1990.
25  Bennett, Leslie, 'k.d. lang Cuts It Close', *Vanity Fair*, August 1993.
26  Starr, Victoria, *k.d. lang: All You Get Is Me* (HarperCollins, London, 1994), p. 82.
27  Author interview, London, 1993.
28  Starr, *k.d. lang*, p. 238.
29  Bennahum, David, *k.d. lang: An Illustrated Biography* (Omnibus Press, London, 1993), p. 43.
30  O'Brien, Lucy, 'One of the Boys', *Guardian*, 3 November 1995.
31  *Ibid.*
32  Author interview, New York, 1993.
33  Powell, Vicky, 'The Sister's Doing It For Herself', *Diva*, July 2001.
34  O'Brien, Lucy, 'The Year Skunk Broke', in Liz Evans (ed.), *Girls Will Be Boys: Women Report on Rock* (Pandora, London, 1997), p. 129.
35  From *Righteous Babes*, Channel 4, 22 December 1998.

**9**   I WANNA DANCE WITH SOMEBODY

1 Author interview, NewYork, 1992.
2 *Ibid.*, London, 1993.
3 *Ibid.*, Rotterdam, 1987.
4 *Ibid.*, London, 1987.
5 *Ibid.*, 1994.
6 Ferguson, Sheila, *Soul Food, Classic Cuisine of the American South* (Weidenfeld & Nicolson, London/NewYork, 1989).
7 From *Top Ten Girl Groups*, Channel 4, January 2000.
8 *Ibid.*
9 Grieg, Charlotte, *Will You Still Love Me Tomorrow?: Girl Groups from the 50s On . . .* (Virago, London, 1989), p. 167.
10 Silver, Dorian, 'Disco Divas', *DJ Magazine*, 11–24 March 1993.
11 Author interview, NewYork, 1994.
12 Dando, Sue, 'It's Whitney Houston's Dad!', *Smash Hits*, 6 April 1988.
13 Rynning, Roald, 'The Making of Whitney', *Record Mirror*, 9 April 1988.
14 DeVries, Hilary, 'Miss Conception', *Time Out*, 16–30 December 1992.
15 Jobey, Liz, 'Still Got the Look', *Independent on Sunday*, 25 October 1992.
16 O'Brien, Lucy, 'Sade', www.nmesoul.com, December 2000.
17 O'Brien, Lucy, 'Essence of Eve', *City Limits*, 13–20 October 1988.
18 Author interview, London, 1987.
19 *Ibid.*, NewYork, 1987.
20 *Ibid.*
21 *Ibid.*, London, 1987.
22 Andrews, Bart, with J. Randy Taraborrelli: *Out of the Madness: The Strictly Unauthorized Biography of Janet* (Headline, London, 1994), p. 125.
23 *Ibid.*, p. 135.
24 *Ibid.*, p. 79.
25 Jonssen, Marianne, 'The Girls En Top', *Vox*, September 1993.
26 Author interview, London, 1993.
27 *Ibid.*, 1994.
28 *Ibid.*, Atlanta, Georgia, 1994.
29 *Ibid.*, London, 1993.
30 *Ibid.*
31 *Ibid.*
32 *Ibid.*
33 Hirshey, Gerri, *We Gotta Get Out of This Place* (Atlantic Monthly Press, New York, 2001), p. 234.
34 Raftery, Brian, 'Lauryn Hill AMG Biography', www.allmusic.com, October 2000.
35 Hirshey, p. 243.
36 Le Gendre, Kevin, 'Mother Earth', *Marie Claire*, March 2001.
37 Deevoy, Adrian, 'Nice Planet, I'll Take It', *Q*, March 2000.
38 *Ibid.*
39 O'Brien, Lucy, 'Top Ten Soul Classics', www.amazon.co.uk, March 2000.
40 Goldman, Vivien, 'Mary J. Blige', The 30th Anniversary, *Rolling Stone*, 13 November 1997.

41  O'Brien, Lucy, 'Hit and Miss', *Style* magazine, *Sunday Times*, 4 April 1999.
42  O'Brien, Lucy, 'Invasion of the Booty-Snatchers', *Q*, November 2000.
43  From *Destiny's Child: MTV Video Diaries*, Channel 5, September 2001.

**10** IN SEARCH OF OUR MOTHERS' GARDENS

1  Author interview, London, 1989.
2  *Ibid.*, New York, 1987.
3  *Ibid.*, London, 1987.
4  *Ibid.*
5  *Ibid.*, Los Angeles, 1993.
6  *Ibid.*, London, 1993.
7  *Ibid.*, New York, 1993.
8  Fadele, Dele, 'Every Dogg Has His Dre', *NME*, 14 May 1994.
9  Jones, Ann, and Neuborne, Ellen, 'Is This Power Feminism?', *Ms.*, Vol. IV. No. 6. 1994.
10  Author interview, New York, 1994.
11  *Ibid.*, 1993.
12  Rose, Tricia, 'Contracting Rap (an interview with Carmen Ashhurst-Watson)', in *Microphone Fiends*, Ross, Andrew, and Rose, Tricia, eds. (Routledge, New York/London, 1994), p. 144.
13  Malone, Bonz, 'Original Flavor', *Source*, May 1994.
14  Author interview, Los Angeles, 1994.
15  Walker, Alice, *In Search of Our Mothers' Gardens* (The Women's Press, London, 1984), p. 232. Reproduced by kind permission of The Women's Press.
16  Morrison, Toni, *Jazz* (Knopf, New York, 1992; Picador, London, 1993), p. 8. Reproduced by kind permission of Chatto & Windus.
17  Harris, Julius, 'Lullabies That Wake You Up', *Interview*, September 1993.
18  Davies, David, 'War Cry', *i-D*, May 1991.
19  Author interview, New York, 1994.
20  *Ibid.*, London, 1993.
21  *Ibid.*, Amsterdam, 1988.
22  hooks, bell, 'Selling Hot Pussy', in *Black Looks: Race and Representation* (South End Press, Boston/Turnaround, London, 1992), pp. 63–5.
23  Marriott, Robert, 'Studio Hoez', *Source*, May 1994.
24  From *Hot Wax: The Notorious Lil' Kim*, BBC 1, September 2001.
25  *Ibid.*
26  Capper, A., Fadele, D. and Robinson, J., 'Got Beef?', *NME*, 30 June 2001.
27  Mulvey, John, 'I Want My Music To Be a Drug', *NME*, 31 March 2001.
28  *Ibid.*
29  Sullivan, Caroline, 'Why the Biggest Music Is Anti-women', *Cosmopolitan*, April 1994.
30  Author interview, London, 1994.
31  *Ibid.*, New York, 1994.
32  Oumano, Elena, 'Daughters of the Dance', *Vibe*, September 1993.
33  Author interview, Kingston, Jamaica, 1994.
34  Johnson, Howard, and Pines, Jim, *Reggae: Deep Roots Music* (Proteus Books, London, 1982), p. 95.

35  Author interview, London, 1994.
36  *Ibid.*, Kingston, Jamaica, 1994.
37  *Ibid.*, London, 1993.


**11** OYE MI CANTO

 1  Graham, Ronnie, ed., *Stern's Guide to Contemporary African Music*, Vol. 2: *The World of African Music* (Pluto Press, London, 1992), p. 85.
 2  Author interview, London, 1994.
 3  *Ibid.*, Paris, 1993.
 4  Graham, *The World of African Music*, p. 14.
 5  Author interview, Brussels, 1994.
 6  *Ibid.*, London, 1994.
 7  *Ibid.*
 8  *Ibid.*
 9  *Ibid.*, Los Angeles, 1994.
10  *Ibid.*, Surrey, 1994.
11  Silver, Dorian, 'Israel Vibrations', *Echoes*, 10 February 1990.
12  Author interview, London, 1994.
13  *Ibid.*
14  *Ibid.*
15  *Ibid.*
16  *Ibid.*, 1992.
17  *China Now*, No. 130.
18  Marre, Jeremy, and Charlton, Hannah, *Beats of the Heart: Popular Music of the World* (Pluto Press, London, 1985), p. 81.
19  *World Music: The Rough Guide*, Broughton, Simon, Ellingham, Mark, Muddyman, David, and Trillo, Richard, eds (Rough Guides Ltd, London, 1994), p. 488.
20  Author interviews, London, 1988.
21  Bone, James, 'Island Queen', *The Times Magazine*, 2 May 1998.
22  Author interview, London, 1993.
23  *Ibid.*, Edinburgh, 1994.
24  Press release, Partridge & Storey, 1994.
25  Author interview, London, 1994.
26  *Ibid.*
27  *Ibid.*
28  *Ibid.*
29  Broughton, S., Ellingham, M., Muddyman, D. and Trillo, R., *World Music: The Rough Guide* (Rough Guides Ltd, London, 1994), p. 278.


**12** TALKIN' TOUGH

 1  Denselow, Robin, *When the Music's Over: The Story of Political Pop* (Faber & Faber, London, 1989).
 2  *The Concise Oxford English Dictionary*, sixth impression (Oxford University Press, Oxford, 1978).
 3  Author interview, London, 1994.

4 Gavin, James, 'For Baby, the Circle Comes Back Around', *International Herald Tribune*, 2 December 1992.

5 Vulliamy, Ed, 'Queen and the Saint', *Guardian*, 25 February 1988.

6 *Ibid.*

7 Author interview, London, 1995.

8 Mellers, Wilfrid, *Angels of the Night: Popular Female Singers of Our Time* (Basil Blackwell, Oxford, 1986), p. 112.

9 Jackson, Alan, 'Polish the Diamonds, Chip Off the Rust', *The Times*, 5 January 1993.

10 Author interview, London, 1988.

11 *Ibid.*, 1987.

12 *Ibid.*, New York, 1993.

13 *Ibid.*, London, 1988.

14 Bradley, Lloyd, 'At the Crossroads', *Time Out*, 27 September–4 October 1989.

15 Smyth, Cherry, 'Tracy's High', *City Limits*, 25 June–2 July 1992.

16 George, Nelson, *Buppies, B-Boys, Baps & Bohos: Notes on Post-Soul Black Culture* (HarperCollins, New York, 1994), p. 113.

17 Denselow, *When the Music's Over*, p. 32.

18 *Ibid.*, p. 177.

19 Sleevenotes to album *Sweet Honey In The Rock: Still On The Journey* (Earthbeat! Records, 1993).

20 Author interview, New York, 1994.

21 Press release, Ensign Records, 1990.

22 Author interview, London, 1992.

23 O'Brien, Lucy, *Dusty* (Sidgwick & Jackson, London, 1989), p. 58.

24 Author interview, London, 1994.

25 Toop, David, 'Abbey Nationalism', *Wire*, December/January 1993.

26 *Ibid.*

27 Author interview, Los Angeles, 1994.

28 *Ibid.*, New Orleans, 1997.

29 *Ibid.*

30 *Ibid.*, London, 1994.

31 Baillie, Stuart, 'She Puts On Women's Clothing', *NME*, 24 April 1993.

32 Author interview, London, 1993.

33 *Ibid.*, 1994.

34 Cosgrove, Stuart, 'Only Women Bleed', *NME*, 16 August 1986.

35 Author interview, London, 1990.

36 O'Brien, Lucy, 'An Inconvenient Woman', *Guardian Weekend*, 26 April 1997.

37 Light, Alan, 'Sinéad Speaks', *Rolling Stone*, 29 October 1992.

28 Sutcliffe, Phil, 'This Time It's Personal', *Q*, September 1994.

39 Clifford, Brendan, 'Torch Singer of Resistance', *Irishways*, No. 4, Winter 1992/3 .

40 Sutcliffe, 'This Time It's Personal'.

41 Author interview, London, 1994.

42 King, Jonathan, 'Annie could give Sinéad a few career tips', 'Letters to the Editor', *Independent*, 13 December 1992.

43 Moore, Suzanne, 'Rock 'n' Roll Rebel with Too Many Causes', *Guardian*, 6 November 1992.

44  *Irish Times*, 10 June 1993.

45  O'Brien, 'An Inconvenient Woman'.

46  Author interview, London, 2001.


**13** TALKIN' BUSINESS

1  Ali, Lorraine, 'Exiled in Guyville', *Rolling Stone*, 6 October 1994.

2  Steward, Sue, and Garratt, Sheryl, *Signed, Sealed and Delivered: True Life Stories of Women in Pop* (Pluto Press, London, 1984), p. 74.

3  Author interview, London, 1993.

4  *Ibid.*

5  *Ibid.*

6  *Ibid.*, Los Angeles, 1993.

7  'Letters to the Editor', *Billboard*, 6 October 1990.

8  Author interview, New York, 1993.

9  *Ibid.*

10  *Ibid.*, 1994.

11  *Ibid.*, 1993.

12  *Ibid.*, 1994.

13  *Ibid.*, 1993.

14  *Ibid.*, Los Angeles, 1994.

15  *Ibid.*, 1993.

16  *Ibid.*, London, 1993.

17  *Ibid.*, 1994.

18  *Ibid.*

19  *Ibid.*

20  *Ibid.*

21  *Ibid.*

22  Barnes, Terry, 'Women in Music and Home Entertainment', A Billboard Spotlight, *Billboard*, 24 April 1993.

23  *Ibid.*

24  Author interview, New York, 1994.

25  *Ibid.*

26  *Ibid.*

27  Barnes, 'Women in Music and Home Entertainment'.

28  Author interview, New York, 1993.

29  Barnes, 'Women in Music and Home Entertainment'.

30  Author interview, New York, 1993.

31  *Ibid.*, London, 1993.

32  *Ibid.*

33  *Ibid.*

34  *Ibid.*, New York, 1993.

35  *Ibid.*, 1994.

36  *Ibid.*, at the opening of her London National Portrait Gallery exhibition, 1994.

37  *Ibid.*

38  *Ibid.*, 1993.

39  *Ibid.*

40 *Ibid.*, 1994.
41 *Ibid.*, 1993.
42 *Ibid.*, 1994.
43 *Ibid.*
44 *Ibid.*
45 *Ibid.*
46 *Ibid.*, New York, 1994.
47 *Ibid.*, Boston, 1994.
48 *Ibid.*, New York, 1994.
49 Women in Music Now, Riverside House, Rattlesden, Bury St Edmunds, IP30 0SF, UK.
50 *Ibid.*, London, 1994.
51 *Ibid.*, referring to her study: 'Women and Pop', Women's Studies MA, University of Westminster, London, 1 June 1994.
52 Author interview, London, 1994, referring to the Annual Tracking Study Report devised by BMRB for HMV UK, 1993–4.
53 Vale, V., ed., *Incredibly Strange Music* (Re/Search Publications, San Francisco, May 1993), Vol. 1, pp. 122 and 130.
54 Bradby, Barbara, 'Lesbians and Popular Music: Does It Matter Who Is Singing?', *Outwrite: Lesbianism and Popular Culture*, ed. Gabriele Griffin (Pluto Press, London, 1993), p. 158.
55 Author interview, London, 2001.

Also useful for this chapter was Carol Jones's 'Becoming "One of the Boys": Female Engineers in the Electronics Industry' in *Women: A Cultural Review*, Vol. 3, No. 1 (Oxford University Press, Oxford, 1992).


**14 GIRLPOWER!**

1 Sawyer, Miranda, 'They Were the Girl Power Rangers', *Observer Life*, 27 December 1997.
2 Deevoy, Adrian, 'We Have Come For Your Children', *Q*, December 1997.
3 O'Brien, Lucy, 'Ker-Runch! Ker-Ching!', *Q*, December 1997.
4 *Ibid.*
5 'Mad About Celebs', *Guardian*, 19 February 2001.
6 Author interview, London, 2001.
7 O'Brien, Lucy, 'Rock 'n' Role', *Guardian*, 21 December 1998.
8 *Ibid.*
9 From *Righteous Babes*, Channel 4, 22 December 1998.
10 O'Brien, Lucy, 'The Great Pretender', *Guardian*, 27 April 1999.
11 Potter, Kerry, 'Mel B: Famous Last Words', *Q*, October 2000.
12 Higginbottom, Adam, 'Tales of Ordinary Madness', *Q*, December 2000.
13 Quatro, Suzi, 'Why Geri's Antics Shame Us All', *Daily Mail*, 9 March 2000.
14 O'Brien, Lucy, 'Rock and Rage', *Express on Sunday Magazine*, 22 November 1998.
15 *Ibid.*
16 Chonin, Neva, 'Liz Phair', The 30th Anniversary, *Rolling Stone*, 13 November 1997.

17  McDonnell, Evelyn, 'Fiona Apple', *Ibid.*
18  Author interview, London, 1998.
19  Mundy, Chris, 'Sarah McLachlan', *Rolling Stone*, 30 April 1998.
20  Author interview, London, 1998.
21  Hamilton, Jill, 'Sheryl Crow', *Rolling Stone*, 13 November 1997.
22  From *Lilith Fair: A Celebration of Women in Music: The Special Edition*, video, High Five Entertainment, 2000.
23  Mundy, 1998.
24  Author interview, London, 1998.
25  *Ibid.*, 1999.
26  *Ibid.*, 1998.
27  *Ibid.*
28  *Ibid.*
29  Bret, David, *Barbra Streisand* (Divas Series, Unanimous Ltd, London, 2000), p. 126.
30  *Ibid.*, p. 34.
31  Jackson, Alan, 'One From the Heart', *The Times*, 29 April 1995.
32  Sinclair, David, 'Belt Up!', *Q*, 52.
33  Davies, David, 'Coo-eee!', *Q*, November 1997.
34  Author interview, Limerick, 2001.
35  O'Hagan, Sean, 'We Are Family', *Guardian Weekend*, 22 July 2000.
36  Thornton, Kate, 'Teen Genie', *Marie Claire*, July 2000.
37  Agnew, Katie, 'There's Something About Britney', *Marie Claire*, March 2001.
38  Madonna, 'Madonna's Intimate Diaries', *Vanity Fair*, November 1996.
39  Eccleston, Danny, 'Sexy Mother', *Q*, March 1998.
40  *Ibid.*
41  Taraborrelli, Randy, *Madonna, An Intimate Biography* (Sidgwick & Jackson, London, 2001), p. 344.
42  *Ibid.*, p. 345–6.
43  Chonin, 1997.
44  O'Brien, 'Rock 'n' Role', 1998.
45  *Righteous Babes*.
46  Author interview, Glasgow, 2001.
47  *Ibid.*, London, 2001.
48  *Ibid.*

# Selected Discography

By no means exhaustive, this album selection highlights just some of the best music available by women written about in this book.

1 Bessie Smith: *Empress Of The Blues* (Charly, 1993)
2 Billie Holiday: *The Voice Of Jazz (The Complete Recordings 1933–1940)* (Charly, 1991)
3 Peggy Lee: *Black Coffee* (MCA, 1987)
4 Dinah Washington: *First Issue: The Dinah Washington Story* (The Original Recordings) (Verve/Polygram 1993)
5 Nina Simone: *My Baby Just Cares For Me* (Charly, 1993)
6 Dusty Springfield: *Goin' Back: The Very Best Of . . . 1962–1994* (Phonogram, 1994)
7 Various: *Motown: The Ultimate Hits Collection* (Motown, 1994)
8 Aretha Franklin: *Queen of Soul – The Very Best Of . . .* (Atlantic/East West, 1994)
9 Dionne Warwick: *Walk On By And Other Favorites* (Charly, 1988)
10 Marianne Faithfull: *Faithfull* (Island, 1994)
11 (Janis Joplin) Full Tilt Boogie Band: *Pearl* (Columbia, 1971)
12 (Grace Slick) Jefferson Airplane: *Surrealistic Pillow* (RCA, 1967)
13 (Moe Tucker) Velvet Underground: *White Light/White Heat* (Verve/Polydor, 1968)
14 Patti Smith: *Easter* (Arista, 1978)
15 Tina Turner: *Private Dancer* (Capitol, 1984)
16 Bonnie Raitt: *Nick Of Time* (Capitol, 1989)
17 (Poly Styrene) X-Ray Spex: *Germ-Free Adolescents* (EMI, 1978)
18 Siouxsie and The Banshees: *The Scream* (Polydor, 1978)
19 (Debbie Harry) Blondie: *Parallel Lines* (Chrysalis, 1978)
20 (Chrissie Hynde) The Pretenders: *Pretenders* (Sire/Real, 1980)
21 The Raincoats: *The Raincoats* (Rough Trade, 1979; reissued Rough Trade, 1994)
22 The Go-Go's: *Return To The Valley Of The Go-Go's* (EMI, 1995)
23 The Slits: *Cut* (Island, 1979)
24 Laurie Anderson: *Home Of The Brave* (WEA, 1986)
25 (Courtney Love) Hole: *Pretty On The Inside* (City Slang/Caroline, 1991)
26 PJ Harvey: *Rid Of Me* (Island, 1993)
27 Kristin Hersh: *Hips And Makers* (4AD, 1993)
28 Joni Mitchell: *Ladies Of The Canyon* (Reprise, 1970)
29 Carole King: *Tapestry* (Ode, 1972)

30  Joan Armatrading: *Joan Armatrading* (A&M, 1976)
31  Kate Bush: *Hounds Of Love* (EMI, 1985)
32  Suzanne Vega: *Solitude Standing* (A&M, 1987)
33  Jane Siberry: *When I Was A Boy* (WEA, 1993)
34  Madonna: *Like A Prayer* (WEA, 1989)
35  The Carpenters: *Only Yesterday – Richard and Karen Carpenter's Greatest Hits* (A&M, 1990)
36  Cyndi Lauper: *Twelve Deadly Cyns . . . And Then Some* (Epic, 1994)
37  (Annie Lennox) Eurythmics: *Savage* (RCA, 1989)
38  Grace Jones: *Nightclubbin'* (Island, 1981)
39  k. d. lang: *Ingénue* (Sire/WEA, 1992)
40  LaBelle: *Nightbirds* (Epic, 1974)
41  Whitney Houston: *Whitney* (Arista, 1985)
42  Sade: *Diamond Life* (Epic, 1984)
43  Anita Baker: *The Songstress* (Beverly Glen, 1983)
44  Janet Jackson: *Control* (A&M, 1986)
45  Salt 'N' Pepa: *Hot Cool & Vicious* (Next Plateau, 1986)
46  MC Lyte: *Ain't No Other* (East West, 1993 – CD has bonus track of 'I Cram To Understand U (Sam)')
47  Queen Latifah: *All Hail The Queen* (Tommy Boy, 1989)
48  Mary J. Blige: *What's The 411?* (Uptown/MCA, 1992)
49  Marcia Griffiths: *Indomitable* (Jet Star, 1994)
50  Oumou Sangaré: *Kosira* (World Circuit, 1993)
51  Gloria Estefan: *Cuts Both Ways* (Epic, 1989)
52  Celia Cruz: *Live at Yankee Stadium (with Fania All Stars)* (2 volumes, Tico, 1975)
53  Angélique Kidjo: *Logozo* (Mango/Island, 1991)
54  Miriam Makeba: Sangoma (WEA, 1988)
55  Joan Baez: *Joan Baez* (Vanguard, 1960)
56  Tracy Chapman: *Tracy Chapman* (Elektra, 1988)
57  Odetta: *Odetta And Larry* (Fantasy US/Acc UK, 1993)
58  Sweet Honey In The Rock: *Still On The Journey (The 20th Anniversary Album)* (Earthbeat!, 1993)
59  Chaka Khan (with Rufus): *Live Stompin' At The Savoy* (2 discs) (Warner Brothers, 1983)
60  Sinéad O'Connor: *Universal Mother* (Ensign/Chrysalis, 1994)
61  Ani DiFranco: *Not A Pretty Girl* (Righteous Babe, 1995)
62  Cesaria Evora: *Sau Vicente di Longe* (BMG, 2001)
63  Erykah Badu: *Baduizm* (Universal, 1997)
64  Lauryn Hill: *The Miseducation of Lauryn Hill* (Sony/Columbia, 1998)
65  Missy Elliot: *Supa Dupa Fly* (East West, 1997)
66  Liz Phair: *Exile in Guyville* (Matador, 1993)
67  Alanis Morissette: *Jagged Little Pill* (Maverick, 1995)
68  Sheryl Crow: *The Globe Sessions* (A&M, 1998)
69  Emmylou Harris: *Wrecking Ball* (Grapevine, 1995)
70  Madonna: *Ray of Light* (Maverick, 1998)
71  Tori Amos: *Strange Little Girls* (East West, 2001)

# Selected Bibliography

Andersen, Christopher: *Madonna Unauthorized* (Signet, London, 1992/Simon & Schuster, New York, 1992).

Balliett, Whitney: *American Singers: Twenty-seven Portraits in Song* (OUP, New York, 1990).

Bayton, Mavis: *Frock Rock: Women Performing Popular Music* (OUP, Oxford and New York, 1998).

Bowie, Angela, with Patrick Carr: *Backstage Passes: Life on the Wild Side with David Bowie* (Orion, London, 1994/Jove Pubns, New York, 1994).

Clarke, Donald, ed.: *The Penguin Encyclopedia of Popular Music* (Penguin, London, 1990).

Clarke, Donald: *Wishing on the Moon: The Life and Times of Billie Holiday* (Viking, London/New York, 1994).

Coleman, Ray: *The Carpenters: The Untold Story* (Boxtree, London, 1995/HarperCollins, New York, 1994).

Cooper, Sarah: *Girls, Girls, Girls: Essays on Women and Music* (Cassell, London, 1995).

Dahl, Linda: *Stormy Weather: The Music and Lives of a Century of Jazzwomen* (Quartet, London, 1987/Limelight Editions, New York, 1989).

Dannen, Fredric: *Hit Men: Power Brokers and Fast Money Inside the Music Business* (Vintage, London, 1994/Times Books, New York, 1991).

Denselow, Robin: *When the Music's Over: The Story of Political Pop* (Faber & Faber, London, 1989).

Eliot, Marc: *Rockonomics: The Money Behind the Music* (Omnibus Press, London, 1990/Citadel Press, New York, 1993).

Evans, Liz: *Girls Will Be Boys: Women Report on Rock* (Pandora, London, 1997).

Faithfull, Marianne, with David Dalton: *Faithfull* (Michael Joseph, London, 1994/Little, Brown, New York, 1994).

Feinstein, Elaine: *Bessie Smith: Empress of the Blues* (Viking Penguin, New York, 1986).

Gaar, Gillian G.: *She's a Rebel: The History of Women in Rock & Roll* (Seal Press, Seattle, 1992).

Garon, Paul and Beth: *Woman with Guitar: Memphis Minnie's Blues* (Da Capo, New York, 1992).

George, Nelson: *Where Did Our Love Go?: The Rise and Fall of Motown Records* (St Martin's Press, New York, 1987).

George, Nelson: *Buppies, B-Boys, Baps and Bohos: Notes on Post-Soul Black Culture* (HarperCollins, New York, 1994).

Green, Lucy: *Music, Gender and Education* (CUP, Cambridge, 1997).

Grieg, Charlotte: *Will You Still Love Me Tomorrow?: Girl Groups from the 50s On . . .* (Virago, London, 1989).

Hirshey, Gerri: *Nowhere to Run: The Story of Soul Music* (Da Capo Press, New York, 1994).

Hirshey, Gerri: *We Gotta Get out of This Place: The True, Tough Story of Women in Rock* (Atlantic Monthly Press, New York, 2001).

Holiday, Billie, with William Dufty: *Lady Sings the Blues* (Penguin, London/New York, 1984).

Joplin, Laura: *Love, Janis* (Bloomsbury, London, 1992/Villard Books, New York, 1992).

Juco, Andrea, and Vale, V., eds.: *Angry Women* (Re/Search Pubns, San Francisco, 1991).

Lee, Peggy: *Miss Peggy Lee* (Bloomsbury, London, 1989/Berkley Pubns, New York, 1992).

Lees, Gene: *Singers and the Song* (OUP, New York, 1989).

McClary, Susan: *Feminine Endings: Music, Gender and Sexuality* (University of Mississippi Press, Mississippi, 1991).

McQuiston, Liz: *Suffragettes to She Devils (Women's Liberation and Beyond)* (Phaidon, London, 1997).

Makeba, Miriam, with James Hall: *Makeba: My Story* (Bloomsbury, London, 1998/NAL Dutton, New York, 1989).

Marcus, Greil: *In the Fascist Bathroom: Writings on Punk 1977–1992* (Penguin, London, 1994).

Mellers, Wilfrid: *Angels of the Night: Popular Female Singers of Our Time* (Basil Blackwell, Cambridge, Mass., 1986).

O'Brien, Karen: *Joni Mitchell: Shadows and Light, the Definitive Biography* (Virgin, London, 2001).

Powers, Ann and McDonnell, Evelyn, eds: *Rock She Wrote: Women Write about Rock, Pop and Rap* (Cooper Square Publishing, New York, 1999).

Press, Joy and Reynolds, Simon: *The Sex Revolts: Gender, Rebellion and Rock 'n' Roll* (Serpent's Tail, London, 1995).

Raphael, Amy: *Never Mind the Bollocks* (Virago, London, 1995).

Ribowsky, Mark: *He's a Rebel: The Truth about Phil Spector, Rock and Roll's Legendary Madman* (E.P. Dutton, New York, 1989).

Roberts, R.: *Ladies First: Women in Music Videos* (University of Mississippi Press, Mississippi, 1996).

Sabin, Roger: *Punk Rock, So What?* (Routledge, London and New York, 1999).

Savage, Jon: *England's Dreaming: Sex Pistols and Punk Rock* (Faber & Faber, London, 1991/St Martin's Press, New York, 1991).

Simone, Nina, with Stephen Cleary: *I Put a Spell on You: The Autobiography* (Pantheon, New York, 1992).

Starr, Victoria: *k.d. lang: All You Get Is Me* (HarperCollins, London, 1994/St Martin's Press, New York, 1994).

Steward, Sue, and Garratt, Sheryl: *Signed, Sealed and Delivered: True Life Stories of Women in Pop* (Serpent's Tail, London, 1991/South End Press, Boston, Mass., 1984).

Sweeney, Philip: *Virgin Directory of World Music: A Guide to Performers and Their Music* (Virgin, London, 1991/Holt, Henry and Co., 1992).

Taraborrelli, Randy: *Madonna, An Intimate Biography* (Sidgwick & Jackson, London, 2001.)

Turner, Tina, with Kurt Loder: *I, Tina* (Penguin, London, 1987/Avon, New York, 1987).

Vermorel, Fred: *The Secret History of Kate Bush (And the Strange Art of Pop)* (Omnibus Press, New York, 1983).

White, John: *Billie Holiday: Her Life and Times* (Omnibus Press, London, 1987).

Wilson, Mary, with Ahrgus Julliard and Patricia Romanowski: *Dreamgirl: My Life as a Supreme* (St Martin's Press, New York, 1986).

# Index of Names

# Index of Albums and Singles